THE COMPLETE
REAL ESTATE
INVESTMENT
HANDBOOK

A Professional Investment Strategy

FOURTH EDITION

C. F. SIRMANS
and
AUSTIN J. JAFFE

PRENTICE HALL PRESS

New York   London   Toronto   Sydney   Tokyo

To ELAINE and LYNN

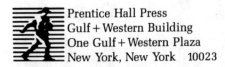

Prentice Hall Press
Gulf + Western Building
One Gulf + Western Plaza
New York, New York   10023

Copyright © 1988 by C. F. Sirmans and Austin J. Jaffe

Originally published in 1985 by Prentice-Hall, Inc.

Library of Congress Cataloging in Publication Data

Sirmans, C. F.
   The complete real estate investment handbook.

   Bibliography: p.
   Includes index.
   1. Real estate investment.   I. Jaffe, Austin J.
II. Title.
HD1382.5.S5   1988   332.63'24   87–43155
ISBN 0–13–162463–6

Designed by Irving Perkins Associates

Manufactured in the United States of America

10   9   8   7   6   5   4

First Prentice Hall Press Edition

ACKNOWLEDGMENTS

A special thanks to Jill Szymanski, Jean Campbell, Deborah Moran, and Wendy Morgan for their valuable assistance. The typing skills of Bessie Avera are also gratefully acknowledged.

CONTENTS _____

PREFACE

INVESTING in income-producing real estate requires detailed analysis of many contingencies that influence profitability. The basic purpose of this book is to provide the investor with a framework for making the investment decision. This framework is referred to as the *real estate investment process*. The process is a series of steps that the investor can apply in an orderly and careful way to analyze the many contingencies and thus reach the optimal investment decision. It can be applied to any type of income-producing real estate investment.

The investment process forms the foundation for a real estate investment strategy. A strategy is the science and art of using the investment process to result in the optimal decision for the investor: to make the best investment decisions and thus reach the objectives. For most investors, there are more potential investments than they are willing or able to undertake. Some investments are "good"; others are "bad." The investment process allows the investor to distinguish between the good and the bad alternatives.

Now more than ever, real estate investing requires careful financial analysis. The purpose of this revision is to provide the techniques necessary for making real estate investment decisions. The Tax Reform Act of 1986 has been incorporated into this revision.

We analyze the real estate investment decision primarily from the viewpoint of the equity investor. Investment, by definition, is the sacrifice of certain outflows in return for expected, but risky, inflows. The inflow of most interest to the investor is the *cash flow* remaining after all expenses have been paid, including operating expenses, mortgage indebtedness, and income taxation expenses. Thus, the investor makes the decision on the basis of the after-tax cash flow. Two potential sources of cash flow must be taken into account: the operation of the investment and its disposition. Any decision that ignores either source could be wrong. Risk—the possibility that the investment will not generate the expected level of cash flow—lies at the very heart of the investment decision.

Real estate investment analysis seeks to estimate *investment value*, or the maximum amount in dollars that an investor would be willing to pay, given assumptions about future expectations. The real estate investor compares his or her estimate of investment value with the *market value*. If the investor's investment value is greater than the market value, the property is "undervalued." If the market price is greater than the investment value, the investor would view the property as "overvalued" or too expensive for what he believes it is worth.

To estimate investment or market value, the real estate investor must analyze local real estate market conditions and make accurate forecasts. The investor must possess a basic understanding of property law, the limitations, and the legal regulations of owning and investing in real property. The modern investor must also be able to make the necessary numerical calculations. These involve analysis of income and expenses, mortgage payments, cash flows, depreciation allowances, and income taxes. Finally, the investor must know what to do once these calculations have been made. Traditionally, investors have relied on a number of well-known "rules of thumb" to help in deciding whether or not to invest. Modern analysis has developed a number of techniques that can be of dramatic assistance in choosing the best investment or investments available.

It should be emphasized that in the entire real estate investment process, probably nothing is of greater importance than reliable forecasts of the costs required and cash inflows expected from a particular investment. The old saying "garbage in, garbage out" is certainly applicable to a real estate investment strategy. Thus estimates of rents, expenses, financing costs, and other cash flow data require careful analysis. Forecasts of each component of the cash flows must be checked and rechecked by the investor before these estimates can be used for selecting "acceptable" and "unacceptable" projects. The investment decision is only as good as the expectations on which it is based.

Part I provides an overview of the framework for the analysis: the real estate investment process. Part II is devoted to an analysis of the environment the investor encounters when making real estate decisions. These elements include analysis of the market, assessment of risk, and legal constraints. Part III encompasses the forecasting of income, expenses, and cash flows that forms the basis of the investment decision. Part IV shows how to use a number of criteria to decide whether real estate investments are acceptable or not, or in many cases, which are preferred. Part V contains a series of case studies and examples of how to use the investment process to form a strategy to solve the many situations facing the real estate investor. We carefully show the reader how to apply the concepts and the principles that are learned to a variety of real estate investment decisions.

I

SOME BASIC INVESTMENT CONCEPTS

INVESTING in income-producing real estate can be viewed as a process: a step-by-step procedure that enables the investor to carefully and systematically analyze each of many factors that affects the rate of return, riskiness, and value of the real estate investment. The real estate investment process takes into account these multitude of considerations and provides the investor with an operational framework to follow to achieve the financial objectives.

The first chapter is devoted to the development of the real estate investment strategy: the identification of investor goals and objectives, the analysis of market conditions and legal constraints, the development of cash flow forecasts, and the investment criteria for making investment decisions. Chapter 2 discusses the reasons why real estate has been and is viewed as an attractive investment and discusses various types of real estate properties available for investors. Chapter 3 shows how to perform the necessary computations to analyze the mechanics of the investment decision, mortgages, and rate of return.

1

THE REAL ESTATE INVESTMENT PROCESS

THE real estate investment process is an overall investment plan of forecasts and decisions that the real estate investor makes to aid in achieving his or her goals. This process involves a careful analysis of the expected risk-return trade-off. It also may be viewed as the art of planning and managing a real estate investment (or a portfolio of investments) to its best advantage: maximization of the equity investor's wealth. To do so requires planning before the investment is made, careful management of the investment during the holding period, and considerations about disposal at the end of the holding period.

THE INVESTMENT PROCESS

As outlined in figure 1.1, there are five basic steps that the investor must take to correctly analyze a real estate investment:

Step 1. *Identify the investor's reasons for investing. What are the constraints on the investor? What are his or her risk-return preferences?*

Step 2. *Analyze the investment climate and the market conditions influencing an investment. What de-*mand forces make the investment potentially successful? What is the competition? What is the legal environment for a particular investment? What is the sociopolitical environment?

Step 3. *Forecast the expected cash flows from the real estate investment.* How much cash inflow is the project expected to generate? What are the cash outflows? What is the level of operating expenses? What are the costs of borrowing for mortgage purposes? Is there a potential for "leveraging" the project? What are the tax impacts? What is the potential for appreciation in value?

Step 4. *Compare the expected cash flows to the cost of investing. All in-*vestments involve risk and return. Does the return compensate for the risks that must be taken?

Step 5. *Decide whether to undertake or reject the investment.*

ANALYZING RISKS AND RETURNS

The purpose of the investment process is to discover whether a specific investment

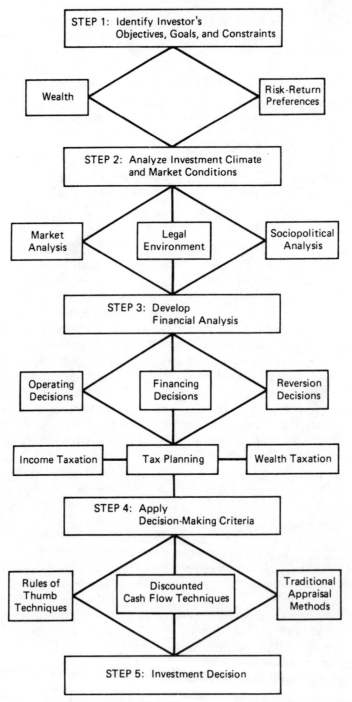

Figure 1.1 The Real Estate Investment Process

is feasible. A real estate investment is feasible when the investor determines that there is a reasonable likelihood of satisfying explicit investment objectives. The specific objectives, which are unique to each investor, must be tested using various criteria against a set of specific constraints. One constraint comes from the investor's own capital position; typically he or she will have only limited resources to invest. To be feasible an investment must meet this constraint. However, the investment must meet the constraints of *all* participants in the decision—not only the equity investor.

The environment, including market, legal, financial, and social factors, imposes another set of constraints. Also, it should be noted that feasibility involves a "reasonable likelihood" of success. The investment process, therefore, does *not* produce a single conclusion but rather involves a range of possible results.

The purpose of the investment process is to treat the investment decision in a systematic manner. The investor can thus be led to an investment decision after a thorough understanding of the expected returns and the risks involved in the investment. The investment process is simply a structure for analyzing risk and return.

STEP 1: IDENTIFYING INVESTOR OBJECTIVES

The first step in the real estate investment process is to identify the objectives and constraints of the investors. There are four basic participants in a real estate investment: the *equity investor*, the *mortgage lender*, the *tenant*, and the *government*, which includes federal, state, and local governments. Figure 1.2 outlines some of the interrelationships among these four participants.

Each of the participants in the investment process has different and often conflicting objectives for participating in the investment. Each places constraints and restrictions on the feasibility of a real estate investment. Failure to analyze any of these will have potentially disastrous results for the equity investor.

THE EQUITY INVESTOR

Because the equity investor is the decision maker, he must make certain that a project meets not only his restrictions and requirements but also those placed on the investment by the other major participants.

The equity investor can use any of several different forms of business entity for ownership of an investment. These include ownership as an individual, a partnership (limited or general), a corporation, or a real estate investment trust (REIT). Each of these forms has advantages and disadvantages. The decision concerning the business entity for ownership can influence the taxation impacts on a real estate investment, the liability for debt to which the equity investor can be exposed, the degree of control the investor has over the investment, and the relative ease of transferal of ownership in the investment. The equity investor must carefully consider the form of business entity for ownership since it will greatly influence the investment decision.

The equity investor is interested in the amount of cash flow from an investment. Cash flow arises from two sources: the annual flow from operations and the flow from the sale (or other disposition) of the investment. In addition, the investor must make certain that he has the rights to the cash flow because without these rights the real estate is valueless and the investment will fail.

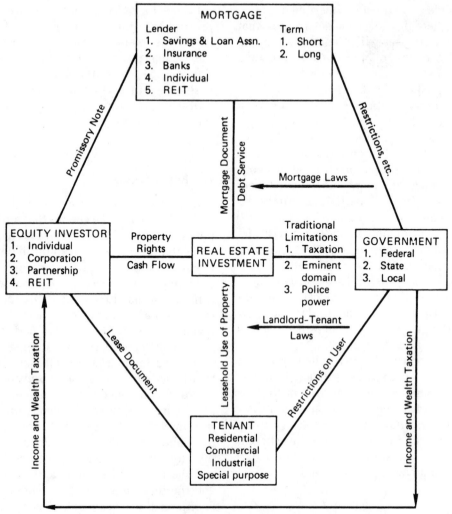

Figure 1.2 Participants in the Real Estate Investment Process

THE MORTGAGE LENDER

Many real estate investments use borrowed funds. There are several reasons for this practice. The first is that most real estate investments require large sums of capital. Next is the concept of *leverage*. Positive leverage enables the equity investor to increase the rate of return by borrowing funds and using them for investment purposes.

Although leverage may increase the rate of return on an investment, it also increases the amount of risk. The investor must be careful of this trade-off between returns to equity and borrowed funds and the increased risk from borrowing.

In general, a *mortgage* is a loan secured by a pledge of real estate as collateral. The *mortgage document* pledges the real estate as security and specifies the conditions of the loan. The *promissory note* is the evidence of the indebtedness and the promise to repay the loan. Each of these documents must be carefully analyzed by the investor.

THE TENANT

The tenant buys the immediate right of possession from the owner in exchange for the payment of rent. The tenant's rights in the real estate is referred to as the *leasehold estate*. The tenant's demands must be carefully analyzed because without him there is no income for the equity investor.

The *lease* binds the equity investor and the tenant. It is a contract under which the tenant (lessee) obtains the right to use the property for a certain period of time in return for payment of rent to the landlord (lessor). All leases should be written, no matter what the period of occupancy.

THE GOVERNMENT

The government influences the interrelationship between the equity investor, the mortgage lender, and the tenant. The government restricts the use of property and restricts the lenders through such actions as portfolio requirements and lending regulations. One of its greatest impacts is *income taxation*. While income taxation influences the investment decision with many complex rules and regulations, one cannot deny the impact of an investment's potential tax benefits and costs.

STEP 2: THE ENVIRONMENT FOR INVESTMENT DECISIONS

The *second step* in the real estate investment process is to analyze the market for investments and to identify investment opportunities. The purpose of this step is to aid the investor in identifying what is gen-

erally called *overall risk*. Business risk can be separated into four categories:

1. Business (market) risk—the possibility that supply and demand factors will vary, thus causing rents, vacancies, and future property values to be different than expected
2. Legal (political) risk—the possibility that government will introduce regulations, tax changes, or other legal restrictions causing profitability to decline
3. Inflation (purchasing power) risk—the possibility that rents and values will decline because of loss in purchasing power
4. Financial (borrowing) risk—the possibility that an investment's income will not cover debt obligation

Aimed at helping the investor identify the factors influencing business risk, this step involves three substeps: analyzing the *market conditions*, analyzing the *legal environment*, and analyzing the *sociopolitical environment*.

MARKET ANALYSIS

Market analysis is concerned with understanding the supply and demand forces that influence the feasibility of a particular investment and it must consider these forces at the national, regional, and local levels. Its focus is on the future potential of the investment for generating after-tax cash flows.

The real estate market is divided into many submarkets that can be grouped in different ways. For example, the market can be divided by type of land use: residential, industrial, and commercial. In turn, these groups can be divided into subgroups. The residential market, for example, can be separated into owner- and renter-occupied properties.

One of the purposes of market analysis is to identify the potential user of the real estate. Income-producing real estate has a user who is different from the owner. Because the user creates the demand for a real estate investment, his characteristics and preferences must be carefully analyzed. Market analysis aids the investor in forming expectations with regard to rents, vacancies, and future trends in the investment's value. Population growth or decline, migration patterns, employment change, income levels, price levels, taxation influences, and governmental policies are examples of the factors that influence an investment's market risk.

LEGAL ENVIRONMENT

As figure 1.2 illustrates, the real estate investment process involves many complex legal relationships that must be carefully analyzed by the investor. Legal constraints are imposed on the real estate, the equity investor, the mortgage lender, and the user of the real estate. All levels of government influence the legal environment of a real estate investment decision.

The ownership of real estate provides the investor with certain *property rights,* including the right to use and to sell the property. The quality and quantity of property rights associated with the ownership of real estate is of great concern to the investor. Real estate without property rights is of no value. Real estate valuation is really the valuation of property rights. Any limitation on these rights influences the value of a real estate investment.

Property rights include possession, control, enjoyment, and disposition. Each of these can be limited, sold, or separated from the others. Indeed, one of these rights

is "sold" in income-producing real estate. The owner (landlord) "sells" the right of use to someone else (the tenant). In return the tenant pays a price (rent) to the landlord.

The traditional governmental limitations on property rights are taxation, eminent domain, police power, and escheat. Taxation includes property taxes, income taxes, gift taxes, and estate taxes. Eminent domain is the right vested in the government to take private property for public use with just compensation. Police power is given to the government to protect the well-being of its citizens. Limiting the use of private property under police power does not require compensation. The most common exercise of police power is zoning laws. Escheat refers to the transferring of ownership to the state when legal heirs cannot be found.

SOCIOPOLITICAL ENVIRONMENT

One of the most difficult areas to analyze is the sociopolitical environment. Any real estate investment, particularly large-scale developments, impinges on the well-being of society as a whole. While there may be a demand for a particular project and while the project may be "legal," public sentiment against it creates a complex situation for the investor.

Community "values" must be dealt with in the decision-making process. In many cases, the investor must be prepared to analyze the compatibility of an investment with community standards and expectations. What is technically legal at any given time may not be politically permissible. Such considerations can place serious constraints on the total feasibility of a particular real estate investment.

STEP 3: CASH FLOW FORECASTING

The third step in the real estate investment process is to forecast the expected cash flows from an investment. The cash flows must be forecast for the period of time over which the investor anticipates holding the investment. It should be emphasized that in making investment decisions the expected cash flows from the investment are never known with certainty. The investor must formulate the expected cash flows carefully.

There are two major sources of cash inflows from a real estate investment—the annual cash flow from rental collections and the cash flow from the future sale (or other disposition) of the investment. The cash flow that is of greatest interest to the equity investor is the amount left after all costs of operating and selling the investment have been paid. These expenses include operating costs, payments on mortgage debt, and income taxes.

ANNUAL CASH FLOW FROM OPERATION

Table 1.1 shows how the cash flow from operating an investment is calculated. Forecasting the expected cash flow is probably the most important task in the analysis of the investment.

Table 1.1 MEASUREMENT OF EXPECTED CASH FLOW FROM OPERATION FOR EACH YEAR

	Estimated rent per unit per year
Times	Number of units
Equals	Potential gross income (PGI)
Minus	Vacancy and bad debt allowance
Plus	Miscellaneous income
Equals	Effective gross income (EGI)
Minus	Operating expenses
Equals	Net operating income (NOI)
Minus	Debt service
Equals	Before-tax cash flow (BTCF)
Minus	Taxes (T)*
Equals	After-tax cash flows (ATCF)

* See Table 1.3.

The development of the annual cash flow statement for a real estate investment can be divided into three subtasks:

1. *Analyze expected rents, vacancies, and operating expenses.* What is the expected level? How will this change over the holding period?
2. *Analyze the impact of financing.* What type of financing is needed? How much should be borrowed? What are the sources of funds? What are the payments?
3. *Analyze the impact of income taxation.* Is the project generating any tax shelter? Which depreciation techniques are permissible?

These are some of the questions that must be answered in forecasting the expected annual cash flows.

Rents, Vacancies, and Operating Expense Analysis. In step 2 of the investment process the investor has identified the demand for the investment and the competition. The number, quantity, and rents of similar properties, which are competing with the investment under consideration, indicate the amount of rent that can be expected from an investment.

The investor must also consider changes in future conditions that would influence the rents on the investment. What is the existing competition? Are projects under construction or being planned that would compete with the investment? Are there legal or political forces, such as rent control, underway that influence the cash flow?

As table 1.1 indicates, there are five levels or categories of future income that the investor must forecast annually: potential gross income (PGI), effective gross income (EGI), net operating income (NOI), before-tax cash flow (BTCF), and after-tax cash flow (ATCF). These levels of income range from the most "gross" to the most "net" from the investor's viewpoint. The bottom line—ATCF—is the most important. This figure is estimated on an annual basis for each year of the expected holding period.

Potential gross income (PGI) is the amount of annual rental receipts the investment would generate if 100 percent occupancy were possible. To calculate PGI, simply multiply the expected rent per unit times the number of units.

Finding PGI

Suppose an investor is considering an apartment building with 100 units. If market analysis indicates that the expected rent would be $200 per unit, then PGI would be $240,000 (100 × $200 × 12).

Obviously, very few investments will be occupied to capacity all the time. The investor must allow for *vacancy*. Income losses can also occur as the result of *bad debts*. These must be deducted from PGI. The investor might also receive some miscellaneous income from the rental of, say, parking spaces (if not included in the rent), vending machines, or laundry facilities. Estimates of this miscellaneous income are added to PGI.

Effective gross income (EGI) is the second category of income from operations. It is calculated by deducting allowances for bad debts and vacancies and by adding miscellaneous income to PGI.

Finding EGI

Suppose the investor is considering an apartment building of 100 units with an expected rent of $200 per month each. He also expects a vacancy of 5 percent and other income losses of 2 percent. The project has 100 parking spaces that the investor expects to rent for $5 per month

each. The forecasted EGI for the first year is $229,200.

Potential gross income (PGI) (annual)	$240,000
Minus vacancy and bad debt (7%)	− 16,800
Plus miscellaneous income	+ 6,000
Effective gross income (EGI) (annual)	$229,200

Operating expenses are deducted next in the expected income statement. Operating expenses are those incurred in generating rental payments and *do not* include payments on mortgage debt, depreciation allowances, or the owner's income taxes.

Operating expenses usually fall into two categories: fixed and variable expenses. The first is not affected by the level of occupancy. Two traditional examples are property taxes and property insurance. The second changes with the level of occupancy. These include management fees, supplies, utilities, personnel expenses, and allowances for repairs and maintenance.

Effective gross income minus operating expenses results in *net operating income* (NOI).

Finding NOI

Suppose the apartment investment example has the following forecasted operating expenses for the first year:

Property taxes	$20,000
Management fee (5% of EGI)	11,460
Salaries	13,000
Utilities	10,000
Insurance	5,000
Supplies	8,000
Advertising	1,500
Repairs and maintenance	22,720
Total operating expenses	$91,680

Net operating income (NOI) would be effective gross income (EGI)	$229,200
Minus operating expenses	−91,680
Net operating income (NOI)	$137,520

Financing Decisions. There are two basic reasons why investors seek financing for an investment. The first is that the investment may require more capital than the investor has, thus he needs to borrow funds in order to complete the transaction.

The second reason is the perceived attractiveness of financial leverage or the use of borrowed funds to increase the rate of return on the equity investment. The larger the proportion of borrowed funds to equity funds, the greater the degree of financial leverage.

Table 1.2 indicates some of the typical costs of borrowing on income properties in recent years. Of particular interest to the investor are the average interest rates, loan-to-value ratio, and the term (maturity) of the mortgage because all of these influence the mortgage constant. The *mortgage constant* is the factor that is multiplied by the loan amount to determine the annual payments (debt service) necessary to amortize the loan over the term and pay the interest cost on the unpaid balance.

As indicated in table 1.1, NOI minus the payment on mortgage indebtedness results in BTCF from a real estate investment. The BTCF is the amount of income available for equity investment before the payment of income taxes.

Finding BTCF

Suppose the payment of debt service on the apartment building is $93,750. The before-tax cash flow is $43,770:

Net operating income (NOI)	$137,520
Minus debt service	−93,750
Before-tax cash flow (BTCF)	$43,770

Tax Planning for Operations. Table 1.3 shows how the taxes from operation are calculated. The federal income tax is vital to real estate investment decision making because changes in tax rates and rules can turn an attractive investment into a problem for the investor.

Taxable income is calculated by deducting interest expenses on mortgage debt, the depreciation allowance, and the amortized financing costs from NOI. In general, the *interest* on mortgage debt is deductible, providing an incentive to finance an investment with interest-bearing debt. We discuss the tax rules in more detail in chapter 8.

The second major deductible item is the *depreciation allowance*, a noncash outlay. The idea behind this deduction is that the asset is "wasting away" and thus the investor should be allowed to recover the cost of the investment over its depreciable life. In real estate investments, only the improvement costs are depreciable.

REVERSION CASH FLOW

The second major source of cash flow from a real estate investment is that obtained at its disposition. The investor must thus estimate the expected cash flow from the sale at the end of the *holding period*, which is the length of time he expects to own the project. The cash flow from sale can have significant impact on the investor's rate of return.

Table 1.4 illustrates the calculation of the cash flow from the sale of real estate investment. First, estimate the expected selling price. From the expected selling price, deduct an allowance for selling expenses, which include brokerage fees and other expenses such as legal fees, title processing, and recording fees.

The estimated selling price minus selling expenses results in the net sales proceeds

Table 1.2 AVERAGE TERMS ON INCOME PROPERTY MORTGAGE LOANS MADE BY LIFE INSURANCE COMPANIES*

	No. of Loans	Amount Committed (× $1,000)	Loan Amount (× $1,000)	Interest Rate (by no.)	Interest Rate (by $)	Loan/Value	Capitalization Rate	Debt Coverage Ratio	Percent Constant	Term (Year/Months)
						AVERAGES				
1981 1st Quarter	155	692,842	4,470	13.90%	13.48%	72.3	12.8%	1.32	14.2%	14/3
2nd Quarter	144	1,206,421	8,378	14.28	13.48	69.0	13.0	1.29	14.5	17/8
3rd Quarter	107	916,068	8,561	14.47	14.34	71.4	13.1	1.28	14.7	17/3
4th Quarter	87	446,974	5,138	14.98	14.77	67.4	13.4	1.34	15.2	13/8
Year	493	3,262,305	6,617	14.32	13.90	70.3	13.0	1.30	14.6	15/10
1982 1st Quarter	135	1,098,020	8,133	15.23	14.63	66.2	12.9	1.39	15.5	14/3
2nd Quarter	137	847,589	6,187	15.23	14.74	66.4	12.8	1.36	15.3	12/2
3rd Quarter	139	750,754	5,401	14.75	14.49	64.9	12.0	1.28	15.1	10/0
4th Quarter	260	2,132,089	8,200	13.26	13.30	67.6	11.6	1.30	13.7	9/6
Year	671	4,828,452	7,196	14.36	14.04	66.5	12.2	1.33	14.7	11/1
1983 1st Quarter	285	2,009,854	7,052	12.89	12.85	69.8	11.4	1.30	13.2	8/9
2nd Quarter	334	2,723,891	8,155	12.25	12.28	70.7	11.0	1.26	12.6	10/0
3rd Quarter	328	2,894,789	8,826	12.29	12.29	69.2	10.8	1.28	12.6	9/10
4th Quarter	234	2,337,340	9,989	12.67	12.57	70.5	11.1	1.23	13.1	9/10
Year	1,118	9,965,874	88,439	12.49	12.46	70.0	11.1	1.27	12.8	9/7

	Number	Amount	Average Size						
1984 1st Quarter	357	3,482,348	9,754	12.59	12.55	70.3	10.8	1.26	12.8	10/0
2nd Quarter	285	3,345,201	11,738	12.97	12.95	68.1	10.5	1.27	13.2	9/10
3rd Quarter	142	2,131,375	15,010	13.40	12.85	72.5	11.2	1.16	13.6	9/9
4th Quarter	354	4,009,911	11,327	12.91	12.90	70.5	10.8	1.22	13.2	9/1
Year	1,138	12,968,835	11,396	12.88	12.81	70.1	10.8	1.24	13.1	9/8
1985 1st Quarter	528	4,405,871	8,344	12.38%	12.28%	70.0%	10.5%	1.25	12.7%	8/7
2nd Quarter	473	4,973,043	10,514	12.17	11.98	70.8	10.2	1.23	12.4	8/1
3rd Quarter	603	5,234,854	8,681	11.42	11.40	71.5	9.9	1.24	11.7	8/3
4th Quarter	555	6,020,011	10,847	11.25	11.20	71.5	9.8	1.25	11.5	8/1
Year	2,159	20,633,779	9,557	11.77	11.67	71.0	10.1	1.24	12.1	8/3
1986 1st Quarter	549	5,986,204	10,904	10.39	10.25	71.6	9.5	1.28	10.9	8/10
2nd Quarter	720	7,769,458	10,791	9.62	9.47	71.2	9.3	1.28	10.4	9/3
3rd Quarter	423	4,713,001	11,142	9.40	9.30	71.4	9.1	1.32	10.1	9/0

* Data are for commitments made by a sample group of life insurance companies. Averages are based on the number of loans.

Source: American Council of Life Insurance, Washington, D.C.

Table 1.3 MEASUREMENT OF TAXABLE INCOME AND TAXES FROM OPERATION FOR EACH YEAR

	Method 1			Method 2
	Effective gross income (EGI)			Effective gross income (EGI)
Minus	Operating expenses		*Minus*	Operating expenses
Equals	Net operating income (NOI)		*Equals*	Net operating income (NOI)
Minus	Interest on debt		*Minus*	Debt service
Minus	Depreciation deduction		*Equals*	Before-tax cash flow (BTCF)
Minus	Amortized financing costs		*Plus*	Principal
Plus	Replacement reserves		*Minus*	Depreciation deduction
Equals	Taxable income (TI)		*Minus*	Amortized financing costs
Times	Investor's marginal tax rate		*Plus*	Replacement reserves
Equals	Taxes from operation (T)		*Equals*	Taxable income (TI)
			Times	Investor's marginal tax rate
			Equals	Taxes from operation (T)

Table 1.4 MEASUREMENT OF EXPECTED CASH FLOW FROM THE SALE OF AN INVESTMENT

	Estimated selling price (SP)
Minus	Selling expenses (SE)
Equals	Net sales proceeds (NSP)
Minus	Unpaid mortgage balance (UM)
Equals	Before-tax equity reversion (BTER)
Minus	Taxes due on sale*
Equals	After-tax equity reversion (ATER)

* See Table 1.5.

Table 1.5 MEASUREMENT OF TAXABLE INCOME AND TAXES DUE ON SALE

	TAXABLE INCOME
	Expected selling price (SP)
Minus	Selling expenses (SE)
Equals	Amount realized (AR)
Minus	Adjusted basis (AB)
Equals	Capital gain on sale (CG)

	TAXES DUE ON SALE
	Capital gain from sale (CG)
Times	Investor's marginal tax rate
Equals	Taxes due on sale (TDS)

(NSP) from sale. The NSP minus the outstanding mortgage balance yields the before-tax equity reversion (BTER). This is the amount of cash flow going to the equity investor before the payment of any taxes due on the sale of the project.

To calculate the taxes due on sale, the investor derives the capital gain as shown in table 1.5. This is then multiplied by the investor's marginal tax rate. The result is the taxes due on sale.

STEP 4: INVESTMENT CRITERIA

The fourth step in the real estate investment process is to apply the criteria for decision making. After the investor has carefully analyzed the expected costs and expected benefits of an investment, some criteria must be used to compare the benefits to the costs. The crucial question is: How much should be paid for a particular investment? Or: If a certain price is paid, what will be the expected rate of return from the investment? Does the expected rate of return "compensate" for the risks that must be taken?

The decision-making criteria available to the real estate investor fall into three categories:

1. Rules-of-thumb techniques
2. Traditional valuation techniques
3. Discounted cash flow models

RULES-OF-THUMB TECHNIQUES

Many investors employ simple "rules of thumb" in making decisions. These techniques are fairly simplistic and have a variety of limitations that make them, at least from a conceptual viewpoint, less desirable as decision-making criteria.

Some of the more popular rules of thumb are the gross income multiplier, the overall capitalization rate, and the equity dividend (or cash-on-cash) rate. The gross income multiplier simply measures the relationship between value (selling price) and gross income from operations. The overall capitalization rate (or its reciprocal, the net income multiplier) is the ratio of net operating income to value (selling price). The equity dividend rate is the ratio of before-tax cash flow (typically for the first year) to the amount of equity invested. The investor could obviously calculate these ratios (as well as a host of others) and use them as criteria for the investment decision. All of the simple rules of thumb have limitations and must be used with extreme care by the equity investor. They may, however, provide useful guidelines for the investor as first approximations in the decision-making process.

TRADITIONAL VALUATION MODELS

The direct sales comparison approach, income approach, and cost approach are additional methods of value estimation.

In the *direct sales comparison approach*, the investor estimates the value of an investment by comparing it to similar properties that have recently been sold. The elements to consider when making this comparison are time, location, physical characteristics, financing, and conditions of the sale. Time is the period between sales of similar properties that may affect the value of the subject property. Location is also important. Physical characteristics such as lot size, building size, and age of building influence property value as much as financing alternatives. Finally, since each property sells under different conditions, these must be carefully analyzed as well.

Under the traditional *income approach*, value is defined as the present worth of the expected income. To estimate value, the investor must forecast the income stream, select an appropriate rate of return, and convert the income to a present worth estimate using the mechanics of discounting.

The *cost approach* technique contends the investor should pay no more for an investment than the cost of producing a similar property. To use this approach, he:

1. Estimates the reproduction cost new of the improvements
2. Estimates the value of the land using the direct sales comparison approach
3. Estimates the loss in value resulting from building obsolescence and the impact of property location
4. Subtracts the loss in value from the reproduction cost new to arrive at the depreciated value of the building
5. Adds the value of the land to the depreciated value of the building to estimate total value

DISCOUNTED CASH FLOW MODELS

The third major set of decision-making criteria includes the discounted cash flow

(DCF) models. These are based on the concept that the value of a real estate investment is equal to the present worth of the future cash flows. So the investor must forecast the expected cash flows and discount the future cash flows back to the present at the appropriate rate of return. The discounted cash flow models recognize that a dollar today is worth more than a dollar tomorrow. This is the essence of *net present value* and the *time value of money*.

There are two DCF models: net present value and internal rate of return methods. With the *net present value method*, discount the expected cash flows using the desired rate of return. If the present value of the cash flows exceeds the present value of the costs of investing, proceed. If the present value of the cash flows is less than the present value of the costs, do not make the investment.

Under the *internal rate of return* (IRR) method, compare the inflows to the costs and calculate the rate of return. The IRR equates the present value of the benefits (cash inflows) with the present value of the costs (cash outflows) of investing. Once this is done, compare this rate to the desired or "hurdle" rate of return. If the calculated rate of return is greater than or equal to the desired rate of return, make the investment. These models are discussed in detail in chapter 10.

STEP 5: INVESTMENT DECISION

If the investor has carefully analyzed all of the foregoing steps, he can make the investment decision. Upon reviewing the estimates and ensuring that all are reasonable and accurate, he will be prepared to make a money-making investment in income-producing real estate according to his goals and preferences or to screen out a possible white elephant. Each of the following chapters examines the investment process in detail.

2

THE INVESTOR'S OBJECTIVES

THE first step in the investment process is to identify the investor's objectives, goals, and constraints. Without this, the feasibility of the investment cannot be determined. In addition to the obvious factors of price appreciation, tax shelter benefits, and financial leverage, we discuss more explicit reasons why individuals or firms invest in real estate. Some investors seek substantial real estate holdings because they feel that real property is more secure, more valuable, and more visible than financial assets. The opportunities for positive cash flows during the holding period of the investment are attractive to many who seek dollar returns. This is reinforced by the relatively small down payment required, the amount of borrowed capital available, as well as the expectation of growth in value of the property when the investor decides to sell. The attractiveness of larger *reversion values* (selling prices in the future) continues to lure investors.

Finally, by making periodic debt service payments for amortizing loans, the investor increases his or her ownership interest through equity buildup over time. Although this accumulation is slow, the repayment of principal over time will add to the owner's equity, assuming the value of the real estate does not fall. It will supplement increases in equity, in addition to property values, which may rise over time.

What is the appropriate goal or objective for the investor? Many investors wish to secure the largest income, profit, cash flow, or tax shelter benefits over the life of the holding period. Others are willing to forego these benefits in the hope of realizing large gains from appreciation at the time of sale. Some attempt to measure this performance by using various rate of return measures while others assess performance by measuring increases in the size of their personal assets, or their net worth (or wealth) positions. However, the best goal for each investor is determined by his own objectives, tolerance for risk, and individual tastes and preferences. For many investors, this goal will be the maximization of wealth or net worth.

WHAT IS INVESTMENT?

Early investment analysis distinguished between investment and speculation. Speculation was associated with large risks for great gains or unsecured gambles where the investor used other people's funds to his own advantage. Investment was viewed as a secure acquisition generally with a steady income and without the use of borrowed funds.

Surprisingly enough, many of these distinctions are still followed today. However, it is difficult to distinguish between speculation and investment. If an individual becomes interested in purchasing some property for significant financial gain, and he analyzes the property in a particular area to the best of his ability, do we call this individual a speculator rather than an investor? Or if the investor has a very short expected holding period, or if the expected rate of appreciation is relatively high due to growth in the community, or if he believes that future rates of appreciation in property of this type will be high, is this so-called speculator different than other investors? Obviously, the answer is no. The historical distinction placed on speculation and investment is not useful and, in some cases, is quite unclear.

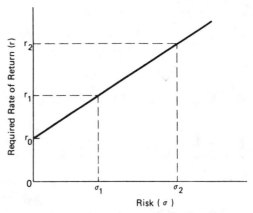

Figure 2.1   Risk-Return Trade-off

RISK-RETURN TRADE-OFF

Risk and return are inseparable. Investment opportunities that promise high rates of return also tend to be high risk. Similarly, those properties that appear to be safer and less risky typically yield less future returns. Given our market economy, the relationship between risk and return must be expected since buyers and sellers in the market are constantly evaluating the effects of changing market conditions on property value. Changes that have dramatic effects on investments have similar effects on the expected return and/or risk of the projects as viewed by the market participants. Therefore, market prices rise or fall according to expected impacts as a result of the change. Since one cannot get "something for nothing" (without superior information that the rest of the market does not possess!), risk and return move together.

Figure 2.1 demonstrates the trade-off between risk and return for investments in income-producing assets. In a market economy, where risk and return move together, one may expect to find the relationship in equilibrium between risk and required rate of return. Without any risk there still is a return, due to the foregone use of funds during the period of the investment. (This is shown by point r_0 in figure 2.1.) However, as an increasing amount of return is desired, it would only come with increasing amounts of risk. In this analysis, the investor is free to pick the amount of risk to be undertaken, which would then translate into an expected return.

Note that the risk-return trade-off offers a risk-free return r_0 and all other combinations of risk and return. For example, suppose an investment contained an amount of risk σ_1 (σ, or the standard deviation of returns, is a well-known measure of risk). The corresponding expected rate of return is shown as r_1. In essence, for risk of σ_1, the investment is expected to return r_0, the risk-free return, and $r_1 - r_0$, the risk premium. For investments with greater risk, for example, σ_2, the corresponding risk premium would be $r_2 - r_0$ and the required rate of return would be $(r_2 - r_0) + (r_0 - 0)$, or r_2.

TYPES OF RISK

There are many types of risk that an investor must analyze in making an investment. These are:

1. *Business (market) risk.* The possibility that an investment will not generate the level of net income that is expected. Many factors could lead to a decline in net income. In general, shifts in supply and demand cause rents and values to increase or decrease.
2. *Inflation (purchasing power) risk.* The possibility that price increases will be greater than expected and result in a decline in future purchasing power.
3. *Legislative (political) risk.* The possibility that the government will change policy or laws that affect the investment, such as changes in tax laws, zoning ordinances, and other elements of the legal environment.
4. *Financial (borrowing) risk.* The possibility that an investment will not generate sufficient income to cover debt obligations.

The point is that *evaluating risk is as important as evaluating return.* The extent to which investment opportunities exist in the real estate market is the extent to which risk must be evaluated as closely as expected returns. Investment analysis *is* the analysis of risk and return for various investment alternatives.

If we allow for the possibility of risky investments (i.e., those that appear to be less probable of success, but given success, will provide a high rate of return) in a well-developed market, the distinction between speculation and investment becomes immaterial. Further, if we "permit" investors to buy and sell from the "market" as they choose, given their beliefs and expectations about the market supply and demand forces

and their tastes and preferences for holding real property, it also seems arbitrary to call a short-term ownership of real property for purposes of financial gain speculation rather than investment. Finally, if investment generally uses only the investor's funds whereas speculation occurs whenever debt is used to acquire the property, few real estate projects could ever be called "investments." Besides, this would result in the forsaking of one of the attractions of real estate as an investment vehicle: the opportunities for financial leverage. Therefore, investing is choosing among market alternatives in order to achieve some financial objective or goal. The basic goal is to maximize the wealth of the investor. The investment decision is the commitment of certain cash outflow in return for risky cash inflows.

EXPECTED, REQUIRED, AND ACTUAL RATES OF RETURN

To understand investment decision making, it is necessary to differentiate between and define three rates of return: the expected rate, the required rate, and the actual (realized) rate.

The investment decision is made by comparing the expected rate of return to the required rate. The *expected rate* is what the investor forecasts that the investment will yield, based on expectations regarding cash outflows in relation to cash inflows. For example, suppose that an investor is considering an investment with an outflow of $1,000 and expects to receive $1,100 after one year. The expected rate of return is 10 percent.

Should the investment be made? To answer this question, the investor must determine the *required rate* of return. Basically, the required rate of return is related to two factors: time and risk. The investor must be compensated for waiting even if there is no risk. The greater the perceived level of risk, the greater the required rate of return. Returning to our example, suppose that the investor decides that a 12 percent rate of return is required. Should the investment be made? No, because the investor requires 12 percent and the investment is expected to pay 10 percent. Because the expected rate is less than the required rate of return, the investment is rejected. However, if the expected rate is greater than the required rate of return, the investment is accepted. For example, if the required rate is 8 percent and the expected is 10 percent, the investment is made.

Now let's extend the example. Suppose that the investment is accepted at an outflow of $1,000, and one year later the investor receives $1,200. Since we know the actual income in this situation, we can calculate the actual (realized) rate of return, which is 20 percent. In this example, the investor required 8 percent, expected 10 percent, and realized 20 percent.

We can calculate the *actual rate* of return only after the investment is made. It is thus an ex *post* number, that is, a historical rate. We make the decision based on the future. Obviously, the actual rate of return may be less than, greater than, or equal to what we expected. Likewise, the actual rate may be different from the required rate of return.

REASONS FOR INVESTING

There are a number of reasons why investing in real estate is favorable. Each is listed below and briefly discussed separately although many are interrelated.

INVESTMENT SECURITY

This is a very old proposition, and under some conditions, quite true. Historically, many investors have held that since the supply of land is essentially fixed, market demand forces will continuously drive up the value. Therefore, real estate appears to be more secure than other investments since the supply of most others can be expanded. This results in a very secure position for the holder since the risk of loss due to a decline in value is very small or nonexistent. Furthermore, it has been argued that real estate returns by nature appear to be less variable over time and are therefore more predictable. Finally, given other factors like inflation protection and leverage gains, investments in property appear to be very safe and secure.

Real estate investments may be viewed as relatively secure if demand for the urban space continues to grow, or at least remains relatively constant. In addition, if the market views the property as very safe, values may have been pushed up so that the investment brings a relatively lower return. Therefore, a safe investment typically will not result in a large return on the investment. Finally, it seems fair to say that while security and safety are favorable attributes, they might result in lower expected returns and less expected risk for an investor.

AVAILABLE CASH FLOWS

The prospect of extra money accruing to the investor after all expenses and debts are paid each period (month or year) is an attractive feature of investing in real estate. (After-tax cash flow is defined as net operating income less debt service less income taxes each period.) *Cash flow* differs from taxable income because the IRS permits deduction of interest payments (but not principal amortization payments) for tax purposes and because depreciation allowances are noncash expenses.

Since positive cash flows enable the investor to acquire new investments or permit additional consumption of personal goods, positive cash flows are almost always attractive to potential investors. Futhermore, since negative after-tax cash flows generally require additional cash outlays on the part of the owner(s), the necessity of obtaining positive cash flows is especially critical. Finally, cash flows are one of the major components in the estimation of investment value for income-producing real estate.

Financial Leverage

Real estate investing allows the investor to borrow a majority of the necessary funds with relatively little cash (or with a low down payment). If the investment rate of return is greater than the cost of borrowed funds, a gain accrues to the investor as a result. In essence, financial leverage requires a comparison of available debt and equity sources.

The drawback, of course, is that the leverage gain occurs only as a result of a corresponding increase in the amount of financial risk in the project. Since increased borrowing results in higher debt service requirements, the leverage gains are accompanied by the greater probability of default. Therefore, leverage is not without its price.

Tax Shelter Benefits

Basically, since depreciation is a noncash expense, the investor may deduct an amount for the "wasting away" of the improvements (building) over time. This depreciation deduction is merely for tax purposes and may have little to do with true change in property value. Since depreciation reduces taxable income and does not involve cash outflow, the tax liability will be smaller. Therefore, depreciation allowances enable tax savings.

Property Value Appreciation

Given that relatively little cash is necessary to acquire the investment and that lenders require periodic fixed dollar payments, the benefits of real appreciation will accrue to the owner/investor. Because well-located and well-maintained property in growing communities or choice sites in urban areas have continued to grow in value in *real* terms, these relative price changes have resulted in large capital gains for property owners. The prospect of continued increases in value at rates greater than those on other assets attracts many investors.

Equity Position

Since the mortgage instrument typically requires a fixed amount of repayment, the accumulation of equity as a result of satisfying the mortgage over time is called *equity buildup*. This advantage to the investor accrues over time independent of the rate of appreciation in the property. The equity buildup helps the investor refinance the property or use the increased equity for additional projects. This process, called *pyramiding*, and changes in the equity position are of critical concern to the investor.

Inflation Hedge

Although property value growth rates have exceeded rates of general price changes for most of the past thirty years, this change in relative prices may not be true for all types of property. In essence, future growth in real estate will be advantageous to the investor only if relative prices of real estate exceed expectations about general price level changes. Therefore, as long as real estate values continue to rise at unexpectedly higher rates than predicted, real estate will be attractive to those seeking protection from falling real values due to price erosion.

PORTFOLIO CONSIDERATIONS

There may be an advantage to adding real estate to an investor's portfolio even if the expected rate of return is not as high for this property as for some of the other alternative investments. If real estate is expected to perform differently than other investments, this may be beneficial for investors. This gain would occur as a result of *diversification* and therefore the overall riskiness of the investor's portfolio would be reduced. If the expected return from real estate inversely moves, or covaries, with the expected return from other investments in the investor's portfolio, real estate investments would be valuable to obtain the gains from diversification. Indeed, one of the key rules in developing an investment strategy is that generally it is not wise to put "all of your eggs in one basket."

NONECONOMIC REASONS

Although market prices should reflect supply and demand pressures, including those that result from noneconomic factors, some investors argue that real estate appeals to them for aesthetic, social, or political reasons. Some investors would rather own twelve-unit luxury apartment buildings in the nicest part of the community for the "social" contribution this makes to the community. Others argue that real property investments are more tangible than alternative investments. Finally, some investors satisfy consumption objectives as well as investment goals when choosing certain types of investment. While these objectives may not always appear to be financially sound, they have been included since some investors place positive values on these nonpecuniary benefits.

THE FUTURE OF REAL ESTATE INVESTING

Housing remains one of the most important needs in modern-day living. Families continue to expand their demands for more and better housing and have more disposable income to spend on it. As a result, single-family housing has become very expensive. In addition, changing demographics will create demand for the conversion of existing property into condominium developments, recreational property, and retirement communities. Investment in commercial and industrial property also appears favorable. Careful market analysis is essential in order to estimate which types of real estate are currently in short supply within market areas. However, the future looks promising for many types of investments.

In terms of financial feasibility, future real estate investments appear to be strong. This does not, however, rule out the "down" cycles that occur in general economic conditions. It appears investors will earn sizable rates of return if they can develop a sound investment strategy. This includes operating and managing property efficiently, analyzing problem areas and correcting them, handling landlord/tenant problems, understanding the role of financing and its effect on investment objectives, and incorporating the role of government in restricting property rights.

COMPARING RATES OF RETURN

It is interesting to compare the relative performance of real estate investments with common stock, bonds, and other financial investments. Recent studies show that, over the long term, returns from real estate and common stock appear to be generally comparable.* This conclusion should be regarded warily for several reasons. First, reliable data for real estate returns is either questionable or unavailable. Second, given the data problems, an overall measure of risk for all investments is not available. Third, because some real estate market characteristics are unique, comparison to common stock markets is difficult. Finally, there is some evidence that real estate markets respond more slowly to economic fluctuation. Information is probably of greater value to real estate analysts than common stock price and investment information is to common stock analysts and brokers. So substantial gains may be made by those investors with the skill to manage this information.

CAN REAL ESTATE INVESTORS OUTPERFORM THE MARKET?

This question is as old as whether real estate returns have exceeded those of common stocks. Although it is difficult to say due to a lack of empirical results, it is unlikely that investors in real estate will, a priori, outperform others seeking alternative investments. In effect, there is little reason to

believe that one investor, using the same market information and analytical skills, will, in the long run, be able to earn superior returns. However, with inside news, efficient data analysis, and/or sophisticated analytical methods, it is likely that such an investor could make better choices than the competition. Real estate markets continue to provide opportunities for investors who obtain better results by reducing "information costs" by using the real estate investment process.

We allow for short-run abnormal gains resulting from "luck" and "good fortune." We even allow for those occasional individuals who seem to have a "nose" for avoiding the "white elephants" and for "picking the winners." These individuals, however few in number, are blessed with the intuitive ability to follow the real estate investment process. If this is you, stop reading and start investing.

TYPES OF REAL ESTATE INVESTMENTS

Although residential investment is a popular form of real estate ownership, there are other types of property that may be attractive to potential investors. Within each type of property, specialized areas may be noted, including residential properties, commercial properties, industrial properties, agricultural real estate, and special purpose properties such as golf courses. Although the investment skills necessary for effective analysis tend to increase with larger and more complicated projects, the basic valuation techniques and the real estate investment process remain the same.

Income-producing real estate may also be classified according to income levels or rent classes and by geographic location. The economic influences of urban location can

* G. Stacy Sirmans, and C. F. Sirmans, "The Returns to Real Estate: The Historical Evidence," *Journal of Portfolio Management* 13 (Spring 1987), pp. 75–90. Stephen E. Roulac, "Can Real Estate Returns Outperform Common Stocks?" *Journal of Portfolio Management* 2 (Winter 1976), pp. 26–43. Robert H. Zerbst and Barbara R. Cambon, "Real Estate: Historical Returns and Risks," *Journal of Portfolio Management* 10 (1984), pp. 5–20. Alexander A. Robichek, Richard A. Cohn, and John J. Pringle, "Returns on Alternative Investment Media and Implications for Portfolio Construction," *Journal of Business* 45 (July 1972), pp. 427–443.

Table 2.1 TYPES OF INCOME-PRODUCING REAL ESTATE INVESTMENTS

Residential	Marinas
Single-family dwellings	Golf courses
Small apartment buildings	Athletic clubs
Duplex	Other commercial uses
Triplex	Theaters
Six-unit	Garages
Others	Special purpose
Low-rise apartments	
Garden-type apartments	**Industrial**
Elevator apartments	Utilities
Large complexes and residential developments	Plants
	Factories
	Warehouses
Commercial	Industrial parks
Single retail stores	Others
Office space	
Single offices	**Agricultural**
Office building centers and clusters	Orchards
Multi-use complexes	Timberland
Hotels and motels	Groves
Recreational property	Farmland
Vacation and second home developments	Others
Waterfront developments	

have such a dramatic effect on property values that an analysis of the economic environment is essential. However, it is obvious that certain uses of land are better suited to certain locations. For example, in newer urban residential areas, the land may be too expensive for a low-density garden-type project. Table 2.1 lists the traditional types of income-producing property.

PITFALLS

In general, any discussion of the attractiveness of investments should also consider the potential downfalls. Since investment involves the giving up of a certain sum for an uncertain inflow, possible changes in the expected inflow leaves the investor in a vulnerable position.

Although the previous discussion listed security, cash flow, leverage, tax shelter, appreciation, equity buildup, and other factors as reasons for the attractiveness of real estate, none of these features are available to the owner of real property without some amount of *risk*. Expected higher returns correspond to higher degrees of risk.

Risk is associated with the inability to forecast a number of variables accurately. Since it is very difficult (or perhaps impossible) to precisely forecast future events with accuracy, the differences between expected and actual results might result in serious problems. Overestimates of rental growth rates or future selling prices, underestimates of operating expenses, or failure to adequately determine equipment replacement expenditures may result in serious cash flow problems. Failure to meet debt service obligations or property tax liens could force foreclosure. All of these points are very relevant to the investor. Accurate analyses can help avert serious losses, inferior investment choices, or financial disaster. Remember that the investment decision is only as good as the expectations on which it is based. Any real estate investment can be made to look "good" if the expected inputs are changed. The challenge facing the investor is to develop a set of rational expectations that are consistent with those of the market participants.

3

REAL ESTATE INVESTMENT MATHEMATICS

THE purpose of this chapter is to review some of the basic mathematical mechanics for making real estate investment decisions. Specifically, we discuss how to do the following:

1. Calculate the present value of a lump-sum future amount.
2. Calculate the present value of a series of unequal future amounts.
3. Calculate the rate of return on an investment. This rate is generally referred to as the *internal rate of return*.
4. Calculate the mechanics of a mortgage including:
   a. Calculation of debt service (payment)
   b. Calculation of amount outstanding at any point of mortgage life
   c. Calculation of the amortization schedule (interest and principal for each payment

The compound interest tables presented in the appendix A of this book are used in making real estate investment decisions. There are three sets of tables:

Table 1. Present value of $1.00 factors (annual)
Table 2. Mortgage constant (monthly payments)
Table 3. Proportion outstanding on mortgages: various interest rates, mortgage maturities, and holding periods

PRESENT VALUE

Table 1 provides the factors for finding the present value of a lump-sum payment to be made in the future at various rates of discount. Table 2 provides the mortgage constant factors for monthly payments. The mortgage constant, when multiplied by the amount borrowed, tells the investor the payment necessary to fully amortize (pay off) the loan. Table 3 provides the proportion outstanding on mortgages. These are useful in allocating the mortgage payment into interest and principal.

How to Calculate Present Value

The present value of $1.00 factors in table 1 of appendix A are constructed using the following equation:

(3.1)
$$PVF_{i,n} = \frac{1}{(1 + i)^n}$$

where:

$PVF_{i,n}$ = the present value of $1.00
factor at rate i for n periods,
i = the rate of discount, and
n = the number of periods.

The present value of any future amount is calculated by multiplying the present value factor by the future amount. In equation form:

(3.2)
$$PV = FV[PVF_{i,n}]$$

where:

PV = the present value,
FV = the future value, and
$PFV_{i,n}$ = the present value factor at rate i for n periods.

Example 3.1: Present Value of a Future Amount. What is the present value of $1,000 to be received six years in the future, discounted at 12 percent per year, using equation 3.2?

Present Value (PV) = $PVF_{i,n}$ [Future

Value]

$$PV = \frac{1}{(1 + .12)^6} [\$1,000]$$

$$= .50663112 [\$1,000]$$

$$= \$506.63$$

Thus, $1,000 to be received six years from now is worth about $506.63 today, at a discount rate of 12 percent. The factor, .50663, for 12 percent interest for six years can be found in table 1 in appendix A by looking under the column labeled 12 percent for six years.

Stated differently, an investor could pay $506.63 today for an investment that would sell for $1,000 six years in the future and earn an annual rate of return of 12 percent.

Example 3.2: Present Value of a Lump Sum. Suppose a real estate investor is considering purchasing a parcel of vacant land. The investor expects to sell the parcel for $25,000 five years from now. How much could be paid today for the investment if the investor wants to earn a return of 15 percent per year?

The present value of $25,000 five years from now at a rate of 15 percent is:

Present Value = Future Value [$PVF_{i,n}$]

$$\text{Present Value} = [\$25,000] \frac{1}{(1.15)^5}$$

$$= \$25,000 (.49717674)$$

$$= \$12,429.42$$

The present value factor, .49717674, can be found by looking in table 1 in appendix A under the column 15 percent for five years. Multiplying this factor by the expected $25,000 results in a price of $12,429. Thus, if the investor paid $12,429 for the investment and sold it for $25,000 in five years, the rate of return would be 15 percent per year.

Example 3.3: Rate of Return. Suppose the investor in example 3.2 paid $13,570 for the parcel of land and sold it five years later for $25,000. What would be the rate of return on the investment?

In this type of situation, we know the present value ($13,570) and the future value ($25,000). What we don't know is the rate that will make the two values equal after a five-year period. The answer can be found as follows:

Present Value = Future Value [$PVF_{i,n}$]

$$\$13,570 = \$25,000 [PVF_{i,n}]$$

$$.5428 = PVF_{i,n}$$

The question is: What rate (i) will make this equation true?

One solution is to simply choose an *i* and solve the equation. Suppose, for example, we were to "guess" 12 percent. Solving the equation yields:

$$.5428 = \frac{1}{(1.12)^5}$$

$$.5428 \neq .56742686$$

Obviously the equation does not hold at 12 percent. Thus we must pick another *i*. Should it be larger or smaller than 12 percent? It should be larger. Why? Because the larger the rate, the smaller the number yielded by the right-hand side of the equation. (The reciprocal of 1.12 raised to the 5th power is larger than, for example, the reciprocal of 1.15 raised to the 5th power. Try it and see.)

Thus, suppose we select 13 percent. Solving the equation:

$$.5428 = \frac{1}{(1.13)^5}$$

$$.5428 = .5428$$

Thus the correct rate is 13 percent. If the investor paid $13,570 for an investment and sold it five years later for $25,000, the rate of return would be 13 percent per year.

Another solution is to take the equation:

$$.5428 = \frac{1}{(1 + i)^5} = PVF_{i,n}$$

and look through the factors in table 1 of appendix A for five years until the factor .5428 is found. This factor is found under the 13 percent column for five years.

Example 3.4: The Present Value of an Unequal Series. A real estate investment is expected to produce the after-tax cash flows (ATCF) shown in table 3.1. What is the present value of these cash flows at a rate of 12 percent? The present value factors (PVF) at 12 percent are shown in column 3. Multiplying these factors by the yearly ATCF yields the present value of each cash flow. Adding the present values results in a total present value of $85,498.68. What does this mean to the investor? It tells the investor that he can pay up to $85,498.68 for the investment and, assuming the investment generates the expected ATCF, earn a rate of return of 12 percent per year.

If the investor paid more than $85,498.68 for the investment, what would happen to the rate of return? It would be lower. For example, if the investor paid $90,289.55, the rate of return would be 10 percent. Should the opposite occur, the investor pays $79,032.51 and the rate of return rises to 15 percent. Thus the lower the price, the higher the rate of return for a given set of cash flows. It should be noted, however, that these changes are based on the assumption that the estimated ATCFs are correct. The

Table 3.1 EXAMPLE OF PRESENT VALUE OF AN UNEQUAL SERIES OF CASH FLOWS

(1) Year	(2) ATCF	(3) Present Value Factor at 12%	(4) Present Value
1	$20,000	.89286	$17,857.20
2	20,400	.79719	16,262.68
3	30,000	.71178	21,353.40
4	20,600	.63552	13,091.71
5	20,200	.56743	11,462.09
6	10,800	.50663	5,471.60
		Total present value =	$85,498.68

actual (realized) rate of return may be different than the expected, if the actual cash flows are different than the expected. The actual return cannot be calculated until an investment is bought, operated, and sold. The actual income streams would then be known with certainty. Investing, however, requires the investor to commit the outflow in the present in return for the expected (but risky) inflows in the future.

HOW TO FIND NET PRESENT VALUE

Example 3.5: The Net Present Value of an Investment. The net present value (NPV) of an investment is equal to the present value of the inflows minus the present value of the outflows. Stated another way, the net present value is the difference between what an investment is worth and its costs. Suppose an investor pays $97,175 in equity for an investment (the costs of the investment). The expected cash flows from operations are shown in table 3.2. What is the net present value of the investment? The concept behind NPV is very simple: If an investment is "worth" more than it "costs," then accept. If not, reject the investment.

Assuming that the investor requires a 12 percent after-tax rate of return, the net present value is $3,016. The decision rules are:

(3.3)
Accept if $NPV \geq 0$,
Reject if $NPV < 0$.

At a rate of return of 12 percent, the present value of the cash inflows exceeds the present value of the outflows by $3,016. Thus, the decision would be to invest. In this example, the cash inflows are "worth" $100,191, but they only "cost" $97,175.

Suppose, however, that the investor requires a higher rate of return. Will the decision to invest still hold if the required rate is 14 percent? To find the NPV at 14 percent (PV of cash inflows minus PV of cash outflows), we discount all of the cash flows at 14 percent (shown in table 3.3).

The NPV of minus $2,865 indicates that an investor requiring a 14 percent rate of return should not invest in this project. As the required rate of return goes up for a given set of cash flows, the NPV decreases.

It seems intuitive that there must be a rate at which the present value of the inflows is equal to the present value of the outflows. This rate is called the *internal rate of return* (IRR) and is illustrated in example 3.6.

HOW TO CALCULATE THE INTERNAL RATE OF RETURN

Example 3.6: The Internal Rate of Return on an Investment. Continuing with the numbers developed in examples 3.4 and 3.5, what is the expected rate of return? The internal rate of return (IRR) is defined as the rate that will make the present value of

Table 3.2 NET PRESENT VALUE OF AN INVESTMENT AT 12 PERCENT

Year	Equity	ATCFs	ATER	PVF at 12%	Present Value
0	− $97,175	—		1.00000	− $97,175
1		$20,000		.89286	17,857
2		20,400		.79719	16,263
3		30,000		.71178	21,353
4		20,600		.63552	13,092
5		20,200		.56743	11,462
6		10,800	$29,000	.50663	20,164
				Net present value =	+ $ 3,016

Table 3.3 NET PRESENT VALUE OF AN INVESTMENT AT **14** PERCENT

Year	Equity	ATCFs	ATER	PVF at 14%	Present Value
0	− $97,175	—		1.00000	− $97,175
1		$20,000		.87720	17,544
2		20,400		.76947	15,697
3		30,000		.67497	20,249
4		20,600		.59208	12,197
5		20,200		.51937	10,491
6		10,800	$29,000	.45559	18,132
				Net present value =	− $ 2,865

Table 3.4 EXAMPLE OF CALCULATING THE INTERNAL RATE OF RETURN **(IRR)**

Year	Equity	ATCFs	ATER	PVF at 13%	Present Value
0	− $97,175	—		1.00000	− $97,175
1		$20,000		.88496	17,699
2		20,400		.78315	15,976
3		30,000		.69305	20,792
4		20,600		.61332	12,634
5		20,200		.54276	10,964
6		10,800	$29,000	.48032	19,117
				Net present value =	+ $ 7

the cash inflows equivalent to the present value of the outflows. Another way to define the IRR is the rate that will make the NPV of an investment equal to zero. There is no simple way to directly compute the IRR without a calculator that performs the function. The alternative is a trial and error (or iterative) approach. When a rate of return is tried and the resulting NPV is positive, the rate should be raised. If the NPV is negative, the rate should be lowered.

Returning to example 3.5, the foregoing analysis indicates that 12 percent is too low a rate since the NPV was a positive $3,016, and that 14 percent is too high since the NPV was a negative $2,865. Therefore, let's try 13 percent (see table 3.4).

The resulting NPV is a positive $7.00 indicating that the IRR is very close to 13 percent; in fact, it is just above 13 percent (13.0022 percent). This rate, 13.0022 per-

cent, will make the present value of the cash inflows equal to the cash outflows. Therefore the expected rate of return on the investment of $97,175—assuming the *expected* cash flows will be realized—is approximately 13 percent. Under these assumptions, the IRR on this investment is 13 percent.

Example 3.7: NPV and IRR. A real estate investor is considering the purchase of a small apartment building. The projected after-tax cash flows are shown in table 3.5. The investor expects to own the property for five years at which time the investment will be sold. The investor's initial equity investment (cash outflow) at the time of investment is $25,000. Note that the investor expects a negative cash flow (meaning more equity must be invested) in year three of the holding period.

Table 3.5 Expected Cash Flows from a Small Apartment Building

Year	Equity	ATCFs	ATER	PVF at 15%	Present Value
0	− $25,000			1.0	− $25,000
1		$3,550		.86957	3,087
2		4,000		.75614	3,025
3		− 2,000		.65752	− 1,315
4		5,000		.57175	2,859
5		6,000	$30,000	.49718	17,898
				Net present value =	554
				Internal rate of return =	15.61%

At a required rate of return of 15 percent, is this a "good" investment? Stated another way, is the net present vaue of the investment positive or negative? Table 3.5 gives the numerical calculations. The present value factors (PVFs) at 15 percent are from table 1 of appendix A. Multiplying these by the cash flows yields the present value for each year. Summing these (shown in the last column) results in a net present value of $554. Since the NPV is positive, it means that the present value of the cash inflows (what the investment is worth) exceeds the present value of the cash outflows (what the investment costs). Thus, this is a "good" investment.

What is the internal rate of return on this investment? That is, at what rate will the present value of the cash inflows exactly equal the present value of the cash outflows? For this example, since the NPV is positive at 15 percent, we know that the IRR (or the expected rate of return since it is calculated on expected cash flows) must be greater than 15 percent (but not much greater). The rate of return, using the trial and error procedure illustrated in example 3.6, is 15.61 percent. Thus, using the IRR method, it is a "good" investment since the expected rate of return (15.61 percent) is greater than the required rate of return (15 percent).

THE MECHANICS OF MORTGAGES

THE MORTGAGE CONSTANT

Tables 2 and 3 of appendix A give the "mortgage constant."

Where i is the interest rate and n is the term of the mortgage:

$$MC_{i,n} = \frac{i}{1 - \dfrac{1}{(1 + i)^n}}$$

When multiplied by the amount borrowed, the mortgage constant results in the amount of debt service (payment) to be made each period. In equation form:

(3.4)

$$\text{Payment} = \text{Amount Borrowed } [MC_{i,n}]$$

where:

MC is the mortgage constant at interest rate i for a maturity of n periods.

Table 2 of appendix A is for payments made monthly.

Example 3.8: Calculating Payments on Monthly Mortgage. Mr. B borrows $75,000 from the City Bank. The loan is at 12 percent interest with payments to be made *monthly* over a period of twenty years. What is the monthly debt service?

Table 2 of appendix A gives the mortgage constant under monthly payments. At 12 percent interest for twenty years, the monthly mortgage constant is .01101. The monthly payment is thus:

$$\text{Payment} = \text{Amount Borrowed} \; [\text{Mortgage Constant}]$$

$$\text{Payment} = \$75,000 \, (.01101)$$

$$\text{Payment} = \$825.75$$

The annual payment is twelve times the monthly payment:

$$\text{Annual Payment} = \$825.75 \, (12)$$

$$= \$9,909$$

Example 3.9: Determining the Outstanding Balance (Monthly Payments). What amount of the $75,000 would be outstanding after six years of monthly payments? The proportion outstanding can be calculated as follows:

(3.5)
$$\text{Proportion outstanding} = \frac{\text{Mortgage constant for total term}}{\text{Mortgage constant for remaining term}}$$

Using the 12 percent, monthly table 2 of appendix A,

$$\text{Proportion outstanding} = \frac{.01101086}{.01231430}$$

$$= .89415$$

The proportion outstanding after six years is found by dividing .01101, the mortgage constant for the total term (12 percent for twenty years, monthly payments), by .01231, the mortgage constant for the remaining term (12 percent for fourteen years, monthly payments).

Multiplying the proportion outstanding, .89415, by the original amount, $75,000,

yields the amount outstanding after six years:

$$\text{Amount Outstanding} = \$75,000 \, (.89415)$$
$$= \$67,061.25$$

Table 3 of appendix A gives the proportion outstanding on mortgages at various interest rates, maturities, and holding periods. These proportions *assume monthly compounding* and are helpful in setting up the mortgage amortization schedule when monthly payments are made.

Example 3.10: Calculating the Amortization Schedule (Monthly Payments). Allocate the payment in example 3.8 between interest and principal for years one through six. Using the proportion outstanding (in table 3 of appendix A), the investor can easily allocate between interest and principal as shown in table 3.6.

The numbers were calculated as follows. The proportion outstanding at the end of each year is found using table 3 under 12 percent, twenty-year (240 months) maturity. The amount outstanding at the end of each year was found by multiplying the amount borrowed ($75,000) by the proportion outstanding at the end of each year (column 2). The amount of principal each year is found by subtracting the amounts outstanding at the end of each year. For example, the principal amount in year one ($961) was calculated by taking the difference between the $75,000 and the amount outstanding at the end of year one ($74,039). The difference between the debt service each year ($9,909) and the principal payment ($961) results in the amount of interest paid in year one ($8,948). This process was continued for each year.

Example 3.11: The Mechanics of a Mortgage. An investor is considering the purchase of a small office building. The price

Table 3.6 AMORTIZATION SCHEDULE FOR $75,000 MORTGAGE AT 12 PERCENT RATE FOR Twenty
YEARS, MONTHLY PAYMENTS

(1) Year	(2) Proportion Outstanding	(3) Amount Outstanding	(4) Annual Debt Service	(5) Interest	(6) Principal
0	1.0	$75,000			
1	.98718	74,039	9,909	$8,948	$ 961
2	.97273	72,955	9,909	8,825	1,084
3	.95646	71,735	9,909	8,689	1,221
4	.93811	70,358	9,909	8,532	1,377
5	.91744	68,808	9,909	8,359	1,550
6	.89415	67,061	9,909	8,162	1,747

is $350,000. The investor anticipates financing the investment with $100,000 in equity and a $250,000 mortgage. The mortgage calls for monthly payments over a term of twenty-five years at an interest rate of 10.5 percent.

What is the monthly payment on this mortgage? Using the mortgage constant factors in table 2 of appendix A yields:

Payment = $250,000 (.00944)

Payment = $2,360

where the factor .00944 is found under the 10.5 percent column for twenty-five years. Thus the monthly payment is $2,360. The annual payment (debt service) would be $28,320, or twelve times the monthly payment.

Table 3.7 contains the amortization schedule for this example. The proportions outstanding are from table 3 of appendix A for a twenty-five-year term at a 10.5 percent rate. Multiplying the proportion outstanding for each year by the original balance of $250,000 yields the amount outstanding at the end of each year. Subtracting the amounts outstanding at the end of each year indicates the amount of principal payment in that year. Since the total payment in any year is known, and since the total payment is the sum of principal and interest, the interest amount in any year can be determined by subtracting the principal payment in any year from the total payment.

To illustrate, let's take the fourth year. The proportion outstanding is .95895. Multiplying this by the original balance of $250,000 yields the amount outstanding at the end of year four of $239,738. The amount outstanding at the end of year three

Table 3.7 AMORTIZATION SCHEDULE FOR A $250,000 MORTGAGE AT 10.5 PERCENT
FOR TWENTY-FIVE YEARS, MONTHLY PAYMENTS

Year	Proportion Outstanding	Amount Outstanding	Annual Debt Service	Interest	Principal
0		$250,000			
1	.99129	247,823	$28,320	$26,143	$2,177
2	.98161	245,403	28,320	25,900	2,420
3	.97087	242,718	28,320	25,635	2,685
4	.95895	239,738	28,320	25,340	2,980
5	.94571	236,428	28,320	25,010	3,310

is $242,718. Thus the difference of $2,980 ($242,718 minus $239,738) is the amount amortized (paid off) in year four. Since the total payment in year four is $28,320, the interest payment is $25,340 (or $28,320 minus $2,980).

SUMMARY

A thorough understanding of these methods can make them a useful tool for real estate investors. This discussion has centered on the key areas for real estate investment decision making. These include how to calculate the present value of future cash inflows, calculate the net present value, and calculate the internal rate of return. Also it is important that the investor understand the mechanics of mortgages. The basic elements are how to calculate the debt service and the mortgage amortization schedule.

II

THE ENVIRONMENT FOR INVESTMENT DECISIONS

THE second step in the investment process is an analysis of the environment in which the decisions are made. Improper, faulty, or insufficient analysis of the setting—market, legal, and sociopolitical—can result in failure for the equity investor.

This analysis is probably the most difficult step in real estate investment decision making. The analysis of market conditions, the sociopolitical climate for investing, and the legal rights at stake are complex issues that are not easy to identify and forecast. And yet, this step is crucial for effective decision making.

Part II introduces the concept of business risk. *Business risk* is best defined as the variation in the expected net income from a real estate investment. This includes net income from operation as well as from the future disposition of the investment. Chapter 4 analyzes the real estate markets for investment decisions. Chapter 5 discusses the legal environment including the impact of traditional property law, the changing legal environment for investing in real property, and relevant considerations for choosing the appropriate ownership form and business entity.

4

ANALYZING REAL ESTATE MARKETS

THE purpose of this chapter and chapter 5 is to examine the second step in the real estate investment process. This chapter examines the market forces, particularly the supply and demand influences, that act upon an investment. The discussion is particularly aimed at identifying and reducing the business risk, the probability that the investment will not generate as much net income as expected, inherent in all real estate investments.

ROLE OF MARKET ANALYSIS IN DECISION MAKING

We have defined real estate investing as the sacrifice of certain outflows for uncertain inflows. Forecasting the future inflows from an investment is risky. The investor must examine the factors influencing the inflows and formulate expectations from this analysis. To begin, he or she must carefully analyze the market forces influencing the investment decision. This analysis is critical: A mistake in the identification of present or future market forces can be costly or result in project failure.

The critical elements of an investment include the quantity and certainty of gross income, operating expenses (operating ratio), and resultant net income over some future time period. Value is a reflection of future income expectations (benefits), and such estimates are risky. The only insurance against risk—and the only clarification (to a limited degree) of uncertainty—is an in-depth market study with a principal thrust concerning supply and demand. Perhaps the most neglected area of real estate investment theory and practice is the requisite market study as a first step in value estimation.

PURPOSE OF MARKET ANALYSIS

What is the purpose of market analysis? The answer is simply to reduce the risk associated with investing. One of the major risks is *market* or *business risk*. Business risk is related to such factors as:

1. National economic trends, such as unemployment or recession
2. A deteriorating economic base
3. Economic obsolescence, perhaps due to changing neighborhood
4. Flood, fire, and other human-made or natural disasters

5. Functional obsolescence, lack of quality construction, or age
6. Properties having high operating expense ratios and requiring very specialized kinds of management (i.e., nursing homes, hotels)
7. Legal restrictions, such as zoning changes
8. Population and sociodemographic trends
9. Changes in income levels, tastes, and preferences of tenants

These are only some of the factors that influence the business risk to which an investment is exposed. Obviously some types of real estate investment are subject to more business risk than others. All have risk, however, and the purpose of market analysis is to analyze this category of risk.

Business risk is a function of general economic conditions and characteristics of the investment and is *not* related to the financial structure (debt–equity mix). Therefore, the variability of net income is generally the most appropriate measure of this type of risk.

A real estate investment produces two potential sources of net income: the annual net operating income and the net income from the future disposition (typically, sale). Because market analysis identifies the variability of net income from these two sources, the investor should know which factors influence the variability. There are several factors, including rent per unit, vacancy level, operating expenses, estimated selling price at the end of the holding period, and selling expenses.

To illustrate the sensitivity of value estimates to changes in rents, suppose an investor is considering a building with 100 units. Market analysis indicates a range in rents from $175 to $200 per month per unit. Therefore, the potential gross income (PGI)

will vary between $210,000 to $240,000 per year, a considerable difference.

An analysis of competing properties indicates a value estimate of 5 times the PGI. This is referred to as the gross income multiplier (GIM). The investor would thus obtain an estimated value between $1,050,000 and $1,200,000.

(4.1)
$$Value = PGI \ (GIM)$$
$$Value = \$210,000 \ (5) = \$1,050,000$$
or
$$Value = \$240,000 \ (5) = \$1,200,000$$

This is a range in value of $150,000, which is a sizable difference in value for only a $25 range in rents. Therefore, investment values are very sensitive to errors or bad estimates.

Market analysis helps narrow the range in the key factors influencing net income—rents, operating expenses, vacancies, and future selling price. Small changes in these inputs to the investment process can make a big difference in the estimated value for an investment and in the expected rate of return.

THE REAL ESTATE MARKET

The real estate investor must focus considerable attention on the real estate market. The real estate market can be defined as a mechanism by which real estate goods and services are exchanged—a mechanism influenced by the wants of the participants in the market as well as by political and governmental intervention into the marketplace.

The purpose of the real estate market is to allocate a scarce commodity. This scarce commodity is real estate, which includes both land and improvements to the land and the property rights associated with the ownership. The real estate market, like any market, allocates this scarce resource by using the price mechanism. Generally, we find that the person willing to pay the most for the real estate acquires the rights associated with that ownership. In some instances, the public has decided that the scarce resource should be allocated by the government. For instance, the implementation of land use controls such as zoning ordinances may be viewed as an example of this type of allocation.

SUPPLY AND DEMAND ANALYSIS

The real estate market links the supply and demand for real estate. There are two types or categories of supply and demand with which the investor must be concerned. The first is the supply and demand for the use of the real estate. This involves the tenant's perspective. The second is the supply and demand for the ownership of an investment or the equity investor's perspective. The equity investor must consider both of these.

THE TENANT'S PERSPECTIVE

The demand for a real estate investment is based on the flow of services that it produces. For example, the demand for an apartment from the tenant's perspective is based on the housing services that are provided. Some of these services are shelter, comfort, prestige, access to work or shopping, safety, and social opportunities. Thus, the tenant is buying a set of services, not merely a physical living unit.

For these services, the tenant pays a "price" called rent. The greater the demand for the services, the greater the rent. Generally we do not observe the rent per unit of services but rather the rent per physical unit, for example, the rent per apartment or

the rent per square foot of retail space. It is important to remember, however, that the tenant is really buying the services. So the investor must be certain that the investment provides the level of services demanded.

THE EQUITY INVESTOR'S PERSPECTIVE

The second type of supply and demand analysis involves the buying and selling of the ownership of the investment. For example, suppose that fifty apartment buildings were bought in a particular real estate market during a given period. We would conclude that there had been a total demand for fifty apartment buildings. This buying and selling involves placing a value (or selling price) on the expected future income (from rental and future disposition).

The value represents the present worth of the expected future income. To illustrate, suppose that an investment is expected to produce $10,000 in net income per year for ten years. In addition, the investment has an expected selling price of $100,000 at the end of the ten years. The investor requires 12 percent return per year on the investment. What is the value of the investment?

To find the value, take the forecasts of income from operation and sale and discount them at the appropriate rate. However, this valuation process raises several questions. How is the expected income determined? What is the risk associated with future income, that is, how certain are we that the investment will generate the expected cash flows? How is the appropriate rate of discount determined?

All of these questions (and others) must be answered from the equity investor's perspective. This is what market analysis is all about. Viewing the investment from the tenant's perspective helps the investor determine the expected net income and variations over the holding period. Market analysis from the equity investor's perspective helps determine the relationship between value, risk, and cash flow from the investment.

So market analysis identifies supply and demand factors from both the tenant's and landlord's (equity investor) perspectives. It also helps to consider market conditions from the seller's and equity investor's perspectives. Changes in factors that influence the number of tenants and the rents tenants are willing to pay also affect the expected income from an investment. These changes can have an impact on the value of the investment from the equity investor's perspective. Likewise, various factors can influence the equity investor's behavior in the marketplace. For example, if equity investors perceive a particular real estate investment as becoming more risky because of international, urban, or neighborhood trends, this increased risk would be reflected in the valuation of the investment.

DECISIONS FROM THE MARKET STUDY

The market study analyzes the likely present and future demand for an investment and the existing and likely future supply of closely competitive facilities. From this, the investor formulates four conclusions:

1. The various prices and their probabilities at which the particular investment (existing or proposed) might be rented and expected future changes in rents
2. An estimate of the quantity (occupancy ratio or, conversely, vacancy ratio), such as apartment units or square feet of office space, likely to be sold or rented per year at those prices
3. A discussion of the specific conditions such as financing terms, sales tech-

niques, or certain amenities, which are required for sale or rental
4. An estimate of the probable future trends in value for the type of investment under consideration in its market environment.

It is obvious that the market study determines the first inputs to the cash flow statement. Remember that cash flow from a real estate investment can arise from two sources: the annual cash flow from operating the investment and the cash flow from the future disposition (usually sale) of the investment.

Market analysis also shows future trends in the expected market value (or selling price) of the investment. Increases (or decreases) in market value are caused by relative price changes or inflation. It is also possible to have both simultaneously. *Inflation* is defined as increases in all prices at the same rate of change. A *relative price change* is one in which the price or value of an investment rises (or falls) relative to prices of the other goods (investments) in the economy.

However, the investor must understand that the present investment value is not influenced by inflation. While inflation affects the future value, it does not influence the present value of an investment. However, expected relative price changes influence both the future and the present value of an investment. This will be discussed further later.

RISK VERSUS UNCERTAINTY

A distinction is sometimes made between risk and uncertainty. *Risk* is associated with situations in which a probability distribution of the returns from investment can be estimated. *Uncertainty* is associated with situations in which estimates of probability distribution are impossible. This distinction is not made in our discussion: Risk and uncertainty are used synonymously.

However, we realize that probability distributions of expected returns can be estimated with some precision. Some investments may have distributions that can be estimated objectively with statistical techniques. When such methods are used, risk is said to be measured by *objective probability distributions*.

In contrast, there are many investment situations in which statistical data cannot be used. The investor may have little or no historical data to use, particularly when the investment is a new project. However, he may rely heavily on historical data for similar projects and personal judgment. This is called *subjective probability distributions*. Thus, risk (or uncertainty) refers to an investment whose return cannot be predicted with certainty but for which an array of alternative outcomes and their probabilities can be estimated. This is a major purpose of market analysis.

RISK OVER TIME

How does the risk for an income stream change over time? Figure 4.1 shows the distribution of expected cash flow from an investment for years one, five, and ten. The distribution becomes flatter over time, indicating that there is more uncertainty about expected cash flows in later years. The dashed lines show the standard deviation, a well-known measure of risk, attached to the cash flow each year. The lines diverge from the expected cash flow over time, which indicates that the riskiness is increasing. If the cash flow in later years could be estimated equally as well as the cash flow in earlier years, that is, if risk was constant through time, the standard devi-

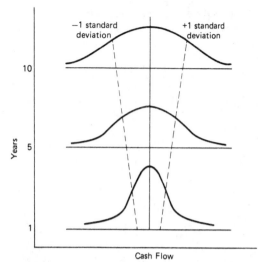

Figure 4.1   Risk as a Function of Time

ation would be constant and the dashed line would not diverge from the expected value.

In setting up the expected cash flow each year, some factors are probably the key to riskiness over time. For example, it is relatively easy to forecast the depreciation deduction and debt service with a fixed rate mortgage in later years, but much harder to forecast the expected rents, vacancies, or selling price. The market forces that cause these factors to vary are difficult to forecast as time increases.

This fact makes the investor base judgments on short-term holding period forecasts of cash flows. It has been argued that, on the average, income-producing properties typically are sold or refinanced within ten years or less of purchase.* Longer term forecasts of the expected cash flows should generally be used only in cases such as long-term leases.

---

* L. W. Ellwood, *Ellwood Tables for Real Estate Appraising and Financing*, 3rd ed. (Chicago: American Institute of Real Estate Appraisers, 1970), pp. 96–97.

INFLATION, RELATIVE PRICE CHANGES, AND MARKET ANALYSIS

Market analysis is particularly aimed at identifying potential relative price changes in an investment. These price changes are caused by shifts in supply and/or demand for a particular investment including real income changes, population growth (or decline), changes in neighborhood characteristics, or changes in tax laws.

It is important to understand the impact of relative price changes. The price of a particular investment can increase or decrease relative to other goods. Unexpected relative price declines have a negative impact on the rate of return for a particular investment. Likewise, unexpected relative price increases have positive effects on rates of return.

To illustrate relative price changes, consider the following simple example. An investor purchases a parcel of land for $10,000. One year later the land is sold for $12,000 (ignoring all holding costs and assuming no inflation). The investor has thus earned a 20 percent return. In present value form:*

$$\$10,000 = \frac{\$12,000}{(1 + r)^1}$$

$$1 + r = \frac{\$12,000}{\$10,000}$$

$$1 + r = 1.2$$

$$r = 1.2 - 1$$

$$r = .20 \text{ or } 20\%$$

But how is the investor able to sell the investment for a higher price? Figure 4.2 illustrates this for the simple case. The curves S and D represent the supply and demand curves for land. Suppose that pop-

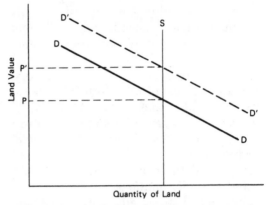

Figure 4.2 A Shift in the Demand for Land

ulation growth shifts the demand curve for land to D'. The price then rises from P to P' in real terms.

The present value of an investment depends on the timing of the estimated future value and the rate of return. Obviously, if the rate of return is held constant and the estimated future value is increased, the present value will be higher. In the simple example, the present value would be $12,000 instead of $10,000 if the expected future value is increased to $15,000 because of a relative price change. If the price is higher because of neutral inflation (or an equal percentage change in all prices), the present value would not be higher because the required rate of return must be increased to compensate for the purchasing power risk to which the investor is exposed.

If we view the required rate of return, $\bar{r}$, as the sum of the risk-free rate r_f, and market risk premium, r_m, and price inflation, r_p, then

(4.2)
$$\bar{r} = r_f + r_m + r_p$$

If there is no inflation, $r_p = 0$. In the example above, if the risk-free rate is 5 percent and the market risk is 15 percent then:

---

* Recall our discussion of present value from chapter 3.

(4.3)

$$\bar{r} = r_f + r_m$$

$$\bar{r} = .05 + .15$$

$$\bar{r} = .20$$

Assume inflation now increases from 0 percent annually to 5 percent annually. In our example, the land that sold for $10,000 a year ago would sell for $12,000 without inflation. However, with inflation, it sells for an additional $500 or $12,500. The question is whether the investor is any better off due to this inflationary effect. The answer is no.

If inflation is 5 percent, then $r_p = .05$. The required rate of return, $\bar{r}$, becomes:

$$\bar{r} = r_f + r_m + r_p$$

$$\bar{r} = .05 + .15 + .05$$

$$\bar{r} = .25$$

The present value of the investment is:

$$PV = \frac{\$12,500}{(1 + .25)^1}$$

$$= \$10,000$$

This may seem surprising since inflation increases the future rather than the present value of the land. However, the important point is that it also increases the required rate of return to keep the real value constant.

Because financial markets anticipate inflation, inflation premiums, r_p, are incorporated into market interest rates. Therefore, since inflation affects all assets in nominal dollars equally, a higher required rate of return means the real value (and return) stays constant.

Obviously, some changes in the value of real estate have occurred due to increasing demand for, or perhaps supply restrictions of, property during recent years. Although accumulated wealth is largely attributed to inflation, it is actually due to changes in demand and/or supply in the real estate market and to changes in the value of indebtedness assumed by borrowers prior to rising interest rates. Market analysis is aimed at trying to uncover potential relative price changes. In order to understand the investment process, one must understand the impact of inflation and relative price changes on present values and required rates of return.

MEASURING RISK AND RETURN

Modern real estate investment analysis defines *risk* as the dispersion of an investment's returns—the positive and negative deviations from the expected return. The most widely used method of risk analysis utilizes the expected (mean) rate of return as an indication of an investment's profitability and the variance (or standard deviation) as an indication of its risk.

Business risk, broadly defined, is the risk inherent in investing in real estate, as measured by the variability in the rate of return for an all equity financed investment. A general way of viewing the rate of return, $\bar{r}$, that should be required on an investment is:

$$\bar{r} = r_f + r_m + r_p$$

The term r_f is the risk-free rate, r_m is the risk premium for business risk, and r_p is the premium for purchasing power risk. The risk-free rate applies to investment where there is no chance that the realized rate of return will be less than the expected rate of return. The risk-free rate is simply compensation for postponing current consumption plans. The risk premium is the additional return necessary to compensate investors for bearing the risk that the realized rate could be lower than expected. Thus, $\bar{r}$ is the required rate of return, and reflects compensation for both waiting and risk.

Expected Rate of Return

A simple measure of the overall rate of return from an investment is calculated as follows:

(4.4)
$$R = \frac{NOI}{V}$$

where:

R = the overall rate of return (sometimes called the overall capitalization rate)

NOI = the expected net operating income

V = the value of the investment

For example, an investment under consideration is expected to generate $100,000 per year. The value is $1,000,000. The overall rate (R) is thus 10 percent ($100,000 divided by $1,000,000).

There is the possibility, however, that the net operating income will not be as expected. Suppose an investor decides that there are six chances out of ten that the actual net operating income will be $100,000. He or she also feels there is a .25 probability that the investment will generate $80,000 and a .15 probability that $110,000 will be realized. These outcomes are summarized in table 4.1.

E(R) denotes the expected rate of return, which is the weighted average of possible rates of return using the probabilities (P_i) as the weights. Thus E(R) can be written as:

(4.5)
$$E(R) = R_1 \cdot P_1 + R_2 \cdot P_2 + R_3 \cdot P_3$$
$$+ \cdots + R_m \cdot P_m$$
$$= \sum_{i=1}^{m} R_i \cdot P_i$$

where:

R_i = the overall return under the ith "state of the world"

m = the number of "states of the world"

P_i = the probability of the ith state of the world

For investment A, the expected rate of return is

$$E(R_A) = .08(.25) + .10(.60) + .11(.15)$$
$$E(R_A) = .0965 \text{ or } 9.65\%$$

Measuring Risk

To measure risk, investment analysis uses *variance* or *standard deviation*. These measure the dispersion of the expected return around the mean (expected) value and provide information on the extent of possible deviations of the actual return from the expected return. The greater the variance in expected return, the greater the risk.

The variance (σ^2) of the mean (equation 4.5) is given by:

Table 4.1 Investment A

Value	Net Operating Income (NOI)	Probability (P_i)	Overall Rate (R_i)
$1,000,000	$ 80,000	.25	.08
$1,000,000	$100,000	.60	.10
$1,000,000	$110,000	.15	.11

(4.6)

$$\sigma^2 = \sum_{i=1}^{m} P_i[R_i - E(R)]^2$$

(σ is the Greek letter sigma. The variance is thus read, sigma squared). To calculate the variance:

1. Calculate the deviation of each possible outcome from the expected value, $[R_i - E(R)]$.
2. Raise this deviation to the second power, $[R_i - E(R)]^2$.
3. Multiply this term by the probability of getting R_i (that is, P_i), $P_i [R_i - E(R)]^2$.
4. Sum these products, $\Sigma\ P_i[R_i - E(R)]^2$ from i to m.
5. The result is σ^2.

It should be noted that the distribution of returns is measured in percentages. The dimension of σ^2 is in "percentages squared," which is economically meaningless. Taking the square root of the variance results in the standard deviation (σ) in "percentages."

(4.7)

$$\sigma = \sqrt{\sigma^2}$$

Because standard deviation also measures the variability of the distribution, it is stated in percentages. For ranking investment proposals, however, either the variance or the standard deviation can be used since both are always greater than or equal to zero.

The standard deviation for investment A is

$$\sigma = \sqrt{.00010225}$$
$$= .01014$$

Thus, for investment A, the expected overall return, $E(R)$, is 9.65 percent with a standard deviation, σ, of 1.014 percent.

THE DECISION RULES

To evaluate investments using the expected return and variance (or standard deviation), there are two decision rules to be applied. Investment A is preferred to investment B if one of the following two conditions holds:

1. The expected return of A exceeds (or is equal to) the expected return of B *and* the standard deviation of A is less than the standard deviation of B.
2. The expected return of A exceeds that of B *and* the standard deviation of A is less than (or equal to) that of B.

In equation form, these decision rules may be written as follows:

A is preferred to B if:

(4.8)
$$E(R_A)\ \geq E(R_B)$$
$$\sigma_A < \sigma_B$$

or

(4.9)
$$E(R_A)\ > E(R_B)$$
$$\sigma_A \leq \sigma_B$$

In the example, the expected return, variance, and standard deviation for investment A is:

Expected Return: $E(R_A) = .0965$

Variance: $\sigma_A{}^2 = .00010225$

Standard Deviation: $\sigma_A = .01014$

Suppose the expected return, variance, and standard deviation for investment B is:

Expected Return: $E(R_B) = .0965$

Variance: $\sigma_B{}^2 = .00015$

Standard Deviation: $\sigma_B = .01225$

Notice that both investments have the same expected return of 9.65 percent. However, investment A is preferred to B by using condition 1. Although the expected return from both investments is the same, investment A has a smaller variance (or standard deviation). Investment B is thus more risky in terms of variance from the expected return.

FURTHER EXAMPLES

The "mean-variance" decision rules help the investor select and, more important, understand the relationship between expected returns from an investment and the risks. To further illustrate these decision rules, suppose an investor has the investment opportunities in table 4.2. Which of these should be selected? Using the decision rules, compare investments C and E. Both have the same expected return but C has less risk since the standard deviation is smaller. Thus, C is preferred to E. Now compare investments C and D. These have the same risk, but D has a higher expected return. So, D is preferred to investment C. Since D is preferred to C and C is preferred to E, investment D is preferred to E. Now, if the investor were to choose among the three, investment D would be selected.

However, there are problems with the mean-variance decision rules. Suppose an investor has the following choice in table 4.3. Which should be picked? We cannot use the mean-variance rules because in this case the expected risk and expected return is greater for investment G than for invest-

Table 4.3 INVESTMENTS F AND G

Investment	Return E(R)	Risk (σ)
F	.11	.02
G	.13	.03

ment F. The question the investor must answer is: Does the increase in return "compensate" for the increase in risk? If it does, then choose G over F. If it doesn't, the investor would prefer investment F. This is a major reason why the investor must identify his or her particular preference on the risk–return trade-off.

COMMON ERRORS IN ANALYZING MARKETS

A recent survey of real estate markets analyses examined the question: "What have been the deficiencies of real estate market and investment analyses that have been prepared, and what can be done to improve them?"* This study examined forty-five feasibility reports prepared by consultants, appraisers, and market analysts with established national and/or regional reputations. It found that the caliber of market analysis reports was substantially below the "state of the art." Six of the most common errors made in analyzing real estate markets are summarized in table 4.4.

Unspecified research direction. The appropriateness of any investment decision can only be evaluated when the investor's goal or objective is known. As previously discussed, the analyst must determine what decision the investor is trying to make.

Table 4.2 INVESTMENTS C, D, AND E

Investment	Return E(R)	Risk (σ)
C	.11	.02
D	.13	.02
E	.11	.03

* Gary W. Eldred and Robert H. Zerbst, "A Critique of Real Estate Market and Investment Analyses," *The Appraisal Journal* 46 (July 1978), pp. 443–452.

Table 4.4 COMMON ERRORS IN ANALYZING MARKETS

Type of Error	% of Reports
1. Unspecified research direction	73
2. Statistics without explanations	82
3. Misspecification of supply and demand	67
4. Failure to correlate supply and demand	60
5. Inattention to economic indicators	76
6. Omission of primary data	49

Source: Gary W. Eldred and Robert H. Zerbst, "A Critique of Real Estate Market and Investment Analyses," *The Appraisal Journal* 46 (July 1978), pp. 443–452.

Statistics Without Explanations. Nearly all market analysis reports contain large amounts of statistics on such factors as population growth, employment levels, income levels, and transportation facilities. The purpose of the market analysis is not to describe but to explain. How do these relate to the problem at hand?

Misspecification of Supply and Demand. As noted previously, market analysis centers on understanding supply and demand for a given investment. What is the market for the investment under consideration? What segment of the market is being served by the project? How does this project compare with competing projects?

Failure to Correlate Supply and Demand. The investor must carefully analyze supply and demand to determine expected vacancy rates for the investment under consideration. From this he must make quantitative decisions regarding the ability to rent the investment.

Inattention to Economic Indicators. The investor must also analyze the possible effects of the regional and national economic climate on local economies and decide how possible downturns will affect the investment. Leading economic indicators may be used in investment decision making.

Omission of Primary Data. Data can be classified as primary or secondary.* *Secondary data* are collected for some purpose other than the study at hand. This type of data is available from such sources as the U.S. Bureau of Census, trade associations, and planning agencies. While typically cost-free, these frequently do not fit the investment process very precisely.

Primary data are gathered specifically for a particular investment decision. Primary data help to determine the tastes and preferences of that special segment of the real estate market toward which an investment is aimed. Types of data include vacancy surveys, rental rates, and the operating expense levels of competing investments.

FACTORS TO CONSIDER IN ANALYZING MARKETS

The general factors influencing real estate investments can be broadly classified as those influencing demand and those influencing supply.

* Arnold L. Redman and C. F. Sirmans, "Regional/Local Economic Analysis: A Discussion of Data Sources," *The Appraisal Journal* 45 (April 1977), pp. 261–272.

Income. Because the demand for real estate is dependent on income, and real estate is used to produce products and services, the investor must carefully consider the demand for the products or services produced using the real estate. For example, the demand for residential units is derived from the demand for housing. The level of income determines the demand for real estate and indicates the ability to obtain financing.

Demographic and Population Factors. Demographics, or charcteristics of the population, are one of the major determinants of the long-term direction of real estate markets. Profiles of age, rates of family formation, fertility, mortality, and migration are extremely important. Migration trends are probably the most difficult to forecast, yet have the most impact on real estate markets.

Supply Factors. The existing supply of real estate includes structures that have been built over a long period of time. New structures added in any one year may exceed the old structures torn down but very seldom is the net increase a very large proportion of the total supply. So the supply of real estate at any point in time is relatively fixed. The characteristics of existing and new supply such as age, location, and physical conditions should be compared to the investment under consideration. These give the investor some idea about how his investment would compete in the market.

Economic Trends. The real estate investor should monitor the important indicators of economic activity that forecast recessions or growth. Some good indicators are interest rates, construction activity, and unemployment levels.

A SAMPLE MARKET ANALYSIS

Table 4.5 illustrates the various types of factors that should be considered in analyzing the real estate market. First, delineate the market area. Second, analyze its demographic characteristics, including population growth, estimated future population growth, age distribution, and number of households. Third, consider those factors influencing employment trends, income data, and the economic base of the neighborhood.

Fourth, analyze the supply side of the market. This includes examining the building and construction industry, housing market, and mortgage market trends, and taking inventory of existing competition. Fifth, analyze the judicial and legal areas. These include land-use planning, zoning, building codes, municipal services, property taxation, and other aspects of the legal environment. Finally, identify the types and sources of data for market analysis.

PHYSICAL CHARACTERISTICS

The physical attributes of land and improvements play a crucial role in the overall feasibility of an investment. These attributes may limit utility or provide opportunities to create competition.

Some of the physical attributes include:

1. Size and shape of the site
2. Topography
3. Storm water drainage
4. Watersheds, springs, or other water factors
5. Soil and subsoil characteristics
6. Utilities
7. Functional layout of the improvements
8. Personal response factors, such as security
9. Transportation access
10. Physical condition of improvements

Table 4.5 REAL ESTATE MARKET ANALYSIS FOR AN INVESTMENT

Delineation of the Market Area

METROPOLITAN AREA

1. Name of standard metropolitan statistical area (SMSA)
2. Identification
   a. County or counties
   b. Principal incorporated and unincorporated urbanized area (10,000 or more population)
3. Geography
   a. Size (land area)
   b. Major topographical features
4. Climate
   a. Rainfall
   b. Temperature changes (monthly, seasonal)
   c. Relative humidity
5. General urban structure; location of facilities
   a. Significant geographic submarkets in SMSA
   b. Employment areas
   c. Shopping areas (central business district, regional, and community shopping centers)
   d. Principal transportation facilities (air, highway, rail, water)
   e. Educational facilities
   f. Community facilities (religious, cultural, recreational)
6. Direction of city growth
7. Commuting patterns (journey to work)
8. Any major community developments and/or special features or characteristics germane to the market analysis

Demographic Analysis

POPULATION

1. Most recent estimate for total population
2. Past trends in population growth
3. Estimated future population
   a. 1985, 1990, 1995 totals and average annual rate of growth
   b. Changes in population due to
      (1) Net natural increase
      (2) Migration
4. Distribution by age groups
   a. 1980 census
   b. Most recent estimates

HOUSEHOLDS

1. Most recent estimates for household formations
2. Past trends in household formations
3. Estimated future total households and average annual rate of growth
4. Current trends in household size (increasing, decreasing)

Economy of the Market Area (Demand Side Analysis)

ECONOMIC HISTORY AND CHARACTERISTICS

1. General description
2. Major economic activities and developments

Table 4.5 *(cont.)*

a. Before 1980
b. Recent and present

EMPLOYMENT, TOTAL AND NONAGRICULTURAL
1. Current estimates
2. Past trends
3. Distribution by industry groups
   a. For each period, past and present
   b. Numerical and as percent of all employment
4. Estimated future employment
   a. Total
   b. By industry groups
5. Trends in labor participation rate
6. Trends in female employment

UNEMPLOYMENT
1. Current level
2. Past trends

ECONOMIC-BASE ANALYSIS
1. Metropolitan area compared to national and state employment data
2. Discussion of principal employers
   a. Primary industries (manufacturing, construction, mining)
   b. Secondary industries (TCU, trade, FIRE, services, governments)
   c. Location and accessibility
3. Payroll data (census of manufacturers, trade, services, governments)

INCOME DATA
1. Personal income by major sources
   a. By type: wage and salary, proprietors
   b. By industry: farm, nonfarm, government
2. Per capita personal income
3. Family income distribution
   a. All families
   b. Owner households
   c. Renter households
   d. Households with female heads
4. Projections for growth in personal income

Construction and Real Estate Activity (Supply Side Analysis)

BUILDING AND CONSTRUCTION INDUSTRY
1. Residential building by type (single family, multifamily, rental, or sales)
   a. Historical and recent trends (past 10 years)
   b. Building permits: monthly for current and previous year
   c. Conversions and demolitions
2. Nonresidential construction
   a. Commercial
   b. Industrial
   c. Institutional
3. High-rise building activity (minimum height of five stories above ground)
   a. Residential

Table 4.5 *(cont.)*

---

    b. Commercial (offices, stores, hotels and motels, multiple use)

    c. Other (governmental, schools, hospitals)

4. Heavy engineering construction

DEMAND-AND-SUPPLY ANALYSIS FOR PROPERTIES OTHER THAN RESIDENTIAL

1. General demand factors in metropolitan area

    a. Number of potential new employees

    b. Number of potential new tenants or owner users

    c. Movement of firms in and out of the area

    d. Recent trends in replacement ratios

2. Existing inventory, by property type

    a. Price: sale or rental rates

    b. Quantity: net leasable square footage

    c. Year built: before 1970, 1970–present, new

    d. Competitive status

    e. Vacancy factors

3. Projected production, by property type

    a. Price: sale or rental rates

    b. Quantity: net leasable space

    c. Probable conditions (financing, marketing, absorption rates)

HOUSING INVENTORY, BY TYPE (SINGLE-FAMILY, MULTIFAMILY)

1. Most recent estimates

2. Past trends including 1980 census

    a. Index of housing value and rents

3. Principal characteristics

    a. Tenure of occupancy

    b. Value of houses and monthly contract rent

    c. Type of structure

    d. Year built

    e. Vacancy ratios: percent of total units (total, homeowner, rental)

RESIDENTIAL SALES AND RENTAL MARKETS

1. General market conditions

2. Major subdivision activity

    a. Current

    b. Past trends

3. Trends in sales prices or monthly rentals

    a. Existing units

    b. New units

    c. Sales prices or monthly rentals adjusted to square-foot basis

4. Unsold inventory of new sales housing

    a. Price ranges

    b. Number of months unsold

    c. Absorption rates

    d. Environmental ratings

    e. Competitive status with other sales properties

5. New rental housing

    a. Date of completion

    b. Type of units and rental ranges

Table 4.5 *(cont.)*

---

     c. Marketing experience to date
     d. Absorption rates
     e. Environmental ratings
     f. Competitive status with existing rental housing
  6. Residential units under construction
     a. Volume
     b. Types of units
     c. Probable environmental ratings
     d. Probable marketing schedules

OTHER HOUSING MARKETS
  1. Public and government subsidized housing
     a. Identification and location
     b. Existing and planned
  2. Specialized submarkets for housing demand and supply
     a. College or university housing
     b. Housing for the elderly
     c. Military housing

REAL ESTATE LOANS AND MORTGAGE MARKETS
  1. Sources and availability of funds
  2. FHA, VA, FNMA, GNMA
  3. Interest rates and terms of mortgages
  4. Recordings of mortgages and/or deeds of trust
  5. Foreclosures
     a. Overall trend
     b. Conventional, FHA, other

Political and Legal Aspects (Legal Environmental Analysis)

LAND-USE PLANNING
  1. Regional
  2. County (counties)
  3. Incorporated cities in SMSA

ZONING
  1. Review of present zoning ordinances for county (counties) and cities
  2. Zoning history and present attitudes of zoning authority
  3. Identify raw land presently zoned for land use of subject property

ORDINANCES, CODES, REGULATIONS
  1. Subdivisions
     a. Submission procedures
     b. Requirements for improvements
  2. Building codes
  3. Health and public safety
  4. Allocation of land for schools, recreational areas, open space

MUNICIPAL SERVICES
  1. Public safety
     a. Fire
     b. Police
  2. Hospitals and health care
  3. Utilities

Table 4.5 *(cont.)*

ECOLOGICAL
1. Environmental impact studies
2. Limited growth policies
3. Floodplains and flood control
4. Solid-waste disposal

PROPERTY TAXATION
1. Tax rate per $1,000 valuation
2. Assessment ratio as percent of market value
3. Special assessment districts

Sources of Information

TYPES OF DATA
1. Population
2. Employment
3. Personal income
4. Planning
5. Building
6. Zoning
7. Other pertinent

SOURCES OF DATA
1. Secondary data sources
   a. Census of population
   b. Census of construction
   c. Census of housing
   d. Bureau of Labor Statistics
   e. National Planning Association
   f. Local planning agencies
2. Primary data sources
   a. Real estate brokers
   b. Appraisers
   c. Construction firms
   d. Mail questionnaires

The investor is obviously concerned with matching the demands in the marketplace to the supply. The key question is whether the investment under consideration provides the services demanded by prospective users.*

---

* For a more detailed discussion, see James A. Graaskamp, *A Guide to Feasibility Analysis* (Chicago: Society of Real Estate Appraisers, 1970), pp. 67–81.

SOCIOPOLITICAL ENVIRONMENT

As we have stated, the purpose of market analysis is to help the investor identify the degree of business risk for an investment. All real estate investments are subject to business risk, since the net income is not known with certainty.

Another important set of factors that influences the decision-making process is re-

Table 4.6 MARKET ANALYSIS OF A POTENTIAL APARTMENT INVESTMENT

Apartment Project	No. of Units	Type	Sq. Ft. Floor Area	Rent per Month	Sq. Ft. Rent per Month	Rent per Room	Estimated Occupancy	COMMENTS
			APARTMENT MIX					
1. Oakbrook Village	52	1BR, 1BA, ST	453	$260	$.57	$ 86.67	98%	Student oriented, well landscaped, two miles from university on student bus route, drapes and carpets, completely furnished, quiet
	55	2BR, 2BA, F	939	400	.43	100.00	99%	
	49	1BR, 1.5BA, TH	729	325	.45	108.33	97%	
2. Tiger Plaza	68	1BR, 1BA, F	709	294	.41	98.00	97%	Large complex, student oriented, drapes and carpets, completely furnished, tennis court and pool, one mile from university, on student bus route
	79	2BR, 1BA, F	893	354	.40	88.50	99%	
	73	3BR, 1.5BA, F	1,044	468	.45	93.60	98%	
3. Plantation Trace	23	1BR, 1BA, 2nd Fl, F	676	295	.44	98.33	97%	Student oriented, drapes and carpets, large closets, washer-dryer connections, pool, tennis court, clubhouse site needs additional landscaping
	24	1BR, 1BA, 1st Fl, F	742	318	.43	106.00	97%	
	24	1BR, 1BA, TH	796	319	.40	106.33	97%	
	25	1BR, 1BA, 1st Fl, F	796	337	.42	112.33	98%	
	27	2BR, 2BA, F	931	397	.43	99.25	99%	
	25	2BR, 1BA, F	864	367	.42	91.75	99%	
	21	2BR, 1.5BA, TH	890	377	.42	94.25	98%	
	21	3BR, 2BA, F	1,168	477	.41	95.40	98%	

4. Place du Plantier	28	1BR, 1.5BA, TH	633	280	.44	93.33	98%	Student oriented, well-maintained landscape, pets allowed, tennis court, clubhouse, well lighted, drapes and carpets, completely furnished, on student bus route
	31	1BR, 1BA, F	633	295	.47	98.33	97%	
	30	2BR, 1BA, F	873	350	.40	87.50	99%	
	30	2BR, 1.5BA, TH	963	360	.37	90.00	99%	
	29	2BR, 2BA, F	962	375	.39	93.75	98%	
	32	3BR, 2BA, F	1,136	440	.39	88.00	98%	
5. Embassy	40	1BR, 1BA, F	735	320	.44	106.67	97%	Student oriented, half mile from university, site needs additional landscaping, very small kitchen space, drapes and carpets, completely furnished
	44	1BR, 1BA, F	595	290	.49	96.67	97%	
	47	2BR, 1.5BA, F	935	400	.43	100.00	99%	
	44	2BR, 1BA, F	727	335	.46	83.75	98%	
6. Sharlo/Sharlo Terrace II	78	1BR, 1BA, F	614	280	.46	93.33	97%	large complex, student oriented, drapes and carpets need replacing, large closets, pool
	74	2BR, 2BA, F	838	370	.44	92.50	99%	
	73	3BR, 2BA, F	980	440	.45	88.00	98%	

Definitions: BA = bathroom, BR = Bedroom, F = Flat, Fl = Floor, ST = Studio, TH = Townhouse.

Source: Compiled by author.

ferred to as the sociopolitical environment. Whereas market analysis is aimed at identifying the demand and supply factors, the sociopolitical environment is concerned with the relationship between an investment and the neighborhood (or community).

While an investment may be legal (say, in terms of zoning), it may not be perceived as "good" by a given neighborhood or community. All real estate investments, and particularly large-scale projects such as shopping centers, create "external" influences on a neighborhood. These externalities—increased property values, increased traffic, noise—must be dealt with by the investor. External effects can be both positive and negative, and a neighborhood may perceive that an investment imposes more negative influences than it does positive. The investor may have to face these questions (and other constraints) in the decision-making framework.

Adverse public reaction to potential investments is as serious a constraint as the possibility of lack of demand or competition. Business risk thus should be viewed in a much larger framework than just supply and demand (economics). The sociopolitical environment is as important, though often much more difficult to identify.

RENTAL AND VACANCY FORECASTS: AN ILLUSTRATION

One of the key purposes of market analysis is to determine the expected rental for the investment under consideration. A major technique for determining expected rents and vacancies is to compare similar properties. Using an apartment investment as the subject property, table 4.6 shows how this is done by analyzing the data on six comparable properties.

In the analysis, the investor first determines the current rental income of the comparable properties. The rent is given per apartment unit, per square foot, and per room. Note that the rent per apartment varies from $260 to $477 per month, and the variation per room is from $83.75 to $112.33, and in terms of square footage, the variation is much lower. The mean rent per square foot is $0.43, with only a $0.06 deviation in either direction (excluding the 1BR, 1BA studio in Oakbrook, which seems not to be typical of market rent). The mean rent per room is $95.95, with a deviation of approximately $12.00 in either direction. This points out the necessity of measuring rent in various units and of comparing rent on a basis most similar to the market.

In the analysis, it is also important to determine who the tenants are and what special services or amenities are necessary to secure this rent. Obviously in a student market, proximity to the university and the availability of public transportation are necessary. Although the apartments usually have identical layouts or floor plans, are there additional features in the subject property such as an extra bath that will make it more appealing? Or are there missing features that will make it less appealing?

Table 4.6 also gives the occupancy rates for the various comparables. This is important in establishing the expectations regarding vacancies for the investment under consideration. The same process is used to forecast rent and vacancies for other types of investments. If the subject property is 100 percent occupied when other similar properties have vacancies, the rent may be underpriced, or vice versa if the subject property is underoccupied.

SUMMARY

Market analysis is a critical step in determining the feasibility of a real estate investment. Rents, vacancies, and future changes in property values have a major impact on the riskiness of a project. Each must be carefully analyzed by the investor in order to minimize risk.

5

THE LEGAL ENVIRONMENT

BECAUSE there is a certain amount of *political risk* involved in making an investment decision, an investor in real estate must pay careful attention to this aspect. Political (or legislative) risk is the probability that the government will change laws that affect the value of the investment. There are many legal implications in many actions. For example, suppose an investor expects to change the use of his or her property in the near future from an apartment building to a condominium. This action will clearly have a direct impact on many members of society. The directly affected members consist of the tenants, or former consumers of urban space, and now, prospective purchasers of condominium units; the mortgage lenders, who have creditor interests in the apartment building and seek satisfaction of the mortgage note prior to the condominium sales; and the various governments who have concerns such as federal taxation of any potential gain from the sale of the apartment building and the potential sales of condominium units.

In each case, the party involved has a set of considerations or "property rights" that the legal system protects. Therefore, any investment analysis necessitates a basic understanding of the modern legal environment in which investment decisions are made. However, the material presented in this chapter is not intended to be all-inclusive or substitute for sound legal counsel.

BASIC DEFINITIONS

Before we study the legal environment for investing in real estate, it is necessary to learn a number of basic definitions. These include the doctrine of property as a bundle of rights, real estate, realty, real property, personalty, personal property, and fixtures.

It is said that real estate interests consist of a set of rights. These may be vast and all-inclusive or few and limited in scope. The complete set of rights is called the *bundle of rights*. So the study of real estate is actually the study of the rights associated with the real estate.

To use the doctrine of the bundle of rights, we must distinguish between real estate and real property. Although often used synonymously, there are distinctions between these terms. Real estate refers to (a) the physical object—land and/or its improvements; (b) the profession of brokers, appraisers, counselors, and others concerned with land and its improvement; and finally, (c) the academic field of study interested in understanding how a limited resource is transformed, used, and allocated among many interested parties. *Real property re-*

fers to the rights associated with the *realty*, or the physical real estate. Therefore, realty and real estate are synonymous. It is obvious, then, that the rights in the realty (real estate) and not merely the physical assets are particularly critical issues in investing in land and improvements.

A similar distinction can be made between personalty and personal property. *Personalty* is defined as movable objects. Since land and improvements to the land are fixed, personalty is anything that is not realty. *Personal property*, however, consists of the rights associated with the personalty. Although these are not as general as real property rights, they are basic to our legal system. For example, the right of possession exists for both realty and personalty and there is a great deal of legal precedent to protect owners of personalty against wrongdoers.

Finally, it is possible for a formerly movable object (i.e., personalty) to become permanently attached and become part of the fixed asset (i.e., realty). Such an object is called a *fixture*. Although the law provides some guidelines in this instance, in some cases, it may be difficult to determine the status of the object. Therefore, we encounter a gray area, which may cause problems for the buyer who valued the property as if the object was a fixture and for the seller who viewed the object as personalty and valued the property to be sold without the personal property included.

Basic Ownership Rights

Under the bundle of rights ownership theory, it is possible, and indeed necessary, to value property according to the number of rights the owner possesses. These include the rights of possession, control, enjoyment, and disposition. Other sources provide further descriptions, but in all cases the "full bundle" enables the holder of the bundle (i.e., the owner) to enjoy the most complete property rights available.

This is not to say, however, that the owner may disregard all others including neighbors, governments, and the public at large. On the contrary, even if the investor owns the real estate in fee simple (the most complete ownership form available), there are still many limitations associated with these rights. Some of the traditional governmental limitations include taxation, police power, eminent domain, and laws regarding public safety. Therefore, absolute ownership rights do not exist; all property rights are limited by law and governmental action.

Finally, it should be pointed out that the property rights may exist in many forms. They may be future interests as opposed to present rights. They may be held individually, jointly, concurrently, or by the state. They may be limited in duration or potentially infinite. The term used to describe specific sets of property rights for interests in real property is *estates* or *estates in land*. Estates vary in degree, duration, nature, and quality. They also form the basis of different ownership rights in real property. Sometimes estates contain so many unusual characteristics that ownership at different points in time may be unclear. It is for these and many other reasons that the study of property law remains such an interesting and challenging subject for the investor.

THE PARTICIPANTS IN INVESTMENT DECISIONS

The basic framework of the legal environment for real estate investors is shown in figure 5.1. Each of the major participants—the equity investor, the mortgage lender, the tenant, and the government—has a partic-

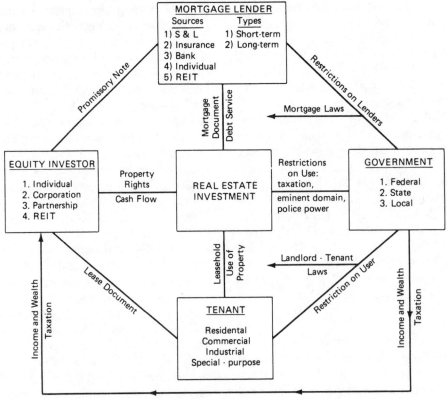

Figure 5.1 Participants in the Real Estate Investment Process

ular legal environment. The equity investor must decide on the appropriate form of business organization. The typical mortgage lender is one of several types of financial institutions, each operating under a different legal environment. The tenant is classified according to the type of property and therefore subject to different legal concerns. And finally, governmental influence will vary according to which level of government is affected: federal, state, or local.

EQUITY INVESTOR

The investor is initially faced with deciding what type of business organization would be best for the investor's objectives. Table

5.1 lists many of the well-known forms available for real estate investment.

The typical equity investor is usually concerned with taxation, liability, market-

Table 5.1 SELECTED ALTERNATIVE FORMS OF OWNERSHIP

Individual (proprietorship)
General partnership
Limited partnership
Ordinary corporation
Subchapter S corporation
Land trust
Real estate investment trust (REIT)
Joint venture
Syndication

ability, management, method of creation of organization, and duration of the organization. After examining all of these, the investor analyzes the overall effect of each form on his objectives and decides which one to use.

Individual (Proprietorship). Individual ownership is very simple to form and operate for a small enterprise. The transferability of assets is easy and inexpensive, and management of the company remains a personal responsibility. For some types of operation, this form is suitable. However, for many small operations, it may not be the most advantageous ownership form. The taxation treatment is according to regular, individual tax rates. In some cases, in the event of large tax shelter depreciation, there may be unused tax losses. Proprietorships have unlimited liability that permits suitors seeking damages to have access to personal, nonbusiness assets. The unlimited liability aspect and sole responsibility for decisions and responsibilities may suggest the use of one of the other forms.

General Partnership. This is very similar to proprietorship. General partnerships are created by agreement of the parties. In general, partnerships offer individual proprietors the advantages of joint decision making and risk sharing with the disadvantage of potential management disagreements and differences of opinion. Tax treatment is according to individual rates but each partner applies the investor's individual tax rate. Potential liability remains unlimited. Although marketability and disposition can be complicated, it is fairly simple in most cases.*

---

* However, there are a number of concurrent estates available that can result in significant differences at the time of disposition.

Limited Partnership. Limited partnership is a relatively new and extremely popular type of business entity. It attempts to secure the best of both worlds for some investors: limited liability on the part of limited partners and tax shelter treatment at personal rates.

This form also requires a general partner (or partners) to serve as managing agent for the entire operation. In addition, termination provisions are typically provided in the agreement. However, marketability is somewhat difficult due to problems with transfer of ownership, and withdrawal of the general partner can terminate the partnership agreement. Therefore, this form would be attractive to investors who seek a passive investment, free of management problems and obligations, and one in which liability is limited to the amount invested, tax losses offset ordinary income, and marketability is not the most important consideration.

Ordinary Corporation. The well-known corporate form is often viewed as the only realistic business form by many investors. There are, of course, advantages such as limited liability, ease of marketability of ownership "shares," generally centralized and constant management, and a perpetual life for the business. However, there are other factors that are less favorable. Income earned by the corporation is taxed twice, once at the corporate rate and again when dividends distributed to shareholders are taxed at ordinary rates. In addition, tax losses can only offset previous tax payments at the corporate rate. Finally, for some small companies, it may be more expensive and time consuming to form a corporation or to dissolve one than for the partnership forms.

Subchapter S Corporation. The Subchapter S corporation is a special form allowed by the 1958 Technical Amendments Act to the Internal Revenue Code. It was designed to avoid the double taxation provision of corporate income and retain the other provisions of corporate treatment. All shareholders must be individuals (partnerships and their corporations are specifically excluded) and residents of the United States. There are some additional income requirements but the basis of this form permits limited liability with tax treatment preferable to the double taxation of corporations. Management considerations depend on the specific organizations and marketability is somewhat affected by the additional requirements and the upper limit on partners.

Land Trust. The land trust is only available in a few states. It was created in Illinois and enjoys the most use there. Under this arrangement, title passes to a trustee who holds the title to property only for the purpose of carrying out the wishes of the owners or beneficiaries. Therefore, the trustee does not take over the operations of the property without the written permission of the beneficiaries.

The land trust has been criticized by tenant groups as being a form that serves no particular purpose, with the exception of hiding the true ownership of property. If a dispute arises between a tenant and the owner, the land trust becomes a shield between the often angry tenant and the trust owner. The trustee, of course, may not be able to make many operating decisions without the permission of the owner.

However, proponents have argued that there is more substance to a land trust. This form permits limited liability on the part of the owners, enables tax treatment at ordinary rates, and offers considerably more ease in marketability than partnerships or Subchapter S corporations. There are other advantages, also. Thus, the land trust remains an attractive option in some states despite legal struggles to prohibit its use.

Real Estate Investment Trust (REIT). The REIT is a special version of an equity trust. It is governed by specific rules and regulations that permit limited liability, tax treatment based on ordinary income, and good marketability. Management is typically handled by an advisory board since an REIT must have at least one hundred shareholders. However, tax losses may not be "passed through" to shareholders as in partnership forms. REITs have enjoyed a boom in recent years as this form of business organization has become more competitive with other forms of real estate ownership.

Joint Venture. This form is a special arrangement which, unlike most of the previous forms, is not expected to be an ongoing concern. Two or more parties are needed to create a joint venture that can take on any legal ownership form. Real estate development is a good example since the developer may need to offer some type of additional incentive to equity holders in order to interest them in somewhat risky ventures. Therefore, joint ventures are the legal arrangement for some real estate investments and are typically partnerships.

Syndication. Syndication, like the joint venture, is not truly an ownership form, but rather a technique to raise capital for investment purposes. The organizer or syndicator is frequently the general partner in a limited partnership and often benefits from management fees and an active role in the operation. Syndicates are really associations for conducting business and thus differ from legal forms of ownership. However, a potential investor may wish to organize a syndicate for investment in larger projects or to attract capital for limited partnerships.

Table 5.2 summarizes the major characteristics of the business organizations discussed in this chapter. It should be emphasized that each investor will have different objectives in selecting the appropriate business organization. Therefore, there is no single organization that is "best" for real estate investing.

MORTGAGE LENDER

The second participant in the real estate investment process is the mortgage lender. An investor seeking sources of funds for investment has a growing choice of financial institutions from which to choose. Table 5.3 presents the breakdown of mortgage originations by institution. Typically, two-thirds of all mortgages are on small (one- to four-family) residential units. This indicates the predominance of mortgage finance for residential property. While savings and loan associations orginated 44.9 percent of all mortgages, commercial banks were a distant second with 24.5 percent of the organizations. Most savings and loan association mortgages consisted of single-family residences and small income-producing buildings (84.6 percent). Mortgage companies, although a much smaller institution, placed 90 percent of their mortgages in this category. In contrast, life insurance companies placed a majority of their funds in mortgages on nonresidential property such as shopping centers and office buildings. Federal credit agencies such as the Veterans Administration, Small Business Administration, and Farm Credit Administration appeared as the sixth largest supplier of mortgage funds to the market. Finally, state and local credit agencies, although small in size, have become one of the largest sources of mortgage funds. In general, mortgages tend to be concentrated in savings and loans and commercial banks with a majority financing single-family and small income-producing property.

The following discussion highlights the major financial institutions and the prospect of each institution as a source of funds for the real estate investor.

Savings and Loan Associations. Savings and loan associations, often called "thrift institutions," specialize in making single-family loans based on time and passbook deposits at their institutions. However, the investor in income-producing real estate may also view savings and loans as a source of funds since many small income-producing properties are financed with loans from these institutions. In recent years, savings and loans have taken a much more active role in the financing of multifamily and commercial mortgages. The savings and loan association of the future may be much less specialized than in the past due to the changing legal environment of financial institutions.

Commercial Banks. Historically commercial banks have been more diversified than savings and loan associations, mutual savings banks, or mortgage companies. In recent years, commercial banks have expanded their operations to include more multifamily and commercial mortgages. They have also been active in short-term construction loans for multifamily housing. The investor in income-producing real estate may use a commercial bank as a source for long-term credit and particular short-term credit such as construction funds.

Mortgage Companies. Mortgage companies are specialized firms that are usually privately owned and that deal mostly with construction and development loans. They

Table 5.2 Summary of Characteristics of Business Organizations

	Taxation Status	Investor's Liability	Transferability	Management	Method of Creation	Duration
Individual	Flow through (single)	Unlimited	Transferable	Personal	Individual	Terminated by death or agreement. Deceased interest becomes part of the estate
General partnership	Flow through (single)	Unlimited	Not transferable	All partners in absence of agreement have equal voice	Created by agreement of the parties	Terminated by death, bankruptcy, or withdrawal of a partner
Limited partnership	Flow through (single)	Limited	Transferable	General partners have equal voice; limited partners have no voice	Created by agreement of the parties	Termination provided in the agreement
Corporation	Nonflow through (double)	Limited	Transferable	Shareholders elect directors who set policy	Charter issued by state	Perpetual
Subchapter S corporation	Nonflow through (single)	Limited	Limited by maximum number of shareholders	Varies with specific organization	Chapter issued by federal tax authority	Terminated by actions of shareholders
Land trust	Flow through (single)	Limited	Very transferable	Beneficiaries	Created by trust document if permitted by state law	Terminated by trustees, beneficiaries, or terms of agreement
Real estate investment trust (REIT)	Modified flow through (tax losses cannot exceed cash distribution)	Limited	Modified	Trustees	Created by agreement of the parties and charter issued by state	Perpetual

Table 5.3 ORIGINATIONS OF LONG-TERM MORTGAGE LOANS ON ALL PROPERTIES (EXCEPT LAND) BY TYPE OF LENDING INSTITUTION (MILLIONS OF DOLLARS)

Annual	Total	Mortgage Companies	Savings & Loans	Comm. Banks	Mutual Savings Banks	Life Companies	Other*
1970	$ 59,835	$11,842	$ 18,303	$ 13,568	$ 4,316	$ 5,843	$ 5,963
1971	93,636	16,425	33,770	21,982	7,036	6,263	8,160
1972	121,605	17,615	46,292	31,173	9,363	7,483	9,679
1973	127,673	14,251	46,830	33,568	10,491	9,975	12,558
1974	111,429	14,375	37,832	28,775	7,051	9,830	13,566
1975	120,717	15,930	49,809	27,062	7,127	8,297	12,492
1976	161,608	17,630	72,583	40,648	9,511	8,594	12,642
1977	229,191	32,754	99,049	58,596	11,860	12,440	14,492
1978	257,208	42,824	101,603	66,863	12,291	15,421	18,206
1979	258,154	53,332	92,337	61,591	11,155	17,388	22,351
1980	197,161	35,694	68,461	45,371	6,990	15,958	24,687
1981	158,043	28,377	47,873	39,151	5,270	12,046	25,326
1982	153,889	30,729	43,499	46,528	5,424	9,066	18,643
1983	293,905	63,430	103,927	79,795	14,593	17,098	15,062
1984	315,204	50,816	129,553	83,753	18,130	17,975	14,977
1985	387,275	68,065	145,624	108,897	21,998	28,984	13,707

* *Other* includes federal and state agencies, pension and retirement funds, and real estate investment trusts.

Source: U.S. Department of Housing and Urban Development.

---

also service loans as well as originate loans for governmental agencies in the secondary mortgage market. The real estate investor seeking short-term construction loans may find private mortgage companies to be sources of capital, although these are smaller institutions compared to the others previously mentioned.

Life Insurance Companies. Life insurance companies are well-established real estate lenders although this does not appear to be true to the casual observer. Despite the fact that these companies have declined in importance in terms of residential loans in recent years, they continue to be a major source of capital for multifamily property and large commercial projects. A real estate developer may find life insurance companies a sound source for long-term permanent financing. (See table 1.2 for the role of life insurance companies.)

Federal Credit Agencies. Federal credit agencies play an important role in the market for single-family loans, multifamily loans, and farm credit. Since most of their assets are held in the form of mortgages, some of the agencies may assist in supplying funds. The available federally subsidized programs are numerous and frequently very detailed with regard to qualifications and program changes. However, for some investors in multifamily housing, the federal agencies may be a viable credit source.

Other Institutions. There are, of course, other institutions such as mutual savings banks, state and local credit agencies, pension funds, and REITs. Each has particular interests and legal requirements. Many may provide funding for certain types of investment projects for a particular investor. All have invested in the real estate market due to its recent history of stable growth and asset protection.

Individuals. The final category is those few individuals with enough liquid money to lend to a real estate investor in the form of a mortgage over a long-term period. A common example is the seller who takes back a purchase–money mortgage or one who accepts a second or junior mortgage in lieu of cash at the time of sale. Such occurrences are not as rare today as they once were due to rapidly rising property values.

TENANT

The third participant is the immediate user of the real estate—the tenant. The tenant in feudal times had very few rights for the duration of the leasehold. However, the development of landlord-tenant law is evidence of the shift toward protection and existence of the rights of tenants. A brief overview of this law will be presented later in this chapter.

There may be different legal ramifications for each type of tenant. One classification divides various leaseholds according to expected duration of the estate. In nearly every case, the legal differences between the tenancies will be directly related to the rights associated with document or lease between the equity investor (or agent) and the tenant (or agent).

Residential Users. This is the most commonly encountered type of tenant for most small income-producing real estate. Residential users consist of tenants in single-family dwellings, small apartment buildings, six-flat apartment buildings, garden-type apartments, large complexes, and others. Residential tenants are primarily interested in suitable living conditions. Depending on the geographical area of the country and on local market conditions, the typical lease for a residential property will extend from a monthly leasehold up to two years or longer. Compared to long-term commercial leases, these are quite short.

Compared to other types of tenants, residential tenants are more concerned with the physical amenities within the building. In most agreements, maintenance is expected to be performed by the lessor on a regular basis and for serious problems, at the notice of the tenant. Failure to provide these services often results in management problems, tenant turnover, and landlord-tenant disputes. In fact, most of the new landlord-tenant laws passed during the past fifteen years are a result of problems encountered with residential property.

In addition, items such as groundskeeping, snow removal, and the overall maintenance of the property's grounds are important to residential tenants. Since residential tenants view their leaseholds as their homes, management should treat the property accordingly. Effective property management is essential in assisting the investor to maintain a good rapport with tenants.

The problems of management are well known to many investors in residential real estate. However, it need not be so if prudent management techniques are followed. The residential tenant may be one of the most difficult management problems for the unsuspecting investor, but without the property manager, income-producing apartment buildings would be valueless.

Commercial Users. There are several types of commercial tenants, or users involved in a commercial or business activity. These include wholesale and retail stores, office buildings, and shopping centers. Commercial tenants tend to be larger, more sophisticated, and often more financially secure. In addition, leases for commercial use frequently involve *percentage leases*. These leases allow for the remittance of a percentage of sales or income for the rental payment. In some cases, this percentage is in addition to a minimum guaranteed rent.

Although some commercial leases are not percentage leases, most are long-term. It is possible to find commercial leases for thirty or forty years for large firms or anchors in some shopping centers. Commercial leases are also frequently quoted on a square foot (or sometimes front footage) basis. This unit of measurement enables quick comparisons in what are often highly competitive markets.

Commercial leases may also have specific clauses that are characteristic of this type of lease. There may be restrictions and requirements regarding the number of hours the firm must be open for business. This is especially common if the percentage lease is in use and gross income is used as a measure of volume sales. In addition, there may be some specific requirement regarding business records and audit procedures, another frequent provision in commercial leases. Finally, the commercial tenant may be limited to only performing certain activities while on the lessor's premises.

Industrial Users. Industrial tenants are generally users of property in which the interior of the buildings is unfinished. Warehouses, plants, utilities, and factories are typical examples. Since this type of property tends to be quite large, industrial leases tend to be quite extensive and are often specially designed for the user. The growth of industrial parks has led to much more careful analysis of the economics of leasing industrial space versus an outright purchase of the property.

Industrial tenants are concerned with access, production efficiency, and safety conditions in the facility. Their leases tend to be long-term in nature and are typically net of maintenance, utilities, and other operating expenses. Because industrial real estate is very competitive, leases must be negotiated very carefully. Since many of the facilities are large, a small error in negotiation may result in a very expensive leasing obligation.

Special-Purpose Users. There are a number of other tenants that lease space for other specific purposes. Some examples of special-purpose users are theaters, assembly halls, and sports arenas. Leasing arrangements and terms vary with each specific use. The requirements of the lessor (landlord) to the lessee (tenant) depend on the value of the economic activity to be performed on the property. Each industry tends to have its own institutional standards regarding leasing terms. For example, a lease for a movie theater may specify a percentage rate with a minimum per-seat guarantee. In addition, the revenue from the concessions may also be included in the lease.

Special-purpose buildings require a much more critical analysis of the activity performed on the premises. Furthermore, more information may be needed to ascertain the riskiness of the tenant and the tenant's ability to make the rental payments. However, in some cases, the profitability of a successful enterprise may result in a very successful real estate investment for the building's owner.

GOVERNMENT

The final primary participant in the real estate investment process is the government. Generally, the impact of government regulation and influence is felt by all of the other participants. Typically, government influence is divided into three categories: federal, state, and local governments. Together these three public sectors greatly affect real estate investment decisions.

Federal. The most visible impact that federal government has on a real estate investment is its ability to tax the income and capital gains from real estate. Chapter 8 is devoted to an analysis of taxation and tax planning to assist the investor in legally avoiding unnecessary tax payments. However, there are other federal regulations on the use of real estate that can be equally important. For example, the right of eminent domain rests with the federal as well as state governments. This right, discussed later in this chapter, permits the taking of private real estate for public purposes as long as "just compensation" is paid. Therefore, if the government decides that your property is needed for a public purpose, it may be obtained through this right, or limitation of your rights of eminent domain.

Federal land-use regulations have resulted from a growing public awareness of conservation and environmental impacts that occur during some uses of land. The federal government has taken an active stance in this area and the future appears to hold an even greater participation by federal authorities.

Finally, the federal government also retains the right of *escheat* or the taking of property when no heirs or will can be found after the death of the owner(s). Further, estate taxes can dramatically affect the returns and worth of property at the time of death.

State. Property law varies from state to state. Although modern property law comes from early English common law and is generally followed throughout the United States,* differences occur as courts and legislatures attempt to deal with various issues. So, most of property law comes from state law.

Various states have defined different estates and interests. Some states have adopted the title theory of mortgages. Others have followed the lien theory. Certain states have created new laws to meet changing conditions in the area of consumer protection of urban tenants in landlord–tenant law or, in some of the western states, in dealing with water rights. Finally, each state has various income, property, and estate tax laws that can significantly affect the value and return of real estate. In general, there are many areas where real estate is affected by state government and its law. Many of these considerations are treated below.

Local. Local government may be the municipality, county, or other political boundary. It is characterized by smaller and more detailed concerns. Examples of local government action include building codes, zoning ordinances, and set-back requirements.

The local government can have a significant influence. Recent moves toward rent control ordinances have been controversial in many communities. Some local governments have also attempted to deal with growth and expansion by limiting (or in some cases forbidding) the issuances of new housing permits. Another example is the recent interest in condominium conversions. Although many real estate developers and investors view local government as an obstacle to their objectives, it is becoming an ever-increasing political force.

---

* This is not true for Louisiana, which follows the French or Napoleonic legal system.

INVESTORS AND THE INVESTMENT VEHICLE

We have described some of the legal aspects of the primary participants in the real estate investment process. Now let us focus on the relationship between the participants and the investment vehicle: the land, the improvements, and the property rights associated with the realty.

PROPERTY RIGHTS AND THE EQUITY INVESTOR

The equity investor, as we have already said, acquires a bundle of rights as an investor in real estate. These entitle him to a cash flow. The magnitude and safety of the cash flow is directly related to the magnitude and quality of the bundle of rights and interests that the investor acquires in taking title to the property. Sometimes the rights are present interests; other times they involve future interests. Some rights are concurrent interests; others are rights in the land of others. All interests that entitle rights to valuable property are presumed to have value. It is very important that the investor understand the basic differences between the many forms of property interests or estates.

Freehold Estates. Freehold estate interests are widely held and represent the most complete interests available in many cases. With the exception of life estates, freehold estates are potentially infinite in duration. The name *freehold* comes from the common law where it referred to the interests in land that were associated with free men. Because they were the only estates that were given full protection of law, they are large and powerful interests today. There are basically four types of freehold estates: fee simple absolute, defeasible fees, fee tail, and life estates.

Fee Simple Absolute or *Fee Simple.* This is the largest and most complete estate available. Potentially infinite as long as heirs can be found, it can be passed on to future heirs without restriction or limitation. A fee simple estate is the complete bundle of rights (subject to the traditional government limitations).

Defeasible Fees. These are identical to fee simple estates except they are defeasible depending on the occurrence of some event. An example would be a grant of property to "Mr. Jones and his heirs as long as the property would be used for the benefit of the children in the community." This is called a *fee simple determinable* or a *qualified fee* since the existence of the fee estate is determined by the event that the property is used "for the benefit of the children in the community." Another example would be if Mr. Brown grants to "Mr. Smith and his heirs but if smoking is permitted on the premises, then Mr. Brown has the right to reenter and repossess the property." Such a grant creates a *fee simple subject to condition subsequent* for Mr. Smith. Clearly, if the specific condition (i.e., smoking) occurs (with permission), then the grant dictates that Mr. Smith may lose his interest and the estate may revert to Mr. Brown, if he elects to take the property.

A final example is a *fee simple subject to executory limitation or devise.* This is really either of two estates. If it is subject to limitation, it is created by deed. If it is subject to devise, it is a creation by last will and testament. As an example, assume Mr. White by deed conveys his property to "Mr. Black and his heirs but if Mrs. Black remarries, then the property goes to Mr. Green and his heirs." In this case, Mr. Black is said to have a *fee simple subject to executory limitations.* The limitation, of course, is that if Mrs. Black remarries, then Mr. Green will take title to the property in fee simple.

Fee Tail. This category of freehold estate is unenforceable in modern law or viewed as a modified fee simple estate. This estate specifies that the property would pass according to the "heirs of his body." If the holder of the fee tail produced a male* heir, then at the time of his death,† the property would pass to the lineal heir. If the line were to be stopped, the property would, by design, revert back to the original grantor (or his heirs). As one can imagine, there were so many problems with this estate that modern law has attempted to eliminate its usage and, in most cases, states will not enforce a fee tail conveyance. Though rarely seen today, it is a reminder of the common law heritage.

Life Estate. There are basically two types of life estates: *conventional life estates* and *legal life estates.* The first is characterized by the words in the deed "for the term of his natural life." The grantee in this case would have a conventional life estate that would entitle him/her to use the property (but not damage it), take "fruits" from it, and even sell the interest to other parties. However, at the time of the life tenant's death, the grantor (or heirs) gets back the interest in the property.

---

* In medieval times, only males could hold title to property at the sufferance of the king. Later, the estate known as *fee tail female* was introduced to specify a line of female descendants.

† Assuming that only males could hold property interests.

It is also possible for the life estate to be measured by the life of someone other than the recipient of the grant. In this case, the life estate is called *pur autre vie* (for another's life). For example, assume Mrs. Howard grants her property to Mrs. Roberts for the life of Mr. Howard. When Mr. Howard dies, Mrs. Roberts' interest is extinguished and the property reverts back to Mrs. Howard.

A common form of *legal life estates* refer to wives' interests in their husbands' property called *dower rights* and husbands' interests in their wives' property called *curtesy rights.* These rights are in disfavor with courts and in many states are no longer enforceable. However, in states that do enforce these rights, these estates refer to rights that may result in surprises at the time of the spouse's death if the grantee is not careful. In many cases, title assurance methods have eliminated much of the risk of "legal life estate surprises."

Clearly, the analysis of freehold estates is complex and intricate. This review exposes the reader to some of the terminology and concepts of estates in land. It is not intended to be a substitute for legal counsel. It should be apparent, however, that there are many kinds of estates available for interests in property.

Concurrent Estates. Concurrent estate interests are used when more than one person desires joint ownership of property. There are four types of concurrent estates: joint tenancy, tenancy in common, tenancy by the entirety, and tenancy in coparcenary. It is important to distinguish between these estates.

Joint Tenancy. An estate that specifies that the surviving tenants will divide the

---

property of the deceased cotenant equally, immediately upon the death of the cotenant, and without entering the estate of the deceased cotenant. All tenants are said to own the entire property as joint owners. The right of survivorship (by the surviving cotenants) is a characteristic of this estate. Finally, in order to create a joint tenancy, one must meet the "four unity tests." This requires that all of the cotenants enter the agreement at the same time (unity of title), all interests are of the same type and duration (unity of interest), and all have an undivided right to use the property (unity of possession). If one or more of these unities cannot be met or are broken over time, the property is not a joint tenancy but a tenancy in common.

Tenancy in Common. A concurrent ownership form where each tenant owns an undivided portion of the property but not necessarily in equal amounts. Further, a tenant may sell his or her interest at will and not disturb the estate. Finally, a tenancy in common permits the passage of property to heirs rather than automatically to cotenants, as in joint tenancy. For several reasons, tenancy in common is preferred by courts and state lawmakers over joint tenancy. The opposite was true in common law, but in modern courts the complications that arise through the use of joint tenancies (and concurrent tenancy in common) has led some states to abolish joint tenancies and still others to apply a very strict interpretation of the four unities test.

Tenancy by the Entirety. Very similar to a joint tenancy, tenancy by the entirety was specifically designed for husbands and wives. It requires an additional fifth unity: unity of person. This means that the husband and wife during marriage are viewed as one legal person in this estate. If one dies, the property automatically goes to the survivor. In addition, neither spouse can voluntarily dispose of an interest in the property without the permission of the other. In a joint tenancy, any tenant can act and be held responsible for the whole tenancy. Finally, in the event of a divorce, the tenancy by the entirety is destroyed and a tenancy in common remains.

Tenancy in Coparcenary. This final tenancy is really an extinct estate which, if found, is typically viewed as a tenancy in common. It was the estate left without male heirs but with at least two female heirs. The female heirs are said to be tenants in coparcenary. Thus, this estate was created by the law of inheritance and receives virtually no legal usage today.

Future Interests. These estates are interests in existing property that will not begin until some future date. These acknowledge that the holder of the future interest has an estate presently: the right to use and enjoy property at some time in the future. In addition, some future interests may never become possessory interests if certain events do not occur. These are called *contingent estates*. These may be contrasted with future interests that are known to occur at some definite point in time or *vested estates*.

All future estates may be classified as one of five types: reversions, possibilities of reverter, rights of reentry, remainders, and executory interests.

Reversions. Future interests that entitle the holder to recover a possessory interest at a future time. An example is the interest at the time of the death of the life tenant.

Since all life tenants will die, reversions are said to be vested interests.

Possibilities of Reverter. Future interests associated with a determinable fee. Recall that in a determinable fee, the owner of the fee may retain the interest for life and pass it to his or her heirs and they to theirs, "as long as" the event specified occurs (or does not occur). Because the future interest may never become a possessory estate, it is classed as a possibility of a reverter.

Right of Reentry. Also the future interest associated with a determinable fee, specifically with a fee simple subject to condition subsequent. The right of reentry gives the original grantor the "right to reenter" the property if certain conditions occur (or do not occur). As noted earlier, the grantee has the right to take back the property. In the case of nearly all of the other future estates, they become possessory estates automatically.

Remainders. The granting away of the reversionary interests. Remainders typically follow life estates but may also follow some fees, fee tails, or terms for years. Remainder interests must become possessory interests.

Executory Interests. Technical future interests that may be created by deed or will and that permit transfer of property rights after the death of the grantor. It is an interest that may become a possessory interest at some future date or due to the occurrence of some event. Courts tend to prefer remainders, contingent upon some event occurring, rather than executory interests for the reason of freer alienation of land.

Interests and Rights in the Land of Others. The final area of property rights of the equity investor consists of a set of related rights of nonpossessory interests. There are four main types: easements, profits, licenses, and covenants.

Easement. Interest in someone else's land that entitles the holder to use and enjoy the land in some manner. A common example is a utility easement for running underground water pipes over a portion of another property owner's land. For investors in real estate, it is important to identify any easements that may stop the use of land in some way and thereby have an adverse effect on the value of the property.

Profit. Similar to an easement, in addition to permitting the use of another's land, it grants the holder of the profit the right to take away the soil or raw materials from the land. Clearly, a profit implies an easement since it encompasses all of the interests of an easement and more. A profit may also be a valuable property right depending on the type of property and the value of the soil and natural resources.

License. A personal privilege granted to the holder to go on another's land without being a trespasser. A license is not an interest in land nor is it a possessory estate. As a mere permission, it is limited in the extent of its rights. Frequently, a license may be revoked by the licensor at his or her discretion.

Covenant. A promise to do or not do a specific thing. In terms of real estate, a covenant may restrict the building of auxiliary buildings in a certain subdivision. Conceptually, covenants are restrictions that stop the owner from using his/her land as he/she pleases. In some cases, this might be a critical factor in the valuation of property. In that event, the existence of a covenant is an important factor for the real estate investor.

MORTGAGE AS SECURITY FOR THE LENDER

The relationship between the mortgage lender and the real estate investment is spelled out in the mortgage document. Although there is a discussion regarding the use of mortgages for real estate finance in chapter 7, the discussion in this section centers on two main parts. The first part reviews the concept of the mortgage instrument as security and the second part highlights the requirements for a valid mortgage.

Nature of the Mortgage Instrument. The mortgage process technically contains a mortgage or the written instrument that pledges real property as security for an obligation and a promissory note or the written promise of one person to repay an amount of money according to agreed terms and conditions. It is important to recognize that the financing process involves both a mortgage and a note. If the note were to be written without a mortgage, it would be, in effect, unsecured. Therefore, both are essential ingredients for the functioning of the mortgage as a secured instrument. Once the note is repaid, a *release* is sought from the lender in order to free the property that was held as security.

The concept of the mortgage instrument has a long history in common law. Over time, however, two "theories" of mortgage law developed: the *title theory* and the *lien theory.** Basically, since states that have

---

* These theories of mortgages are also discussed in chapter 7.

adopted the title theory view the adoption of a mortgage as a change in possession and a conveyance of title, the use of a mortgage in a title state is paramount to a conveyance of property rights between the equity holder (mortgagor) and the mortgage lender (mortgagee). In states that have adopted the lien theory, by far the majority, different results occur. In lien theory states, the existence of a mortgage implies that the mortgagee merely has a claim against the property in the event of a default. Therefore, there is no conveyance of title and fewer property rights have been transferred.

Finally, in some states, a device that is quite similar to a mortgage is used for security. This device is called a *deed of trust* or *trust deed.* Unlike the ordinary mortgage, the deed of trust involves a third person. In using it, the borrower (or *trustor*) transfers the title to the real estate to a *trustee* who holds it in trust for the lender (or *beneficiary*) for performance of the obligation owed by the borrower to the lender. When the obligation is fulfilled, the title is reconveyed to the trustor by the trustee.

Requirements for a Valid Mortgage. A number of elements are necessary for a mortgage to be free of defects. However, in some cases, the law may hold that certain defects in the mortgage document can result in the mortgage remaining as a so-called *equitable mortgage.* A valid mortgage must name the mortgagor and the mortgagee. It must contain the words of conveyance to clearly indicate that a mortgage is being agreed upon. It must specify the debt to be secured and it must be recorded.

The mortgage must adequately describe the realty being mortgaged. In title states, the mortgage must clearly state the conditions on which the title will be defeated. This is called the *defeasance clause.* The mortgage must be signed by the mortgagor and in some states must be sealed and witnessed. The document must also be delivered and accepted.

Finally, mortgage law has specified other requirements regarding satisfaction of the mortgage, acceleration of the note, possible extensions of the mortgage, assignment of the mortgage, and release of the mortgage. A full discussion of these clauses is beyond the scope of this book but in many cases the advice of experienced counsel is very helpful. These instruments are the only way the mortgage lender can specify his or her legal rights to the real estate.

TENANT AND THE LEASEHOLD ESTATE

The tenant also acquires a set of legal rights that include more than the use of the property for the period of the lease. The tenant has a legal interest in the real estate called a *nonfreehold* or *leasehold estate*. Each is frequently classified according to its expected duration.

Nonfreehold (Leasehold) Estates. Generally, there are four types of tenancy: tenancy for years, tenancy from period to period, tenancy at will, and tenancy at sufferance. With the exception of the last one, all are estates since they represent interests and rights in land.

Tenancy for Years. A leasehold estate in which the beginning and end of the estate are clearly specified. For instance, if you have an estate for twenty years, at the end of that period, the property would automatically revert to the lessor.

Tenancy from Period to Period. This lasts as long as a tenancy for years but implies that the tenant may stay on the premises for consideration of rent according to the

terms stated in the original tenancy. This implied tenancy may be terminated with sufficient notice given by either party. Sufficient notice may be defined within the document, or measured by local law or tradition. A typical period of notice is six months.

Tenancy at Will. The least structured. In this leasehold, the lessor offers the lessee (tenant) to continue the estate "for as long as the lessee wishes." Thus, a tenancy at will is an estate of indeterminate duration and involves fewer restrictions on either party than any of the other leasehold estates. The notice period for termination is typically stated in the lease or is determined by state statute or state court precedent.

Tenancy at Sufferance. This is the legal term for the tenant who remains after the expiration of a previous lease. The tenant who continues without the consent of the lessor is "at the sufferance" of the lessor. Thus, it is not an estate but a possession without legal right. It is said that a tenancy at sufferance differs from a trespasser only because the original entry was legal. Although tenants at sufferance possess civil and human rights, they have no real property rights.

Lease Analysis. The lease is the legal document that conveys a legal interest (leasehold) in real property. However, as we shall see, the lease also represents a contract between landlord and tenant that contains a set of express and implicit conditions that bind the parties. The typical conditions are discussed below.

It should be pointed out that the major legal difference between a leasehold and other interests where the owner conveys rights (such as licenses, easements, or profits) is that the lease conveys the right of exclusive possession. Interests in the land of others convey the right to use the land but do not convey the right of possession. The legal test to determine if a conveyance is a leasehold is whether or not the transaction of rights results in a transfer of possession. If so, then a leasehold state has been created.

The essential elements of a lease include identification of landlord and tenant, both of whom must be of legal age and otherwise capable of entering the agreement; identification of the leased premises with sufficient precision to avoid ambiguity; specification of the amount of rent to be paid and the time and method of payment; and an indication of the term or length of the leasehold to which the parties have agreed. As indicated above, however, there are some leaseholds where the term is not specifically agreed on at the time of signing.

In addition, and depending on the legal requirements of the state, other clauses are also found in most leases. A frequently used covenant describes the permissible uses allowed under the lease. For commercial property, this clause specifies what types of activities will be permitted by the lessor. In the case of a shopping center, this clause is critical since the selection of tenants is made according to economic function as well as risk and safety of the lessee. In residential leases, this clause ensures a minimum amount of conflict between tenants since all are presumed to want peaceful and quiet use of their rental space.

Another important covenant provides specific information about the maintenance and repair responsibilities of the landlord. However, consistent with recent changes in landlord–tenant law, landlords are held responsible for physical maintenance and repair of appliances and urban services even

if these promises are not expressly provided.

Leases also have provisions for assignment and subleasing, specifying the rights of the lessee should he wish to convey the rights of the leasehold before the end of the lease.

Finally, leases frequently include clauses concerning the status of the leasehold in the event of condemnation, casualty loss, or destruction. Although the outcomes may vary according to express covenants and state laws, the typical result is that the lessee is freed from rental obligation if the physical premises are "uninhabitable."

Other Considerations. The development of landlord–tenant law during the seventies and eighties is one of the major changes in property law. As a result, the landlord is now required to deliver possession to the tenant at the beginning of the lease.* A famous New Jersey case decided in 1968 that the "covenant of quiet enjoyment" was implied by all leases and if the landlord failed to provide this provision, the tenant could argue that he/she could not enjoy the premises and, in effect, that the leasehold was being terminated by "constructive eviction."[†]

Additional responsibilities of the landlord include the landlord's duty to deliver habitable premises. This shift from common law was based on the doctrine held by the court for all urban dwellings of "the implied warranty of habitability."[‡] Courts also shifted the burden of repair and main-

---

* Whether this consists of "actual" or "legal" possession varies according to state. According to the majority view, the English rule is followed that requires actual possession to be delivered to the tenant.

† See *Reste Realty v. Cooper* (1968).

‡ See *Javins et al. v. First National Realty Corp.* (1970).

tenance more squarely on the shoulders of the landlord. Now landlords have a larger responsibility than ever for repairing "defects that interfere with basic habitability."

GOVERNMENTAL LIMITATIONS

Government laws and regulations can have a dramatic impact on real estate investments. Much of this area remains controversial and deals with politically sensitive issues. Resolution of conflicting land uses and protection of public interests by land use control* are two areas that merit discussion.

Conflicting Land Uses. The law attempts to resolve matters where a conflict of usage creates a problem. Four common types of conflicts concern nuisance, lateral support, water rights, and air rights.

Nuisance. This law requires that a user of property operate in such a way that the use does not interfere with neighboring use or with the public's right to use the property. Public nuisances are of particular concern since such activities cause "injury to the public health, morals, safety, or general welfare of the community." Nuisance doctrine is much less specific, and often the rulings are based on a case-specific analysis. In general, it protects holders of property interests from injury due to interference from others.

Lateral Support. A property right that entitles the owner of property to have his or her land supported by adjoining land.* For example, the owner of an apartment building that begins to lean due to a weakening of the lateral support from the adjacent land is entitled to seek legal remedies. Although the property holder does not own the adjacent land, his right to receive lateral support is "an absolute right inherent in the land itself."

Water Rights and *Air Rights.* These are two of the most visible areas in which interests may conflict. However, each area has developed a body of case law regarding the central question: Who owns what? Water rights refer to the title of lands under water and the rights of the water itself. This is clearly an important area in some of the arid states and also where two adjoining land owners share a water supply or rely on a common water source for their livelihood. Many of the problems regarding water rights arise from the differences between two conflicting theories of water use: the riparian rights theory and the prior appropriation doctrine. The *riparian rights theory* holds that the water rights belong to the adjacent landowner and no one can use water at the deprivation of others with an equal opportunity to use it. This theory has been rejected by many western states in favor of the *prior appropriation doctrine* that establishes a priority schedule for users. Those there first have the best claim to use of the water.

Air rights also involve conflicts of usage. Traditionally this was an area of torts but

---

* Many potential conflicting land uses involve private property rights exclusively and, thus, no government activity is necessary. However, many of these disputes seek governmental authority to rectify the issue, often by taxing the wrongdoer based on a measure of the damages to the plaintiff. Economists have shown that governmental action may not be needed in many of these disputes since the conflicting parties can negotiate the damages between themselves.

---

* A similar notion is the doctrine of subjacent support that gives property holders the right to expect support from beneath the surface of the land once a structure is erected.

with the development of technology these property rights are becoming more important. Formerly, planes had free access to the "paths in the sky" since the sky was considered to belong to the public. However, if damage is done to property on earth, modern property law holds that this is a taking of property and that compensation must be paid to the property owner. This area is also controversial and the courts will probably provide more rulings and precedents in the next few years.

Land Use Control. For the urban property holder, land use control has become one of the most important legal areas of interest. As noted earlier, some of the limitations result from local governmental action, while others are due to state or local law. In many urban areas land use control has been a hotly contested issue and one that will be important for years to come.

Some of the main techniques and methods that the public sector uses for land use control include but are not limited to zoning laws, regulation of land development, urban land use planning, eminent domain takings, environmental controls, and aesthetics as a land use goal.

Zoning laws have been passed by most municipalities throughout the United States. These local ordinances typically provide a "master plan" by which the urban and nearby rural land will be used in a systematic and organized fashion. The issues of the value of zoning ordinances, their implementation, the costs of their use, and the changes in property rights associated with the adoption of zoning ordinances have become well known to economists, city planners, politicians, and to many potential investors in real estate. The issues are far too complex for a cursory treatment here, but it is apparent that zoning and other

land use planning programs are becoming an increasingly important consideration with regard to real estate development and investment.

Other regulations of land development have also grown in recent years. Some cities hope to limit the extent of urban growth by refusing to issue building permits or by limiting the number to be issued each year. Another method is to limit the "urban service boundary" outside of which police, fire, water, and other local services will not be extended. Once again, the issues can become complex and often raise the emotional levels of those involved. To some, this activity is called economic or legal extortion, since builders and developers are frequently asked by the local municipalities to pay development fees to help offset the additional costs to the city of having to provide extra urban services. To others, this type of regulation appears to be the only hope for rationing growth in urban areas among potential users.

The government may also take property by condemning it and using it for public purposes. This power, called *eminent domain,* requires that just compensation, or an amount in dollars equal to the market value of the loss, be paid to the former holder of the real property. Frequently, eminent domain proceedings are controversial and make headlines. However, empirical studies have shown that just compensation is not always equal to the owner's loss in market value.

Environmental controls are also becoming a relevant issue for much real estate development. Many municipalities now require environmental impact statements prior to the approval of large developments. These concerns have become more prevalent as cities pay more attention to growing problems in the areas of energy, resource demands, and urban structure.

Finally, a new movement has argued for aesthetics as a land use goal. Although traditionally the law of nuisance failed to uphold "unsightliness" as a legal nuisance, recent municipal ordinances have sought, in the interest of society's welfare, to limit the use of billboards, signs, and other "visual pollution." This is a relatively new and highly controversial area for government intervention and indicates the extent to which the investor must examine the role of governmental influence before investing in real estate.

Figure 5.2 classifies the major property rights of real estate participants. Nearly all of the property rights that appear in the figure were discussed in this chapter.

LINKS BETWEEN PARTICIPANTS

Each of the four primary participants in the real estate investment process has a specific legal relationship with the real estate investment itself. In this section, we shall look at the links between each of them.

EQUITY INVESTOR AND MORTGAGE LENDER

The link between the equity investor and the mortgage lender is the *promissory note* signed by the investor. This specifies that the maker of the note (investor) promises to repay a specific sum of money to the payee (lender). The note may be negotiable or nonnegotiable. *Negotiable notes* may be passed to other persons for cash or sold in the market for negotiable notes. *Nonnegotiable notes* lack this marketability and, for this reason, are used less frequently.

Two common types of promissory notes are used in real estate: straight notes and installment notes. *Straight notes* require that only interest be paid during the term of the note and that principal be repaid at the end. *Installment notes* require periodic interest and principal reduction payments. In the usual case, the note is repaid in the level amortization payment plan, which enables a decreasing portion of a given level periodic payment to be attributed to interest and an increasing portion to principal reduction. It is also possible to only partially amortize the note and make the final payment larger to cover the remaining balance. This final payment is called a *balloon payment* and the mortgage in which it appears is called a *balloon mortgage.*

There are a number of common provisions in promissory notes. Frequently, the same provisions appear in the mortgage (or deed of trust). Together the note and the mortgage make up the agreement between the parties. Some of the provisions typically included are the date and place of the creation of the note, the amount of the note, the names of the payee and the maker, the time in which interest will begin and the effective rate to be charged, the results in the event of a default, and a statement regarding the use of a mortgage as security. Other issues include acceleration provisions, prepayment clauses and penalties, and the use of escrows. In general, for complex transactions, legal counsel is advisable.

EQUITY INVESTOR AND TENANT

The legal link between the investor and the tenant is the *lease.* This is a type of contract in which one party (lessor) conveys to another (lessee) for consideration the right to use a specified property for a period of time. However, as we have seen, the changing nature of landlord–tenant laws has moved the analysis of leases further away from the law of contracts. Therefore, the lease is an instrument that is based on a blend of contract and property law.

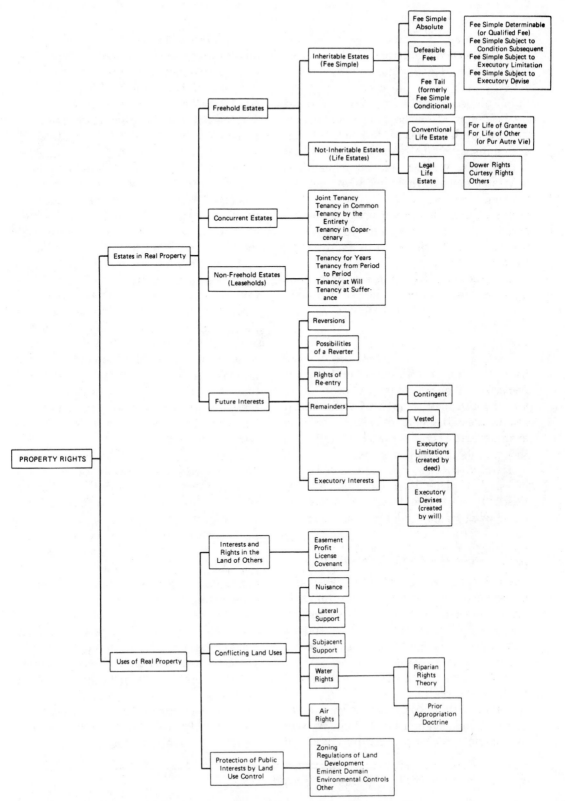

Figure 5.2 Classification of Interests in Real Property

In order to create a valid lease, at least six essential elements must be included:

1. A statement of the correct names and the signatures of the competent parties.
2. An identifiable description of the leased premises, typically including but not limited to the address of the location.
3. A statement of the consideration to be paid.
4. A statement of the purpose(s) for which the premises are expected to be used.
5. A statement of the beginning and ending dates of the leasehold.
6. A statement of the rights and obligations of each party. This may be a simple statement or many pages of clauses and covenants.

Many of the clauses are important to specifying the rights of the lessor and lessee. A well-written lease will help to prevent potential problems that may arise. Finally, it is necessary to spend some time carefully examining the clauses in the lease used in the real estate. If real estate is to be viewed as a bundle of rights, then the establishment of leasehold extends certain rights to the lessee. It is of paramount importance to know what rights the lessee possesses.

EQUITY INVESTOR AND GOVERNMENT

All levels of government have the authority to impose the burden of taxes. Taxation may consist of taxes on income; taxes on real property, typically used for local purposes; and taxes on the gain from selling assets. In income tax systems at the federal and most state levels, the government taxes both income and wealth.

Chapter 8 is devoted exclusively to the complex and detailed tax system. We will see that not only is tax planning useful, but also in many cases it is necessary in order to earn a competitive return. Tax avoidance is expected; tax evasion is illegal and punishable by law.

However, there are other taxes that affect real estate investment. These include personal property taxes, payroll taxes, estate taxes, and others. One of the more controversial issues in recent years has been the extent to which property taxes should be used to finance public expenditures such as schools. The Proposition 13 revolt made the clear point that in the minds of many homeowners and real estate investors, the tax burdens had grown significantly, often to 3 percent or more of market value.

Another way to view taxation is called the *tax capitalization theory.* This notion argues that if, for example, many investors believe that property (or other) taxes will increase in the near future, they will evaluate that expectation in analyzing investments. Thus, their investments and the values placed on property will take the tax burden into account.

Whether most or all of the tax burden is "capitalized" into the value of the investment property is an empirical question that remains unanswered. Evidence indicates that at least some of the tax burdens on real property are capitalized into selling prices by investors in the real estate market. At the same time, however, the investor is also concerned with the influence of various government programs on the investment's value. For example, the monies collected from the property tax is used to support schools, build roads, support police and fire protection, and so forth. These programs could very well increase the property value. So the investor should be concerned with the net effect: the decrease associated with the property tax and the increase from "quality" neighborhoods.

MORTGAGE LENDER AND TENANT

This is perhaps the most fragile of all of the legal links between the participants. The lender never encounters the tenant directly. However, if the tenant is not financially secure, this may result in default on the promissory note. Poor tenant selection by the equity investor or the management agent may therefore directly affect the mortgage lender.

A major part of the mortgage lender's review of the investor's application for funds is an analysis of the investor's projected income statement. Since the income to be generated from the real estate is directly a function of the tenants' willingness and ability to pay rent, the lender ought to analyze the financial position of major tenants. The lender's willingness to make the loan may be contingent upon the type and quality of tenants in the property, particularly in large-scale projects where long-term financing becomes available after the leases are signed.

The lender may require tenants to pass certain income and credit tests. This is especially true in residential income-producing real estate where tenants may not have as easy access to credit markets as large corporations in commercial and industrial property.

MORTGAGE LENDER AND GOVERNMENT

The mortgage lender is linked to the government by a set of legal restrictions placed on the lender. Clearly the nature of these restrictions depends on the lender involved. Those placed on savings and loan associations, for example, will differ from those placed on commercial banks or life insurance companies. Federally chartered savings and loan associations are largely confined to lending on residential real estate.

There are also limits placed on the maximum amount that may be loaned on any particular property as well as restrictions on maximum loan-to-value ratios, the length and amount of term loans, and requirements regarding the geographic locations of properties held as loan security.

Commercial banks, however, are permitted to engage in many more financial services. Although banks were not permitted to make real estate loans until after 1913, their interest has since grown to where they represent a major source of real estate loans (table 4.3). However, there are regulations regarding the use of deposits for real estate loans, including limits on the ratio of mortgages to deposits and loan-to-value restrictions. Banks also do a good deal of short-term (construction) and interim financing that have other requirements.

TENANT AND GOVERNMENT

The final link is between the tenant and government. This link involves additional restrictions on tenant use as well as an ongoing interpretation of lessee's rights. The changing nature of landlord–tenant law has forced many governments to pass new laws to reflect the new legal environment. Laws such as those requiring itemized lists of damages for which charges were deducted when returning security deposits or those requiring fire alarms and smoke detectors in apartment buildings in some cities and towns exemplify the changing legal emphasis.

Some observers feel the government has no business in some of these areas. Builders frequently argue that, although the intention may be good, many of the new laws result in higher construction costs and often higher rents charged to tenants. The problem for builders and investors, of course, is that the rents are not always increased in proportion to the increased costs. Sometimes only part of the additional cost is "passed on" to the tenant.

Proponents of government intervention in these areas argue that there is no market mechanism to correct safety, health, or other hazards. Therefore, they view the problem as a governmental duty. Whether either side is correct more often than the other is a matter of conjecture. What is clear is that lessee's rights are continually being refined and reinterpreted with each new governmental action.

OTHER AGREEMENTS

Four other linkages are important to the real estate investor:

1. *Listing agreement.* The link between the investor wishing to sell or trade property and the selling agent (salesperson or broker).
2. *Purchase option.* The link between the investor who offers a potential buyer the right to purchase the property at some time during the future.
3. *Sales contract.* The link between buyer and seller at the time of sale.
4. *Management agreement.* The link between the investor who seeks assistance in managing the investment and the managing agent.

The listing agreement may be one of several types: net listings, open listings, exclusive listings, and multiple listings. Each includes different property rights extended by the investor to a broker or brokers in exchange for a sales commission to be paid upon completion of the sale. The written agreement specifies a definite expiration date. Since the agreement lacks consideration, it is generally revocable by either party prior to the end of the agreement. In essence, listing agreements give rights (sometimes exclusive rights) to real estate agents to sell the owner's property.

The purchase option is a less well-known agreement since most agreements to buy or sell property are for a shorter period of time. Such agreements are typically used as sales contracts and require specific performance (i.e., sale) at a specified date. The purchase option gives the holder the right to buy a specified property at a specified price within an extended period in the future. Although the valuation of such an option is complex, it is clear that the value of the option to buy a piece of property is a function of the expected future value of the property itself. An option to buy a property that has become very valuable is itself a valuable property right.

Finally, the management agreement links the investor and the party hired to operate the real estate. It is a detailed document that should clearly specify the rights and obligations of the management agent. For this work, the agent is given a management fee based on a percentage of gross income.

The right to manage and operate property is inherently associated with the private ownership of real estate. If for one of several reasons the investor in real property hires a property manager, the agent acquires some property rights in the investor's properties. Because these property rights may result in problems between the investor and the managing agent, the investor must be very careful about which rights he retains and which rights are extended to the agent.

SUMMARY

Because real estate investment analysis is a very legal process, a large portion of investing in income-producing real estate in an effective manner involves the use of sound legal advice and planning. Furthermore, since many transactions are or become quite complex, legal problems may easily arise, especially if ownership forms, financing arrangements, tax status, or governmental attitudes change during the life of the investment. Finally, there may be many legal decisions and choices that must be made beyond those briefly discussed in this chapter. This includes various types of transfers of ownership such as wills and inheritance laws, sales contracts, deeds, the use of escrows, gifts, estate planning, title assurance and insurance, and others.

It is necessary to have a basic understanding of the legal environment prior to analyzing the financial opportunities associated with the investment. However, merely to possess a descriptive understanding of the various partnership forms or the breakdown of estates is rarely sufficient. The real estate investor must understand the impact of the legal environment on the decisions he faces. Only then will the legal environment matter to the decision maker.

III

CASH FLOW FORECASTING

THE measurement of cash flows begins with the forecasting of gross income and concludes with the after-tax cash flow. In between, the investor must analyze operating expenses and operating leverage, financial leverage and the decision to borrow, and finally, tax planning including the measurement of taxes from operation and decisions regarding the taxation of disposition.

Chapter 6 deals with the estimation, measurement, and evaluation of operating expenses. This chapter demonstrates various techniques and tools for the analysis of expenses and explains the importance and value of professional management.

Chapter 7 addresses the real estate financing decisions, including how much to borrow, the impact of financial leverage, and the measurement of borrowing costs. Finally, chapter 8 discusses the tax implications of real estate investing, including depreciation policy, tax shelter, tax planning for disposition, and tax deferral.

6

OPERATING EXPENSE ANALYSIS

IN the general area of real estate investment analysis and specifically in the analysis dealing with income-producing property, a careful evaluation of operating expenses is critical. Some investors concentrate on other aspects of the investment such as financing or tax planning. However, few considerations affect the investor's return and the value of the property more than changes in operating expenses. Since operating expenses can change rapidly, occasionally despite forecasts to the contrary, and since these changes directly affect net operating income and may be significant in size, a careful analysis of the components of total operating expenses for an income property is very important.

This chapter shows how to extend the cash flow statement from effective gross income to net operating income. The difference between these income accounts is operating expenses. In equation form, this reads as follows:

(6.1)
Effective Gross Income
− Operating Expenses
= Net Operating Income

Typically, many of the items are required expenses for the everyday upkeep and operation of the property. Others, however, are less obvious. We also discuss some of the important techniques the investor can use in analyzing operating expenses. These include an understanding of the relationship between operating expenses, net operating income, and the investment value of the property; the impact of changes in rents and expenses over time; the impact that operating expenses exert on net income multipliers; financial ratios and operating expenses; and more sophisticated techniques such as break-even analysis and operating leverage. This discussion will help the investor to better understand the importance of operating expense analysis. Value creation is often enhanced by careful management of operating expenses.

ESTIMATING OPERATING EXPENSES

One of the investor's most critical tasks is to estimate the types and amounts of operating expenses associated with an income property investment. Errors in forecasting operating expenses can have a substantial impact on real estate decision making. This is true for the potential investor who is contemplating the purchase of income property as well as for the owner who is currently holding the income-producing real estate.

OVERVIEW OF OPERATING EXPENSES

Traditionally, for valuation purposes, all of the required outlays associated with the regular operation of the property have been called the *operating expenses* of the investment. Expenditures of a more permanent and larger nature that improve, upgrade, or rehabilitate the property are called *capital improvements* and are not regarded as operating expenses. The investor should remember that the types and levels of operating expenses vary with the different types of real estate investments.

It is sometimes useful to separate the various operating expenses into categories: variable expenses, fixed expenses, and the reserve for replacement. *Variable expenses* differ from *fixed expenses* in that the former varies with the occupancy and general operation of the property. These items include electricity and water, garbage removal, supplies, repairs, bookkeeping services, management fees, and others. *Fixed expenses* are periodic in nature and in the short run remain constant or level throughout the period, independent of the operation of the property. The best-known fixed expenses are property taxes and property insurance. Recent dramatic changes in property values and, thus, in property taxes suggest that in some cases, taxes may not be fixed for the relevant period. In the long run, of course, all expenses tend to vary. However, this categorization is based on the income reporting period, typically a year. Traditionally, however, since property taxes are based on the tax rate and assessment base, these taxes are treated as fixed each period (year). Other fixed expenses include additional taxes and local fees.

The final expense category is the *reserve for replacement*. This category is frequently misunderstood by beginning investors because it does involve an immediate outflow of cash and is not deductible for tax purposes. It is really a reserve account used to set aside funds that will eventually be used to replace worn-out appliances, furniture, or machinery. This reserve adjusts the value of the cash flow to reflect the fact that some of the appliances will need to be replaced in the near future. This is one of the ways that cash flow differs from income for accounting purposes.

Since the funds are not spent each period (monthly, quarterly, semiannually, or annually) like other expenses, the Internal Revenue Service will not permit its deduction from gross income for tax purposes. However, it should be included as an expense item for investment purposes (i.e., when calculating cash flow). By assuming that either the assets to be replaced have economic lives equal to the building (which in most cases is unlikely) or that these assets will not wear out (which is most unlikely if not impossible for most items), failure to include this reserve would result in overstating the value of the property. In any event, inclusion of this expense gives the investor an accurate net operating income figure at each point in time. (This argument can still be made even if the investor does not set aside funds for this purpose. The point is that the income and cash flow streams must be evaluated under the realistic assumption that expenditures will be required to replace some of these short-term assets.)

Table 6.1 is a typical operating expense statement for an income-producing real estate project. Note that this statement includes only the expenditures for the past reporting period, in this case one year. In valuing the property, the investor would es-

Table 6.1 TYPICAL OPERATING EXPENSE
CATEGORIES

Variable Expenses
  Utilities
  Repairs and maintenance
  Services
  Administration and payroll
  Supplies
  Decorating
  Management
  Miscellaneous expenses
    Total variable expenses

Fixed Expenses
  Real estate taxes
  Insurance
  Other taxes and fees
    Total fixed expenses

  Total operating expenses = variable plus
  fixed

timate future expenses and use these to gauge net operating income. It would be quite reasonable to forecast changes in certain expense items for future periods. It should also be noted that items such as management fees and the reserve for replacement may not be included on past operating expense statements, especially if these were made by the previous owners. This would be true if the previous owner personally managed the property or if he or she failed to establish a reserve for re-

placement. As already noted, the replacement reserve is not a true expense but rather an account established for valuation purposes. Table 6.2 presents a sample replacement for reserve account for an apartment investment.

Data compiled by the Institute of Real Estate Management (IREM) shows that the typical operating expenses as a percentage of gross potential income per room for income-producing residential properties were 13.9 percent for utilities, 5 percent for repairs and maintenance, 2 percent for decorating, and about 9 percent for payroll and management. Total variable expenses averaged about 33.2 percent of potential gross income and about 34.5 percent of effective gross income. Total fixed expenses averaged nearly 15 percent. Therefore, for this type of property, total operating expenses averaged about 48 percent of potential gross income and about 50 percent of effective gross income.

Another recent study by IREM indicated that rent collected for suburban office buildings was typically allocated as indicated in table 6.3.

The study was based on a sample of data from 532 suburban office buildings. The occupancy level for the entire sample was 94 percent. These buildings were within a 30-mile radius of a metropolitan location, outside the central business district, and had a minimum floor area of 5,000 square feet,

Table 6.2 REPLACEMENT RESERVE ACCOUNT

Asset	Number	Cost ($)	Expected Econ. Life (yrs.)	Annual Reserve Amt. ($)
Refrigerators	24	350	15	560
Stoves	24	300	15	480
Air conditioners	48	150	8	900
Carpeting	24	500	6	2,000
Drapes	24	150	6	600
Total replacement reserve				$4,540

Table 6.3 Typical Suburban Office
Building Expenses

Type of Expense	Percent of PGI
Utilities	15.8
Janitorial, maintenance, repair	14.6
Real estate taxes	10.2
Insurance and services	3.5
Administration and payroll	5.5
Total expense ratio	49.6

at least 80 percent of which was occupied by office space.

Variable Expense Items

Utilities. Utility expenses include most power and water services found in most urban properties, including electricity, gas, heating fuels, telephone charges, sewer or other sanitary system charges, and water. Many utility expenses are relatively fixed in nature; however, an investor may be able to restrict unnecessary usage of some of these items by following recommended management prevention techniques. For example, the investor may be able to reduce electricity use by checking and replacing worn or insufficient insulation in the walls and ceilings and by installing energy-efficient storm windows and thermopane glass. The caulking and weather stripping of windows and doors may further reduce unnecessary electrical usage. Similarly, he should regularly check plumbing fixtures for worn rings and seals. As energy becomes more expensive, it will be to the investor's advantage to make the most efficient use of utility services.

Repairs and Maintenance. There are two types of repairs and maintenance expenses: those that are minor and are expected to occur at various intervals and those that are

potentially more serious and mostly unexpected. Items typically classified as repairs include breakdowns of elevators, heating and cooling systems, refrigerators and stoves, and other mechanical items. Maintenance items include the general upkeep of the building's common space and the exterior grounds, minor maintenance of appliances on a regular basis (preventive maintenance), and regular maintenance of equipment. When cash flow problems occur in residential income property, some owners tend to postpone certain maintenance and repair items. This deferred maintenance strategy often results in even greater maintenance expenses in the future, falling property values, and very unhappy tenants.

Services. Many items can better be handled by outside professional services. The more obvious ones are garbage removal, regular extermination and pest control, building security, and fire safety control. However, some investors also may be interested in other services such as professional bookkeeping and accounting, maintenance and building cleaning, and window washing. In many ways, the benefits of professional services accrue to both owners and renters. The owners may wish to employ specialists who are more familiar with the problems of the job and are trained to handle various situations. Tenants will appreciate the results.

Administration and Payroll. Administration and payroll expenses encompass employees who have been hired by the investor (or the management firm) for various tasks. These people include regular maintenance staff, secretarial assistance, groundskeepers, or others. Administrative expenses consist of small operating expenses such as the costs of preparing credit reports on prospective tenants, legal expenses, and petty cash items.

Supplies. This item refers to materials and small items incidental to the operation of the property. Hardware items and other minor maintenance items purchased by the investor or manager fall into this category. Although supplies constitute a very small percentage of expenses, the owner or manager who neglects this part of the upkeep is inviting trouble in the future.

Decorating. Sometimes included in services, decorating is listed separately here because it is an important way to insure an investment's success. The newly redecorated income-producing building allows the investor to attract tenants at the highest rents. It is also regarded as a sign of good management. In many cases, the expenses can be easily justified by the increases in rental receipts.

Management. This is one of the more controversial expense items. If the owner manages the property himself, then for accounting purposes, there are no management expenses. Since the owner provides the service, the investor would pay no monthly management fee.

Traditionally, management is compensated on a percentage of gross income. Therefore, the management firm is useful to reduce vacancies and maximize gross possible income. Management fee percentages vary between 5 percent and 8 percent for smaller and problem properties. The rate is largely determined by custom and local market conditions.

It is up to the investor to decide whether or not to hire a management company. Such a company may run the property efficiently and, in the long run, will make more money for the investor.

Real Estate Taxes. Real estate taxes are one of the more permanent expenses that owners of real property must pay. Based on local assessment, these taxes are *ad valorem* or "according to value." Each state defines the relationship between *assessed value* and *market value* (that requires all property to be assessed at the same percentage). The total amount of tax liability is determined by the tax rate times the assessed value. If the owner feels that his property assessment is too high relative to his estimate of market value and the state's assessment-to-market value ratio, he may request a reassessment.

Insurance. Property insurance is another important area for analysis. Although entire books are available on the subject, the basic purpose for acquiring insurance protection is to reduce or limit unforeseen casualty losses. Insurance firms offer various packages of protection including fire insurance, extended coverage policies (with additional protection against floods, hail, tornados, and other disasters), casualty coverage against robbery, theft, and on-the-job accidents, and liability. Property insurance is a fixed expense. In addition, there are other taxes that may be included as fixed expenses. Examples of these are franchise taxes, personal property taxes, or similar levies or fees.

ROLE OF PROPERTY MANAGEMENT

Property management is one of the frequently misunderstood areas of analysis. Typically defined as "the branch of real estate composed of renting, supervising, collecting, paying, and the overall maintaining and managing of real estate for others,"* many investors believe that the expense associated with professional property management is unnecessary. After all, many of the managerial duties and activities may be undertaken by the equity investor. However, since the amount of time required and the types of skills needed may be more than some investors possess, professional property management is a service that warrants consideration. Also, there are other investors for whom the employment of a professional management firm arises out of choice, not necessity.

The decision of whether or not to employ a management firm is often difficult. The advantages are there, however, for the firm may be more familiar with the market and with the latest construction and maintenance procedures to help increase the efficient use of property. Finally, it may have more resources available for bookkeeping, advertising, and preparing financial reports.

Although these factors and others are helpful, the investor does not acquire them without expense. The decision, then, is whether the services are worth the cost. In many cases, they are.

IMPACT ON INVESTMENT ANALYSIS

One way to determine whether or not the employment of one or more professional services is worth it is to measure its potential impact on the return and value of the investment. For example, if the advice and policies of the property management firm increased the value of the property significantly, it is easy to justify its employment. If, however, it could not do so and

the other services offered were either too expensive or unnecessary, the investor would do better by acquiring the services of others or of none at all.

Recent studies have shown that property management significantly influences investment values.* Since the professionally trained property manager can best deal with factors affecting income and operating expenses, he is quite valuable to the investor. The following discussion demonstrates some of the other ways in which professional property management may be of considerable help.

ANALYSIS OF EXPENSES AND VALUATION

Given that the investor is able to carefully forecast expected operating expenses, there are a number of ways in which to analyze the relationships between income, expenses, value, return, and risk. These techniques aid in the investment decision-making process and are discussed next.

OPERATING EXPENSES AND VALUE

One of the most common ways of valuing property is to estimate an average (or "stabilized") net operating income figure based on market and investment analyses and capitalize this amount by the appropriate discount or capitalization rate. If the investor wanted to find out how much value he placed on the property, this approach suggests that the investor would make a re-

* From *Illustrated Encyclopedia Dictionary of Real Estate Terms* by Jerome S. Gross. © 1969 by Prentice-Hall, Inc. Published by Prentice-Hall, Inc., Englewood Cliffs, N.J. 07632.

* See David W. Walters, "Just How Important Is Property Management?" *Journal of Property Management* 38 (July/August 1973), pp. 164–168; Austin J. Jaffe, *Property Management in Real Estate Investment Decision-Making* (Lexington, Mass.: Lexington Books, D. C. Heath and Co., 1979).

liable estimate of net operating income and divide it by the capitalization rate for projects of this risk class and type of investment. The result is an estimate of investment value.

The *operating expense ratio* is defined as follows:

(6.2)

$$OER = \frac{TOE}{EGI}$$

where:

  OER = operating ratio
  TOE = total operating expenses
  EGI = effective gross income

Net operating income is determined by multiplying effective gross income by (1 − OER):

(6.3)

$$NOI = EGI \times (1 - OER)$$

where:

  NOI = net operating income

Net operating income is "capitalized" into value by dividing the capitalization rate into the net operating income figure.

(6.4)

$$V = \frac{NOI}{R}$$

where:

  V = investment value
  R = (overall) capitalization rate

For example, using an operating expense estimate of $25,000, if effective gross income is expected to be $50,000, the operating expense ratio would be .50 and net operating income would be $25,000.

$$OER = \frac{\$25,000}{\$50,000}$$

$$= .50$$

and

$$NOI = \$50,000 \, (1 - .50)$$

$$= \$25,000$$

Finally, if the capitalization rate is 10 percent, the investment value is $250,000.

$$V = \frac{\$25,000}{.10}$$

$$= \$250,000$$

Suppose that the effective gross income increases by $55,000 due to increased demand for rental space. The analysis shows that the investment value would increase from $250,000 to $300,000, holding everything else constant.

$$OER = \frac{\$25,000}{\$55,000}$$

$$= .4545$$

and

$$NOI = \$55,000 \, (1 - .4545)$$

$$= \$30,000$$

Therefore:

$$V = \frac{\$30,000}{.10}$$

$$= \$300,000$$

The same result would occur, of course, if total operating expenses decreased from $5,000 to $20,000, *without an accompanied change in rents*. In this case, net operating income would also be $30,000 ($50,000 minus $20,000) and the investment value would also be $300,000.

Finally, the investor could forecast changes in income and expenses and translate those combinations of changes into capitalized value. This is shown in the next section. It is important to emphasize that the calculation of investment value using net operating income as well as other measures of income and an overall capitalization rate is very sensitive to changes in operating expenses.

Although income capitalization is only one method of valuation, operating expenses play a major role in the value of an investment. Since net operating income is the difference between effective gross income and total operating expenses, changes in total operating expenses affect the estimated size of net operating income. Sizable changes in net operating income when divided by the overall capitalization rate result in significant changes in investment value. Therefore, a careful analysis of the changes in operating expenses over time is vital to ensure that the investment (and market) values of the property are not seriously damaged.

Similarly, the investor who is able to eliminate unnecessary expenses or who is able to raise rents by making significant improvements in the physical facilities can greatly increase the value of the property. One of the benefits of professional property management firms is their ability to eliminate unnecessary expenses and recommend programs for upgrading and rehabilitation that may result in higher rent schedules despite additional outlays. These actions raise net operating income and therefore the value (and return) of the investment.

OPERATING EXPENSES, OPERATING EXPENSE RATIO, AND VALUE

A question that frequently arises in estimating net operating income is the relationship between changes in operating expenses, changes in the operating expense ratio, and the value of property. This is a very important area since changes in the operating expense ratio directly result from changes in income as well as expenses.

The operating expense ratio is a key factor in making real estate investment decisions.* As a rule of thumb, the investor can predict whether or not the value of the property will change by comparing the expected changes in rents and expenses with the operating expense ratio. For example, suppose income is only expected to increase at a rate of 5 percent annually, but expenses were expected to increase at a rate of 10 percent annually. If the operating expense ratio (total operating expenses divided by effective gross income) was less than .50, then investment value would still increase.

The basic relationship is:

If a = expected growth rate in (effective gross) income and

b = expected growth rate in (total operating) expenses,

then:

OER = operating expense ratio

value will increase when:

(6.5)
$$\frac{a}{b} > OER$$

value will remain the same when:

(6.6)
$$\frac{a}{b} = OER$$

value will decrease when:

(6.7)
$$\frac{a}{b} < OER$$

---

* Austin J. Jaffe and C. F. Sirmans, "The Relationship Between Growth Factors, Operating Expense Ratio, and Valuation," *The Real Estate Appraiser* 44 (July/August 1978), pp. 30–34.

In this example:

$$\frac{a}{b} = .50$$

If OER is less than .50, the value will increase. If OER is greater than .50, the value will decline.

This result may seem paradoxical to some readers. In this example, expenses were expected to rise twice as much as income, and yet if the OER was less than .50, the investment value would rise. The explanation is that the investor must pay careful attention to the relationship between operating expenses and the operating expense ratio and how these items affect the value of property. He simply cannot make a proper decision by only looking at changes in income and expenses.

GROSS AND NET INCOME MULTIPLIERS

These are reasonably simple investment measures which relate value and effective gross or net operating income. Each has a particular meaning in relation to the analysis of operating expenses. The gross income multiplier (GIM) technique is more commonly used. However, since operating expense levels and, thus, ratios vary among different pieces of property, this technique may be less useful for comparative purposes. However, a well-known article suggests that this technique may be very reliable in making investment decisions.*

The GIM is defined as follows:

(6.8)

$$GIM = \frac{MV}{EGI}$$

---

* Richard U. Ratcliff, "Don't Underrate the Gross Income Multiplier," *The Appraisal Journal* 39 (April 1971), pp. 264–271.

where:

GIM = gross income multiplier
MV = market value
EGI = effective gross income

If the effective gross income of an income property is $15,000 per year and the market value of the property is $100,000, the gross income multiplier would be 6.67.

$$GIM = \frac{\$100,000}{\$15,000}$$

$$= 6.67$$

The investor would then compare this GIM to others for sale in order to evaluate investment alternatives.

The net income multiplier (NIM) is defined as value divided by net operating income. The reciprocal of the NIM, called the overall rate, is widely used in valuation of real estate.

Since V = NOI/R, value is also equal to NOI times 1/R. The net income multiplier (NIM) is defined as 1/R. For example, if value is equal to $200,000 and net operating income is $20,000, the net income multiplier is 10.

(6.9)

$$NIM = \frac{MV}{NOI}$$

where:

NIM = net income multiplier

$$= \frac{\$200,000}{\$20,000}$$

$$= 10.0$$

The NIM is also equal to 1/R.

(6.10)

$$NIM = \frac{1}{R}$$

In addition to R, the capitalization rate may be expressed as the NIM reciprocal.

(6.11)
$$R = \frac{1}{NIM}$$

Using the same numbers as in the above example of V = $200,000, NOI = $20,000, and NIM = 10, then R is .10, since the capitalization rate is the reciprocal of NIM.

$$R = \frac{1}{10.0}$$
$$= .10$$

In any event, real estate analysts and experienced investors urge that a great deal of judgment must be used when developing multipliers. Since these measures are relatively simple to compute, the data requirements minimal, and the results easy to interpret, care must be taken to avoid inaccuracies.

To the extent that the gross income multiplier technique is preferred to the net income multiplier, the investor is minimizing the impact that *different sets of operating expenses* can have on various properties. Although comparable properties may vary significantly, comparisons on the basis of gross income multipliers may not pose any significant problems for some income-producing real estate. The problem is when operating expenses vary for other comparable properties. In this event, the net income multiplier (or its reciprocal) is a better measure.

Consider the alternatives shown in table 6.4. Although projects A and B have identical expected selling prices and annual effective gross income, the NIM method or direct capitalization using R gives different results. Obviously, an investor would not be indifferent to each project, despite the same GIM. The example shows that Project B re-

Table 6.4 PROJECTS A AND B

	A	B
Expected selling price	$500,000	$500,000
Effective gross income	$100,000	$100,000
Total operating expenses	$ 40,000	$ 50,000
Net operating income	$ 60,000	$ 50,000
GIM	5.00	5.00
NIM	8.33	10.00
R	12%	10%

quires a greater NIM (or lower R) than A. Stated differently, if the capitalization rate R was chosen to be 12 percent for both investments, Project B would be valued at $416,667. Therefore, Project A would be preferred if both were viewed as equally risky. Only after the net income multiplier (and the capitalization rate) is considered is the analyst able to choose Project A over Project B. Using the gross income multiplier, the investor does not consider differences in expenses among alternatives.

FINANCIAL RATIOS

Some of the well-known financial ratios involve operating expenses directly or indirectly. Three of the more common ones are the operating expense ratio, the break-even cash flow ratio, and the debt coverage ratio. Each of these measures is important in the analysis of income, expenses, and value of real estate.

A high *operating expense ratio* may indicate that some expenses currently being charged against the property are unnecessary or that rent levels are too low compared to similar property on the market. The investor should carefully monitor this ratio over time to pick up any danger signals in low or falling net operating incomes.

The *break-even cash flow ratio* is the sum of the operating expenses ratio except that the debt service is added to expenses as a percentage of gross income. This measure indicates the extent to which the investment is able to provide enough cash flow to pay all of the required expenses and financial obligations. If the break-even cash flow ratio approaches 80 percent to 85 percent, this indicates that the required obligations relative to gross income are reasonably high. Since financial expenses (principal and interest payments) tend to be fixed when a level-payment amortization is used, changes in the break-even cash flow ratio reflect changes in operating expenses, in gross income, or in both of these. In any event, this ratio may help identify periods of tight cash flow and years when the operation of the real estate may require further attention.

The *debt coverage ratio* is net operating income divided by the debt service. A measure of financial risk, it determines the ability of the investment to cover the fixed mortgage payment. Typical ratios for large income-producing properties range from 1.2 to 1.5. The importance of this ratio in terms of operating expenses is that if operating expenses are forecasted to increase in the near future, this may result in a lower net operating income (dependent on any expected changes in rental income). If the net operating income falls sharply, the debt coverage ratio may fall dangerously close to 1.00 (or perhaps even less), which would mean serious cash flow problems for the investor. This might occur if operating expenses rose rapidly relative to rental income or if rents fell suddenly due to increasing market risk.

For example, if effective gross income was expected to be $40,000 for the upcoming year and total operating expenses were estimated to be $20,000, net operating income would be expected to be $20,000. If the debt service for the year is $14,500, the debt coverage ratio is 1.38.

(6.12)
$$\text{Debt Coverage Ratio} = \frac{\text{Net Operating Income}}{\text{Debt Service}}$$
$$= \frac{\$20,000}{\$14,500}$$
$$= 1.38$$

Suppose operating expenses were expected to increase by 25 percent (to $25,000) for next year without any increase in income. The new debt coverage ratio would be:

$$\frac{\$15,000}{\$14,500} = 1.03$$

A debt coverage ratio of 1.03 indicates the lack of safety available to the investor to meet the debt service requirements from net operating income. Therefore, analysis of the debt coverage ratio can help identify a changing operating expense position. Table 6.5 summarizes the basic measures and relationships of operating expense analysis.

FINANCIAL TOOLS FOR THE ANALYSIS OF OPERATING EXPENSES

One of the more vital areas in the analysis of operating expenses is the relationship between fixed expenses, variable expenses, and income. If there are no fixed expenses associated with the property and rents are greater than variable expenses, net operating income will always be positive. However, it is unrealistic to assume that real estate investments will have no fixed expenses. Most have sizable mortgage payments as well. Therefore, it is wise to determine how much rental income is needed to break even in order to cover variable and fixed expenses. *Break-even analysis* provides this information.

Table 6.5 SUMMARY OF OPERATING EXPENSES ANALYSIS: DEFINITIONS AND RATIOS

1. Net operating income and value

$$\text{Investment value} = \frac{\text{Net operating income}}{\text{Capitalization rate}}$$

2. Operating expenses, operating expense ratio, and value

Increase in investment value if: $\dfrac{\Delta \text{ Effective gross income}}{\Delta \text{ Operating expenses}} > \text{OER}$

No change in investment value if: $\dfrac{\Delta \text{ Effective gross income}}{\Delta \text{ Operating expenses}} = \text{OER}$

Decrease in investment value if: $\dfrac{\Delta \text{ Effective gross income}}{\Delta \text{ Operating expenses}} < \text{OER}$

3. Gross and net income multipliers

$$\text{Gross income multiplier} = \frac{\text{Market value}}{\text{Effective gross income}}$$

$$\text{Net income multiplier} = \frac{\text{Market value}}{\text{Net operating income}}$$

4. Financial ratios

$$\text{Operating expense ratio} = \frac{\text{Operating expenses}}{\text{Effective gross income}}$$

$$\text{Break-even cash flow ratio} = \frac{\text{Operating expenses} + \text{debt service}}{\text{Effective gross income}}$$

$$\text{Debt coverage ratio} = \frac{\text{Net operating income}}{\text{Debt service}}$$

Break-even Analysis. Since most income-producing properties have fixed expenses, the investor wants to be able to identify the amount of income needed (and, therefore, the number of apartments that must be occupied) in order to break even. The break-even point is the amount of income where revenues would just cover all costs (variable, fixed, and financial expenses). In order to use this type of analysis, one must make some assumptions about the revenues and expenses of the property.

First, assume that all of the rental units are rented at the same rates. Second, estimate the amount of variable expenses per rental unit and assume that this amount

will be constant for each additional rental unit occupied. Finally, assume that the fixed expenses remain constant throughout the analysis.

Break-even for Number of Units. In order to find the minimum number of rental units that must be occupied in order to break even, we can perform the following analysis.

The following definitions are used:

GI = Gross income
OE = Operating expenses
FE = Fixed expenses
ve = Variable expenses per unit

gr = Gross rent per unit
Q = Number of rental units occupied
DS = Debt service
TC = Total costs
VE = Total variable expenses

Using algebra, we get the following results:

(6.13)
$$TC = OE + DS$$

(6.14)
$$VE = ve \times Q$$

(6.15)
$$GI = gr \times Q$$

(6.16)
$$TC = VE + FE + DS$$

The break-even point for occupied units, BEP(Q) is where gross income equals total costs.

(6.17)
$$\text{Gross income} = \text{Total costs}$$
$$(gr \times Q) = VE + FE + DS$$

By algebra:

(6.18)
$$gr \times Q - ve \times Q = FE + DS$$
$$(Q)(gr - ve) = FE + DS$$
$$BEP(Q) = \frac{FE + DS}{gr - ve}$$

For example, assume an investor is considering investing in ABC Properties, a 50-unit two-bedroom apartment building. Each apartment can be rented at $250 per month. Variable expenses are estimated to be $100 per month per unit, fixed expenses are estimated to be $1,250 per month, and the monthly debt service is $4,000. How many apartments must be rented in order to break even?

$$BEP(Q) = \frac{\$1,250 + \$4,000}{\$250 - \$100}$$
$$= \frac{\$5,250}{\$150}$$
$$= 35$$

Therefore, the owners of ABC Properties must rent 35 of the 50 available units to break even (i.e., achieve a zero cash flow). These results are demonstrated in table 6.6.

Therefore, 35 units is the minimum occupancy required to break even or a 70 percent occupancy rate.

Break-even Gross Income. It is also possible to calculate break-even points in terms of rental income rather than number of units. This may be useful in cases where there is more than one type of rental unit in a particular investment.

If the break-even point in dollars, BEP($), is consistent with BEP(Q), then gross income must equal total costs.

(6.19)
$$GI = VE + FE + DS$$

By algebra and substitution:

(6.20)
$$(gr \times Q) - (ve \times Q) = FE + DS$$
$$\frac{GI}{Q}Q - \frac{VE}{Q}Q = FE + DS$$
$$Q\left(\frac{GI - VE}{Q}\right) = FE + DS$$

(6.21)
Since $Q = \dfrac{GI}{gr}$, then:

$$\frac{GI}{gr}\left(\frac{GI - VE}{GI/gr}\right) = FE + DS$$
$$GI\left(\frac{GI - VE}{GI}\right) = FE + DS$$
$$GI\left(1 - \frac{VE}{GI}\right) = FE + DS$$
$$GI = \frac{FE + DS}{1 - \dfrac{ve}{gr}}$$

Using the same numbers from the ABC Properties example, we get results consistent with table 6.6.

$$BEP(\$) - \frac{\$1{,}250 + \$4{,}000}{1 - \dfrac{\$100}{\$250}}$$

$$= \frac{\$5{,}250}{.60}$$

$$= \$8{,}750$$

In other words, $8,750 is needed in rental income per month to break even for this property.

Break-even for Rental Income per Unit. In addition, it may be useful to derive the break-even point in dollars per unit. The algebra is shown below:

(6.22)

$$Q = \frac{FE + DS}{gr - ve}$$

$$Q(gr - ve) = FE + DS$$

$$Qgr - Qve = FE + DS$$

$$Qgr = FE + DS + Qve$$

$$gr = \frac{FE + DS + Qve}{Q}$$

If the investor forecasts that he can rent 35 units, what rent per unit would be necessary to break even?

$$\frac{BEP}{(\$ \text{ per unit})} = \frac{1{,}250 + 4{,}000 + 35(100)}{35}$$

$$= \frac{8{,}750}{35}$$

$$= \$250$$

Although all the results deal with hypothetical *monthly* income statements, the break-even analysis will work for other periods (i.e., annually) as well. However, the ability to perform useful break-even analysis for annual periods is based on access to annual data. If it is available and forecasts can be made for the upcoming year, the break-even analysis will work.

Of course the usefulness of the different break-even methods discussed here will vary among analysts, situations, and types of property. The break-even analysis for number of units is best suited for residential income-producing real estate in which all of the units are identical in rental price. The methods that measure break-even in dollars and dollars per unit enable the investor to select any gross income and variable expense combination and get a break-even point in dollar terms. Since fixed expenses and debt service are constant, the denominator is always constant for break-even analysis for rental income (in this example, .60) with correct combinations of gross income and variable expenses. Finally, the last method solved for a break-even amount per unit when the number of units was known.

Table 6.6 ABC PROPERTIES ANALYSIS OF BREAK-EVEN CASH FLOW

Gross income ($250 × 35)		$8,750
Less expenses		
Variable expenses ($100 × 35)	$3,500	
Fixed expenses	$1,250	
Operating expenses		$4,750
Net operating income		$4,000
Less debt service		$4,000
If zero, break-even cash flow is correct		$ 0

OPERATING LEVERAGE

*Operating leverage** is the fact that a relatively small increase in gross income can result in a large increase in net operating income. Using the example of ABC Properties again, we have seen that if 35 units are rented at $250 per month, the cash flow will be equal to zero. Similarly, table 6.7

---

* This term, although somewhat related in concept, should not be confused with the term *financial leverage*, which we will discuss in a later chapter.

Table 6.7 ABC Properties Analysis of Operating Leverage

Number of units occupied	30	35	40	45	50
Gross income	$7,500	$8,750	$10,000	$11,250	$12,500
Less expenses					
Variable expenses	$3,000	$3,500	$ 4,000	$ 4,500	$ 5,000
Fixed expenses	1,250	1,250	1,250	1,250	1,250
Operating expenses	$4,250	$4,750	$ 5,250	$ 5,750	$ 6,250
Net operating income	$3,250	$4,000	$ 4,750	$ 5,500	$ 6,250

Assumptions: Rent per unit = $250
Variable expenses per unit = $100
Fixed expenses = $1,250
Income taxes and bad debts = $0

demonstrates changes in net operating income as a result of changes in occupancy rates.

If, for example, the investor were to increase occupancy from 40 to 45 units (or increase gross income from $10,000 to $11,250), a 12.5 percent increase, the resulting net operating income would increase from $4,750 to $5,500, or 15.79 percent. Therefore, a small percentage change in occupancy (or gross income) *levers* net operating income into a larger amount. All of this is due to the manner in which the investor uses fixed expenses. As long as the rent per unit is larger than the variable cost per unit, favorable operating leverage will magnify the changes in occupancy into larger changes in income.

Specification of the percentage change in net operating income resulting from a percentage change in occupancy or gross income is called the *degree of operating leverage* (DOL) and can be calculated at any occupancy level. If the change in net operating income is equal to $\Delta Q(gr - ve)$, since FE is constant, the net operating income at any Q occupancy level is $Q(gr - ve) - FE$, so the percentage change in net operating income is:

(6.23)
$$\frac{\text{Percentage change}}{\text{in NOI}} = \frac{\Delta Q(gr - ve)}{Q(gr - ve) - FE}$$

If the percentage change in occupancy is $\Delta Q/Q$, the percentage change in net operating income to occupancy is defined as follows:

(6.24)
$$\begin{aligned} \text{DOL} \\ \text{(at occupancy} \\ \text{level, } Q) \end{aligned} = \frac{\dfrac{\Delta Q(gr - ve)}{Q(gr - ve) - FE}}{\dfrac{\Delta Q}{Q}}$$

$$= \frac{\Delta Q(gr - ve)}{Q(gr - ve) - FE} \times \frac{Q}{\Delta Q}$$

$$= \frac{Q(gr - ve)}{Q(gr - ve) - FE}$$

For example, the degree of operating leverage at 40 units is 1.26.

$$\begin{aligned} \text{DOL at} \\ Q = 40 \end{aligned} = \frac{40(250 - 100)}{40(250 - 100) - 1250}$$

$$= 1.26$$

Therefore, for each one percent increase in occupancy after 40 units, net operating income will increase by 1.26 percent.

SUMMARY

Operating expense analysis is an important component of the investment decision. Variations in operating expenses have a major impact on the value and expected rate of return for an investment. In the next chapter we turn our attention to the financing decision.

7

FINANCING DECISIONS

THE financing decision is one of the most important for the investor in real property. This chapter begins by analyzing the reasons why investors borrow. It is often said that the investor in real estate has an advantage over the investor in other assets since the typical real estate investor needs only a relatively small amount of cash in order to acquire the investment. The investor often borrows a relatively large amount of money to finance the investment, pays the cost of obtaining outside debt sources out of the income stream from the investment, and therefore acquires ownership of the property with only a fraction of the cash required.

Some investors suggest borrowing as much as possible so that investing in the income-producing real estate requires as little equity capital as possible. Thus, they conclude, the use of other people's money is the key to real estate finance and investment analysis.

This chapter explains why borrowing is advantageous and how to evaluate various financing alternatives; it discusses the impact of financing on investment value and rate of return and examines financial leverage and its role in making real estate investment decisions. A brief introduction to alternative financing methods concludes the chapter.

WHY BORROW?

An individual who wishes to invest in real estate (or other assets) and has enough cash to pay for the investment outright has two choices: pay cash for the entire property or borrow a portion and pay cash for the remaining amount. What should this potential investor do?

Analysis shows that even if individuals have enough cash for this particular investment (but not enough to satisfy all needs), the value of the funds he or she has may be viewed as more valuable than the cost of borrowing. The investor can acquire more assets by using debt because the same equity can be "stretched" into more investments, more assets, or more consumption. So individuals (and firms) borrow because they believe they will be better off as a result.

In order to consume goods and services now rather than wait, investors must pay a price: the interest for the use of the money over the period. It is clear, then, that investors would only borrow if it is perceived to be in their best interests. However, if these situations exist, we would expect to see them borrowing as much as possible all of the time. The problem is that the gains from leverage are associated with increasing amounts of financial risk—the probability of defaulting on financial obligations. Obviously, the more debt that is acquired, the higher the required interest payments and the greater the probability of not having enough income to cover obligations. Thus, financial leverage is not free or riskless, although no investor borrows without expecting favorable financial leverage.

In general, financial leverage is the major reason for borrowing. When the expected rate of return from the investment is greater than the cost of borrowing, favorable financial leverage exists for those who have borrowed to finance the project. If, however, the returns fall short of expectations and return less than the cost of debt used to finance the investment, unfavorable financial leverage exists. Not even an extremely optimistic real estate investor is happy about unfavorable leverage. Unfavorable leverage means two things: First, the investor would have been better off using equity instead of borrowing (or perhaps not investing until later); second, the investor should not intentionally use this means to achieve his financial goals.

EVALUATING FINANCING ALTERNATIVES

If the key financing decision involves the measurement of financial leverage and its impact on the wealth of the investor, it is necessary to compare various financing alternatives in order to decide which would be preferable.

For instance, you could compare the annual debt services of each loan plan. (This is very similar to using the mortgage constant as a cost of borrowing since the mortgage constant is the proportion of debt service to the original loan.) The problem with this method is that it is possible to mistakenly choose the more expensive alternative.

For example, in table 7.1, suppose a loan

Table 7.1 WHICH $1,000,000 LOAN IS CHEAPER?

	Bank A	Bank B
Interest rate	10.5%	11.5%
Term (years)	20	30
Debt service	$121,493	$119,564

from Bank A is available for $1,000,000 at a rate of 10.5 percent for twenty years. If the loan is to be repaid in equal annual payments using a regular amortization schedule, the annual payment will be $121,493. However, you could borrow the same amount, $1,000,000, from Bank B at a rate of 11.5 percent for thirty years. The annual payment would be $119,564. By comparing the annual debt service of the loans, we conclude that the loan from Bank B has a lower debt service. Accordingly, Bank B's loan also has a lower mortgage constant (.1196) compared to Bank A's (.1215). The problem is, that despite much widespread use by real estate investors, the loan from Bank B is *not* cheaper than Bank A.

Another way to see that the loan with lower debt service is not automatically cheaper than another is to compare the investor's position at the end of the shorter of the two loans. If the loan from Bank A was accepted, it would be repaid at the end of twenty years. However, if the investor borrowed at Bank B, ten more years of debt service would remain. This situation causes problems for those evaluating alternative financing packages by debt service (or mortgage constant).

A better method is one that measures the true cost of the loan or the effective cost of borrowing. This net cost distinguishes loans on the basis of the annual interest rate on a time adjusted basis of borrowing and repaying interest.

A final method evaluates the impact that various loan arrangements can have on the investment value and/or rate of return of the investment. Sometimes this can be done by using the effective cost of borrowing.

MECHANICS OF THE MORTGAGE

Once the investor has decided to borrow, he must become familiar with the mortgage since it is the most commonly used financial debt instrument. We might point out that the word *mortgage* can be used as a noun or a verb. The instrument of a mortgage is the document that provides security to the lender who seeks repayment of a note. In many states, the typical instrument is a trust deed rather than a mortgage but the results are almost identical. However, an investor may also mortgage a piece of property. In this sense, he pledges the property as security in order to receive cash for some purpose.

The Mortgage Instrument

The formal use of mortgages began during the fourteenth century in England, although its roots can be traced to the first century B.C. The mortgagee (lender) had most of the property rights. If the mortgagee wished to evict the mortgagor (borrower) he generally could do so. However, the development of common law resulted in more rights for the mortgagor. The mortgage instrument consisted of a description of the property held as security in order to satisfy the note owed. In addition it also specified the one day each year on which the mortgagor could pay the debt. This was known as *Debt Day* and the law permitted the satisfaction of the note and the cancelling of the mortgage according to the *defeasance clause*.

If the mortgagor failed to pay the debt, he forfeited any interest in the land. This led to the development of the *equitable right of redemption* in the beginning of the seventeenth century. This permitted mortgagors to regain their interests during a grace period after the default. The mortgagors could pay interest and costs to the mortgagee and redeem the property. If the grace period expired, then the mortgagor *foreclosed* and took the property.

This common law led to modern foreclosure practices. Foreclosure today limits the period of redemption of the mortgagor by the mortgagee's action. In modern law, there are two doctrines which may be followed: *strict foreclosure* and *statutory foreclosure*. Strict foreclosure is followed only by a few states and closely resembles common law treatment of mortgagors. Statutory foreclosure permits a taking by the mortgagee only to the extent of his debt, and court proceedings are usually required before an exchange of title can take place.

Analysis of Mortgage Terms

The typical terms of a mortgage loan consist of the interest rate, the amount borrowed relative to the total value (the loan-to-value ratio), the period over which the borrower repays the loan (maturity), and the method and timing of repayment. These interrelationships determine the amount of debt service required each period for repayment of the loan.

Interest Rate. The interest rate is the most commonly recognized mortgage lending term. One characteristic of the mortgage market in the past has been the fixed interest rate over the amortization period. Unexpected inflation has posed serious problems for mortgage lenders during the last decade. Because the interest rate must include an allowance for inflation risk, the lender must analyze inflation trends over the amortization period. This led to the development of the variable rate mortgage, which allows the mortgage interest rate to fluctuate as the market adjusts.

Loan-to-Value Ratio. The proportion (or percentage) of the total property value represented by the amount borrowed is called the *loan-to-value (L/V) ratio*. For example, an investment with a value of $500,000 against which $400,000 is borrowed has a loan-to-value ratio of .80 or 80 percent. This ratio is set partially by state and federal laws for different types of lenders as well as by lenders' policies. Obviously, the loan-to-value ratio plus the equity-to-value ratio must equal 100 percent. It should also be noted that a higher loan-to-value ratio increases the lender's risk.

A higher loan-to-value ratio means higher leverage and increased risk to the equity investor. If the interest rate and the amortization period are held constant, the loan-to-value ratio, the amount borrowed, and the debt service will be greater. For example, consider 70 percent and 80 percent loans on a $500,000 property at 10 percent interest. On the 70 percent loan, the interest payment is $35,000 per year. On the 80 percent loan, the interest payment is $5,000 higher.

Amortization Term. The amortization term (sometimes called the maturity) is the length of time over which the loan is to be repaid. For example, a twenty-year loan is one which is to be fully repaid at the end of twenty years. As with loan-to-value ratios and interest rates, the amortization term is set partly by state and federal laws and partly by the lenders' policies. If all of the other mortgage terms are held constant, a greater amortization term means lower debt service.

THE MORTGAGE CONSTANT

The payment on a mortgage is generally referred to as the debt service, which is found by multiplying the mortgage constant by the amount borrowed. The mortgage constant relates the interest rate and the amortization term. (Table 2 in appendix A provides the mortgage constant at various interest rates for various amortization terms.)

Suppose a twenty-five-year loan is made for $500,000 at 11 percent with monthly

Table 7.2 AMORTIZATION SCHEDULE FOR A $100,000 MORTGAGE AT 10 PERCENT INTEREST RATE FOR TWENTY YEARS (MONTHLY PAYMENTS)

Year	Proportion Outstanding	Amount Outstanding	Debt Service	Interest	Principal
0	1.0	$100,000			
1	.98345	98,345	$11,580	$9,925	$ 1,655
2	.96517	96,517	11,580	9,752	1,828
3	.94498	94,498	11,580	9,561	2,619
4	.92267	92,267	11,580	9,349	2,231
5	.89802	89,802	11,586	9,115	2,465
•	•	•	•	•	•
•	•	•	•	•	•
•	•	•	•	•	•
18	.20912	20,912	11,580	2,585	8,995
19	.10976	10,976	11,580	1,644	9,936
20	0.0	0	11,580	604	10,976

payments. How much payment is necessary to amortize the loan over the twenty-five years? Use the 11 percent column to find the mortgage constant of .00980. Multiply this by the amount borrowed to yield a monthly payment of $4,900. The annual payment is twelve times that, or $58,800.

The Amortization Schedule. One problem that the investor must handle is the allocation of annual debt service between interest and principal repayment. Interest is deductible for tax purposes but principal repayment is not. For instance, a loan for $100,000 at 10 percent interest is made for twenty years with monthly payments. The mortgage constant is .1158, which results in a debt service of $11,580 per year (using the monthly mortgage constant, .00965, times twelve months). The monthly mortgage constant is from table 2 of appendix A. Table 7.2 illustrates the distribution of this debt service for the first five years of the mortgage. Recall our discussion in chapter 3.

SPECIAL LOAN PROVISIONS

Modern mortgages include many clauses. Some require that the mortgagor pay additional fees, penalties, or charges. Others require payments at specific times. The investor must be able to evaluate these common loan provisions.

Early Repayment. Although many mortgages extend to twenty or thirty years, few income-producing investments are held that long. In many cases, the property is sold to repay the loan and satisfy the lien against the property. In other instances, an investor makes payments on the promissory note before they are due. What effects do these actions have on the rate of return or the value of the investment?

Assume that the early repayment of a level-payment fully amortized loan has no effect on the cost of borrowing and, therefore, on the wealth of the investor. Since the amount to be repaid consists of the present value of the outstanding balance to be paid that year, the investor bears no additional costs when repaying. The additional payment is applied directly to the reduction of the principal and results in lower interest charges in the next period. However, this does not occur if closing costs were paid at the time the loan was originated.

Financing Costs. These are charges assessed by the mortgagee to the mortgagor when making the loan. Typical financing costs include loan origination fees, appraisal fees, recording fees, title insurance, past inspections, and credit reference expenses.

Closing costs are divided into two general categories: (1) costs incurred in placing the mortgage and (2) costs incurred in acquiring the property. The first type is amortized on a straight-line basis over the mortgage maturity for tax purposes. The second type is capitalized, thereby increasing the property's depreciable basis. Neither type is tax deductible in the year in which it is paid.

For example, if the mortgagor borrows $50,000 for thirty years and agrees to repay $5,500 at the end of each year, the effective cost of borrowing is 10.44 percent. If closing costs amount to $2,000 and these costs are paid when the loan is originated, the borrower really pays $5,500 per year for thirty years and receives $50,000 minus $2,000 at the time of borrowing, or $48,000. The effective cost of borrowing is really 10.95 percent or more than a half percent higher. Therefore, closing costs increase the effective cost of borrowing.

This is further complicated by the fact

that early repayment also increases the cost of borrowing. And note that the calculated APR does not take early repayment into account. For example, suppose the investor wished to repay a thirty-year $50,000 loan at the end of five years and that he had paid $2,000 closing costs. The effective cost of borrowing becomes 11.55 percent or 60 basis points higher than if it were repaid over the thirty-year agreement.

Prepayment Penalties. Some loans also require prepayment penalties to be assessed if the mortgagor chooses to prepay. These penalties are usually a flat 1 percent to 3 percent of the remaining balance. Another method charges six months' interest at the time of prepayment.

Prepaid Interest. In some transactions, the mortgagee seeks prepaid interest when the loan is originated. This buffer is frequently used for short-term loans and construction financing. It is often included as

a part of closing costs although technically it is not a closing cost. Using the same example, assume that the lender also required prepaid interest of $1,000. The balance to be paid off at the early repayment date of five years would be $48,693. If the closing costs remained at $2,000 and the repayment penalties were 3 percent, the new effective rate of borrowing would be 12.05 percent.

Discount Points. This is another charge typically paid by the mortgagor. These points are often added to the loan origination fees but, if treated separately, increase the yield to the lender beyond the rate charged on the loan. Assume the discount points amount to $2,000. This charge, added to all of the others, raises the cost of borrowing to 13.26 percent.

Mortgage Insurance. Finally, if the loan-to-value ratio of the loan is relatively high, the lender may require private mortgage insurance. This is particularly true for resi-

Table 7.3 SUMMARY OF IMPACT ON COSTS OF BORROWING BY VARIOUS LOAN PROVISIONS

Description	Effective Cost of Borrowing (%)
1. Basic example: $50,000 mortgage, payable in $5,500 annual payments over 30 years	10.44
2. Impact of financing costs: $2,000 paid of time of loan origination	10.95
3. Additional impact of early repayment: Repayment of note at end of 5 years	11.55
4. Additional impact of prepayment penalty: Penalty of 3% of outstanding balance, paid at time of prepayment	12.02
5. Additional impact of prepaid interest: $1000 paid at time of loan origination (affects outstanding balance and prepayment penalty)	12.05
6. Additional impact of discount points: $2,000 paid at time of loan origination	13.26
7. Additional impact of mortgage insurance: Annual premium of 1/4 of 1% of original mortgage loan	13.56

Note: Each provision assumes that the previous ones applied. Therefore, if some did not, the effective costs of borrowing would be altered.

dential single-family loans. Although the mortgage insurance premium is small (typically about $\frac{1}{4}$ of one percent of the original loan) it, too, increases the effective cost of borrowing. Typically, a front-end initial premium of about 1 percent is also included. The total of all of these charges: an effective cost of borrowing of 13.56 percent.

Other Provisions. These include acceleration clauses, assignments and assumptions, and the use of balloon payments. In addition, there are different tax effects: certain closing costs are deductible from taxable income. This is particularly important since these result in tax savings. Prepayment penalties, prepaid interest, and discount points are also tax deductible, but in different ways.

Table 7.3 summarizes this analysis. Clearly, the cost of borrowing is directly related to the investor's mortgage agreement. If all of these factors applied, the before-tax cost of borrowing would have increased from 10.44 percent to 13.56 percent. This is strong evidence of the importance of analyzing mortgage loan provisions.

FINANCIAL LEVERAGE

One of the attractions of income-producing real estate is the ability to finance a large portion of the investment with debt. However, the reason why this is so advantageous to the investor is often misunderstood. As we suggested earlier, the investor uses debt because he believes the rate of return earned by the investment will be greater than the cost of borrowing. This important factor is called *financial leverage*.

DEFINITION OF FINANCIAL LEVERAGE

Financial leverage involves the use of funds for which the investor pays a fixed cost in the hope of increasing his equity return. It has two possible outcomes—favorable or unfavorable. Positive leverage results when the cost of borrowing is less than the overall rate of return on investment. Unfavorable leverage results when the opposite is true.

IMPACT OF FINANCIAL LEVERAGE

The financing of a real estate investment involves the use of two types of funds: debt (mortgage) and equity. The use of debt to finance an investment can have two impacts: The rate of return to the equity position can be increased and so can the expected risk of the equity position. Thus the investor must face this question: Does the increase in the expected return offset the increased risk? If it does, the investor should use the debt. If it does not, the debt should not be used.

To illustrate the impact of borrowing on the expected risk and return, consider the example in table 7.4.

The investor has two financing options:

1. Financing with 100 percent equity and no debt.
2. Financing with 75 percent debt, 25 percent equity. The debt has an interest rate of 10 percent with a maturity of twenty-five years, monthly payments. The debt service is $40,905 per year.

Table 7.4 FINANCING EXAMPLE

An investor has the opportunity to invest in an apartment building. The cost of the investment is $500,000. The investment is expected to produce the following net operating incomes:

State of the World	NOI	Probability
Pessimistic	$55,000	20%
Most likely	60,000	60%
Optimistic	65,000	20%

Impact on Rate of Return. To illustrate the impact of the two financing options on the rate of return, the following simple rate of return measure is used.

(7.1)
$$EDR = \frac{BTCF}{E}$$

where:

E = Equity
EDR = Equity dividend rate
$BTCF$ = Before-tax cash flow
$Equity$ = Equity investment

The EDR is a simple but widely used measure of the rate of return from an investment. In essence it is a cash-on-cash measure of return.

Now look at the example. The expected rate of return is the weighted average of the return for each "state of the world" multiplied by the probability for each "state." Thus, in equation form, the expected rate of return is:

(7.2)
$$E(EDR) = \sum_{i=1}^{m} P_i(EDR_i)$$

where

E = Equity
$E(EDR)$ = Expected equity dividend rate
P_i = Probability under each "state of the world"
EDR_i = Equity dividend rate under each "state"

m = Number of states of the world
Σ = Summation symbol

To implement this equation, look at the first financing option. If the investor uses option one, the scenario of table 7.5 would occur:

Under the pessimistic state of the world, the investor feels that the NOI would be $55,000. The debt service is zero, since option one involves no debt. The equity investment is thus the total cost of $500,000. The before-tax cash flow (BTCF) is the net operating income minus the debt service, or $55,000. The equity dividend rate (EDR) for the pessimistic outcome is:

$$EDR = \frac{BTCF}{E}$$
$$= \frac{\$55,000}{\$500,000}$$
$$= .11 \text{ or } 11\%$$

The probability of this outcome is 20 percent. Likewise the EDRs for each of the other possible states of the world are calculated as 12 percent for the most likely and 13 percent for the optimistic.

Using equation (7.2), the expected EDR is

$$E(EDR) = \sum_{i=1}^{m} P_i(EDR_i)$$
$$= .2(.11) + .6(.12) + .2(.13)$$
$$= .12 \text{ or } 12\%$$

So the investor expects the investment to generate a 12 percent EDR if financing option one (all equity) is used.

Table 7.5 EVALUATION OF FIRST FINANCING OPTION

State of the World	NOI	Debt Service	BTCF	EDR	Probability
Pessimistic	$55,000	$0	$55,000	11%	.2
Most likely	60,000	0	60,000	12%	.6
Optimistic	65,000	0	65,000	13%	.2

Table 7.6 EVALUATION OF SECOND FINANCING OPTION

State of the World	NOI	Debt Service	BTCF	EDR	Probability
Pessimistic	$55,000	$40,905	$14,095	11.28%	.2
Most likely	60,000	40,905	19,095	15.28%	.6
Optimistic	65,000	40,905	24,095	19.28%	.2

What is the expected EDR (return on equity) if the second financing method is employed? This is illustrated in table 7.6.

Under the second financing option, the investor borrows 75 percent, or $375,000, of the total cost. The equity investment is thus $125,000. Under outcome one, the NOI is $55,000. The debt service is $40,905, which leaves $14,095 in BTCF. The equity dividend rate is 11.28 percent ($14,095 divided by $125,000). The probability is 20 percent. The EDR for the most likely outcome is 15.28 percent and 19.28 percent for the optimistic outcome.

The expected equity dividend rate is

$$E(EDR) = \sum_{i=1}^{m} P_i(EDR_i)$$
$$= .2(.1128) + .6(.1528)$$
$$\quad + .2(.1928)$$
$$= .1528 \text{ or } 1528\%$$

Now, let's compare the rates of return expected for each financing option in table 7.7. Notice that by borrowing money, the expected rate of return on the equity investment increased from 11 percent to 15.28 percent.

Does this mean that the investor should always use debt? The answer lies in understanding that the risk of the investment has also increased.

Table 7.7 COMPARISON OF FINANCING OPTIONS

Financing Option	E (EDR)
Option 1	11.00%
Option 2	15.28%

Impact on Risk. The risk associated with the use of debt is called *financial risk*. This refers to the probability that the debt obligations will not be met. Notice that in the preceding examples, the debt claim has priority over the equity position. Thus, the equity position is the "residual" and bears the impact of the risk of borrowing.

To illustrate the impact of borrowing on the risk, let's define risk as the variation around the expected rate of return. A measure of variation is the standard deviation, abbreviated by the Greek letter sigma, σ. The equation for calculating the standard deviation, σ, is

(7.3)

$$\sigma = \sqrt{\sum_{i=1}^{m} P_i(EDR_i - E(EDR)^2}$$

The steps for calulating σ are:

1. Calculate the deviation of each possible outcome from the expected EDR, $[EDR_i - E(EDR)]$.
2. Raise this deviation to the second power, $[EDR_i - E(EDR)]^2$.
3. Multiply this term by the probability of getting EDR_i (that is, P_i), $P_i[EDR_i - E(EDR)]^2$.
4. Sum these products, $\Sigma P_i[EDR_i - E(EDR)]^2$.
5. Take the square root of this sum.

To illustrate, let's first calculate the standard deviation for financing option one. This is shown in table 7.8.

The equity dividend rate under each state

Table 7.8 ANALYSIS OF RISK OF FIRST FINANCING OPTION

State of the World	EDR$_i$	EDR$_i$ − E(EDR)	[EDR$_i$ − E(EDR)]²	P$_i$	
Pessimistic	.11	− .01	.0001	.2	.00002
Most likely	.12	0	0	.6	0
Optimistic	.13	.01	.0001	.2	.00002
				Σ =	.00004

$$\sigma = \sqrt{.00004}$$
$$\sigma = .0063$$

of the world (EDR$_i$) was calculated previously. The expected equity dividend rate [E(EDR)] was 12 percent under financing option one. Using the steps outlined, the resulting standard deviation is .0063 or .63 percent.

For financing option two, the same procedure can be followed as in table 7.9.

Thus for financing option two the standard deviation is .0253 or 2.53 percent.

What do these numbers mean? The results are summarized in table 7.10.
Notice that the use of debt increased the expected return on equity from 11 percent to 15.28 percent. But also notice that the standard deviation increased from .63 percent to 2.53 percent. Thus, expected return and expected risk increased by the use of debt.

Should the investor use the debt? To answer this question, the investor must ask himself if the increase in return is enough to cover the increased risk. The answer would vary depending on the preference of each investor. For some investors the answer is yes—meaning that the debt should

be used. For other investors, the answer is no—indicating the debt should not be used.

CAN LEVERAGE INCREASE WEALTH?

If the investor can become wealthier by borrowing, why shouldn't an investor borrow as much as possible as long as the expected overall rate of return on the investment exceeds the cost of borrowing? The answer depends on the amount of (financial) risk that the investor takes on by borrowing. But this is not sufficient to answer the question.

Imagine that the investor views the financing opportunities available in the market as favorable. This implies that the investor would be wealthier by substituting debt for equity in financing the investment. In fact, it may imply that the more debt that is used (or the less equity employed), the wealthier the investor. The problem is that it is unreasonable to expect that, in the long run, lenders would be willing to supply funds to investors at a rate less than the rate that could be earned if the lenders invested

Table 7.9 ANALYSIS OF RISK OF SECOND FINANCING OPTION

State of the World	EDR$_i$	EDR$_i$ − E(EDR)	[EDR$_i$ − E(EDR)]²	P$_i$	
Pessimistic	.1128	− .04	.0016	.2	.00032
Most likely	.1528	0	0	.6	0
Optimistic	.1928	.04	.0016	.2	.00032
				Σ =	.00064

$$\sigma = \sqrt{.00064}$$
$$\sigma = .0253$$

Table 7.10 Summary of Financing Example

Financing Option	Expected Return/E(EDR)	Risk (σ)
1	11.00%	.63%
2	15.28%	2.53%

directly into the projects. In essence, if the overall rate of return on one investment was expected to be higher than on another, the trade-off between risk and return implies that the risk associated with the former would be greater. (If not, all investors would prefer the first investment.) If the first investment had a higher expected return and higher level of risk, we would not expect lenders to offer debt finance at so "low" a rate. Therefore, theoretically, without any tax effects, we would not expect to find investors increasing their wealth simply by borrowing; if it were generally possible, lenders could become wealthier by borrowing the money themselves and investing in projects for their own accounts!

COMBINING THE EFFECTS OF OPERATING AND FINANCIAL LEVERAGE

The previous chapter showed how operating leverage dramatically increased net operating income of an investment. In ana-

lyzing financial leverage, the return on assets and the cost of debt were presumed to be determined independent of operating leverage. A more careful examination reveals that the two effects are interrelated.

Because of this interrelationship, an investor expects a trade-off between operating and financial leverage. If he reduces the operating leverage, this could permit an increase in his financial leverage. Conversely, if financial leverage were reduced, this would permit an increase in operating leverage. The key is that the different leverage elements can be increased or decreased without altering the overall risk.

Table 7.11 illustrates the equity investor's financial leverage. By subtracting the entire debt service interest and principal, the repayment of principal is a "cost of borrowing." Therefore, the cash flows to the equity holder are measured after the entire debt service payment is made.

If the investor wishes to calculate the combined leverage effect, or the product of the degree of operating leverage times the

Table 7.11 ABC Properties Revisited Analysis of Operating and Financing Leverage

Number of units occupied	30	35	40	45	50
Gross income	$7,500	$8,750	$10,000	$11,250	$12,500
Less expenses					
Variable expenses	3,000	3,500	4,000	4,500	5,000
Fixed expenses	1,250	1,250	1,250	1,250	1,250
Operating expenses	$4,250	$4,750	$ 5,250	$ 5,750	$ 6,250
Net operating income	$3,250	$4,000	$ 4,750	$ 5,500	$ 6,250
Less debt service	4,000	4,000	4,000	4,000	4,000
(Before-tax) cash flow	$(750)	$ 0	$ 750	$ 1,500	$ 2,250

Total leverage effect = (TLE)

$$\frac{Q(gr - ve)}{Q(gr - ve) - FE - DS}$$

degree of financial leverage, he may use the following formula:

$$\text{Total leverage effect} = \frac{Q(gr - ve)}{Q(gr - ve) - FE - DS}$$

Assuming an occupancy level of 40 units with $250 rent per unit, variable expenses of $100, fixed expenses of $1,250, no income taxes nor bad debts, and $4,000 annual debt service, then the total leverage effect is 8.0.

$$\text{Total leverage effect} = \frac{40(250 - 100)}{40(250 - 100) - 1250 - 4000}$$
$$(\text{at } Q = 40) = 8.0$$

Therefore, for each one percent increase in occupancy after 40 units, before-tax cash flow will increase by 8 percent. If occupancy were to increase (by 25 percent) to 50 units, the total leverage effect of 8.0 suggests that cash flow will increase by 200 percent. With 50 units occupied, net operating income equals $6,250 (see table 7.11) and cash flow (BTCF) equals $2,250.

(7.5)

$$\begin{aligned} BTCF &= Q(qr - ve) - FE - DS \\ &= 50(\$250 - \$100) - \$1,250 \\ &\quad - \$4,000 \\ &= \$2,250 \end{aligned}$$

These measures of operating leverage, financial leverage, and total leverage effect provide additional information about the possible changes in cash flow as a result of changes in the management and operation of the property, the debt financing arrangements, or both. Since various financing options exist, the measurement and analysis of financial leverage can be very useful. However, many of the leverage opportuni-

ties involve specific techniques that we will discuss next.

ALTERNATIVE FINANCING METHODS

Despite the widespread use of conventional fixed-rate, amortized mortgages, modern financing techniques offer various alternatives. Some of the more common ones are discussed here.

The list below outlines some of the basic aspects of any creative financing method that the real estate investor must analyze and outlines some of the questions the investor should answer in using any creative method. To correctly apply and understand each financing method, the investor should understand the implications for all involved, particularly the lender and the borrower. The mechanics of the technique, the tax implications, the legal aspects of the method, and the decision-making implications must be carefully analyzed before using any financing method.

1. The mechanics of the technique. How does it work? What is the expected yield (from borrower's perspective—the cost of borrowing) both before and after tax?
2. The tax implications. What are the tax rules related to this financing method? What are the implications for both the lender and the borrower? Are there unique tax implications in the event of default? What unique tax problems does this method create?
3. The legal aspects of the method. What legal problems does the method create? How is the legal instrument different from the traditional? What are the typical clauses in such an instrument?
4. The decision-making implications. When would such a financing method be used? Under what investment situa-

tions would it be more advantageous than other financing methods?

PURCHASE-MONEY MORTGAGE

A purchase-money mortgage is where the seller takes back a note from the buyer and retains a lien against the property until the value of the note is satisfied. The major difference between this and a conventional mortgage is that the purchase-money agreement is between the buyer and the seller only. Therefore, purchase-money mortgages have very high legal priority in the event of a default. This technique is often used since financing can affect an offer's attractiveness. Sometimes the investor may lack the necessary equity. However, through negotiation, the seller may accept a purchase-money mortgage with a balloon payment or a second mortgage.

INSTALLMENT SALES CONTRACT

The installment land sales contract is used when the buyer can provide only a low down payment. It is similar to the purchase-money mortgage because the financing arrangements are made exclusively between the buyer and the seller. However, the major difference between these two arises in the event of a default. In this method, if the buyer defaults prior to fulfillment of the contract, the seller can recover the full value of the property under contract law. Under a purchase-money mortgage, the defaulting buyer is liable (in most states) for only the balance on the note. We discuss installment sales further in the next chapter.

BALLOON PAYMENT MORTGAGES

This is a very general financing technique that requires a large outlay as a final payment (hence the term *balloon payment*). In some forms, the balloon payment amounts to an agreed sales price in a future year, after a period of interest payments. In others, the balloon payment takes place at the end of some period of time over which regular amortized payments were made. This accelerates the repayment of the loan but keeps the level of the repayment of principal plus interest at the original term. This form is sometimes called a *balloon mortgage*.

JUNIOR LIENS

Junior liens are claims by creditors against the asset(s) pledged as security for which there exists a senior or prior lien (typically, a first mortgage). These are also called second mortgages and result in a secondary satisfaction in the event of a default and subsequent foreclosure. It should be noted that a purchase-money mortgage may be a junior lien.

Junior liens are inherently more risky from the borrower's point of view due to their secondary priority in claims against the secured assets. To compensate for this risk, lenders often seek higher rates of interest. However, the availability of second mortgages opens up new avenues of finance for the investor. If investment opportunities develop, investors with equity in their property can acquire additional real property interests by using second mortgages and increasing their wealth through positive financial leverage. An example of the use of second mortgages is given in chapter 12.

SALE-LEASEBACK

This is a special financing technique which is used in some markets when more traditional financial arrangements are not acceptable. It is often used between large investors and large manufacturing firms. In sale-leaseback, the investor purchases real estate that is owned and operated by a well-established income-producing firm. At the same time, he leases property back to the firm.

In recent years, this form of financing has become quite popular because equity capital is either more expensive or unavailable for commercial real estate investment. In addition, there are advantages to both sides of the transaction. For the leasing firm, this arrangement frees equity for other uses. For the investor, the expected returns from the leaseback are relatively long in term and typically large in size. There are other advantages if the value of the property appreciates at a higher rate than expected. Finally, there are income tax advantages for both sides. See chapter 12 for an example.

INCOME AND EQUITY PARTICIPATIONS

Income and equity participations allow the institutional lender to participate in future income in addition to receiving the contracted debt service repayment. For this benefit, the lender often accepts a less secure financial position.

The income property mortgage market has developed a wide variety of ways of participating in the income. Examples include taking a percentage of the gross income, net operating income, or the before-tax cash flow and/or a percentage of the income from sale. This participation by the lender increases the yield to the lender on

the mortgage loan. Conversely, it increases the cost of borrowing to the investor.

For tax purposes, the payment to the lender under the participation agreement is generally treated as interest paid by the borrower/investor. As such, it is deductible as interest from the investor's taxable income from operations. If the agreement is written as interest payments, the payment due in the year of sale would be deductible like a prepayment penalty.

To illustrate a participation loan, consider the following example. A real estate investor is considering the purchase of a small shopping center. The lender has agreed to make a mortgage for $200,000 at an interest rate of 12.5 percent with monthly payments over twenty years. The mortgage constant is .13632 per year. The annual debt service is $27,264. In addition, the lender requires a participation of 2 percent of the annual effective gross income (EGI). The expected cash flow for years one through five is shown in table 7.12.

Table 7.12 also contains the EGI for each year, the operating expenses, and the resulting net operating income. From this the investor subtracts the $27,264 payment on the debt service and the participating interest of 2 percent of EGI each year. The result is the before-tax cash flow.

For tax purposes the participating amount each year is deductible from the investor's taxable income from operations. While we have constructed this example as

Table 7.12 A PARTICIPATING MORTGAGE EXAMPLE

Year	Effective Gross Income	Operating Expenses	Net Operating Income	Debt Service	Participation Interest	BTCF
1	$55,000	$22,000	$33,000	$27,264	$1,100	$4,636
2	57,750	23,100	34,650	27,264	1,155	6,231
3	60,600	26,000	34,600	27,264	1,212	6,124
4	63,600	28,600	34,980	27,264	1,272	6,444
5	66,750	30,000	36,750	27,264	1,335	8,151

participation in the effective gross income, the loans have been written for net operating income or before-tax cash flow participation as well.

WRAPAROUND MORTGAGES

A wraparound mortgage is a financing alternative in which an older, cheaper loan is maintained and a second, larger loan is "wrapped around" it instead of being paid off by the larger commitment. This maintains a high leverage position at a relatively low cost. Therefore, given transaction costs of borrowing and special loan provisions, wraparound mortgages are attractive alternatives for investors when interest rates escalate rapidly. Like junior liens, wraparound mortgages are secondary liens against the property.

A wraparound mortgage is a loan that is subordinated to an existing first mortgage and is of a greater amount than the first mortgage. The seller of the real property continues to make payments on the first mortgage using the debt service payments made on the "wrap" by the buyer.

A wraparound mortgage usually will be of benefit to both buyer and seller. First, because of the lower interest rate on the first mortgage, it is often in the best interest of both parties to preserve this mortgage if possible. However, there are situations in which the existing first mortgage should not be kept. If the current loan constant on the first mortgage is higher than the loan constant available on new loans from conventional sources, the first mortgage should not be retained. Second, since the seller provides the wrap, more liberal financing terms may be offered than institutions. This should make the property more marketable for the seller, since it will be more attractive to potential buyers. Obviously, the holder of the existing low-interest rate first mortgage

is the losing party in the use of the wraparound mortgage.

The following is an example of a situation in which a wrap may be used to the advantage of both buyer and seller. Suppose the owner of a property is interested in selling an investment for $2 million. A buyer is interested in the property but is only willing to make a $400,000 down payment. Suppose more traditional lenders are only willing to lend $1.4 million at a rate of 13 percent. On the basis of this alternative, it does not seem that the deal will go through.

However, the owner has a mortgage on the property that can be wrapped. The mortgage was originally for $1 million at 8 percent over a twenty-five-year term. Monthly payments on this loan are $7,718. The loan has been in existence for seven years, so the current balance is $882,057.

Because of the existing mortgage, the seller is willing to offer a wrap for $1.6 million at 12 percent with a twenty-five-year amortization schedule, but requiring a balloon payment at the end of five years. Since the wrap is for $1.6 million and the balance on the first mortgage is $882,057, the seller is in essence financing $717,943.

The buyer will make monthly payments of $16,851 on the wrap. This is shown in table 7.13. The total annual payment is $202,212. Table 7.13 also contains the interest–principal split for each payment over the five-year life of the mortgage. From the total payment, the seller must cover the debt service on the existing first loan. The amortization schedule for the existing first loan is shown in table 7.14.

To calculate the seller's before-tax yield on the wraparound, it is necessary to calculate the before-tax cash flow to the seller. This is shown in table 7.15. From the total payment of $202,212 on the wraparound the seller must pay $92,616 on the debt service of the first mortgage. Thus the net to the

Table 7.13 A Wraparound Example: Amortization Schedule*

Year	Annual Payment	Principal Payment	Interest Payment	Amount Outstanding
0	—	—	—	$1,600,000
1	$202,212	$10,714	$191,498	1,589,286
2	202,212	12,197	190,015	1,577,089
3	202,212	13,753	188,459	1,563,336
4	202,212	15,366	186,846	1,547,970
5	202,212	17,434	184,778	1,530,536

* See text for assumptions.

Table 7.14 Amortization Schedule for the Existing First Mortgage*

Year	Annual Payment	Principal Payment	Interest Payment	Amount Outstanding
0	—	—	—	$882,057
1	$92,616	$22,879	$69,737	859,178
2	92,616	24,800	67,816	834,378
3	92,616	26,803	65,813	807,575
4	92,616	29,081	63,535	778,494
5	92,616	31,423	61,193	747,071

* See text for assumptions.

seller is $109,596. Remember that the seller financed $717,943 for the buyer. The yield on the wrap is approximately 16.6 percent. This is calculated by finding the rate that will equate to expected before-tax cash inflows to the amount financed.

Table 7.15 Before-tax Cash Flows to Seller from the Wraparound Mortgage

Year	Amount Financed	Before-Tax Cash Flow
0	$717,943	$109,596
1		109,596
2		109,596
3		109,596
4		109,596
5		893,061*

* This includes the $109,596 from debt service plus the $783,465 net difference between the amount outstanding on the wrap and the first mortgage.

ADJUSTABLE RATE MORTGAGES

Depending on the plan selected, alternative mortgage instruments allow the investor to acquire a mortgage with a variable interest rate, mortgage term, or debt service repayment schedule. Because these vary with interest rates, the price of the alternative mortgage instrument may be higher or lower than the price of a conventional mortgage. Mortgages that allow the interest rate to vary according to some agreed on index have become necessary to protect lenders from the risks associated with unexpected inflation.

Another common alternative financing method is the so-called *adjustable rate loan*

Table 7.16 AN ADJUSTABLE
RATE MORTGAGE EXAMPLE

Years	Interest Rate per Year (%)
1	12.5
2	13.5
3	14.0
4	12.0
5	11.0

(also known as the variable rate loan or the renegotiable rate loan). As the name implies, the interest rate is subject to adjustment, and thus the debt service is subject to the change in some index to which the interest rate is tied.

These types of loans create no unique tax problems for the investor. They do, however, create cash-flow forecasting problems, since the investor must forecast the interest rate on the loan for future time periods. In effect, the risk of changes in interest rate is shifted from the lender to the equity investor.

To illustrate the mechanics of such a loan consider table 7.16. A real estate investor is considering the purchase of a duplex for $70,000. The lender has agreed to loan 75 percent of the purchase price with a maturity of twenty-five years with the interest rate adjusted every year. Debt service is payable on a monthly basis. The initial interest rate is 12.5 percent per year for the first year. The investor/borrower expects the interest rate to be as indicated in table 7.16 for the first five years of the loan.

The first year's mortgage constant is .0109. This mortgage constant is then multiplied by the loan amount ($52,500) to result in the monthly payment of $572.44. At the end of year one, the borrower has an outstanding balance of $52,175.44.

Now we must recalculate the mortgage constant using an annual interest rate of 13.5 percent since this is what the investor expects. What is the maturity of this new loan? It is twenty-four years, or 288 six-month periods. The new mortgage constant is .01172. This is multiplied by the amount outstanding ($52,175.44) to result in the new debt service of $611.35 for each month of the second year. At the end of year two, the borrower has a balance of $51,864.09.

This process is continued for each year. The final result is shown in table 7.17. This table shows the amortization schedule for the adjustable rate loan: the debt service for each year at the assumed interest rates, the amount outstanding at the end of each year, and the allocation between interest and principal for each payment.

As a final note on adjustable rate mortgages, they could obviously include points, fees, and prepayment penalties as in a fixed rate mortgage. The items are treated for tax purposes as in the fixed rate mortgage.

Table 7.17 AMORTIZATION SCHEDULE FOR AN ADJUSTABLE RATE LOAN

Year	Mortgage Constant	Amount Outstanding	Annual Debt Service	Interest	Principal
0		$52,500.00			
1	.01090	52,175.44	$6,869.28	$6,544.72	$324.56
2	.01172	51,864.09	7,336.24	7,024.89	311.35
3	.01216	51,535.43	7,569.08	7,240.51	328.57
4	.01078	51,025.99	6,666.24	6,156.80	509.44
5	.01019	50,367.67	6,238.67	5,580.35	658.32

8

TAX PLANNING DECISIONS

THE previous chapters discussed the measurement of cash flows (operation and reversion) on a before-tax basis. This chapter will take the final step in cash flow forecasting—the influence of taxation on real estate investments.

CASH FLOW VERSUS TAXABLE INCOME

It is important to understand the difference between the *cash flow* from a real estate investment and the *taxable income* from the investment. The investor is interested in cash flow—the amount of income after all expenses, including taxes, from the investment. An investment generates two potential sources of cash flow: the after-tax cash flow from operation and the after-tax cash flow from sale, referred to as the after-tax equity reversion. In contrast, the taxing agency (government) is interested in the taxable income from both operation and reversion (sale, exchange).

Table 8.1 illustrates the measurement of expected after-tax cash flows from operation. The investor forecasts these cash flows for each year of operations: the holding period. Table 8.2 shows how to measure the expected ordinary income taxes for each year of operations. Table 8.3 measures the

after-tax equity reversion from the sale of an investment at the end of the expected holding period. Table 8.4 tells how to calculate taxes due on sale when straight-line depreciation is used.

REAL ESTATE AS A TAX SHELTER

As Table 8.2 illustrates, the ordinary taxable income (TI) from operating a real estate investment is:

$$TI_t = NOI_t - Int_t - Dep_t + RR_t - AFC_t$$

where:

TI_t = ordinary taxable income from operations in year t

NOI_t = the net operating income from the investment in year t

Int_t = the interest deduction in year t

Dep_t = the depreciation deduction in year t

RR_t = the allowance set aside for replacing short-lived property (replacement reserves) in year t

AFC_t = the costs of borrowed funds, such as fees and points, deductible over the life of the mortgage

Table 8.1 MEASUREMENT OF CASH FLOW FROM OPERATION FOR EACH YEAR

	Estimated rent per unit per year
Times	Number of units
Equals	Potential gross income (PGI)
Minus	Vacancy and bad debt allowance
Plus	Miscellaneous income
Equals	Effective gross income (EGI)
Minus	Operating expenses
Equals	Net operating income (NOI)
Minus	Debt service
Equals	Before-tax cash flow (BTCF)
Minus	Taxes from operation*
Equals	After-tax cash flow (ATCF)

* See table 8.2.

Table 8.3 MEASUREMENT OF EXPECTED CASH FLOW FROM THE SALE OF AN INVESTMENT

	Estimated selling price (SP)
Minus	Selling expenses (SE)
Equals	Net sales proceeds (NSP)
Minus	Unpaid mortgage balance (UM)
Equals	Before-tax equity reversion (BTER)
Minus	Taxes due on sale*
Equals	After-tax equity reversion (ATER)

* See table 8.4.

Taxes from operations are equal to taxable income (TI) multiplied by the marginal tax rate.

It is easy to see how a real estate investment shelters taxes. If the depreciation deduction, interest, and amortized financing costs are exactly equal to the net operating income plus replacement revenues, taxes are equal to zero, since taxable income is zero. Taxes are equal to the taxable income multiplied by the tax rate. If the net operating income and replacement reserves are greater than the depreciation deduction, interest, amd amortized financing costs, taxable income is greater than zero. Some of the cash flow is sheltered, but not all of it. If the net operating income and replacement reserves are less than the depreciation deduction and interest costs, the taxable income is negative. This does not mean that cash flow from the investment is negative; rather, that for *tax purposes*, the investment

Table 8.2 MEASUREMENT OF TAXABLE INCOME AND TAXES FROM OPERATION FOR EACH YEAR

Method 1		Method 2	
	Effective gross income (EGI)		Effective gross income (EGI)
Minus	Operating expenses	Minus	Operating expenses
Equals	Net operating income (NOI)	Equals	Net operating income (NOI)
Minus	Interest on debt	Minus	Debt service
Minus	Depreciation deduction	Equals	Before-tax cash flow (BTCF)
Minus	Amortized financing costs	Plus	Principal
Plus	Replacement reserves	Minus	Depreciation deduction
Equals	Taxable income	Minus	Amortized financing costs
Times	Investor's marginal tax rate	Plus	Replacement reserves
Equals	Taxes from operation	Equals	Taxable income
		Times	Investor's marginal tax rate
		Equals	Taxes from operation

Table 8.4 TAXES DUE ON SALE

	TAXABLE INCOME
	Selling price (SP)
Minus	Selling expenses (SE)
Equals	Amount realized (AR)
Minus	Adjusted basis (AB)
Equals	Capital gains (CG)

	TAXES DUE ON SALE
	Capital gain
Times	Investor's marginal tax rate
Equals	Taxes due on sale

Table 8.5 CLASSIFICATION OF TAXPAYER'S INCOME

1. Active income such as wages, salaries
2. Portfolio income such as interest, dividends
3. Passive income
   Trade or business in which the investor does not materially participate
   Rental activities
   Limited partnership activities

is generating a loss. Under certain forms of ownership, this loss can be used to offset the investor's other taxable income.

ANALYZING TAX IMPACTS

To analyze the expected taxes from a real estate investment, the investor must do the following:

1. Determine the tax classification of the investment.
2. Determine the tax status of the investor, that is, corporate or noncorporate.
3. Estimate the investor's marginal tax rate by examining the investor's taxable income.
4. Estimate the taxable income that arises from both operations and disposition (such as sale, exchange, etc.).
5. Compute the estimated taxes using the expected tax rate and the expected taxable income.

For tax purposes, two types of classifications exist with real estate. The first classifies it into four categories: property held as personal residence, property held for sale

to customers, property held for use in a trade or business, and property held for investment. Each of the categories, as we will see, has different tax rules. It should be noted that, within the tax code's definition, most real estate investments are classified as trade or business property and not investment property.

Real estate has been further classified by the Tax Reform Act of 1986 (TRA 1986). A taxpayer's income has been subdivided into three categories: active, portfolio, and passive income. Table 8.5 depicts the three categories and gives some examples. The basic implication of this categorization is that losses derived from passive activities cannot be used to offset income from either active or portfolio activities. Thus, passive losses may be used only to offset income; however, these losses may be carried forward (suspended losses) to offset future passive income. Passive activities are defined as activities in which the investor does not materially participate; specifically included in this are rented and limited partnership activities.

Active participation in real estate rental activities does not change the status to active. However, an exception is granted to individuals who actively participate in a rental real estate activity with at least 10 percent interest. The exception results in a $25,000 loss deduction (total deductions and equivalent credits) against active and portfolio income. A limitation is imposed on this exemption for taxpayers with income greater than $100,000. For every dollar greater than $100,000 the exemption is reduced 50 percent, resulting in a total phase-out for incomes exceeding $150,000. Thus this exception allows taxpayers of medium incomes to offset some of their current rental losses.

The tax status of the investor is important since both tax rates and taxable income are determined differently for the corporate and the noncorporate investor. Certain business organizations, such as partnerships, are not taxed separately. The income from a partnership is taxed on the individual partner's tax return.

The tax rates vary depending on the taxable income of the taxpayer. The crucial one for making investment decisions is the *marginal* rate, which has been reduced from past rates by TRA 1986. Marginal tax rates are as high as 28 percent for the noncorporate investor, while corporate investors face marginal tax rates as high as 34 percent. This means, for example, that the noncorporate taxpayer in a 28 percent bracket would owe 28 cents in taxes out of every one dollar increase in taxable income. Likewise, a one dollar decrease in taxable income would save the investor 28 cents in taxes.

The next step is to estimate taxable income. The operation and sale of real estate produces two types of income taxes: (1) tax on ordinary income and capital gains and (2) tax on preference and adjustment items in the computation of the taxpayer's alternative minimum tax (discussed later). Taxable income is also measured according to the investment's tax classification and the investor's tax status.

The final step is to estimate the taxes using the tax rates and the taxable income.

These estimates are then subtracted from the before-tax cash flow (from operation or reversion) to arrive at the estimated after-tax cash flow. We will discuss each step more thoroughly in the following sections.

CLASSIFYING REAL ESTATE FOR TAX PURPOSES

The classification of a taxpayer's real property controls the tax influence on the investment. It is extremely important for this reason. The four classifications are property for personal use, property for the sale to customers, property for investment (for the production of income), and property for use in a trade or business. Table 8.6 outlines some of the key differences in the tax treatment of each of these.

One distinguishing characteristic of property held for personal use is that all expenses incurred for personal, living, or family purposes as well as expenses of repair or maintenance are nondeductible. The owner is also not permitted to deduct an allowance for depreciation. In the case of sale, any loss incurred is nondeductible. Interest paid on a mortgage loan and real property taxes incurred on a home, however, are deductible if the owner itemizes deductions. An additional limitation is placed on interest if it exceeds the cost of the home and improvements. This excess interest is not deductible if it is not used to pay educational or medical expenses. The owner of a personal residence is also permitted to defer all or part of the gain realized on a sale if the purchase of another home is made within a specified period of time.

Table 8.6 also displays some important differences between property held for sale to customers and investment property. When the owner of a real estate investment

Table 8.6 CHARACTERISTICS OF VARIOUS CLASSIFICATIONS OF REAL ESTATE FOR TAX PURPOSES

TREATMENT OF CHARACTERISTIC FOR TAX PURPOSE

Tax Classification	Depreciation Allowance	Treatment of Gain from Sale	Treatment of Loss from Sale	Operating Expense Deduction	Property Tax Deduction	Interest Deduction	Tax Deferred Exchange	Selling Expenses
1. Personal residence	No	Capital gain (can be deferred)	Loss not deductible	No	Yes	Yes	No	Yes
2. For sale to customers	No	Ordinary income	Ordinary loss	Yes	Yes	Yes (limited)	No	Ordinary business expense
3. Trade or business	Yes	Capital gain (Section 1231)	Fully deductible	Yes	Yes	Yes	Yes	Deductible from sales price
4. Investment	Yes	Capital gain	Deductible (limited)	Yes	Yes	Yes (limited)	Yes	Deductible from sales price

holds it "primarily for sale to customers in the ordinary course of his trade or business" he is a dealer. However, if he holds property primarily as an investment for the production of income or for use in his trade or business, he is an investor. There are several differences in the treatment of the investor and the dealer in real estate.

One of the most important drawbacks on property held for investment purposes is that the interest paid on mortgage indebtedness is subject to limitations for the noncorporate taxpayer. Investment interest is defined as interest paid or accrued on indebtedness incurred or continued to purchase or carry property for investment.

Generally, the tax code considers real estate owned and operated for the purpose of deriving rental income to be property used in a trade or business a passive activity. Transient lodging such as hotels and motels are excluded from this passive activity classification. As previously mentioned, losses derived from passive activities are generally not deductible against active and portfolio income. However, upon the sale of such an activity any suspended losses would be allocated in the following order:

1. Gain from the sale of the passive activity
2. Income from other passive activities
3. Active or portfolio income

Thus, upon the sale of a passive activity, the investor may be able to use some of its losses against active or portfolio income.

Real estate held for use in a taxpayer's trade or business receives the most favorable treatment. The owner is entitled to deduct all operating expenses related to the investment, as well as an allowance for depreciation.

On the sale of trade or business property held for more than six months, the investor is entitled to treat the gain or loss as a Sec-

tion 1231 transaction. As we will see, Section 1231 transactions enjoy the greatest tax benefits with respect to capital gains and losses. Also, all interest expenses are deductible and the investor can take advantage of the tax deferral exchange provisions.

Table 8.7 shows the personal tax rates for 1988 taxable income. Table 8.8 shows the graduated phase-out of the lower 15 percent

Table 8.7 NONCORPORATE TAX RATES: TAXABLE INCOME YEAR 1988

SINGLE TAXPAYERS NOT QUALIFYING AS HEADS OF HOUSEHOLDS	
$0–$17,850	15%
$17,850 & above	28%
MARRIED TAXPAYERS FILING JOINTLY	
$0–$29,750	15%
$29,750 & above	28%
MARRIED TAXPAYERS FILING SEPARATELY	
$0–$14,875	15%
$14,875 & above	28%
UNMARRIED TAXPAYERS QUALIFYING AS HEADS OF HOUSEHOLDS	
$0–$23,900	15%
$23,900 & above	28%

Table 8.8 GRADUATED PHASE-OUT RANGES*

SINGLE
$43,145–$89,560
MARRIED FILING JOINTLY
$71,900–$149,250
MARRIED FILING SEPARATELY
$35,950–$113,300
HEAD OF HOUSEHOLD
$61,650–$123,790

* For incomes falling within these ranges an additional 5 percent tax will be imposed to phase out the 15 percent bracket.

bracket for incomes above a specified level. Marginal tax rates on personal income are either 15 percent or 28 percent with higher incomes taxed at a flat rate of 28 percent. The taxpayer is categorized according to one of the following tax classifications: unmarried, married filing a joint return (or surviving spouse), head of household, or married filing a separate return. For instance, suppose a taxpayer, married filing a joint return, has a taxable income of $70,000. The taxes due are computed as follows:

Taxes on income up to $29,750 at 15%	=	$ 4,462
Taxes on income excess at 28%	=	11,270
Taxes due	=	$15,732

Suppose the taxpayer makes a real estate investment that generates a taxable income of $10,000. The total taxable income is now $80,000 ($70,000 + $10,000) and taxes due are computed as follows:

Taxes on income up to $29,750 at 15%	=	$ 4,462
Taxes on income excess at 28%	=	$14,070
Amount of 15% phase-out = [($80,000 − $71,900) × .05)]	=	405

The taxes increased $3,205 while taxable income increased $10,000. Due to the phase-out of the 15 percent bracket, this investment was subject to a 32.05 percent marginal tax. If the taxpayer's income had already been above the phase-out range the investment would only have been subject to the 28 percent rate.

Corporate tax rates have also been reduced through TRA 1986. Additionally, the number of tax brackets has decreased from five to three. A similar type of phase-out range has been imposed so that corpora-

Table 8.9 CORPORATE TAX RATES*

$0–$50,000	15%
$50,001–$75,000	25%
$75,001 and above	34%

* A phase-out rate of 5% is imposed on income between $100,000–$335,000. Thus, corporations with incomes in excess of $335,000 will be subject to a flat rate of 34%.

tions with incomes over $335,000 will not be able to take advantage of the lower tax brackets (table 8.9).

TAXABLE INCOME FROM OPERATIONS

The taxable income from operations is calculated as shown in table 8.2. The gross income is adjusted for operating expenses, financing costs, and depreciation deduction. The following sections discuss each of the categories as they relate to the determination of taxable income from operations.

OPERATING EXPENSES AND TAXES

In general, the expenses of operating, maintaining, and repairing real estate investments are deductible in the year that such expenses are paid or incurred. However, operating expenses are cash outflows, which makes them less valuable to the equity investor compared to the depreciation deduction.

Suppose the investor is in a 28 percent marginal tax bracket. Suppose that the net operating income is $50,000 that year. The investor incurs an unexpected operating expense of $5,000. This reduces the NOI to $45,000. The deductibility of this operating expense reduces the after-tax cost to the investor to $1,400 (28 percent of $5,000). While the expense generated a tax savings of $1,400, it cost the investor $3,600.

The test of whether an expenditure is an

operating expense or a capital expenditure depends on the nature of the expenditure and its relationship to the operating, care, and maintenance of the property. A repair is deductible whereas the cost of a capital addition is depreciable over the improvement's useful life. A repair is an expenditure that only maintains the value or useful life of real property. A capital expenditure, in contrast, increases the useful life or the value of the property, adding to the owner's basis for the property. The costs for capital expenditures can be recovered through depreciation allowance or upon a taxable disposition of the investment. Since the owner's basis (cost) has increased through the capital expenditure, the tax due on the sale as a result of capital gain would be lowered.

Because repairs and capital improvements are similar, it is often difficult to distinguish between them. The following itemizations show how general types of expenditures are treated for tax purposes:

Type	Repair
Roofing	Patching leaks and replacing a limited number of shingles
Wiring	Mending or temporary replacements
Plumbing	Mending and minor part replacements
Fire damage	Cleanup, removal, and temporary replacement

Type	Capital Addition
Roofing	Adding a new roof or major replacements
Wiring	New installations or general replacements
Plumbing	Major replacements
Fire damage	Modernization incidental to restoration of former facilities

The same problem occurs in the case of an expenditure made in protection of income versus defense of title. Only expenditures to conserve income are deductible. Costs of protecting title must be capitalized as part of the cost of the property and are thus depreciable. The costs of acquiring an investment, such as legal costs and appraisal fees, also are not deductible in the year paid but are added to the depreciable basis and thus are depreciable.

Real estate taxes are deductible by the owner in the year paid or incurred, even on property held for personal use. In the case of a personal residence, however, the taxes are deductible only if the owner foregoes the use of the standard deduction and itemizes.

Another category that the investor must consider is allowance for replacements. In some instances, he should set aside an allowance for the replacement of personal property, such as carpets and appliances. Such reserves, while treated as operating expense for cash flow purposes, are not operating expenses for tax purposes. Therefore, replacement reserve allowances must be added to taxable income from operation. Personal property in the investment can be depreciated.

FINANCING AND TAXES

Mortgage financing of real estate investments has four fundamental tax consequences. These are:

1. The mortgage debt is included as part of the depreciable basis.
2. The interest costs are, in general, deductible.
3. Borrowed money does not represent taxable income.
4. The costs associated with placing the mortgage are, in general, not deductible

in the year in which they are paid but can be amortized over the life of the loan.

Depreciable Basis and the Mortgage.

First, if an investment is being purchased, the investor can include the amount of any borrowed money used to finance the purchase as part of his cost basis when computing the allowance for depreciation. Although only a part of the money is equity, the investor is entitled to take the entire price paid for his cost basis. This includes his own money as well as the borrowed money. Thus, a substantial portion of the net income from a property may be received as a tax-free allowance for depreciation. The investor is also in a position to increase his equity in the investment by paying off the mortgage debt out of the monies contributed to the depreciation allowance.

So, suppose an investor is purchasing a property valued at $500,000. Suppose the property has a $350,000 mortgage that the investor assumes and in addition invests $150,000 in equity. The total cost of the investment is $500,000 on which the investor would calculate his basis for depreciation purposes. The depreciable basis is independent of any mortgage amount. The result is the same regardless of whether an investor buys a property and takes out a new loan, buys a property and assumes an old loan, or buys a property subject to an existing loan.

Interest Deductibility.

What are the tax effects of various payments and charges made or received by the mortgagor or mortgagee during the life of the mortgage? Repayment of the principal of the mortgage debt is neither income to the mortgagee nor a deductible expense to the mortgagor. However, the payment of interest on a debt is both income to the mortgagee and a deductible item to the mortgagor.

Interest paid by an investor on a mortgage debt is deductible even though the investor might not have assumed personal liability for the debt. The distinction between investment property and property held for trade or business is important because the interest expense paid on a mortgage is subject to limitation if the property is for investment purposes. The limits on the deductibility of investment interest—defined as interest paid or accrued on indebtedness incurred or continued to purchase or carry property held for investment—is equal to the sum of net investment income. This applies only to the noncorporate investor. Real estate investments classified as portfolio activities encompass this deduction, but it does not include interest from passive activities or a personal residence, which are basically fully deductible.

Refinancing and Tax.

The third major advantage of using a mortgage is that borrowed money does not represent taxable income to the borrower. Thus an investor who wishes to liquidate a portion of an investment in real property can do so by borrowing against the property. The cash received on borrowing for nonpersonal use property is not taxable, even though the amount borrowed is in excess of the property's basis. The investor's price for borrowing is the payment of interest, an expense that is normally deductible.

Deductibility of Financing Costs.

The costs of placing a mortgage on nonpersonal use property are not deductible as expenses in the year in which they are paid. The investor may, however, be entitled to amortize these costs over the life of the mortgage loan. These costs include commissions, brokerage fees, points, and any other expenses of obtaining the loan.

The deduction of the financing cost is

taken as an annual amount over the mortgage maturity. For instance, suppose an investor borrows $500,000 against an office building. He pays a $1,500 commission for arranging the loan, $1,000 for title insurance in favor of the lender, $750 in legal fees related to the loan, and $10,000 in points to the lender. The loan maturity is twenty years. The total loan costs are $13,250, of which $\frac{1}{20}$ (5 percent) can be deducted each year. Thus the amortized financing costs for annual tax purposes are $662.50.

The unamortized remainder of the costs is deductible in full in the year of sale if the investment is sold prior to the mortgage maturity. Using the same example, suppose the investor sells the property after eight years. The total amount amortized is $5,300 ($662.50 times 8) with a balance of $7,950 ($13,250 minus $5,300) that can be deducted in the year of sale. Any prepayment penalties associated with a mortgage loan are also deductible against operating income.

If the loan is taken out against non-business property, such as personal residence, the financing costs cannot be deducted or amortized. Except for points paid, the costs are not added to the owner's basis. These points are deductible as interest in the year paid.

At-risk Limitations. One additional exception to the deductibility of real estate losses besides passive activities has resulted from the TRA 1986 inclusion of real estate as being subject to at-risk rules. At-risk rules limit the amount of losses an investor may deduct to the amount at which he is actually at risk or personally liable. Usually loans in which the investor was not liable (nonrecourse) were excluded; however, with respect to real estate, certain types are included in the amount of an investor at risk. Loans must be from a qualified lender who may not have an equity interest but may be a related party as long as the terms of the loan are similar to others without these relationships. Loans that are acquired from the seller, which may be the bank itself, cannot qualify as at-risk amounts. Therefore, an investor buying property must be careful when securing his mortgage.

DEPRECIATION DEDUCTION

The third item in the calculation of taxable income from operations is the depreciation deduction. This is the key to the shelter aspect of real estate investing. In order to calculate the depreciation deduction in any year, the taxpayer must determine three factors: the amount being depreciated, the useful life of the asset, and the depreciation method.

What Is Depreciation? The depreciation deduction allows the taxpayer to recover the costs of the depreciable property from his taxable income. Depreciation produces tax deductions *without* any cash outlay. A maximum depreciation deduction reduces taxable income, which in turn reduces tax liability and increases the after-tax cash flow.

Cumulative depreciation deductions usually bear little or no relationship to the *actual* change in the value of the property. Typically the situation is such that the taxpayer has a deduction for depreciation while the property value is rising. The net result is the creation of a tax-free cash flow.

Two types of property are allowed depreciation deductions:

1. Property used in trade or business
2. Property held for production of income (investment)

Property used by the taxpayer for personal purposes, such as the taxpayer's residence, is not depreciable.

Depreciation is only allowed on property with a limited useful life, such as building and machines. Land is not depreciable since it has an infinite useful life. Although certain land improvements such as paving curbs and gutters may be depreciable, the depreciation of land improvements in general depends on whether they permanently improve the land or improve it only as long as a particular building remains useful.

The depreciation deduction in any year is the aggregate amount set aside over the useful life of the asset to equal the cost or basis of the property. Therefore, the depreciation deduction depends on:

1. The costs or basis (that is, the amount to be depreciated)
2. The period of time over which the asset is to be depreciated
3. The classification of the asset for depreciation purposes

Since much of the investment in a real estate asset is depreciable, the deduction may have three results:

1. All of the before-tax cash flow from an investment may be sheltered from taxes.
2. Part of the before-tax flow from an investment may be sheltered.
3. More than the before-tax cash flow from the investment may be sheltered from income taxes. This reduces the taxpayer's other taxable income and other income taxes.

All real estate investments create a tax shelter to some degree. The amount of the tax shelter is determined by the relationship between the depreciation deduction and the net operating income from the invest-ment, the interest payment on mortgage debt, the amortized financing costs, and any adjustment for replacement reserves. The depreciation deduction affects the operating taxable income as well as the taxable income from the sale of the investment.

Determining the Depreciable Amount.

The first step in estimating the depreciation deduction is to determine the amount to be depreciated. *Basis,* the term used to describe the value of property for income tax purposes, generally means the cost of the property. The basis is important for (1) determining the amount of annual depreciation deductions and (2) determining the investor's gain or loss on the property at the time of sale. The total depreciable amount is generally the original cost *plus* the cost of any capital improvements less the cost of the land.

Basis includes cash, mortgages, and other real estate given in exchange for the investment. For example, if an investor purchases a property for cash and also assumes a mortgage, the cash and the mortgage amount are combined to form the basis of the investment.

Certain items may affect the cost of an investment and change the depreciable basis. These include expenditures for capital improvements, certain legal fees, and the cost of title insurance. Other items, such as financing costs, do not affect the basis. However, these financing costs are deducted over the life of the mortgage.

To determine the depreciable amount, the investor must allocate the total cost between land and building.

Basis Allocation.

From a tax perspective, a real estate investment consists of a depreciable building and nondepreciable land. The allocation between land and building is based on the market value of each at the time of acquisition. You can determine the allocation by using a professional appraisal or by other methods. For example, suppose you make an investment for a total cost of $100,000. If the building to total value ratio is 75 percent, the depreciable amount is $75,000. However, if the ratio were to increase to 85 percent, the depreciable amount would increase to $85,000. The increase or decrease in depreciable amount represents a considerable increase or decrease in depreciation deductions, which in turn translates into savings or losses in taxes.

A second means of allocation is to use tax assessor estimates. For instance, suppose the tax assessor has assessed the value of the building at $50,000 and the value of the land at $15,000. This represents a building total assessed value ratio of $50,000/$65,000, which is equal to 77 percent. Using the ratio, the investor would allocate $77,000 of the $100,000 cost to the building and the remaining $23,000 to land value.

Time Depreciated. Another major factor influencing the depreciation deduction is the length of time over which an investment is to be depreciated. The TRA of 1986 has modified the depreciable lives for real estate. Under the new law, real estate has been divided into two categories: residential real property, which has a life of 27.5 years (including low-income housing); and nonresidential real property, which must be depreciated over 31.5 years. Both types must also be depreciated on a straight-line basis. The effect of this has substantially reduced the amount of depreciation deduction the taxpayer is allowed to take from previous years. Depreciation in the year the property is placed in service is based on the mid-month convention. This assumes that an asset is placed in service on the fifteenth of the month regardless of the actual day. Table 8.10 shows the percentage deduction for residential property depreciated on a 27.5-year basis for the years in service. To use this table, choose the vertical column that shows the recovery year and move across to the month of depreciation. The percentage will be applied to the total amount to be depreciated. For example, if a real estate investment was placed in service in June, the first year's proportion would be .020 and the second year would be .036. A similar proportion would be used over the balance of the life. If the property is sold before the end of the life, the deduction for the year of disposition is based only on the number of months the property was in service during that year.

Classification of Assets. The final step in determining the depreciation deduction is to select the method. The 1986 tax revision

Table 8.10 Mid-Month Convention for Residential Real Property Depreciation (27.5 Years)

Year of Recovery	MONTH PLACED IN SERVICE											
	Jan.	Feb.	Mar.	Apr.	May	June	July	Aug.	Sept.	Oct.	Nov.	Dec.
1	.036	.032	.029	.026	.023	.020	.017	.014	.011	.008	.005	.002
2–27	.036	.036	.036	.036	.036	.036	.036	.036	.036	.036	.036	.036
28	.029	.032	.035	.036	.036	.036	.036	.036	.036	.036	.036	.036
29	0	0	0	.002	.005	.008	.011	.014	.017	.020	.023	.026

allows real estate investors basically the option to depreciate on a straight-line basis of either 27.5 years of 31.5 years for residential rental property and nonresidential real property, respectively.

Certain other types of assets such as improvements are subject to accelerated methods of depreciation based on their ACRS class lives. Table 8.11 depicts the types of real estate assets that would fall into this category. The investor also has the option of depreciating these assets on a straight-line rate. The ACRS methods are applied using a mid-year convention; however, if 40 percent of the assets are acquired in the last quarter of the year the taxpayer must follow a mid-quarter convention. Table 8.12 shows the accelerated depreciation percentages for these class lives using the mid-year convention. The depreciation deduction is computed by multiplying the proportion each year by the depreciable basis. This process is continued for each year.

ALTERNATIVE MINIMUM TAX

In addition to generating ordinary taxable income, a real estate investment can also potentially generate what is known as tax-preference income. This tax-preference income is subject to the minimum tax.

There are two sources of tax preferences of income from real estate investments: appreciated property given to charities and accelerated depreciation on property in service prior to 1987. For appreciated property that is donated, the excess appreciation of all donated property is a tax preference item and thus is added back to the taxable income. For property in service prior to 1987, an accelerated method of depreciation was available. In the computation of alternative minimum tax, the excess of the accelerated method of depreciation over the straight-line method results in a tax preference item. In addition to real estate there are five other types of tax preferences, and as shown in Table 8.13, these are added back to taxable income to arrive at the alternative minimum tax.

Table 8.13 shows how to compute the alternative minimum tax. To calculate this, tax preferences are added to taxable income. Certain adjustments are either added or subtracted to this sum depending on their tax treatment. These adjustments include, among others, depreciation of real and personal property in service after 1986, passive activity losses, installment sales of dealer property, alternative net operating loss deduction, and certain itemized deductions.

Table 8.11 CLASS LIVES FOR CERTAIN REAL-ESTATE-RELATED ASSETS

3-year	Property with class lives of 4 or less years; includes such items as carpeting, draperies, furnishings
5-year	Property with class lives between 4 and 10 years; includes cars, energy-saving devices
7-year	Property with class lives between 10 and 16 years; includes office equipment, fixtures
10-year	Property with class lives between 16 and 20 years; includes mobile homes and prefab houses
15-year	Property with class lives between 20 and 25 years; includes landscaping, sidewalks, improvements
20-year	Property with class lives of 25 or more years; includes sewer pipes and farms

Table 8.12 DEPRECIATION RATES FOR CERTAIN ASSET CLASS LIVES

Year of Recovery	CLASS LIFE 3	5	7	10	15	20
1	.33	.200	.143	.100	.050	.038
2	.45	.320	.245	.180	.095	.072
3	.15	.192	.175	.144	.086	.067
4	.07	.115	.125	.115	.077	.062
5		.115	.089	.092	.069	.057
6		.058	.089	.074	.062	.053
7			.089	.066	.059	.049
8			.045	.066	.059	.045
9				.065	.059	.045
10				.065	.059	.045
11				.033	.059	.045
12					.059	.045
13					.059	.045
14					.059	.045
15					.059	.045
16					.030	.045
17						.045
18						.045
19						.045
20						.045
21						.017

For depreciation of real property in service after 1986, depreciation must be calculated on a forty-year life. When subtracted from the regular depreciation any excess must be added back; however, following the 27.5 or 31.5 life to which the property applies, the amount will result in reduction of taxable income. Additionally an exemption is allowed to reduce the minimum tax liability under the TRA of 1986. This amount is $30,000 for single taxpayers and $40,000 for married taxpayers; however, a phase-out of 25 cents over certain levels of alternative minimum taxable income is applied. These levels are $112,500 for single and $150,000 for married taxpayers. Thus, when these incomes exceed $232,500 and $310,000, respectively, no exemption will be allowed.

To illustrate, suppose a married real es-

Table 8.13 CALCULATION OF MINIMUM TAXES ON PREFERENCE INCOME (AMT)

	TAXABLE INCOME
Plus	Tax preferences
Plus or Minus	Adjustments
Equals	Alternative minimum taxable income
Minus	Exemption

	TAX BASE
Times	21%
Equals	Minimum tax before reduction
Minus	Regular income tax
Equals	Alternative minimum tax

tate investor had a taxable income of $150,000. He also had property in service prior to 1986 with an excess of accelerated depreciation over straight-line depreciation of $25,000 and positive adjustments of $40,000. Using the formula in table 8.13, the amount of alternative minimum tax would be as follows:

Taxable income	$150,000
Tax preferences	25,000
Adjustments	40,000
Alternative minimum taxable income	$215,000
Exemption*	(23,750)*
Tax base	$191,250
	.21
Minimum tax before reduction	$ 40,163
Regular tax†	(35,000)†
Alternative minimum tax	$ 5,163

* $40,000 − .25 ($215,000 − $150,000)
† Assume the taxpayer's regular tax was $35,000.

Therefore, in addition to the taxpayer's regular tax, he must pay an additional $5,163. This would then reduce the investor's after-tax cash flow.

TAXES ON THE SALE OF AN INVESTMENT

The disposition of a real estate investment is generally referred to as the reversion. The tax impact on the sale of the real estate investment depends on its tax classification and form of ownership. We have already discussed the four tax classifications of property in relation to federal income taxes. This section deals primarily with the tax impact on the sale of property held for investment purposes or for use in a trade or business by the individual and the corporate investor.

For the individual taxpayer capital gains and losses must be netted together, and short-term and long-term gains or losses are computed separately. If a capital gain results, it is subject to tax at the investor's ordinary rate or a maximum of 28 percent. However, if a capital loss is the result, the deduction in the year of sale is limited to $3,000. This must first be used against short-term losses and then against long-term losses. Any loss in excess of $3,000 may be carried forward indefinitely, but the distinction between short-term and long-term must remain.

For the corporate taxpayer, capital gains and losses are also netted together and short-term and long-term are kept distinct. However, they are not subject to a minimum tax of 28 percent and losses may only offset gains. Thus the corporate taxpayer is not allowed to deduct $3,000 of loss against his regular income. He is further limited in the respect of carrying his losses forward. A corporate taxpayer is subject to a three-year carryback and five-year carryforward. Additionally these corporate carryovers and carrybacks are then classified as short-term. Thus the taxpayer cannot offset them against future long-term gains.

Table 8.4 illustrates the calculation of taxes due on the sale of the real estate investment. The selling price less selling expenses results in the *amount realized*. Subtract the *adjusted basis* from the amount realized in order to arrive at the *total gain* from the sale. The adjusted basis is the original total cost of the property plus the cost of capital improvements made to the property, less the accumulated depreciation deduction over the holding period. For any nondepreciable investment, such as unimproved land, the adjusted basis equals the original cost.

After arriving at the total gain from the sale, the *capital gain* (loss) on the sale of a real estate investment is multiplied by the investor's marginal tax rate to compute the taxes due on sale.

Capital Gains and Losses

Gains or losses from the sale are treated as either short-term or long-term depending on the length of time the investment is owned. If the period of ownership is more than six months, the gains or losses will be long-term. Holding periods of six months or less are short-term.

If the investor has both long-term gains and losses, he must compute the net long-term gain. If he has short-term gains and losses, he must compute the net short-term gain or loss. A net short-term gain is treated as ordinary income. A net short-term loss may be used to offset a long-term gain.

All real estate qualifies for capital gains treatment unless it is held primarily for sale to customers in the ordinary course of business. Real estate used in trade or business and held for more than six months qualifies as Section 1231 property. Within the tax guidelines, Section 1231 property receives more favorable tax treatment than other investment real estate, referred to as capital assets. Real estate held as neither a capital asset nor Section 1231 assets results in an ordinary gain or loss, whereas Section 1231 and capital assets receive more favorable tax treatment of gains, yet have different guidelines for losses.

The disposition of Section 1231 assets can result in more favorable tax treatment than that given to capital assets because:

1. A net gain from all sales of Section 1231 assets is taxed as a long-term capital gain.
2. A net loss from such sales is fully deductible against other income without the limitations imposed on the deductibility of losses of capital assets.

Net long-term losses on capital assets may be deducted from ordinary income. There is a limitation of $3,000 on the deductibility of long-term losses for individuals. Short-term losses for the individual are used dollar for dollar to offset taxable income, subject to the $3,000 limitation. The benefits of the carryforward of a capital loss are available to an individual taxpayer until used up or until his death.

For the corporate investor, the full amount of the capital gains is included in a corporation's taxable income before the corporate tax rate is applied. Capital losses can only be deducted against capital gains. A corporation can carry back capital losses for three years to obtain a refund on taxes paid during that period or it may carry losses forward five years for the same purpose. The benefit of any capital loss must be used in this carryback or carryforward period or it is lost to the corporate taxpayer.

Minimum Taxes on Sale

The second type of taxes to consider on a sale is minimum taxes. The following section discusses minimum taxes for corporate entities.

Minimum Taxation of Corporations. The corporate investor calculates the tax preference income by the formula in table 8.14.

Corporate tax preference items must be added back to taxable income. These include, among others, bad debt reserves, tax-exempt interest, and charitable contributions of appreciated property. Thus, these will all increase the base that the corporation is taxed upon. Adjustments may be either added or subtracted from taxable income. One of the major new items included as a result of TRA 1986 is the depreciation on all of a corporation's personal property. In the computation of AMT, personal prop-

Table 8.14 CORPORATE ALTERNATIVE MINIMUM TAX

	Taxable Income
Plus	Tax preferences
Plus or	
Minus	Adjustments
Minus	Amount net operating loss
	Alternative minimum taxable income
Minus	Exemption
	Net alternative minimum tax
Times	.20
	Alternative minimum tax before credits
Minus	Foreign tax credit
	Alternative minimum tax
Minus	Regular tax
	Additional tax due (credit carryover)

erty that may have been subject to higher ACRS percentages must be computed on a 150 percent declining-balance method over the asset's class life. The treatment of depreciation of real property acquired after 1986 is handled in the same manner as the noncorporate taxpayer.

AMT net operating loss is computed, and the new tax law allows it to be deducted for up to 90 percent of AMT. Upon this deduction the corporation arrives at alternative minimum taxable income (AMTI) from which the exemption is subtracted to arrive at net AMTI. The exemption for corporations is $40,000; however, it is also subject to a phase-out between $150,000 and $310,000 of 25 percent, which is calculated similarly to the noncorporate phase-out. From this the allowable foreign tax credit and regular tax is subtracted to arrive at the additional tax a corporation must pay. However, unlike the noncorporate taxpayer, this amount may be used in future years as a credit to offset future alternative minimum taxes.

Assume the corporation has taxable in-

come of $350,000, including a charitable contribution of appreciated property of $200,000 that had a cost of $50,000. It also has excess depreciation on personal property of $20,000 and a carryforward net operating loss of $70,000. Its regular tax liability for the year amounted to $119,000. Using the formula in Table 8.14, the additional taxes due would be computed as follows:

Taxable income	$350,000
Tax preferences	150,000
Adjustments	20,000
Net operating loss	(70,000)
Alternative minimum taxable income	$450,000
Exemption	0*
Net alternative minimum taxable income	$450,000
	.20
Alternative minimum tax	$ 90,000
Regular tax	(119,000)
Additional tax due	0

* Exemption is phased out for incomes over $310,000.

Thus, since the alternative minimum tax did not exceed the corporation's regular tax liability, no additional tax is imposed. The purpose for establishing the alternative minimum tax is to ensure that everyone will pay some amount of tax on their income generated throughout the year.

To summarize briefly, the sale of a real estate investment creates two potential sources of tax liability: ordinary and capital gains taxes, and minimum taxes. The investor must carefully analyze the expected tax consequences *before* undertaking an investment. These taxes are subtracted from the before-tax equity reversion (BTER) to arrive at the after-tax equity reversion (ATER), as shown in table 8.3. The investor makes the investment decision based on the expected cash flow after taxes from operation and sale.

METHODS OF DEFERRING TAXES ON DISPOSITION

The two most common methods of deferring taxes on the disposition of a real estate investment are the installment sale and the tax-deferred exchange.

THE INSTALLMENT SALE

When the seller does not receive the entire amount at sale and provides some financing for the buyer, it is possible to defer the tax liability. The installment sale allows the seller to spread the gain from the sale over a period of time rather than to report it all in the year of the sale. However, tax laws affecting the installment sale have recently been changed by the Tax Reform Act of 1986.

The installment method of reporting taxable income has advantages over the ordinary method of reporting the entire gain in the year of sale. Some of these advantages are:

1. Only a pro rata share of the down payment and a portion of the taxpayer's indebtedness is recognized as taxable income and therefore subject to tax. If the entire gain were taxable in the year of the sale, most of the down payment, or more, might be used in payment in tax on the gain.
2. The seller may postpone the payment of tax on part of the gain until the time in which he receives payments that include the proportionate share of the gain.
3. The seller may save some of the total tax if he uses the installment method, and

if the gain on the sale is taxed as ordinary income. Due to the progressive tax rate structure, the seller's gain will be taxed at lower rates if reported over a period of years than if it is reported all in one year.

4. The seller risks a possibility of changing tax rates. Since taxes are computed according to the tax rates in effect in the year in which the gain is reported, if tax rates decrease in the future, the total tax will be less if the sale is spread out. However, if the tax rates increase, so will the total tax liability.

Basic Requirements. Basically, the installment sale method is where the buyer pays the seller in a series of payments. The investor is relieved of the obligation to pay tax on income not received and allows him to include only the gain portion of principal in his gross income.

The effect of an installment sale is to spread the gain and tax over the years during which the installment payments are received. This is achieved by applying a gross profit percentage (gain divided by contract price) to the amount of cash received and the taxpayer's allocable installment indebtedness. Losses may not be reported on the installment method. The total gain is equal to the sales price less the taxpayer's adjusted basis and selling expenses. The contract price is the sale price reduced by mortgages or other indebtedness assumed (or taken subject to) by the buyer and payable to a third party.

If a minimum amount of interest is not provided for, the IRS will impute interest—each installment payment is divided between interest and principal, and the interest portion will be ordinary income to the seller and deductible interest to the buyer. An investor is deemed to have allocable installment indebtedness when his installments receivable over the sum of installments renewable and the adjusted basis of his assets times his average quarterly indebtedness exists. This amount is then multiplied by the gross profit percentage to arrive at the investor's gain attributable to his installment obligations. Upon receipt of installment obligations, any amount previously taxed will be excluded from tax.

The Tax Reform Act of 1986 holds that certain property in an installment sale will be subject to the allocable installment indebtedness. Types of property include trade, business, or investment property with a sales price greater than $150,000, any other trade or business property, and personal inventory. Moreover, in the case of affiliated groups owning property, they will be treated as one taxpayer.

Installment Sale Procedure. To illustrate the concepts discussed and the basic mechanics of an installment sale, the following steps are employed:

Step 1. Compute the after-tax cash flow in year of sale as illustrated in table 8.15.
Step 2. Compute the after-tax cash flow each year from installment receipts as illustrated in table 8.19.

ATCF in Year of Installment Sale. Table 8.15 illustrates how to calculate the after-tax cash flow in the year of installment sale. From the cash received (down payment), the investor deducts any selling expenses (such as brokerage fees) and the taxes due in the year of installment sale. Table 8.16 shows how to calculate the tax due in the year of installment sale. The investor's total receipts for tax purposes in the year of sale is the sum of the down payment plus the excess of the mortgage given up over the adjusted basis plus selling expenses and al-

Table 8.15 ATCF in Year of Installment Sale

	Down payment
Minus	Selling expense
Minus	Taxes*
	ATCF in year of sale

* See table 8.16.

locable installment indebtedness (see table 8.17). Then this is multiplied by the profit percentage as shown in table 8.18. This results in the taxable amount in year of installment sale.

After-tax Cash Flow from Installment Receipts. Table 8.19 shows how to calculate the after-tax cash flow from the installment receipts each year. Since the seller is also the lender, the purchaser will make a payment to the seller each year. Some taxes must be paid on the payment received by the seller. These are ordinary income taxes on the interest portion of the debt service and on the gain portion of the principal portion of the debt service. Additionally, any amount of gain that was previously taxed due to allocable installment indebt-

Table 8.16 Tax in Year of Installment Sale

	Excess of mortgage over adjusted basis and selling expenses
Plus	Down payment
Equals	Payment received in year of sale
Plus	Allocable installment indebtedness*
Equals	Total gain in year of sale
Times	profit percentage†
Equals	Taxable income in year of sale
Times	Marginal tax rate
Equals	Tax in year of sale

* See table 8.17.

† See table 8.18.

Table 8.17 ALLOCABLE INSTALLMENT INDEBTEDNESS

	Installments receivable
Divided by	Installments receivable plus
	Adjusted basis of assets
Equals	Installment percentage
Times	Average quarterly indebtedness
Equals	Allocable installment indebtedness

Table 8.19 AFTER-TAX CASH FLOW FROM INSTALLMENT RECEIPTS

	BTCF (Debt service)
Plus	Balloon payment
Minus	Taxes*
Equals	ATCF from installment receipts

* See table 8.20.

edness is shielded from further tax to avoid double taxation (table 8.20). Chapter 12 provides a detailed example of an installment sale.

TAX-DEFERRED EXCHANGES

Section 1031 of the Internal Revenue Code provides an exception to the general rule requiring recognition of gain or loss upon the sale or exchange of property. Under this section, no gain or loss is recognized if the property held for productive use in a trade or business or for an investment is exchanged solely for property of a like kind to be held for productive use in a trade or business or for investment. The application of the section for deferring the taxes due on

Table 8.18 PROFIT PERCENTAGE ON INSTALLMENT SALE

	Sale price
Minus	Selling expenses
Minus	Adjusted basis
Equals	Total gain
	Sale price
Plus	Excess mortgage over basis and selling expenses
Minus	Mortgage balance assumed
Equals	Contract price
	Total gain
Divided by	Contract price
Equals	Profit percentage

the disposition of a real estate investment is referred to as the deferred exchange.

Why Exchange? Exchanging real estate rather than selling it and reinvesting the proceeds stems from two basic motivations. The first reason is that exchanging an investment is an attractive method of marketing real estate when a sale does not appear possible. The second, and probably the most important motivation, is the availability of income tax deferral. Thus taxes that would be paid on an outright sale may be postponed under the use of the exchange.

To illustrate the importance of the tax deferral concept of the exchange, consider the following simple example. Suppose that an investor has a property with a market value of $250,000 and an adjusted basis of $150,000. If the property were sold for an amount realized in cash of $250,000, the taxable income (assuming all capital gains) from the sale is $40,000 (40 percent of the $100,000 total gain). If the investor is in a 40 percent marginal tax bracket, the tax on

Table 8.20 TAX DUE ON INSTALLMENT RECEIPTS

	BTCF (Debt service)
Minus	Taxes (t)*
Equals	ATCF

* Less any amount previously taxed if applicable.

the taxable capital gain is $16,000. Thus, as a result of the taxes, the investor is left with less capital to reinvest.

The investor, however, must ask the following question: Am I better off by selling, paying the tax due on sale, and reinvesting, or by avoiding current taxation by means of the tax deferred exchange? Since the exchange has other important tax implications (the most important of which is that, in general, the basis of the property given up becomes the basis of the property acquired by the exchange), there is not a simple answer to the question.

Basic Exchange Requirements. Under Section 1031, no gain or loss is recognized if property held for use in a trade or business or for investment is exchanged solely for property of "like-kind" to be held either for productive use in a trade or business or as an investment. The first requirement of a tax-deferred exchange is that property is held for productive use in a trade or business or for an investment.

The exchange qualifies for Section 1031 treatment as long as the properties involved fit into either class. Therefore, property held for use in a trade or business may be exchanged for property held for investment and vice versa. Recall from chapter 2 that for tax purposes, real estate is divided into four categories. Property held as a personal residence and property held primarily for sale do not qualify under Section 1031. However, investment property and property for use in a trade or business may be exchanged and qualify in any combination: investment for investment, investment for business, or business for business.

The second requirement for tax-deferred treatment under Section 1031 is that the properties involved in the exchange must be of "like-kind," which refers to the nature or character of the property and not to its grade or quality. Under Section 1031, one kind or class of property may not be tax-deferred exchanged for property of a different kind or class. The fact that any real estate involved is improved or unimproved is immaterial because this relates only to the grade or quality of the property and not to its kind or class.

In general, like kind refers to the distinction between real and personal property. Real property may be exchanged for real property as long as the first requirement is met. The exchange of real property for personal property does not qualify under Section 1031 for nontaxable treatment. For example, an exchange of an apartment building will qualify even if it was exchanged for a farm. Also, a commercial building for business use could be exchanged for an apartment building. However, an exchange for an apartment building for government bonds would not qualify under Section 1031 for tax-deferred purposes.

Few real estate exchanges are completely nontaxable for all participants. Property value differences usually require the balancing of the equities with what is known as "boot." Boot can take several forms and, by definition, does not qualify as like-kind property. The third requirement of a real estate exchange is the identification of the amount of boot and the amount of taxes due on the exchange.

Boot includes such items as stock, bonds, cash, notes, or personal property received in a real estate exchange. Boot also may be received in the form of relief from indebtedness, which is treated as a receipt of cash. While boot is generally perceived as value given to entice the other investor to trade, its meaning has greater impact when it is considered in the light of tax consequences to the party who receives it.

How the Exchange Works. To analyze the real estate exchange, we must do the following:

Step 1. Balance equity positions and identify the value of like-kind and unlike-kind (boot) property.
Step 2. Calculate the realized gain in an exchange.
Step 3. Calculate the recognized gain in an exchange.
Step 4. Identify the taxable gain (the lower of amounts in step 2 or step 3).
Step 5. Calculate the ATCF and equity position after exchange.

Table 8.21 shows how to calculate the value of the equity position for each investor. The investor's equity is the difference between the market value of property given up minus the outstanding mortgage debt against the property. In any real estate exchange, the net equity positions must be equal for all parties. There are numerous ways to balance the equity positions. Generally, this involves the use of "boot," or unlike property, cash, or net loan relief. Table 8.22 shows how to calculate the net equity position. This is the equity given minus the equity received. If the net equity is negative, it means that the investor must give something of equal value, such as cash or other property, like-kind or unlike-kind.

How to Balance Equities. There are several alternatives for balancing the equities in an exchange. A partial list includes:

Table 8.21 CALCULATION OF THE EQUITY POSITION

	Market value of property given
Minus	Outstanding mortgage debt
Equals	Equity

Table 8.22 CALCULATION OF NET EQUITY POSITION

	Equity given
Minus	Equity received
Equals	Net equity*

* If net equity is negative, this indicates the amount of "boot" cash to be paid or of the like-kind property; if positive, the amount to be received.

1. Add cash by investor with lower equity.
2. Add note and mortgage by investor with lower equity.
3. Refinance the property with the higher equity.
4. Add another like-kind investment.
5. Add unlike-kind property (bonds, stocks, etc.).
6. Investor with least equity could pay down the outstanding mortgage, thus increasing equity.
7. Any combination of the above that is acceptable and meets the objectives of each party.

Table 8.23 shows how to calculate what is called the *realized gain*. The realized gain is in essence the gain that the investor would have had if the property was sold rather than exchanged. The realized gain (table 8.23) is the market value of the property given, minus the adjusted basis of the property given, minus the transactions costs such as brokerage commission and legal fees.

Next we must calculate the amount of

Table 8.23 CALCULATION OF THE REALIZED GAIN IN AN EXCHANGE

	Market value of property given
Minus	Adjusted basis of property given
Minus	Transactions costs
Equals	Realized gain on exchange

Table 8.24 CALCULATION OF RECOGNIZED GAIN IN AN EXCHANGE

	Boot (or cash) received
Minus	Boot (or cash) given
Plus	Net loan relief*
Minus	Transactions costs
Equals	Recognized gain†

* Net loan relief is the difference between the mortgage debt on the property given minus the mortgage debt on the property received. It is deemed unlike property (taxable) only to the extent that the debt on the property given up *exceeds* the mortgage on property received.

† The amount of recognized gain subject to taxation cannot exceed the realized gain.

Table 8.25 CALCULATION OF THE ADJUSTED BASIS OF PROPERTY ACQUIRED IN AN EXCHANGE

	Value of property received
Minus	Realized gain
Plus	Taxable gain*
Equals	Adjusted basis of property acquired

* The taxable gain cannot exceed the realized gain.

gain that is taxable. Table 8.24 shows how to calculate the recognized gain in an exchange as follows: the boot received (value of unlike property) or cash, minus the boot (or cash) given, plus the net loan relief, minus the transactions costs. The net loan relief is the difference between the amount of debt on the property given and the amount of debt on the property received. The net mortgage relief is considered unlike property only to the extent that the difference between the two mortgage balances is positive. Thus, there is no "negative" net mortgage relief. The investor pays tax on the lower of the recognized gain or the realized gain. Thus, taxable gain is equal to recognized gain as long as recognized gain does not exceed realized gain.

The final step in analyzing the tax impact of an exchange is to calculate the adjusted basis of the property acquired in the ex-change. Table 8.25 shows this calculation. The adjusted basis is the value of the property received minus the realized gain plus the recognized gain.

In chapter 12 we provide an example of a tax-deferred exchange using this procedure.

OTHER METHODS OF DEFERRING TAXES ON DISPOSITION

When property is involuntarily converted or condemned, the gain or loss may be recognized. If certain requirements are met, the taxpayer may defer the tax liability on the gain by replacing the property within certain time limits. The basis of the replacement property is reduced so that future disposition reflects the postponement.

An involuntary conversion results when property is stolen, requisitioned, condemned, or destroyed, and other property or money is received in payment. Examples of an involuntary conversion are the receipt of insurance proceeds if the property is destroyed or the receipt of condemnation payment if the property is destroyed. If an owner has his property condemned, no gain or loss is recognized if he receives similar property as compensation.

OTHER ITEMS AFFECTING TAX PLANNING

An investor is allowed a tax credit, which reduces the amount of taxes he pays dollar for dollar, for certain rehabilitations he provides. Minor repairs are not included because to qualify for the credit substantial rehabilitation must take place. Substantial rehabilitation consists of either $5,000 or the adjusted basis of the property, whichever is greater. Property that qualifies for this credit is of two types, either certified historic structures in service before 1936 or other nonresidential buildings in service before 1936. The credits are 20 percent and 10 percent, respectively, of the rehabilitation expenditures. Any amount of credit taken will reduce the basis of the property.

Low-income housing previously enjoyed a variety of tax benefits. Although there are still benefits to investment in low-income housing, the Tax Reform Act of 1986 has rearranged these incentives into tax credits for the purchase, construction, and rehabilitation of such property. For the rehabilitation or new construction a 9 percent credit is available, and a credit of 4 percent for the purchase of an existing structure. The 9 percent credits will be reduced to 4 percent if any tax-exempt financing or federal subsidies are used to pay for part of the project.

Requirements are imposed to establish criteria for low-income status. The main criteria is based on an area's particular median income. At least 20 percent of the units must be rented to individuals whose income is not more than 50 percent of the area's median income, or at least 40 percent of the units must be rented by individuals whose income is not more than 60 percent of the area's median income.

Low-income housing receives special treatment with regard to its passive activity status. The credit may be used against passive income or $25,000 of it may be used against active income. The $25,000 when used against active income is subject to a higher phase-out range of $200,000 to $250,000.

SUMMARY

As one can see the effect of taxes plays a major role on the return an investor derives from his investments. Changing tax laws such as the Tax Reform Act of 1986 can widely impact existing and future real estate projects. Some of the changes from the past reform that have been mentioned previously include changes in depreciation status of real estate from accelerated to straight-line, repeal of the tax treatment of long-term capital gains, recalculation of the individual and corporate alternative minimum tax, and the recognition of gain on indebtedness in installment sales. All of these have affected the way present and future real estate decisions will be made.

IV

INVESTMENT CRITERIA

PART IV discusses the fourth step in the investment process—applying the investment criteria. Using these investment criteria, the investor takes step 5—the investment decision. In general, the decision is made by comparing the costs of investing with the expected cash flows.

The investment decision can be viewed from two perspectives:

1. How much should be paid for an investment given some required rate of return from the investment?
2. What will be the expected rate of return given that some price is paid for the investment?

Real estate investors have three major categories of investment criteria:

1. Rules-of-thumb techniques
2. Traditional appraisal techniques
3. Discounted cash flow techniques

Each of these categories have several methods for comparing the costs and benefits of an investment. Chapter 9 discusses the rules of thumb and traditional appraisal techniques. Chapter 10 discusses the more complex discounted cash flow models.

9

TRADITIONAL INVESTMENT CRITERIA

MANY real estate investment decisions are made using various "rules of thumb" criteria. The widespread use of these measures is acknowledged in real estate investment literature. These criteria are examined in this chapter along with the limitations with which the investment analyst should be familiar. The investor should also be familiar with traditional appraisal techniques for value estimation.

Surveys of real estate investing practices suggest that the number of different criteria used has been limited only by investors' ingenuity in devising additional variations of existing profitability measures. After examining each of the measures, this chapter briefly looks at the current practices in estimating investment value. It concludes with a review of the traditional valuation methods of the direct sales income and cost approaches for value estimations.

GENERAL CHARACTERISTICS OF RULES-OF-THUMB CRITERIA

The rules-of-thumb criteria fall into one of two classes: the payback methods (or its reciprocal rates of return) and the average rate of return methods. Table 9.1 summa-

rizes the rules-of-thumb criteria. Notice that the overall capitalization rate is simply the reciprocal of the net income multiplier. Likewise, the equity dividend rate and the after-tax rate are reciprocals to the before-tax and after-tax cash flow multipliers.

Many of these rules of thumb have a number of general characteristics in common. First, all of these measures can be derived using data available from the forecasted cash flow for the investment. The necessary cash flow items include gross income, net operating income, before-tax cash flow, and after-tax cash flow. Other items required are total investment costs and total (or initial) equity. All of these measures are easily derived by calculating percentages of costs to cash flow (or income) or cash flow (or income) to costs.

Second, many of these rules attempt to measure the same conceptual item: either a multiplier (a rate of return as a reciprocal) or an average rate of return. The difference is that each measure relates different items in the cash flow statement to equity or total investment. For example, the equity dividend rate is similar to the after-tax rate except that the cash flow of the former is before-tax while the latter is after-tax. With the same denominator (equity costs), the

Table 9.1 Rules of Thumb: A Summary

Payback Methods

MULTIPLIERS

1. Gross income multiplier (GIM) $= \dfrac{\text{Total investment}}{\text{Gross income}}$
(Potential or effective)

2. Net income multiplier (NIM) $= \dfrac{\text{Total investment}}{\text{Net operating income}}$

3. Before-tax cash flow multiplier $= \dfrac{\text{Equity investment}}{\text{BTCF}}$

4. After-tax cash flow multiplier $= \dfrac{\text{Equity investment}}{\text{ATCF}}$

RATES OF RETURN

1. Overall capitalization rate (R) $= \dfrac{\text{Net operating income}}{\text{Total investment}}$

2. Equity dividend rate (EDR) $= \dfrac{\text{BTCF}}{\text{Equity investment}}$

3. After-tax rate (ATR) $= \dfrac{\text{ATCF}}{\text{Equity investment}}$

Average Rates of Return

1. Average rate on net operating income $= \dfrac{\text{Average net operating income}}{\text{Total investment}}$

2. Average rate on before-tax cash flow $= \dfrac{\text{Average before-tax cash flow}}{\text{Equity investment}}$

3. Average rate on after-tax cash flow $= \dfrac{\text{Average after-tax cash flow}}{\text{Equity investment}}$

after-tax rate will obviously be different than the before-tax equity dividend rate. The point is that these measures produce different results that may influence different investment decisions.

Third, these techniques are unadjusted for the time value of money. In the case of the payback methods, all of the measures are "single-period measures." This means that the multipliers and rates of return are calculated using only a single period measure of income or cash flow that severely constrains its usefulness because income or cash flow is expected to change over time.

In the case of the average rate of return, the average income and cash flow figures are (1) only averages and thereby prone to significant undervaluing in some periods and overvaluing in others, (2) unadjusted for the timing of the true cash flows and, therefore, less useful from an investment standpoint, and (3) inconsistent with investment criteria using the time value of money concept. Since none of these measure changes in expected future income of cash flow streams, they are generally imprecise and subject to error.

While the simple rules of thumb have several problems from a theoretical point of view, they *are* widely used by real estate investors because they are easier to implement than the more complex discounted cash flow models. This ease of use, from both a cost as well as an investor understanding viewpoint, makes them valuable as a first approximation to the investment decision.

ANALYSIS OF RULES OF THUMB

The *payback period* is simply the number of years required to recover the initial investment outlay from an investment's future cash flow. Often the payback period is expressed in reciprocal form, that is, as a rate of return (see table 9.1).

PAYBACK PERIOD METHODS

In equation form, the payback method may be expressed as:

(9.1)

$$\text{Payback period} = \frac{\text{Investment cost}}{\text{Income}}$$

Alternatively, in the rate form,

(9.2)

$$\text{Rate of Return} = \frac{1}{\text{Payback period}}$$

$$= \frac{\text{Income}}{\text{Investment cost}}$$

As we discussed earlier, there are five measures (or levels) of income from the operation of a real estate investment:

1. Potential gross income
2. Effective gross income
3. Net operating income
4. Before-tax cash flow
5. After-tax cash flow

Payback periods (or rates of return) for these five types of inflow can be calculated by using equations (9.1) and (9.2).

Gross Income Multiplier. One of the most widely used payback methods for estimating both market and investment value is the gross income multiplier (GIM).

The GIM can be expressed as:

(9.3)

$$\text{GIM} = \frac{\text{Total investment}}{\text{EGI}}$$

The GIM simply tells the analyst how many years it would take to recover the total investment costs (purchase price) if all of the gross income were allocated to recovery. To illustrate, suppose an investor is considering an investment with an asking price of $500,000. The estimated effective gross income in the first year is $100,000. So the GIM is:

$$\text{GIM} = \frac{\$500,000}{\$100,000}$$

$$= 5.00$$

Hence, if all the gross income were used, it would take five years to recover the total cost of the investment.

Net Income Multiplier (Overall Capitalization Rate). A second type of payback criteria can be calculated by using net operating income (NOI) instead of gross income. The method is typically called the *overall capitalization rate*. Thus, using equation (9.2), the overall rate is:

(9.4)

$$\frac{\text{Overall}}{\text{capitalization rate}} = \frac{\text{NOI}}{\text{Investment cost}}$$

This overall capitalization rate is sometimes called the "free and clear" rate of return.

Suppose the investment considered has a purchase price of $500,000 and a net operating income of $50,000. The overall rate is:

$$\text{Overall capitalization rate} = \frac{\$50,000}{\$500,000}$$
$$= 10\%$$

Or, in payback form, the net income multiplier (NIM) would be the reciprocal of the overall rate using equation (9.1):

$$NIM = \frac{\$500,000}{\$50,000}$$
$$= 10.00$$

So it would take ten years to recover the total investment cost if all the net operating income was allocated to recovery. Notice that the reciprocal of the NIM (10) is the overall capitalization rate (10 percent).

Before-tax Cash Flow Multiplier (*Equity Dividend Rate*). A third payback period rate is the equity dividend rate (EDR) or the cash-on-cash return. The before-tax cash flow (BTCF) is used to calculate the rate. In equation form, the equity dividend rate is:

(9.5)
$$EDR = \frac{\text{Before-tax cash flow}}{\text{Equity investment}}$$

Notice that with this method, the cost of the investment is measured by the amount of equity rather than the total investment costs.

For instance, suppose the investment has a total cost of $500,000 of which $400,000 is financed with a mortgage and $100,000 with equity. Assume that the BTCF is $12,000 in the first year. The equity dividend rate would be

$$EDR = \frac{\$12,000}{\$100,000}$$
$$= 12\%$$

In multiplier form the reciprocal of the EDR would be:

$$\frac{\text{Before-tax cash}}{\text{flow multiplier}} = \frac{\$100,000}{\$12,000}$$
$$= 8.33$$

Thus, it would take 8.33 years to recover the original equity investment using before-tax cash flow.

After-tax Cash Flow Multiplier (*After-tax Rate*). The final payback rate of return is calculated using the after-tax cash flows rather than before-tax. In equation form, the after-tax rate (ATR) is:

(9.6)
$$ATR = \frac{\text{After-tax cash flow}}{\text{Equity investment}}$$

In the continuing example, suppose the investment is generating some tax shelter, but the taxable income is still positive so that the after-tax cash flows are less than the before-tax cash flows. Assuming an ATCF of $7,500, the ATR is

$$ATR = \frac{\$7,500}{\$100,000}$$
$$= 7.5\%$$

Alternatively, the payback period of the equity investment of $100,000 (assuming a level yearly ATCF of $7,500) is 13.33 years.

Table 9.2 summarizes and compares the results using the payback methods for the example. All of the results are single period income and cash flow figures, and all required outlays are taken at their initial amounts.

Table 9.2 COMPARISON OF RESULTS USING PAYBACK METHODS*

Method[†]	Multiplier (Years)	Rate of Return (%)
Gross income multiplier	5	20
Net income multiplier (overall rate)	10	10
Before-tax cash flow mutliplier (Equity dividend rate)	8.33	12
After-tax cash flow multiplier (After-tax rate)	13.33	7.5

* Example: Selling Price = $500,000
           Effective Gross Income = $100,000
           Net Operating Income = $50,000
           Mortgage = $400,000
           Equity = $100,000
           BTCF = $12,000
           ATCF = $7,500

[†] See table 9.1 for the equations.

AVERAGE RATE OF RETURN METHODS

The second major category of rules of thumb techniques is the average (or accounting) rates of return. These methods are not as popular as the payback methods.

An average rate of return is calculated by dividing an investment's average annual income (or average before- or after-tax cash flow) by the total investment or equity costs. In equation form, the average rate of return can be expressed as

(9.7)
$$\text{Average rate of return on total investment} = \frac{\text{Average cash flow}}{\text{Investment cost}}$$

There are three commonly found forms of the average rate of return.

Average Rate on Net Operating Income.

This is very similar to the overall capitalization rate. If, for example, the net operating income of the investment is constant each period, the average rate on net operating income and the overall capitalization rate would be identical. Thus the average rate on net operating income is expressed as:

(9.8)
$$\text{Average rate on net operating income} = \frac{\text{Average NOI}}{\text{Total investment}}$$

This measure tells the investor the average rate of return on net operating income to investment cost over an expected number of years.

As an example, consider the following: A property is purchased for $250,000 of which $200,000 is financed with a mortgage having an interest rate of 10 percent with annual payments for twenty-five years. The equity investment is $50,000. The property is sold ten years after purchase for $300,000. The annual net operating income is $26,000.

The mortgage terms result in a mortgage constant of .10904, thus requiring a debt service of $21,809. The resultant before-tax cash flow is $4,191 ($26,000 minus $21,809). The before-tax equity reversion is $130,877. This is calculated using the sale price of $300,000 less the unpaid mortgage balance of $169,123 after 10 years. Assume straight-line depreciation over 27.5 years, 80 percent of the total cost is depreciable, and a 28 percent income tax rate.

The average rate on net operating income would be:

$$\text{Average rate on net operating income} = \frac{\$26,000}{\$250,000}$$

$$= 10.400\%$$

As indicated, the overall capitalization rate is also 10.400 percent.

Average Rate on Before-tax Cash Flow. This calculates the average before-tax cash flow as a percentage of equity investment. Therefore, the average rate on before-tax cash flow is defined as:

(9.9)

$$\text{Average rate on before-tax cash flow} = \frac{\text{Average BTCF}}{\text{Equity investment}}$$

Using the example, we can get the following results:

Annual before-tax cash flow	$ 4,191
Holding period (years)	× 10
Total before-tax cash flow	$41,910
Average before-tax cash flow	$ 4,191
Average rate on before-tax cash flow	$ 4,191
	$50,000
	= 8.382%

Average Rate on After-tax Cash Flow. This average rate of return is calculated in the same way as the before-tax except the cash flows are on an after-tax basis. This measure is defined as:

(9.10)

$$\text{Average rate on after-tax cash flow} = \frac{\text{Average ATCF}}{\text{Equity investment}}$$

However, it requires many more calculations to get this result as table 9.3 shows. Note that the interest payment falls as the loan is amortized. Since the interest portion is deductible, taxable income varies each period.

Depreciation is also deductible, assuming that 80 percent of the total cost, or $200,000, is depreciable over 27.5 years. In this case, the straight-line method is used, so each year $7,273 is deducted from taxable income. Taxable income multiplied by the tax rate (28 percent) is equal to the tax liability. The tax liability is subtracted from BTCF to yield ATCF each year. Therefore, from table 9.3, we get the average rate on after-tax cash flow equal to 8.378 percent.

Adjusting for Reversion. The average rates of return methods can be improved by adjusting the average income and/or cash flow figures to reflect the fact that the selling price (or reversion) is expected at the end of some holding period. Although this adjustment is an improvement, the adjusted average rates of return still contain several problems.

The impact of the selling of the property on the average rate on net operating income would be as follows:

Total net operating income ($26,000 for 10 years)	$260,000
Net selling price (after 10 years)	300,000
Total cash return	$560,000
Cost of total investment	$250,000
Profit	$310,000

Average profit:
$310,000/10 = $31,000

Table 9.3 Calculation of Average Return on After-tax Cash Flow*

Cash flow		YEAR								
	1	2	3	4	5	6	7	8	9	10
Net operating income	$26,000	$26,000	$26,000	$26,000	$26,000	$26,000	$26,000	$26,000	$26,000	$26,000
Less interest	−19,915	−19,716	−19,497	−19,255	−18,988	−18,692	−18,366	−18,000	−17,607	−17,168
Less depreciation†	−7,273	−7,273	−7,273	−7,273	−7,273	−7,273	−7,273	−7,273	−7,273	−7,273
Taxable income	(1,187)	(989)	(770)	(528)	(261)	35	361	722	1,120	1,560
Times tax rate	.28	.28	.28	.28	.28	.28	.28	.28	.28	.28
	$ (332)	$ (277)	$ (216)	$ (148)	$ (73)	$ 10	$ 101	$ 202	$ 314	$ 437
Before-tax cash flow (BTCF)	$ 4,191	$ 4,191	$ 4,191	$ 4,191	$ 4,191	$ 4,191	$ 4,191	$ 4,191	$ 4,191	$ 4,191
Less taxes	−(332)	−(277)	−(216)	−(148)	−(73)	−10	−101	−202	−314	−437
After-tax cash flow (ATCF)	$ 4,524	$ 4,468	$ 4,407	$ 4,339	$ 4,264	$ 4,181	$ 4,090	$ 3,989	$ 3,878	$ 3,754

Total ATCF = $41,894
Holding period (years) = 10
Average ATCF = $4,189

Average rate on after-tax cash flow = $\dfrac{\$4,189}{\$50,000}$ = 8.378%

* See text for assumptions.

† Depreciable basis of $200,000; useful life of 27.5 years; straight-line depreciation method.

153

Adjusted average rate
on net income $ 31,000
                                 $250,000
                                 12.400%

If we include the impact of the before-tax equity reversion on the average rate on before-tax cash flow, we would get:

Total before-tax cash flow
($4,191 for 10 years) $ 41,910
Before-tax equity
reversion   130,877
Total cash return $135,068

Cost of equity investment $ 50,000
Profit $ 85,068

Average profit:
$85,068/10 = $8,507
Adjusted average rate
on before-tax cash flow $ 8,507
                                 $50,000
                                 17.014%

Finally, if we include the impact of the after-tax equity reversion on the average rate on after-tax cash flow, we must calculate the after-tax equity reversion as follows:

Taxes Due on Sale

Expected selling price $300,000
Adjusted basis
($250,000 − $72,730)   − 177,270
Capital gain $122,730
Investor's marginal tax rate   .28
Tax on capital gain $ 34,364

After-tax Equity Reversion

Expected selling price $300,000
Unpaid mortgage   − 169,123
Tax on capital gain   − 34,364
After-tax equity reversion $ 96,513

Next, the adjusted average rate on after-tax cash flow would be:

Total after-tax cash flow $ 41,894
After-tax equity reversion   96,513
Total cash return $138,407
Cost of equity investment   − 50,000
Profit $ 88,407

Average profit:
$88,407/10 = $8,841
Adjusted average return on
after-tax cash flow $ 8,841
                                 $ 50,000
                                 17.682%

Table 9.4 summarizes the results of this example. It is important to note that in all cases the rates of return increase with inclusion of the expected sales proceeds. Also, it is clear that taxes have a decreasing effect on the rates of return.

DECISION RULES

How does the investor use the rules-of-thumb criteria to make an investment decision? Obviously, for example, an investment with a gross income multiplier of 5 means nothing by itself. The investor must compare this with something in order to make the decision.

In using the payback methods, the investor wants to minimize the payback period. Alternatively, if expressed as a rate, the investor wants to maximize this rate of return. For example, if an investment had a calculated net income multiplier of 10 (or equivalently an overall rate of 10 percent), the investor could compare this to multipliers (or rates) on similar investments. If similar properties had multipliers of 12, the investor might conclude that the first project is preferable, since he would prefer the one with the shorter payback period. The first investment may not be acceptable, however.

In using the average rate of return measures, the investor obviously prefers invest-

Table 9.4 SUMMARY OF AVERAGE RATES OF RETURN FOR AN INVESTMENT

	Without Reversion	With Reversion
Average rate on net operating income	10.400%	12.400%
Average rate on before-tax cash flow	8.382%	17.014%
Average rate on after-tax cash flow	8.378%	17.682%

ments with the highest rates of return. A rate of return of 10 percent for one investment is preferred to another investment with a rate of return of 8 percent using the same measure.

Perhaps a more important problem is the fact that there are no standards that permit the analyst the opportunity to decide whether or not a particular investment is acceptable. In the case of the payback methods, what is the maximum acceptable payback period? How is it determined? In the case of the rates of return, what is an acceptable rate of return? How is this determined?

LIMITATIONS OF RULES OF THUMB

Table 9.4 summarizes the results of the analysis of average rates of return. One of the most serious problems with these measures is that the rate of return varies according to the various measures used. Furthermore, one could compare these rates of return to better measures (such as the internal rate of return discussed in the next chapter) and get surprisingly large differences.

The most serious defect in both the payback methods and the average rates of return measures is that no provision is made for the discounting of the future cash flow. Consider the hypothetical investments shown in table 9.5. The investor can only acquire one project and each costs $100,000.

Each investment expects to return the effective gross income amounts during various years as indicated. If the investor were to use the gross income multiplier to decide which investment is preferred, Investments A, B, and C would all be evaluated equally attractive, since each has a GIM of 4.

However, a more careful look indicates that as long as there is a time value of money, Investment B would be preferred to C, and both would be preferred to A. The time value of money consideration implies that, for the same amount, the investor prefers income (or cash flow) in the present rather than the future. In this example, Investments A, B, and C are expected to return $25,000 at the end of year one. However, Investments B and C promise $125,000 in returns over four years while Investment A promises only $100,000. Even if a "zero

Table 9.5 ALTERNATIVE INVESTMENTS

Year	A	B	C	D
0	($100,000)	($100,000)	($100,000)	($100,000)
1	25,000	25,000	25,000	—
2	25,000	50,000	—	—
3	25,000	—	—	—
4	25,000	50,000	100,000	—
5	—	—	—	150,000

capitalization rate" is used, Investment A is unacceptable even for a four-year holding period, since it only promises to return $100,000 over four years for a $100,000 outlay. However, the GIM method fails to distinguish it from Investments B and C.

The GIM approach also views Investments B and C as identical. A more careful look indicates that Investment B is preferred to Investment C for any positive time value of money. This is because we always prefer income now if the amounts are identical. Therefore, the GIM approach fails to select Investment B over C even though the former is clearly preferable.

Finally, if we use the GIM, Investment D is not really considered since it pays back after the other three. So there are serious doubts about the use of payback methods as investment criteria.

Moreover, the average rate of return measures are inappropriate when cash flows change over the investment holding period. To illustrate this point, consider the following investments.

The positive numbers in table 9.6 represent the before-tax cash flows for each mutually exclusive investment. Each investment requires $150,000 equity. The cash flows from Investment R are expected to increase as shown. The before-tax cash flows for Investment S are constant, and they are decreasing for Investment T.

The average rate on before-tax cash flow is clearly identical for all of the investments: ($50,000/$150,000 = 33.33 percent). Using

this measure, the investor might conclude that all are equally attractive. A more careful examination suggests that if money has a time value, Investment T is most attractive since it returns more cash flow more quickly, and Investment R is the least attractive for the same reason.

CURRENT PRACTICES

Recent studies on real estate investment decision-making criteria reveal a diversity in rate-of-return criteria and valuation methods. Why are shortcut methods used despite the overwhelming evidence in favor of discounted cash-flow methods? The answer may be that they provide reliable information on which to make investment decisions. The DCF models require the investor to estimate both the timing and the magnitude of the cash flow for each period. These estimations take considerable expertise and expense. Hence, the investor may be able to make reliable investment decisions without the added expense. This is not to say, however, that he *should* make the decision in this manner. Even minor deviations of the rules of thumb from the time adjusted rate of return may lead to decision errors.

The development of computerized discounted cash flow models have reduced the calculation problems for investors. In a survey of real estate return measures, Wiley found that 91 percent of the investors used some form of before-tax return while 54 percent used some after-tax measure.* Wiley's survey included seventy-two life insurance companies, forty-nine REITs, and thirty-seven real estate corporations. Table 9.7

Table 9.6 ALTERNATIVE INVESTMENTS' EXPECTED BEFORE-TAX CASH FLOWS

Year	R	S	T
0	($150,000)	($150,000)	($150,000)
1	25,000	50,000	75,000
2	50,000	50,000	50,000
3	75,000	50,000	25,000

---

* Robert J. Wiley, "Real Estate Investment Analysis: An Empirical Study," *The Appraisal Journal* 44 (October 1976), pp. 586–592.

Table 9.7 INVESTMENT CRITERIA USED BY INVESTORS

BEFORE-TAX INVESTMENT RETURN CRITERIA

	% of 72 Ins. Cos.	% of 49 REITs	% of 37 Corps.	% of all Respondents
Gross income/purchase price	13	6	11	10
Net income/initial investment	40	35	30	36
Before-tax cash flow/initial equity investment	54	69	49	58
Payback period (time to recapture initial equity investment)	11	8	14	11
Investment yield (time-adjusted rate of return on initial equity investment)	40	27	24	32
Other measures used	6	12	3	7
No before-tax measure	7	2	24	9

AFTER-TAX INVESTMENT RETURN CRITERIA

	72 Ins. Cos.	% of 49 REITs	% of 37 Corps.	% of all Respondents
Earnings after tax (first year)/initial equity investment	11	8	19	12
After-tax cash flow (first year)/initial equity investment	24	12	46	25
Payback period	7	8	11	8
Time-adjusted rate of return	32	10	16	22
Method: Net present value	7	2	11	6
Internal rate of return	29	8	8	18
Profitability index	0	2	3	1
Tax-shelter benefits	19	12	24	18
Other measures	1	0	5	2
No after-tax measure	40	67	27	46

Source: Robert J. Wiley, "Real Estate Investment Analysis: An Empirical Study," *The Appraisal Journal* 44 (October 1976), pp. 586–592.

shows the type of before- and after-tax measures used by the respondents.

Wiley also found that:

1. Return on equity is emphasized. Only 10 percent of the surveyed companies specifically identified the purchase price rather than initial equity investment as the basis for their rate-of-return measures. This suggests that most real estate equity investors analyze their real estate investment proposals in relation to the equity investment.

2. The emphasis is placed on *cash flows.* The survey indicates that the most widely used relative return measures involve cash flow instead of gross income, net income, or other accounting income. The use of cash flow return measures implies that debt service payments are deducted from net income in measuring periodic investment returns. The large percentage of investors reporting the use of after-tax cash flow measures and tax-shelter measures reflects their concern with depreciation and other tax-related

features attendant to ownership of investment properties.

3. There is widespread use of discounted cash flow models. While the single most important return measure (on both before- and after-tax bases) was before-tax cash flow divided by initial equity investment (the equity dividend rate), a large percentage of the investors reported using some form of after-tax discounted cash flow model; the internal rate of return was the most popular variation. Also, 32 percent used some form of time-adjusted return measure on a before-tax basis.

TRADITIONAL APPRAISAL METHODS

The three traditional appraisal methods are the market comparison, income, and cost approaches. These methods also can be used, and should be used, as investment criteria by the real estate investor since he is particularly interested in the market value of the property. Real estate appraisal advocates the use of the comparison approach as the best method for value estimation. Obviously the investor does not want to pay more than the market value for the investment, even if it is worth more to him.

MARKET COMPARISON APPROACH

Using the market comparison (or direct sales comparison) approach, the investor estimates value by comparing the subject property with similar properties in the market. Recently sold comparables are selected, and the appraiser identifies and adjusts for the factors that affect the value. In essence, the skilled interpretation of recent sales in the marketplace of similar property leads to the value estimate.

The comparison approach removes the bias a particular investor might have regarding future income appreciation or depreciation and internal rate of return. The comparison approach gives an indication of the expectations of and the return sought by the "typical" investor. This decision-making process is reflected in the market price of recent sales.

The most serious limitation of the comparison approach is the lack of sales data. The appraiser (investor) must have an adequate number of truly comparable sales in order to estimate the value. Since no two properties are exactly alike, the appraiser (investor) must adjust for differences to arrive at a final value estimate. In general, there are five major categories of adjustments:

1. *Time.* Since sales are historical, the comparables should be adjusted for time. For example, suppose the investor observed a comparable that sold six months ago. How have things changed over this period? Has there been new construction of this type of property? Have factors influencing demand for the property changed? What has the inflation rate been over the period? All of these considerations will influence value, either positively or negatively. Taking these factors into consideration, how much would the property sell for today?

2. *Location.* The location of a property can have a significant impact on the value. Obviously, if the comparable is in the same neighborhood, no adjustment would be necessary. However, if the comparable is in a different neighborhood, the investor must compare the relative advantages and disadvantages of each neighborhood. An adjustment must be made to reflect these differences.

3. *Financing.* Different methods of financing can have a significant impact on the behavior of investors and on the selling prices in the market. It is important to know what type of financing is available at the present time and the terms of financing on the comparable property as well.

4. *Conditions of sale.* The appraiser (investor) must be certain that the buyers and sellers are motivated by ordinary market motives. Factors such as the inclusion of a significant amount of personal property in the sale, inordinate bargaining strength, unusual pressure, and a poorly informed buyer or seller renders a sale useless as a comparable.

5. *Physical characteristics.* This category of adjustment involves many factors, such as size of building, number of rooms, age of the comparable, and lot size, to name a few.

The appraiser (investor) should select a set of comparables and adjust these to the five key categories. The investor is asking the question: What would the comparable have sold for if it were like the subject property?

The Market Approach: An Example. To illustrate the market approach to value estimation, suppose an investor is considering the purchase of an apartment building. Table 9.8 gives the information collected on four comparable properties and shows the unadjusted prices per apartment and per room. Notice that the sales price indicates a range from $12,492 to $17,088 per apartment. The sale price per room ranges between $3,217 and $3,924. Also given is the gross income multiplier, which ranges between 5.44 and 6.10.

Table 9.9 gives the adjustment grid for the comparables. In this example, we only adjusted for time, location, and condition of the building. The adjustments are based on the price per room. Notice that sale 1 was not adjusted for time or location but there was a 10 percent upward adjustment for building condition. Obviously, the appraiser decided that the building condition on comparable 1 was 10 percent inferior to that of the subject. Sales 2 and 3 are adjusted upward by 10 percent for time and sale 4 was adjusted upward by 15 percent for time. Likewise, the other adjustments shown in table 9.9 were made. Positive adjustments were made if the comparable was inferior to the subject, and negative adjustments were made if the comparable was superior. The net result was a price per room that ranged from $3,858 for comparable 4 to $4,088 for comparable 3.

The subject property contains 2,171 rooms. Multiplying the number of rooms by the estimated value per room results in a total value, as shown in the last line of table 9.9, between $8,375,700 and $8,875,000. The final value estimate depends on how much weight each of the comparables is given.

How could the investor use this value estimate to make the investment decision? First, he would compare this estimated market value to the asking price for the property. Suppose, for example, that the asking price was $4,300 per room. The investor would probably conclude that the property is overpriced since the maximum indicated value from the comparison approach is only $4,088. So he would use the estimate from comparison as the standard by which to make the investment decision.

COST APPROACH

The value of an investment is calculated by adding the estimated land value to the depreciated value of the building. The steps in the cost approach are as follows:

Table 9.8 COMPARABLE APARTMENT SALES: AN EXAMPLE

Sale Number	Sale: Months Ago	Sale Price	Number of Apartments	Price per Apartment	Number of Rooms	Price per Room	Gross Income	Gross Income Multiplier
1. Mill Grove Apartments	2	$5,456,000	338	$16,142	1,525	$3,578	$950,000	5.74
2. Plymouth Park Apartments	24	$3,674,000	234	15,700	1,035	3,550	674,500	5.44
3. Towne Coast Apartments	28	$4,497,000	360	12,492	1,398	3,217	783,700	5.73
4. Chatham Village Apartments	35	$5,639,000	330	17,088	1,437	3,924	923,200	6.10

Source: William M. Shenkel, *Modern Real Estate Appraisal* (New York: McGraw-Hill Book Company, 1978), p. 441.

Table 9.9 APARTMENT ADJUSTMENT GRID: AN EXAMPLE

Sale Adjustment Factors	Sale 1	Sale 2	Sale 3	Sale 4
Sale price	$5,456,000	$3,674,000	$4,497,000	$5,639,000
Number of rooms	1,525	1,035	1,398	1,437
Price per room	$3,578	$3,550	$3,217	$3,924
Time adjustment	0	+10%	+10%	+15%
	$3,578	$3,905	$3,539	$4,513
Condition of building	+10%	0	+10%	−10%
	$3,936	$3,905	$3,893	$4,061
Location	0	0	+5%	−5%
	$3,936	$3,905	$4,088	$3,858
Indicated value, subject property, 2,171 rooms	$8,545,000	$8,478,000	$8,875,000	$8,375,700

Source: William M. Shenkel, *Modern Real Estate Appraisal* (New York: McGraw-Hill Book Company, 1978), p. 442.

1. *Estimate reproduction cost of the improvements.* Improvements include the building as well as other site alterations, such as paving and landscaping. Reproduction cost is the cost of constructing a replica that is identical in shape, structure, materials, and workmanship. Generally, the cost estimate is derived from the costs of recently constructed buildings in the same locality and with the same materials as the building under appraisal. The most widely used cost estimation procedure is the unit comparison on a square-foot or cubic-foot basis.

2. *Estimate the loss in value to the improvements.* In the cost appraisal, depreciation means the loss in value to the building due to deterioration and obsolescence. Deterioration is the normal wear and tear over time. Obsolescence can be either functional or economic in nature. Functional obsolescence is the loss in value resulting from changes in design, technology, or tastes and preferences of the market. Economic obsolescence refers to changes in the neighborhood and market conditions, external of the property itself. Thus, depreciation is the difference between the cost of the building new and the actual price it could command in the present market.

3. *Subtract the loss in value from the reproduction cost.* This results in the depreciated value of the improvements.

4. *Estimate the land value.* Land values are generally estimated using the market comparison approach.

5. *Add the estimated depreciated building value to the land value.* The result is the estimated total value of the property.

It should be noted that depreciation in the cost approach is not the same as depreciation for income tax purposes. The former is a loss in value while the latter is simply a deduction for tax purposes.

Cost Approach: An Example. To illustrate value estimation using the cost approach, suppose the following. The investor has an apartment building that contains 100,000 square feet of area. The estimated reproduction cost from comparable properties recently constructed is $45 per square foot. The building is not new and thus it is estimated that the loss in value from physical depreciation is 20 percent of the new cost. There appears to be no economic or functional loss in value. The land value is estimated at $700,000.

Using these assumptions, the value under the cost approach would be as follows:

1. Reproduction cost of $4,500,000 (100,000 square feet times cost of $45 per square foot). Paving and landscaping costs of $25,000
2. Loss in value: Physical depreciation of 20%, or $905,000. Economic depreciation—none, functional depreciation—none
3. Depreciated value of building and other improvements: $4,500,000 plus $25,000 minus $905,000 equals $3,620,000
4. Estimated land value of $700,000
5. Total value: land value plus depreciated building value, or $4,320,000

The cost approach is criticized as a method for estimating value primarily because cost is not necessarily equal to value. Simply because it costs $4,320,000 to build the investment does not necessarily mean that this is its total value. However, the cost approach serves as a useful check along with other methods.

The Income Approach

In chapter 2, we argued that the major objective of the real estate investor is to maximize wealth from investments. Value was defined as the present worth of the expected future stream of income received from ownership of the property. The amount an investor is willing to pay to acquire a property takes into account the expected annual cash flow as well as the reversion at the end of the holding period.

Operationally, the definition of value is expressed in the following equation:

(9.11)

$$V = \frac{NOI}{R}$$

where:

V = Value

NOI = Expected income stream

R = Rate of capitalization

For example, for an investment with an expected income stream of $100,000 and with a rate of capitalization of 10 percent, the value is $1 million.

Equation (9.11) is the basis of the income approach to value estimation. Basically the appraiser/investor faces two questions in order to estimate value.

1. What is the expected income stream?
2. What is the "cap" rate?

The steps in the traditional income approach to value estimation are:

1. Estimate potential gross income.
2. Estimate and deduct a vacancy and bad debt loss allowance to derive effective gross income.
3. Estimate and deduct expenses of operation to derive net operating income.
4. Estimate remaining economic life (or the duration) and pattern of the projected income stream.
5. Select an applicable capitalization method and technique.
6. Develop the appropriate rate or rates.
7. Select the method to derive a value estimate using the income approach.

The basic premise of the income approach is expressed as in equation (9.11). Because the income referred to in this relationship is net operating income (NOI), the first three steps in the procedure are designed to estimate it, as we have previously discussed.

Once NOI is determined, the appropriate rate must be derived. The economic life and pattern of the income stream should be considered before selecting a capitalization method.

Deriving Capitalization Rates. There are several methods used to derive capitalization rates. The first method extracts the rate from comparable sales in the market.

Suppose that an investor observes three recently sold properties that are similar to the investment being valued. The rate can be derived from the market (as shown in table 9.10) using equation (9.11) and solving for R. The market extracted rate in this example would be about 11.8 percent.

When deriving a rate from the market, it is very important that the properties be similar in terms of age, location, quality, condition, and other significant factors. Additionally, if the sales occurred at different points in time, market and financing conditions must also be similar. For example, suppose the investment under consideration had an NOI of $50,000; the value, using the rates from table 9.10, would be:

$$V = \frac{\$50,000}{.118}$$

$$V = \$423,729$$

A second method of rate derivation is called the band of investment or mortgage–equity analysis. This method considers the return required by the mortgage lender, as indicated by the annual mortgage constant (*MC*), and the return required by equity investors, as indicated by the equity divi-

dend rate (*EDR*). Mortgage and equity returns are weighted by the proportion they contribute to total value. The rate (*R*) is derived using the following:

(9.12)
$$R = L/V\,(MC) + E/V\,(EDR)$$

The following example illustrates the band of investment method. An investor is able to obtain a 75 percent loan at 11 percent, with a thirty-year term. The investor demands a 13 percent equity dividend rate on the investment. The overall capitalization rate is calculated as follows:

$$.75 \times .1143 = .0857$$
$$\underline{.25 \times .13\ \ \ = .0325}$$
$$R = .1182$$

In order to satisfy the requirements of the mortgage and equity, the investor would pay the price indicated by capitalizing the NOI of the property at a rate of 11.82 percent. Since the information used in the band of investment is taken from the market, the rate derived by this method should be an indication of the overall capitalization rate in the market. For example, supposing the investment under consideration had an NOI of $50,000, the value would be:

$$V = \frac{\$50,000}{.1182}$$
$$V = \$423,012$$

SUMMARY

Appraisal techniques consist of a variety of methods used to evaluate an investment. The payback methods and the average rates of return methods have been illustrated in this chapter with corresponding examples. These methods may be used when com-

Table 9.10 EXAMPLE OF MARKET-EXTRACTED CAPITALIZATION RATE

	Sale 1	Sale 2	Sale 3
NOI	$ 40,000	$ 53,150	$ 47,500
Sale price	$340,000	$450,000	$400,500
Indicated R	11.76%	11.81%	11.86%

paring an investment with other possible investments, providing the investor with a selection tool for his decision. As previously mentioned, an inherent limitation in these methods is the lack of regard for the time value of money. This is taken into consideration in chapter 10, as attention is turned to the discounted cash flow models.

10

DISCOUNTED CASH FLOW MODELS

DISCOUNTED cash flow (DCF) models have a long tradition in finance but have only recently been applied to real estate investment analysis. The concept of time-adjusted investment techniques and discounted cash flow measures, such as the internal rate of return, are the next logical step in analysis, given the use of present value tables (chapter 3), the problems and inconsistencies with many of the traditional investment criteria (chapter 9), and the nature of the cash flows being valued in real estate investment analysis (chapters 4 through 8).

This chapter examines the discounted cash flow approach including a discussion of the basic model, the importance of discounted cash flow techniques versus traditional methods, the problems with data requirements such as the necessity of accurate estimation of future cash flows, the measurement of risk, and the application of present value tables for real estate investment analysis. The core of the chapter derives the basic valuation model that can measure the net present value of equity (NPV) and the internal rate of return on equity (r). The final sections compare the investment value and the internal rate of return approaches and briefly discuss additional advanced techniques and risk analysis.

THE DISCOUNTED CASH FLOW APPROACH

Modern real estate investment analysis has generally adopted the discounted cash flow approach to valuation. There are many reasons why this approach is favored. First, it can measure cash flows throughout the life of the investment, as well as the impact of the reversion at the time of sale. Second, the measure of benefits used, after-tax cash flows, is selected since this measure takes into account factors such as operating expenses, financing expenses, depreciation and interest, tax shelter, and taxation. Third, the after-tax equity reversion takes into account the selling expenses, the repayment of outstanding principal, and taxes at the time of sale. Fourth, this approach permits any or all of these variables to change over time, at individual rates of change, if the analyst believes such changes are necessary. Fifth, since expected cash flows in the future and the expected equity reversion at a future selling date are not received by the investor today, this technique incorporates a consideration of the time value of money to permit the adjustment of actual dollars into present-value, time-adjusted dollars. Finally, the various types of risk may be incorporated into the discounted cash flow approach. In addition, changing risk levels may also be treated although this may become a difficult task. Therefore, for these and other reasons, the discounted cash flow approach enjoys a prominent place among investment criteria for real estate investment analysis.

The use of discounted cash flow models requires the understanding of more technical methods of analysis, additional data requirements and estimates, and additional time and effort on the part of the analyst. We believe that familiarity with the basic approach and an understanding of the concept of discounted models can help investors improve their analysis of potential real estate investment, and in many cases, eliminate reliance upon the traditional rules of thumb.

The Basic Discounted Cash Flow Model

The entire chapter is oriented around the discounted cash flow to equity valuation model. A review of the topics covered from chapters 4 through 8 reveals that each chapter deals with a particular step in the real estate investment process. This process assists in making real estate investment choices. The model introduced in this section is the criterion on which real estate investment decisions may be made. Therefore, this model is very important in completing the final step in the real estate investment.

Given the estimation of effective gross income (chapters 4 and 5), we presented an analysis of operating expenses (chapter 6). The difference between these two measures is called net operating income. Debt service

from financing decisions (chapter 7) can be subtracted from net operating income to get before-tax cash flow. Since investors base their investment decisions on after-tax cash flow, the tax treatment of income and tax shelter benefits need to be included (chapter 8). After the deduction of taxes from before-tax cash flow, the investor arrives at after-tax cash flow (ATCF).

A similar development takes place in the other form of cash flow: the reversion. Selling price less selling expenses yields the net selling price. The unpaid mortgage balance is then calculated and subtracted from the net selling price to get the before-tax equity reversion. Finally, the taxes due on sale are deducted to arrive at after-tax equity reversion (ATER).

The investor can make the investment decision by applying the basic equity valuation model:

(10.1)
$$E = \sum_{i=1}^{n} \frac{ATCF_i}{(1 + k_e)^i} + \frac{ATER_n}{(1 + k_e)^n}$$

where:

E = Investment value of equity

$ATCF$ = After-tax cash flow each ith period

$ATER$ = Expected after-tax equity reversion in the nth period

k_e = Investor's required rate of return on equity

n = Expected holding period

Since $ATCF_i$, $ATER_n$, n, and k_e are typically known (or able to be forecasted), the unknown for which the analyst solves is E. *The investment value of equity is the greatest amount of equity (total value less mortgage debt) that the investor would be willing to invest to acquire the property.*

Alternatively, the basic model can be written as the net present value, NPV, as:

(10.2)
$$NPV = \sum_{i=1}^{n} \frac{ATCF_i}{(1 + k_e)^i} + \frac{ATER_n}{(1 + k_e)^n}$$
$$- (MV - MD)$$

where:

NPV = Net present value

MV = Market value at the time of purchase

MD = Morgage debt

IMPORTANCE OF DISCOUNTED CASH FLOW ANALYSIS

Real estate investment is basically a capitalization process: Investors give up a known, certain amount in exchange for an expected, but uncertain, stream of future cash flows. Capitalization is the conversion of an expected future stream of benefits into a present value sum. Therefore, capitalization of income or cash flow is an integral part of investment analysis.

There are four major reasons why discounted cash flow models are superior to the traditional methods discussed in chapter 9:

1. Changing income (and cash flow) streams.
2. Changing levels of risk.
3. Differing size and types of expected future benefits.
4. The time value of money concept.

Changing Benefit Streams. Unlike other investments such as corporate bonds and some common stocks, the financial benefits of real estate investments vary each period. In the case of apartment houses, for example, despite the fixing of contract rent and the predominance of level-payment amortized mortgages, operating expenses may vary significantly throughout the leasing period. This causes net operating income to vary. As net operating income varies, so does before-tax cash flow with the fixed debt service payment.

Futhermore, discounted cash flow techniques rely on after-tax cash flow payments in calculating value and return. Chapters 1 and 8 showed that after-tax cash flow differs from before-tax cash flow by the amount of income tax to be paid each period. Since income taxes are calculated by the investor's tax rate times the amount of taxable income, changes in taxable income (or the tax rate) will result in changes in after-tax cash flow. The cash flow statement in chapter 1 also showed that taxable income varies according to changes in interest payments and depreciation allowances (if an accelerated depreciation method is used). Therefore since the equity valuation model uses after-tax cash flow as a measure of benefits, changes in net operating income, interest payments, depreciation allowances, or tax rates expected in the future will result in the changing benefit stream from the investment.

Finally, if rental and income payments vary due to monthly lease agreements, if vacancies vary, or if bad debt problems are particularly relevant, effective gross income and potential gross income will vary. If multiple financing options are used, causing financial expenses to vary from period to period, measures relating to the equity position also may be altered. These possibilities suggest that changing benefit streams are more likely to occur than not, and as a result, discounted cash flow models are much more suited to handling these problems.

Changing Levels of Risk. Since financial and economic markets are dynamic in nature, events frequently occur that affect the risk/return opportunities of investments.

For example, at the time the investment is being evaluated, there is a certain amount of market risk associated with the investment, as discussed in chapter 4. If the amount of risk is expected to vary over the expected holding period of the investment, the analyst is concerned with the fact that as the riskiness of the investment increased (decreased), the investment value would fall (rise) in response to the change in risk. Similarly, changes in the required rate of return on equity would occur in proportion to changes in the riskiness of the investment.

Discounted cash flow models are better suited to handle this measurement problem than direct capitalization or other single-period rules of thumb. In some cases, the necessary adjustment can be made to income estimates when risk is expected to increase. Other models show that expected increasing risk levels result in falling values of income or cash flows. Finally, complex models may be used to account for expected changes in future risk levels in a discounted cash flow approach. Although this development is beyond the scope of this book, it demonstrates the fact that discounted cash flow models can be extremely flexible and therefore are valuable for real estate analysts.

Some investors suggest that increasing the capitalization rate by using traditional rules of thumb has the same effect as raising the risk-adjusted discount rate used in discounted cash flow models. In some cases, it may be possible to get consistent or identical results. However, in view of other limitations and problems with the earlier techniques, the measurement of expected changes in risk is best handled in the discounted cash flow approach.

Differing Sizes and Types of Benefits. Another advantage is the ability to ac-curately account for income or cash flow figures that are expected to vary significantly from year to year. Traditional techniques have either disregarded future benefit streams which were expected to be significantly different than the current one, averaged the expected income or cash flow for the next few years, or stabilized the benefits in some fashion. The ability of discounted cash flow models to reflect the expected size of the income or cash flow in the year in which it is expected to occur is a major improvement over other techniques.

Real estate investment analysis often involves property where an income is earned over the holding period and a capital gain is expected at the time of sale. Thus, the investor actually expects to receive two types of benefits: periodic cash flow receipts and a lump sum cash flow at the end of the holding period. These benefits cause significant problems for investors using rules of thumb.

Discounted cash flow models can adequately account for both types of benefits. Furthermore, estimates of benefit sizes can be made without specifying the capitalization rate or investment value. Discounted cash flow procedures also help the investor to account for rising property values, equity buildup, or rising income levels due to changes in demand. The investor who uses rules of thumb either takes rough averages of the changing variables, assumes the changes have no effect on the investment and does nothing about them, or is unable to evaluate the effects of these changes on income-producing real estate.

Time Value of Money. Finally, discounted cash flow techniques are important due to the existence of the time value of money in productive market economies. The concept of the time value of money is critical to investment decisions because returns from the investment often occur at various intervals throughout the holding period. The present value of all of the expected income or cash flow payments is less than the sum of the payments, even without inflation or risk, and the analyst must evaluate investments on a time-adjusted basis. Discounted cash flow models help the investor to take into account the *timing* and the *amount* of payments and receipts. Then this factor is incorporated into the decision criteria.

The traditional single period measures either ignore the time value of money or assume these are consistent with discounted cash flow models. However, the former action leads to inferior investment choices while the latter is more general and flexible and therefore preferable.

Discounted cash flow models were developed due to the effect of declining values of future benefits. As we will see, comparisons based on total dollar receipts (income, cash flows, etc.) disregard the measurement of the time value of money and therefore result in a wrong choice. This point is demonstrated in the following example. An investor wishes to decide between investments G and H. Each costs the same amount. Investment G is expected to yield $100 per year for ten years. Investment H is expected to yield $1,000 at the end of the tenth year. Each investment is believed to be in the same risk class. Should he assume that these two are similar? Obviously, the answer is no. Although both yield the same total dollars of benefits, $1,000, investment G will yield some return each year. Since investment H is not expected to return any dollars until the end of ten years, the time value of money theory says that investment G is preferred to investment H at any positive discount rate.

Therefore, discounted cash flow analysis can be a very powerful and useful tool for analysts. It forms the framework for most modern real estate investment analysis and is flexible enough to permit adjustments according to market changes. Finally, it permits a treatment of the time value of money considerations that are so crucial in making financial decisions.

FORECASTING FUTURE CASH FLOWS

One of the most difficult requirements is the need to estimate future cash flows for use in the discounted cash flow analysis. Some proponents of the rules-of-thumb techniques point out that failure (or inability) to accurately forecast expected future cash flows results in discounted cash flow methods that are no more reliable than the rules of thumb and therefore no more powerful or useful. The extent to which future cash flows cannot be estimated very precisely, they argue, is the extent to which rules of thumb are as adequate a technique.

This argument has a certain degree of merit. A relatively accurate estimate of future cash flows is necessary for effective investment decision making. Obviously, using unreliable numbers in a formula results in an almost meaningless exercise. Therefore, the use of discounted cash flow techniques requires a careful forecast and estimation of future cash flows and possible trends in their amounts.

Since one does not really *know* what will happen in the future, forecasts of cash flows can be very risky. Of what value is a technique that depends heavily on the reliability of such a forecast?

Normally, we would expect a high margin of error in such a forecast. Nonetheless, this is somewhat better than no forecast at all because the investment choice must be made, and some analysis is needed to screen out poor investments. Since an investment choice is made after every analysis, the analyst is better off making his choice with poor data rather than with no data.

The ability to estimate future cash flows is particularly critical. If an analyst was *certain* about the future cash flows, the investment problem would be solved. He would be able to calculate the rate of return and value of the investment, and whether or not to buy it given the asking price. The analysis would be quick and easy, but in fact, moot. But since this is not the case, risk must be incorporated into the analysis.

ACCOUNTING FOR RISK IN DISCOUNTED CASH FLOW MODELS

There are many ways of accounting for risk and uncertainty using discounted cash flow models. Although others could be added, we include some of the well-known techniques: (a) conservatism, (b) risk-adjusted discount rates, (c) certainty-equivalent approach, (d) measures of variability, (e) decision trees and sensitivity analysis, (f) probabilistic modeling and simulation, and (g) modern capital market measures.

CONSERVATISM

A rudimentary method of assessing risk is to choose low estimates of cash benefits, high estimates of cash outflows (costs), and to evaluate the net benefits using a relatively high discount rate. These actions result in a low value estimate or a high required rate of return estimate. If the analyst accepts the project as a good investment, he or she feels even more anxious to make the purchase since this analysis assumed bad outcomes in every case. So, a conservative outlook regarding benefits and costs limits potential projects to the best alternative.

The problem with this method is that the estimates used are more conservative than what the analyst believes will occur and if the analyst seeks to maximize his wealth, conservative action results in the exclusion of some projects that would be acceptable under normal conditions.

RISK-ADJUSTED DISCOUNT RATES

As we discussed in chapter 4, as the risk associated with an investment rises, the nominal (or market) rate (or required rate of return) on that investment increases as the risk is incorporated into the discount rate. The analyst accomplishes the same thing by applying higher risk-adjusted discount rates in order to lower the investment value of the project.

Conceptually, this approach is not difficult. However, some analysts find it hard to assess discount rate levels for each type of risky investment as well as the relevant increase in rates due to the perceived increase in risk levels.

CERTAINTY-EQUIVALENT APPROACH

This financial technique offers an alternative to the risk-adjusted discount approach. This approach argues that it is conceptually equivalent and operationally easier to account for the risk associated with the likelihood of the cash flows than it is to account for the time value of money using the risk-free discount rate.

Here the analyst applies a *certainty-equivalent coefficient* to each income or cash flow payment. This coefficient may vary from 0.00 to 1.00 depending on the degree of certainty associated with the receipt of the payment. Typically, one expects cash flows in the immediate future to be more easily estimated than those in the distant future. In the instance of one year, a certainty-equivalent coefficient of almost

1.00 would be multiplied by the expected cash flow. Those expected five years hence may warrant a coefficient of .50. The final year's cash flow is far less certain so .20 may be used. Obviously, the analyst must decide on the relative sizes of the certainty-equivalents based on when the cash flow will occur. In this sense, the risk of the cash flow not occurring is accounted for independently of the consideration of the time value of money.

The certainty-equivalent approach is attractive for a number of reasons. First, it provides a conceptual basis for accounting for risk that is consistent with more traditional methods. Second, it may be easier to use because risk and the time value of money are treated separately. This may be important depending on the risk characteristics of the project in question. Third, the certainty-equivalent approach requires no new information over the risk-adjusted discount rate approach. Finally, it is easier to derive investment results when risk is not constant over time. Since risk tends to be resolved over time, this last condition offers a strong argument for its adoption.

MEASURES OF VARIABILITY

Traditionally, measures of risk and uncertainty in finance gauge the expected variability of cash flows from the expected value. The most common of these measures are the *variance* and the *standard deviation*.

There are many reasons why these measures are useful. First, both are operationally consistent with each other since, by definition, the standard deviation is the square root of the variance. Second, both use deviations of outcomes from expected values to measure the degree of variability in the distribution of outcomes to measure risk.

Finally, modern statistical analysis demonstrates that *confidence intervals* and *hypothesis testing* are possible using these measures of variability. Confidence intervals permit analysts to develop a range of possible outcomes based on the expected value and the variance (or standard deviations) of outcomes. Hypothesis testing permits the analyst to statistically investigate the likelihood of achieving certain goals or objectives. Although these techniques are complex, they are very useful in providing information about risk. However, they are also beyond the introductory nature of this book (see the bibliography).

DECISION TREES AND SENSITIVITY ANALYSIS

Two additional well-known techniques for measuring risk are *decision trees* and *sensitivity analysis*. Decision trees require the analyst to estimate the likelihood of each outcome at every expected decision point in the future. In this manner, he will grasp an understanding of the relationships between each decision and the probabilities of occurrence. Sensitivity analysis is the estimation of investment values by systematic alteration of the inputs. This technique is characterized by the question, "What if . . . ?" In other words, the analyst might ask "What if effective gross income fell by 10 percent?"

These techniques are helpful in judging the links and inputs of various investment decisions (decision trees) and the sensitivity of value of return to changes in certain input values (sensitivity analysis). Furthermore, this type of analysis is available to most analysts in real estate investment.

PROBABILISTIC MODELING AND SIMULATION

A logical extension of decision trees and sensitivity analysis is the incorporation of random elements directly into the decision-making process. *Probabilistic modeling* involves the use of subjective probability distributions around various input variables. For example, the analyst estimates the distribution of outcomes around effective gross income, operating expenses, debt service, growth rates in income and expenses, growth rate in property values, and others. The probabilistic model then uses this information to make a valuation estimate. *Simulation* is an integral part of this process since the distributions of inputs for a large set of observations are typically generated by a computer program. Many computer services now offer these types of programs to investors.

Modern Capital Market Measures

The final method measures risk by integrating risk and return into a modern capital market approach. This involves measuring the risk of an asset as a function of variability with other investments (covariability), or with the real estate market in general rather than variability of its own possible outcomes. This *covariance* is essential to modern portfolio theory.

To the extent that the risk of real estate investments is viewed as a function of the relationship between the expected returns of one investment with the expected returns of other investments in the market, the development of market measures of risk incorporating principles of diversification, portfolio theory, and capital market theory may be useful. Recent attempts to modify financial models for real estate investments have made some gains in this direction although more development is expected.

USING THE REAL ESTATE INVESTMENT TABLES

Discounted cash flow models use discount rates based on the time value of money and,

in the typical case, a risk premium. Therefore, valuation factors have been applied to these models to help account for these. A set of real estate investment tables is included in appendix A to assist in making real estate investment calculations.

Present Value of Single Sums and Future Selling Prices

The time value of money shows that a future amount of money is worth less than the same amount to be received in the present. For example, if an expected $100 cash flow is to be received in five years, the value will be less than $100 today. How much less depends on the rate of discount.

In this case, we find that at an annual rate of 9 percent, the $100 expected in five yeas will be equal to $64.99 on a present value basis.

(10.3)
$$
\begin{aligned}
\text{Present value} &= \text{(Single sum)} \\
\text{of single} &\quad \times \text{(Present value of \$1)} \\
\text{sum} &= \$100 \times .64993 \\
&= \$64.99
\end{aligned}
$$

Table 1 in appendix A gives the value of the annual factors.

Another application of this table is to estimate the present worth of a property that is expected to sell for $500,000 in ten years. For this example, we do not seek to value the entire investment; we simply need an estimate of the value of the future expected selling price. The model to value the entire investment will be presented later in the chapter.

We need a rate indicative of the time value of money plus the risk associated with the investment. Assume we estimate this rate to be 12 percent. The answer then is:

(10.4)

$$\text{Present value of future selling price} = \text{(Future selling price)} \times \text{(Present value \$1 factor)}$$

$$= \$500,000 \times .32197$$

$$= \$160,986.50$$

In other words, using 12 percent as a discount rate, the expected future selling price is $160,986.50.

PRESENT VALUE OF UNEQUAL SERIES OF CASH FLOW

Table 1 of appendix A also can be used to calculate the present value of a set of payments to be received by the investor at various points in the future. For example, the investor may wish to know the present value of the following set of after-tax cash flows in table 10.1. If the investor chooses to use a discount rate of 12.5 percent and all payments are expected to occur at the end of each year, he could find the present value of the unequal series of each flow in the table as well. The present value factors are from table 1 in appendix A. These multiplied by the expected cash flow to get the present value. All of these are summed to yield the total present value. Thus, today, the owner of this stream of expected cash flows would value it at $14,780.67.

Note that the sum of the six cash flows equals $25,000. The use of the present value tables will always result in a present value amount which is less than the sum of the discounted cash flows, assuming some positive rate.

PRESENT VALUE OF EQUAL SERIES OF CASH FLOW (ANNUITY)

Assume an investor wishes to find the present value of the stream of after-cash flows in table 10.2.

In this case, the investor expects to receive eight cash flow payments of $5,000 at the end of each year. The present value of the payments is calculated, at 11 percent, as shown in the table. Therefore, an investor would value the ownership of this equal series at $25,730.62.

If the series is long (say twenty-five years), the calculations can become quite tedious. However, it is not necessary to calculate the present value of each cash flow if the payments are equal. In this case it is called an annuity and tables are available that permit the calculation of the present value of an annuity.

As an example, let us assume an investor wishes to value the following set of cash flows and, at the end of the fifteenth year, he expects to receive a final cash payment (equity reversion), shown in table 10.3. The investor also chooses a discount rate of 12 percent to reflect the risk associated with this investment.

Table 10.1 PRESENT VALUE OF A SERIES OF UNEQUAL CASH FLOWS

Year	ATCF	Present Value Factor at 12.5%	Present Value
1	$ 1,000	.88889	$ 888.89
2	2,000	.79012	1,580.25
3	3,000	.70233	2,107.00
4	4,000	.62429	2,497.18
5	5,000	.55493	2,774.65
6	10,000	.49327	4,932.70
		Total present value =	$14,780.67

Table 10.2 Present Value of an Annuity at 11 Percent

Year	ATCF	PVF	Present Value
1	5,000	.90090	$ 4,504.51
2	5,000	.81162	$ 4,058.11
3	5,000	.73119	$ 3,655.96
4	5,000	.65873	$ 3,293.65
5	5,000	.59345	$ 2,967.26
6	5,000	.53464	$ 2,673.21
7	5,000	.48166	$ 2,408.29
8	5,000	.43393	$ 2,169.63
		Total present value =	$25,730.62

Table 10.3 Illustration of Equal Cash Flows

Year	Cash Flow	Equity Reversion
	($)	($)
1	10,000	
2	10,000	
3	10,000	
.	.	
.	.	
.	.	
15	10,000	250,000

Using table 1 in appendix A, compute the present value of each of the fifteen cash flows as if each cash flow was in an unequal stream and the present value of the future selling price. The investor would conclude that the present value of the expected cash flow and equity reversion is $113,782.76 using a 12 percent discount.

Obviously, the value derived above is contingent upon the choice of discount rates. Table 10.4 shows the effect of changing discount rates on the present value of the previous example.

An analysis shows that the higher the discount rate, the lower the present values.

THE INVESTMENT VALUE OF EQUITY (E)

Given the basic method demonstrated in the preceding section, we can now develop the *investment value of equity* (E) model. This model provides the investor with an approach that can then be compared to the market (or asking) price to see if it is an acceptable investment. This measure emphasizes the equity position of the investor and values two major components: *after-tax cash flow* and *after-tax equity reversion*. Of course, emphasis is also placed on the decision rules for making the analysis.

Operating After-tax Cash Flow

The preceding example calculated investment values using cash flows as measures of benefits. In valuing the portion attributable to the equity holder, the analyst can choose which type of cash flow measure to use. However, there are many reasons why

Table 10.4 Impact of Rate on Present Value

Discount Rate (%)	Present Value of Cash Flow ($)	Present Value of Equity Reversion ($)	Present Value of All Cash Payments ($)
7	91,078.83	90,611.50	181,690.33
8	85,594.45	78,810.50	164,404.95
10	76,060.67	59,848.00	135,908.67
12	68,108.76	45,674.00	113,782.76
14	61,421.67	35,024.00	96,445.67
18	50,915.72	20,079.00	70,994.72
20	46,754.75	16,226.25	62,981.00

an investor would prefer to use an after-tax cash flow figure.

Chapter 1 defined after-tax cash flow as net operating income less debt service less tax payments. This can be represented as:

(10.5)
$$ATCF_i = NOI_i - DS_i - T_i$$

where:

$ATCF_i$ = After-tax cash flow in the ith period

NOI_i = Net operating income in the ith period

DS_i = Debt service in the ith period

T_i = Income tax liability in the ith period

Furthermore, we can split debt service into two components: interest expense and principal amortization:

(10.6)
$$DS_i = I_i + A_i$$

where:

I_i = Interest expense in the ith period

A_i = Principal amortization in the ith period

Recall that income taxes are calculated by multiplying the investor's marginal tax rate times net operating income plus the replacement reserve less expense less depreciation, or:

(10.7)
$$T_i = t(NOI_i + RR_i - I_i - D_i - AFC_i)$$

where:

t = Investor's marginal tax rate

RR_i = Reserve for replacement in the ith period

I_i = Interest deduction in the ith period

D_i = Depreciation allowance in the ith period

AFC_i = Amortized financing costs in the ith period

By substituting equations (10.6) and (10.7) into equation (10.5), we get:

(10.8)
$$ATCF_i = NOI_i - (I_i + A_i)$$
$$- t(NOI_i + RR_i - I_i$$
$$- D_i - AFC_i)$$

It is interesting to note that independent of the method selected by the analyst and permitted by the IRS, the depreciaiton allowance affects the after-tax cash flow only in the last term of equation (10.8). The benefit of depreciation result from a reduction in income tax liability and in this way, depreciaiton allowances alter the after-tax cash flow to the investor.

The discounted value of the after-tax cash flows is:

(10.9)
$$PV \text{ of } ATCF = \frac{ATCF_1}{(1 + k_e)^1} + \frac{ATCF_2}{(1 + k_e)^2}$$
$$+ \frac{ATCF_3}{(1 + k_e)^3} + \cdots$$
$$+ \frac{ATCF_n}{(1 + k_e)^n}$$
$$= \sum_{i=1}^{n} \frac{ATCF_1}{(1 + k_e)^i}$$

where:

$PV \text{ of } ATCF$ = Present value of after-tax cash flow stream

k_e = Required rate of return on equity

This formula represents the discounted value of after-tax cash flows for the expected holding period. It permits after-tax cash flow estimates to be constant each period as in an annuity, or permits the cash flows to vary from year to year, as in the typical investment.

The After-tax Equity Reversion

However, equation (10.9) fails to take into account the expected selling price at the end of the nth year, the satisfaction of the unpaid mortgage note, or taxes due at the time of sale (capital gains, recapture, or minimum taxes). A better valuation model would take account of these factors since these affect the cash flow to the investor at the time of sale. Therefore, the analyst needs to incorporate these considerations into one model. Equation (10.10) provides the necessary measure: the after-tax equity reversion.

(10.10)
$$ATER_n = SP_n - SE_n - UM_n - TDS_n$$

where:

$ATER_n$ = After-tax equity reversion at the end of the nth period

SP_n = Estimated selling price at the end of the nth period

SE_n = Selling expenses

UM_n = Unpaid mortgage balance at the end of the nth period

TDS_n = Taxes due on sale at the end of the nth period

Since ATER does not result in cash flow for the investor until the nth period (year), the value of this component can be found as follows:

(10.11)
$$PV \text{ of } ATER = \frac{ATER_n}{(1 + k_e)^n}$$

where:

$PV \text{ of } ATER$ = Present value after-tax equity reversion

Therefore, by combining equations (10.9) and (10.11), we get the complete equity valuation model.

(10.12)
$$E = (PV \text{ of } ATCF) + (PV \text{ of } ATER)$$
$$= \frac{ATCF_1}{(1 + k_e)^1} + \frac{ATCF_2}{(1 + k_e)^2} + \frac{ATCF^3}{(1 + k_e)^3}$$
$$+ \cdots + \frac{ATCF_n}{(1 + k_e)^n} + \frac{ATER_n}{(1 + k_e)^n}$$
$$= \sum_{i=1}^{n} \frac{ATCF_i}{(1 + k_e)^i} + \frac{ATER_n}{(1 + k_e)^n}$$

where E = Investment value of equity

Whenever $ATER_n$ is positive, analysts who neglect the impact of the after-tax equity reversion and rely solely on the operating after-tax cash flow benefits will calculate a lower value than desirable. Therefore, the inclusion of the reversion is important to valuing income-producing real estate, and equation (10.12), which measures the investment value of equity (E), is a more realistic model.

An Example

To illustrate how to compute the value of the equity, consider an investment with the NOI and expected sale price as shown in table 10.5. Further assume that the reserve for replacements is $1,000 per year. Interest payments vary according to a level-payment amortization schedule for a $75,000 mortgage (9 percent interest rate for 20 years and monthly payments); financing costs are $1,500. Table 10.6 contains the amortization schedule for the mortgage.

Table 10.5 Example of Use of Discounted Cash Flow Model

Year	NOI	SP
1	$10,000	
2	12,000	
3	15,000	
4	15,000	
5	20,000	$150,000

Table 10.6 AMORTIZATION SCHEDULE FOR $75,000 MORTGAGE AT 9 PERCENT RATE, TWENTY-YEAR MATURITY, MONTHLY PAYMENTS

Year	Proportion Outstanding	Amount Outstanding	Debt Service	Interest	Principal
0	1.0	75,000			
1	.98127	73,595	8,098	6,693	1,405
2	.96077	72,058	8,098	6,561	1,537
3	.93836	70,377	8,098	6,417	1,681
4	.91384	68,538	8,098	6,259	1,839
5	.88703	66,527	8,098	6,087	2,011

Depreciation is deducted on a depreciable basis of $90,000 over a life of 27.5 years, assuming the property is classified as residential and using the straight-line method. The estimated land value is $35,000. The investment is expected to sell for $150,000 at the end of 5 years with expected selling expenses of 6 percent. The investor's marginal tax rate is 28 percent and the required rate of return is 15 percent. Tables 10.7 and 10.8 compute the cash flows and taxes from operations based on the example.

Table 10.7 AFTER-TAX CASH FLOWS FROM OPERATION

		YEAR				
		1	2	3	4	5
	Net operating income (NOI)	$ 10,000	12,000	15,000	15,000	20,000
Minus	Debt service (DS)	$ 8,098	8,098	8,098	8,098	8,098
Equals	Before-tax cash flow (BTCF)	$ 1,902	3,902	6,902	6,902	11,902
Minus	Taxes (savings) from operation (TO)*	$ 269	865	1,746	1,790	2,923
Equals	After-tax cash flow (ATCF)	$ 1,633	3,037	5,156	5,112	8,979

* See table 10.8.

Table 10.8 MEASUREMENT OF TAXABLE INCOME AND TAXES FROM OPERATION FOR EACH YEAR

		1	2	3	4	5
	Effective gross income (EGI)	$ 10,000	12,000	15,000	15,000	20,000
Minus	Operating expenses (OE)	$ 0	0	0	0	0
Equals	Net operating income (NOI)	$ 10,000	12,000	15,000	15,000	20,000
Minus	Interest on debt (I)	$ 6,693	6,561	6,417	6,259	6,087
Minus	Depreciation deduction (D)	$ 3,273	3,273	3,273	3,273	3,273
Minus	Amortized financing costs (AFC)	$ 75	75	75	75	1,200
Plus	Replacement reserves (RR)	$ 1,000	1,000	1,000	1,000	1,000
Equals	Ordinary taxable income (OTI)	$ 959	3,091	6,235	6,393	10,440
Times	Investor's marginal tax rate (t)	0.28	0.28	0.28	0.28	0.28
Equals	Taxes (savings) from operation (TO)	$ 269	865	1,746	1,790	2,923

Table 10.9 AFTER-TAX EQUITY REVERSION

	Expected selling price (SP)	$ 150,000
Minus	Selling expenses (SE)	$ 9,000
Equals	Net sales proceeds (NSP)	$ 141,000
Minus	Unpaid mortgage balance (UM)	$ 66,527
Equals	Before-tax equity reversion (BTER)	$ 74,473
Minus	Taxes due on sale (TDS)*	$ (9,062)
Equals	After-tax equity reversion (ATER)	$ 65,411

* See table 10.10.

Table 10.9 computes the after-tax equity reversion ($65,411) by deducting selling expenses, unpaid mortgage, and taxes due on sale from the expected selling price in year five. Table 10.10 computes the taxes due by deducting selling expenses and adjusted basis from the selling price to reach the total loss. This loss is then multiplied by the investor's marginal tax rate to obtain the taxes due on sale. Table 10.11 computes the present value of the equity cash flows using the 15 percent required rate of return. This value is found by multiplying the ATCFs (table 10.7) and the ATER (table 10.9) by the appropriate present value factors at 15 percent and summing these products. The total present value of the equity cash flows is $46,746. The total investment value of the project is the mortgage amount ($75,000) plus the value of the equity ($46,746), or $121,746.

Table 10.10 TAXES DUE ON SALE

Taxable Income

	Expected selling price (SP)	$ 150,000
Minus	Selling expenses (SE)	$ 9,000
Equals	Amount realized (AR)	$ 141,000
Minus	Adjusted basis (AB)	$ 108,635
Equals	Capital gain on sale (CG)	$ 32,365
Times	Investor's marginal tax rate (t)	0.28
Equals	Taxes due on sale (TDS)	$ 9,062

THE NET PRESENT VALUE OF EQUITY

The difference between the total value ($122,014 in our example) and the mortgage amount ($75,000) is the present value of the investor's equity ($47,014). The net present value of equity is the excess value if the investment value for the total is greater than the market value. As long as the net present value is positive, the project should be accepted.

HOW TO CALCULATE NPV OF EQUITY

The net present value of equity is equal to the present value of the cash flows calculated at the required rate of return minus the required equity (MV − MD). In equation form:

$$\begin{array}{c} NPV \text{ of equity} \\ (NPV) \end{array} = \sum_{i=1}^{n} \frac{ATCF_i}{(1 + k)^i} + \frac{ATER_n}{(1 + k)^n} \\ - [MV - MD]$$

This formula is illustrated in table 10.12 with three examples. In example 1, the same data from the previous example is used where the market value is assumed to be $122,014. Given this data, the net present value is equal to zero since the present value of the ATCFs and ATER are equal to the equity. In this case, the investor would be indifferent about choosing this project. Example 2 has a market value of $100,000 and

Table 10.11 PRESENT VALUE OF EQUITY CASH FLOWS

Year	ATCF	ATER	PV at 15%	PV
0			1.00000	
1	$1,633		.86957	$ 1,420
2	3,037		.75614	2,296
3	5,156		.65752	3,390
4	5,112		.57175	2,923
5	8,979	$65,411	.49718	36,985
			Total PV of equity (E) =	47,014

a positive NPV of equity ($22,014) so the investor would accept the project. Example 3 has a market value of $150,000 and negative NPV, so the investor would not accept the project.

NPV DECISION RULE

When using investment models, it is important to decide whether an investment is acceptable or not and, if so, how attractive it is relative to other alternatives. In fact, one of the major criticisms of the rules of thumb is the lack of consistent decision rules. For example, how short a payback period should the minimally acceptable project have, if payback methods are used? How high can the gross income multiplier become before the investment ceases to be attractive? Clearly, there are no objective answers to these questions. The traditional answers often result in more rules of thumb.

Using the net present value of equity model developed in this section, we can define an acceptable investment project as one that is expected to earn the required rate of return. Using equation (10.12), we get a value for E. Since the initial amount of mortgage debt, MD, must be known in

---

Table 10.12 NET PRESENT VALUE OF EQUITY

$$\text{Net present value (NPV)} = \sum_{i=1}^{n} \frac{ATCF_i}{(Itke)^i} \frac{ATER_n}{(Itke)^n} - \text{equity}$$

Where: Equity = market value − mortgage debt

1. Assume market value = $122,014

$$\text{NPV} = \frac{\$1,633}{(1.15)^1} + \frac{\$3,037}{(1.15)^2} + \frac{\$5,156}{(1.15)^3} + \frac{\$5,112}{(1.15)^4} + \frac{\$8,979}{(1.15)^5} + \frac{\$65,411}{(1.15)^5} - (\$122,014 - \$75,000)$$

$$= 0$$

2. Assume market value = $100,000

$$\text{NPV} = \frac{\$1,633}{(1.15)^1} + \frac{\$3,037}{(1.15)^2} + \frac{\$5,156}{(1.15)^3} + \frac{\$5,112}{(1.15)^4} + \frac{\$8,979}{(1.15)^5} + \frac{\$65,411}{(1.15)^5} - (\$100,000 - \$75,000)$$

$$= \$22,014$$

3. Assume market value = $150,000

$$\text{NPV} = \frac{\$1,633}{(1.15)^1} + \frac{\$3,037}{(1.15)^2} + \frac{\$5,156}{(1.15)^3} + \frac{\$5,112}{(1.15)^4} + \frac{\$8,979}{(1.15)^5} + \frac{\$65,411}{(1.15)^5} - (\$150,000 - \$75,000)$$

$$= (\$27,986)$$

order to calculate the debt service, we next develop an investment value for the total investment by adding E and MD. Then this sum is compared to the market value. If this value (E + MD) is greater than the market's sales price (or market value), the investor should invest in the project because he would earn more than the required rate of return and increase wealth. If the market value is greater than the sum of E and MD, the investor would not be able to achieve the required rate of return and should reject it.

Therefore, if the investment value for the total capital is greater than the market value, this excess value is the net present value (NPV) of the investment. As long as the net present value is greater than zero, investment in the project will increase the investor's wealth, and he should accept all projects with positive net present values.

Decision rule 1: Using investment value of equity and mortgage debts if:

$$(E + MD) \geq MV,$$

then NPV ≥ 0, therefore accept and if:

$$(E + MD) < MV,$$

then NPV < 0, therefore reject

Following the example, E is calculated (in table 10.11) to be $47,014 and MD is $75,000. Since $122,014 is greater than the assumed $100,000 market value, the decision rule tells the investor to accept the investment (NPV is equal to $22,014).

An alternative approach is to develop a decision rule using E directly. Since equation (10.12) calculates E, some investors might prefer a decision rule using E, which indicates whether or not to accept the investment. This can be accomplished by modifying Decision Rule 1 as follows:

Decision rule 2: Using investment value of equity, if:

$$E \geq (MV - MD),$$

then NPV ≥ 0, therefore accept and if:

$$E < (MV + MD),$$

then NPV < 0, therefore reject

Using the numbers from the example, $47,014 is greater than the $25,000 required equity, so this decision rule also tells the investor to accept the investment. The NPV of equity is $22,014 at a market value of $100,000.

Obviously, Decision Rules 1 and 2 are consistent. Both provide identical measures of net present value. Both indicate whether or not the wealth of the investor will increase if the investment is acquired.

THE INTERNAL RATE OF RETURN ON EQUITY

An alternative framework for making real estate investment decisions uses a measure called the internal rate of return. It is similar to net present value but potentially inconsistent with the foregoing techniques. The internal rate of return is defined as the rate that equates the present value of the cash inflows with the present value of the cash outflows. In real estate investment analysis, the internal rate of return on equity (r) is the measure preferred by most investors.

How to Calculate Internal Rate of Return on Equity

The internal rate of return (IRR) is the rate that will equate the present value of the cash inflows with the present value of the outflows. When the IRR is found, this is also the rate that will make the NPV = 0. The IRR on equity is shown in equation form as:

(10.13)

$$NPV = 0 = \frac{ATCF_1}{(1 + r)^1} + \frac{ATCF_2}{(1 + r)^2} + \frac{ATCF_3}{(1 + r)^3}$$

$$+ \cdots \frac{ATCF_n}{(1 + r)^n} + \frac{ATER_n}{(1 + r)^n}$$

$$- (MV - MD)$$

$$0 = \sum_{i=1}^{n} \frac{ATCF_1}{(1 + r)^i} + \frac{ATER_n}{(1 + r)^n}$$

$$- (MV - MD)$$

Table 10.13 illustrates the calculation of IRR using the different assumptions for the previous example. The first example uses the data with a market value of $122,014. The IRR on equity is found to be 15 percent

(which is also the required rate), so the investor would be indifferent as to choosing this project. The second example uses a market value of $100,000 and the IRR is 32.60 percent, which signals the investor to choose this project (since the IRR exceeds the required rate of 15 percent). The third example uses a market value of $150,000 and yields an IRR of 3.85 percent, which is less than the 15 percent required rate so the investor would reject this project.

However, technically, a multiperiod internal rate of return cannot be calculated directly. The analyst must: (1) approximate the internal rate of return by trial-and-error and center in on the value, (2) use a calculator or computer to approximate the answer using one of several mathematical techniques, or (3) find the rate of return, r, which makes E equal to (MV − MD), (i.e.,

---

Table 10.13 INTERNAL RATE OF RETURN ON EQUITY

1. IRR on Equity (r)

$$0 = \frac{ATCF_i}{(1 + r)^1} + \frac{ATCF_2}{(1 + r)^2} + \frac{ATCF_3}{(1 + r)^3} + \frac{ATCF_n}{(1 + r)^n} + \frac{ATER}{(1 + r)^n} - (MV - MD)$$

$$= \sum_{i=1}^{n} \frac{ATCF_i}{(1 + r)^i} + \frac{ATER_n}{(1 + r)^n} - (MV - MD)$$

2. MV = $122,014

$$0 = \frac{\$1,633}{(1 + r)^1} + \frac{\$3,037}{(1 + r)^2} + \frac{\$5,156}{(1 + r)^3} + \frac{\$5,112}{(1 + r)^4} + \frac{\$8,979}{(1 + r)^5} + \frac{\$65,411}{(1 + r)^5}$$

$$- (\$122,014 - \$75,000)$$

r = 15%

3. MV = $100,000

$$0 = \frac{\$1,633}{(1 + r)^1} + \frac{\$3,037}{(1 + r)^2} + \frac{\$5,156}{(1 + r)^3} + \frac{\$5,112}{(1 + r)^4} + \frac{\$8,979}{(1 + r)^5} + \frac{\$65,411}{(1 + r)^5}$$

$$- (\$100,000 - \$75,000)$$

r = 32.60%

4. MV = $150,000

$$0 = \frac{\$1,633}{(1 + r)^1} + \frac{\$3,037}{(1 + r)^2} + \frac{\$5,156}{(1 + r)^3} + \frac{\$5,112}{(1 + r)^4} + \frac{\$8,979}{(1 + r)^5} + \frac{\$65,411}{(1 + r)^5}$$

$$- (150,000 - 75,000)$$

r = 3.85%

---

where NPV = 0). This last suggestion is actually the condition under which the internal rate of return on equity is derived.

THE IRR DECISION RULE

After a value for r is derived, the analyst must evaluate the attractiveness of the investment. The following decision rule is applicable:

Decision rule 3: Using internal rule of return on equity, if:

$$r \geq k_e$$

then NPV $\geq$ 0, therefore, accept and if:

$$r < k_e$$

then NPV < 0, therefore reject

In our example at a market value of $100,000, the IRR of 32.60 percent is greater than 15 percent, so the investor should invest in the project. Basically, the IRR decision rule says: If the expected rate of return (r) exceeds (is less than) the required rate of return (k), then accept (reject) the investment.

A few words of clarification are in order. First, although the use of the investment value of equity model and the internal rate of return on equity are closely related, there are some important differences. A comparison of Decision Rules 1 and 2 with Decision Rule 3 reveals that in all of the rules, a favorable project is indicated by a positive net present value. Whenever one of the rules indicates an accept signal, the other two will indicate it as well. Therefore, it is impossible to get conflicting accept–reject signals between the net present value (investment value of equity) and internal rate of return (on equity) techniques. Second, although the decision rules are consistent about final outcomes, they *may not rank*

projects identically. Finally, despite the close relationship between these two approaches, there is much to lose if the analyst chooses the internal rate of return as a matter of preference.

COMPARISON BETWEEN NPV AND IRR TECHNIQUES

It may seem that the NPV and IRR techniques are interchangeable when making investment decisions, and that the choice of technique is immaterial. However, the following discussion will prove that these presumptions are dangerously misleading, relatively unsubstantiated, and in some cases, absolutely incorrect. The analysis of these techniques is divided into three major issues: ranking problems, reinvestment of cash flows, and the possibility of nonexistent or multiple r solutions.

RANKING PROBLEMS

Frequently the investor encounters several investment alternatives simultaneously. If discounted cash flow analysis is performed, the investor may discover many projects with positive net present values [where $(E + MD) > MV$ and/or where $E > (MV - MD)$ and where $r > k_e$]. Careful analysis suggests ranking the various projects according to the highest net present value greater than zero. The analyst might also rank the projects according to the highest internal rate of return on equity greater than the required rate of return on equity.

There may be instances when, at a relatively low required rate of return on equity, investment A has a higher net present value than alternative B. This suggests investing in A since it has a higher net present value and the choices are mutually exclusive. However, investing in B could yield a higher

Table 10.14 POSSIBLE RANKING PROBLEMS USING NET PRESENT VALUE AND INTERNAL RATE OF RETURN

	Investments	
	A	B
Net present value*	✓	
Internal rate of return		✓

* At certain required rates of return on equity.

internal rate of return than A. This would suggest investing in B. Table 10.14 illustrates the problem.

Thus, the investor would choose one investment if he used the net present value method and the other if he used the internal rate of return. What should he do?

One way to solve this problem is to evaluate his wealth position under each alternative. In choosing A, he is better off because the net present value is greater. By choosing B, the internal rate of return is higher, but the net present value is lower. Therefore, following the internal rate of return rule results in the selection of a project which is less valuable for the investor despite its higher rate of return. This result may shock those who prefer the internal rate of return approach. Nonetheless, the investor would not benefit by choosing the investment with the lower net present value, even if it has a higher internal rate of return.

REINVESTMENT OF CASH FLOWS

Another basis for comparison is what happens to the cash flows earned by an investor during the investment period. Is there any difference in the presumption about the reinvestment of cash flows using the net present value method or the internal rate of return method?

Some may argue that there is no reinvestment presumption at all since E and r do not imply that anything must be done with the cash flows. In other words, the investor may be just as well off by spending cash flows than by reinvesting them. However, to the extent that the analyst must value the opportunity cost of the reinvested proceedings by spending the cash flows, it seems much more appropriate to use the discount rate, k_e, rather than r as the rate. Following this line of reasoning, the internal rate of return method poses a problem regarding the choice of a reinvestment rate.

MULTIPLE INTERNAL RATE OF RETURN SOLUTIONS

It is also possible to have two or more internal rates of return that are each mathematically correct. This may occur when negative cash flows are expected to appear in a future period with positive cash flows expected the period(s) before and after the negative one(s). This condition renders the calculation of internal rate of return useless.

In the event that more than one value for r solves the formula, the investor would have a difficult time deciding the investment's rate of return. Suppose an investment has two rates (say 30 percent and 10 percent). Let us assume that the required rate of return is in between (20 percent). If the right rate of return is 10 percent, the investor rejects the investment. However, it could be either. The analyst cannot determine what to do if a multiple solution is found.

Some analysts suggest solving for E, using the required rate of return on equity of 20 percent, in this case. If the net present value is greater than zero, accept the investment and the problem is solved. What this means is that one must use the net present value approach to make the decision because the internal rate method will not result in a solution in this case.

ADVANCED TECHNIQUES AND MEASURES

Additional methods have been developed to improve previous measures or to evaluate different problems. This brief section introduces some of the concepts and techniques typically found in more advanced books. (The bibliography at the back of this book will serve as an excellent source of reference for those people interested in pursuing more advanced study.)

BENEFIT/COST RATIO

One of the criticisms of the internal rate of return techniques is that comparisons on the basis of values of r failed to consider the size of the investments. In order to deal with this problem, analysts relied on the *benefit-cost ratio* (sometimes called the profitability index). This provided a measure of benefits per dollar of cost and corrected a shortcoming of the internal rate of return.

The trouble with this measure is its consistency with net present value for some projects. In other words, choosing the investment with the highest benefit-cost ratio instead of another investment can result in giving up an investment with a higher value of E and higher net present value. So this finding casts grave doubts on the usefulness of benefit-cost ratios for real estate investment.

ADJUSTED INTERNAL RATE OF RETURN

This category contains a number of techniques which were motivated by dissatisfaction with the original internal rate of return. The typical adjustments deal with either the reinvestment rate problem or the possibilities of the multiple rate of return problems. Some models deal with both.

The results vary, although some of the advanced models avoid some of the internal rate of return problems. Much of this work was done by analysts who sought to get a rate of return method free of the problems outlined in the previous section. An example is a recent article by Strung.*

The major difficulty with these models is that for the most part, no new information is derived by a "perfected internal rate of return." After all, if there are ranking problems compared to net present value, differences will remain between the investment value of equity approach and the adjusted internal rate of return approach. If a particular model solves all of the inconsistencies with wealth-maximization criteria (i.e., maximizing net present value), then nothing new is gained since the net present value result is already available. The point is that this argument raises some serious questions about the benefits to be gained by investors using these measures.

FINANCIAL MANAGEMENT RATE OF RETURN (FMRR)

One of the more highly regarded measures is the *financial management rate of return*. Developed in 1975, it has attracted a wide following in a very short time.† It is basically a rate of return model that purports to solve the reinvestment presumption problem and the possibility of multiple rates of return. It uses a holding period rate

---

* Joseph Strung, "The Internal Rate of Return and the Reinvestment Presumptions," *The Appraisal Journal* 44 (January 1976), pp. 23–33.

† Stephen D. Messner and M. Chapman Findlay III, "Real Estate Investment Analysis: IRR Versus FMRR," *The Real Estate Appraiser* 41 (July–August, 1975), pp. 5–20.

of return measure which may result in differences from an internal rate of return calculation.

There are many attractive elements about the FMRR model. However, much of the conceptual basis and the reinvestment presumptions have been questioned in recent years. Still, it is too early to judge the degree of acceptance and the amount of reliance placed on this technique.

PROBABILISTIC MODELING

One of the major developments in modern real estate investment analysis is the interest in simulation and probabilistic modeling.* With the development of computerized real estate investment analysis, many large-scale investors use these techniques to improve investment decision making where they formerly relied on deterministic, single-point estimates or sensitivity analysis.

This technique uses subjective probability distributions around many of the necessary inputs into the investment decision. In this manner, the investor can acquire, process, and evaluate more information about the riskiness of the investment. Because many of the models are complex, an investor may require computer assistance to generate the necessary data. Most of these models also require expert assistance to evaluate the data. Still, this type of analysis may be well-embedded in real estate investment analysis in the future.

---

* Stephen A. Pyhrr, "A Computer Simulation Model to Measure the Risk in Real Estate Investment," *The Real Estate Appraiser* 39 (May–June, 1973), pp. 13–21.

V

Developing an Investment Strategy

PREVIOUS chapters identified and discussed the diverse factors that the investor analyzes in making an investment decision. This part discusses the development of a real estate investment strategy—an overall plan by which the equity investor makes decisions that lead to good investments. The real estate investment process forms the basis for a general real estate investment strategy.

An investment strategy requires taking risks in order to gain financial rewards. In chapter 1, we defined an investment as the sacrifice of certain (known) cash outflows in return for uncertain (risky) cash inflows. Although the future is never known when making an investment, this does not mean that the investor cannot form a set of rational expectations regarding future outcomes. These expectations are the basis for the investment decision.

An investment strategy is the art of planning and managing a real estate investment (or a portfolio of investments) in such a way that the investor reaches the most advantageous position from the investment. The basic objective is the maximization of wealth. A strategy requires planning before the investment is made, careful management of the investment during operations, and correct decisions concerning disposition.

Chapter 11 provides a detailed case study of an income-producing residential investment. Using the investment process outlined in the previous chapters, we analyze the many factors influencing the investment decision. Chapter 12 provides additional examples of making the real estate investment decision. Alternative financing and acquisition methods are illustrated for various types of real estate investments.

11

RESIDENTIAL INCOME PROPERTY: A CASE STUDY

IN the previous chapters, we have outlined and discussed the real estate investment process. In this chapter, we apply this decision-making process in a detailed case format. The investment situation is a real estate investor considering the purchase of a small apartment building.

We first review some of the basic elements of a real estate investment strategy. Then, we walk the investor step-by-step through the decision-making process. The reader is encouraged to work all of the numerical calculations and use the text as an answer key. Only by such a detailed analysis will the mechanics of real estate investment decision making be understood.

ELEMENTS OF AN INVESTMENT STRATEGY

Investment analysis involves identifying the factors that influence risk and return of alternative investments. There are several key elements in the development of an investment strategy. These include diversification, legal environment, choices of ownership entity, choices of management strategy,

choices of financing options, tax planning, choices of decision criteria, and inflation expectations. Let's discuss each of these elements.

DIVERSIFICATION

To make optimal decisions, resources must be allocated to real estate in consideration with other types of investments, such as stocks and bonds. This area of investment analysis is referred to as *portfolio analysis*. A portfolio is a combination of different types of investments or investments with different characteristics. Through diversification, the investor can lower the overall risk to which he is exposed.

Diversification involves investing equity into a number of different investments. An ideal portfolio of investments is one in which the returns for each investment are inversely related to each other.

One method of diversification would be to choose the same type of real estate investment but in a spatially varied fashion. A particular investor, for example, may prefer residential investments. He or she could diversify the real estate portfolio by spreading investments across different housing markets.

An investor could also diversify equity capital into different types of real estate investments (residential and commercial) and different locations for the various investments (i.e., different neighborhoods, cities, or even states). In this case, the investor may be able to improve the investment portfolio by carefully analyzing different expectations regarding the type and location of property.

LEGAL ENVIRONMENT

The development of a real estate investment strategy must include an understanding of the legal environment. The legal environment affects the investment decision in a number of ways. For example, the type of legal estate involved in the transaction can dramatically affect the value of the investment. The value of real property can significantly differ depending on the estate's limitations, duration, and conception. Therefore, the investor must understand the legal implications involving investing and making a real estate investment strategy.

To analyze an investment strategy, the investor has two choices: He can accept the legal environment as a constraint and work within it to achieve his financial outcome, or he can adopt a more active stance regarding the legal environment and use the law to his best interests.

While the first is a more passive approach, it should not be viewed as less aggressive or less ambitious. It seeks to achieve financial results, given a set of expectations and legal outcomes that legal counsel will support.

The second approach views the legal environment as a changing area that can be molded to fit the particular situation and requirements. In this case, the analyst seeks legal counsel as an active participant in the decision-making process.

OWNERSHIP ENTITY

Another important issue is the choice of business entity for ownership. Since this choice can mean the difference between the achievement of financial objectives or bankruptcy, or between fixed (or limited) liability and complete (or unlimited) liability in the event of suit against the owner, the choice of ownership entity is not to be overlooked. Furthermore, the choice of ownership varies according to the rights of control and operation, which may lead to problems concerning the ownership of property.

MANAGEMENT STRATEGY

Another important consideration is an analysis of the managerial decisions during the period of ownership. Many things occur during this time that affect the value of the property.

Because many operating decisions are delegated to the property manager when one is employed, the property manager may be one of the most important participants in the real estate investment process. Many of the production, operations, and financial decisions made by this person (or firm) may determine an investment strategy for the owner.

FINANCING OPTIONS

Financing is another major area. The investor must answer some important questions, such as: What is the appropriate level of debt? Is there an appropriate time to refinance in the case of a level-payment amortized loan? Should second mortgage sources be sought in order to expand the holdings of real estate investments when an attractive property becomes available? The answers to these and other questions involve dealing with financing policy and the solutions are not easily derived.

TAX PLANNING

Income taxation has a great impact on real estate investment decisions. The cash flow on which to make investment decisions is the amount after taxes. The amount of taxes depends on the taxable income and the investor's tax rate. A real estate investment strategy for income-producing property must involve considerable tax planning. The value of tax shelter provisions and the tax implications at the time of sale are important, too.

In general, since income taxation remains one of the basic ways in which federal and state governments collect money, tax planning is a necessary prerequisite for maximizing the equity investor's wealth. Those who choose to analyze projects on a before-tax basis can select inferior projects over better ones or in many cases overstate values or expected returns.

DECISION CRITERIA

There are various methods of measuring expected returns and investment values. The more traditional criteria are called rules of thumb because they are more easily used and require less data for analysis. The more sophisticated criteria require more data, more complex estimation procedures, and employ a stronger conceptual basis. The investor interested in developing a real estate investment strategy must decide on which criterion (or criteria) the decision will be made. For some investors, many measures and criteria will be used to provide as much relevant information as possible. For others, experience may show that only a select few are needed. Finally, a few investors may rely only on one or two approaches to make the investment decision.

Effective real estate investment decision making requires that the investor make the best choice, given his or her objectives and a set of alternatives. Implicit in this statement is the presumption that a wrong choice is costly in terms of giving up expected income, cash flow, or wealth.

INFLATIONARY ENVIRONMENT

In the past few years, inflation has soared to double digits in the United States. Many observers believe this will probably continue for the next decade as well. Real estate is traditionally regarded as an inflation hedge because some empirical evidence shows that the nominal value of property has increased at a faster rate than other goods. Although this really represents a change in relative prices due to changing demand, it nonetheless supports the notion that real estate investments provide real rates of return to investors.

THE INVESTMENT STRATEGY: A CASE STUDY

To illustrate the development of the real estate investment strategy, we will use a detailed case study of an apartment building investment. While it is impossible to illustrate all the problems faced by an investor, this example is a step-by-step discussion of an investment strategy based on the investment process discussed in the preceding chapters.

STEP 1: IDENTIFYING INVESTOR OBJECTIVES

The initial step is to identify the objectives of the investor. There are several different reasons for investing, such as tax shelter, inflation hedge, and cash flow.

The investor in this project decides that he wants to earn a 15 percent rate of return on his equity investment on an after-tax basis. This desired rate of return is determined after considering the other investment opportunities and the relative risk of the project. The investor's major objective is to decide whether the project is expected to generate the required return of 15 percent.

STEP 2: ANALYSIS OF THE INVESTMENT ENVIRONMENT

The second step is to analyze the environment in which the investment decision is made. This consists of three categories: market, legal, and sociopolitical.

Market Analysis. Two major categories of risk include the possibility that an investment will not generate the expected level of net income (market risk) and the possibility that income increases will not keep pace with inflation (purchasing power risk). Market analysis is designed to aid the investor in identifying the factors that influence these categories of risk.

The basic components of a market study include:

1. Definition and delineation of the market area for an investment.
2. Analysis of the demand factors. Demand for housing is dependent on number of households, income levels, and other demographic aspects, such as sex, age, and education.
3. Analysis of supply factors. This includes the existing competition in the market area, a survey of projects currently under construction, and an understanding of projects under consideration. It is most

difficult to obtain information about this latter category. However, real estate lenders, appraisers, brokers, developers, and other real estate professionals can provide this type of information. Vacancy rates for existing competition should be carefully considered along with rent levels and operating expenses.

4. The physical aspects of any proposed or existing project must be reviewed. Such factors as the compatibility with existing uses, size, shape, topography, zoning regulations, density requirements, deed restrictions, and others must be analyzed.

The market study must also provide information about such items as anticipated rent levels, vacancy rates, and forecasts of future property values. Table 11.1 summarizes the assumptions based on market analysis.

Legal Analysis. A second major category is legislative (legal) risk. This is the pos-

---

Table 11.1 ASSUMPTIONS FROM MARKET ANALYSIS

1. Investment type: apartments; residential.
2. The asking price is $500,000.
3. The total number of rentable units is 25.
4. The age of the investment is 10 years.
5. Rents are expected to range between $300 and $375 per unit per month.
6. Vacancy and bad debt losses are expected to be between 3 percent and 7 percent per year.
7. Rents are expected to increase at an annual rate between 3 percent and 7 percent.
8. Demand is expected to be strong. There appears to be a growing population base.
9. The location is excellent relative to shopping and employment centers.
10. The building is in good condition with little deferred maintenance. This should help keep demand strong.

sibility that the government will change the laws and introduce restrictions and regulations that cause incomes and/or property values to decline. Examples of this type of change would be increased taxation, change in zoning ordinances, and the exercising of the right of eminent domain.

Legal risk can also arise from the interrelationships between the other participants in the investment process (see figure 1.2 in chapter 1). For example, there may be deed restrictions which limit the use of the property or outstanding mortgage liens against the property that create a "cloud" on the title.

The investor must realize that property rights are bought and sold in the real estate market. The investor must be certain that the seller possesses the property rights. The buyer (investor) cannot acquire more rights than the seller has to sell. Table 11.2 illustrates the assumptions from the legal analysis.

Sociopolitical Analysis. Another area to be analyzed involves potential social constraints related to an investment. While a project may be legally permissible, it may not be feasible from society's point of view. Social controls in real estate investment

analysis have received increased attention in recent years.

A real estate investment creates external effects on the neighborhood and society in general. Some of these external effects are positive while others are negative. Potential external effects and their possible benefits and costs affect the risk and return expected from an investment. Examples of these effects include increased traffic and lowered (or increased) property values.

In this case, the apartment building's value should reflect these external effects. If it were a proposed project, the investor would be more concerned with the sociopolitical constraints. Is there any adverse neighborhood reaction to the investment? Table 11.3 indicates no expected sociopolitical problems with the investment.

STEP 3: FORECAST OF CASH FLOWS

The third step in the development of the investment strategy is to forecast the expected cash flows (both in and out) for the expected holding period (length of ownership). The cash inflows are derived from two sources: the annual cash flows from rental collections and the cash flow from the disposition (typically sale) of the investment. The investor is interested in the expected after-tax cash flow from these two sources. This represents the amount of cash that the investment is expected to generate after all obligations, including income taxes, have been met.

Table 11.2 ASSUMPTIONS FROM LEGAL ANALYSIS

1. The property conforms to current building code and zoning restrictions.
2. There is no threat of rent control in the community.
3. Property rights to be acquired are fee simple, subject to existing easements and government restrictions.
4. Current easements do not appear to have a significant impact on the value.
5. The current liens are property taxes (not in arrears) and an existing mortgage (nonassumable) that will be paid off on sale.

Table 11.3 ASSUMPTIONS FROM SOCIOPOLITICAL ANALYSIS

Positive effects	None
Negative effects	None

There appear to be no sociopolitical problems associated with this investment.

Cash flows are those that the project is expected to generate. The investor will not know the actual cash flows until the investment has been acquired, operated, and sold. This is what investing is all about—sacrificing outflows for expected inflows. There is always the possibility that an investment will not produce the investor's expected level of cash flow. To formulate the expected cash flows, the investor must make decisions and assumptions regarding operations, financing, reversion, and tax planning.

Operating Decisions. To formulate the expected cash inflow, the investor must make assumptions regarding the operation of the investment. This operating plan should include expenses such as maintenance, repairs, utilities, property taxes, and insurance.

Table 11.4 shows the projected level of operating expenses in the first year. These expenses are expected to increase at a rate between 3 percent to 7 percent each year.

In the first year, the expected operating expenses require approximately 45 percent of the effective gross income (EGI). The investor must compare this expected level of expenses to the competition. After doing so, he decides that the operating expense ratio (OER) will probably vary between 45 percent and 50 percent.

Table 11.4 FORECAST OF FIRST-YEAR OPERATING EXPENSES

Expense Category	% of Most Likely EGI (rounded)
Real estate taxes	12%
Insurance	3%
Utilities	12%
Administrative (management)	8%
Maintenance and operation	10%
Total operating expenses	45%

Financing Decisions. The next area of analysis in formulating the expected cash flows is the financing decisions. Financing involves two sources: debt and equity.

Table 11.5 summarizes the financing decision assumptions. Total mortgaged debt is $350,000 and the equity required is $164,000. The required rate of return on the equity is 15 percent. This rate reflects the risks to which the equity position is exposed (market risk, inflation risk, legal risk, and financial risk).

Table 11.6 gives the mortgage amortization schedule. This shows the distribution between interest and principal for each year of the holding period. The debt service is expected to be $44,100 per year.

Reversion Decisions. The second category of cash flow is that from the expected sale of the investment. The investor must forecast the expected changes in the property value over the expected holding period. The

Table 11.5 FINANCING DECISION ASSUMPTIONS

Debt Financing

1. The investor can borrow $350,000 from a local lender. This results in a loan-to-value ratio of 70 percent.
2. The mortgage interest rate is 10.5 percent.
3. The mortgage maturity is twenty-five years with monthly payments.
4. Financing costs, including points and fees are 4 percent of the amount borrowed or $14,000 ($350,000 × .04).
5. Prepayment penalties are 5 percent of the outstanding balance.

Equity Financing

1. The equity investment is $150,000 plus the $14,000 financing costs. Total equity is thus $164,000.
2. The desired rate of return on the equity position is 15 percent after tax.

Table 11.6 MORTGAGE AMORTIZATION SCHEDULE

Total cost: $550,000
Amount borrowed: $350,000
Interest rate: 10.50%
Maturity term: 25 years
Payments: Monthly
Annual mortgage constant: .11330
Debt service: $39,656

Year	Proportion Outstanding	Amount Outstanding	Debt Service	Interest Payment	Principal Payment
0	1.0	$350,000			
1	.99128	346,950	$39,656	$36,606	$3,050
2	.98161	343,564	39,656	36,270	3,386
3	.97087	339,805	39,656	35,897	3,759
4	.95895	335,632	39,656	35,483	4,173
5	.94571	330,999	39,656	35,023	4,633
6	.93102	325,855	39,656	34,512	5,144
7	.91470	320,145	39,656	33,946	5,710

investment horizon is eight years. Table 11.7 summarizes the reversion assumptions.

Tax Planning Decisions. The last major area of analysis in forecasting the expected cash flows is tax planning. Table 11.8 lists the assumptions for tax planning. The important elements are the tax rate and the depreciation deduction. The amount of the depreciation deduction depends on the depreciable basis, useful life, and depreciation method. Table 11.9 gives the depreciation schedule based on the assumptions in table 11.8.

Table 11.10 summarizes the assumptions necessary to forecast the expected cash flows. These assumptions are based on the market, financing, operations, reversions, and tax planning analyses. The investor has formulated expectations on three possible "states of the world": most likely, optimistic, and pessimistic. These three possible outcomes provide him with information regarding the sensitivity of the investment decision based on the assumptions. It is obvious that the investor will not know the actual state of the world until he buys, op-

erates, and sells the property. The investor must, however, make a decision today based on the expectations. The next section develops the expected after-tax cash flows from operations and sale under these three possible outcomes.

The Expected Cash Flow from Operations. Using the assumptions from the preceding analysis, the expected after-tax cash flows from operations, under the most likely, optimistic, and pessimistic outcomes, are given in tables 11.11 through 11.16.

Tables 11.11 and 11.12 show that for the most likely outcome, the investment generates a negative taxable income for each year through six and year eight. It might be noted that using these most likely assumptions, rents are estimated to be approximately $470 per unit per month at the end of seven years.

Tables 11.13 and 11.14 give the ATCF and the taxes from operations for the optimistic assumptions. Under these assumptions, rents after seven years are estimated to be approximately $560 per month per unit.

Tables 11.15 and 11.16 give the expected ATCF and the taxes from operations under the pessimistic assumptions. Here, rents are forecast to be approximately $360 per unit per month at the end of the holding period. Also, note that the investment generates a tax shelter for each year of the holding period. Notice that in year seven BTCF is negative. The ATCF is positive due to the tax shelter benefits. The investment does, however, have a declining expected ATCF for each year. The declining ATCF results from the fact that rents are not rising as fast as operating expenses, which causes NOI to decline.

The Expected After-tax Cash Flow from Sale. The expected after-tax cash flow from sale (ATER) is given in tables 11.17, 11.19, and 11.21 for the most likely, optimistic, and pessimistic assumptions regarding future values of the property. Tables 11.18, 11.20, and 11.22 give the taxable income and the taxes due on sale for these three possible outcomes.

STEP 4: APPLYING THE DECISION-MAKING CRITERIA

The preceding section developed the expected cash flow from operations and sale. Now we turn to the decision-making criteria: rules of thumb and discounted cash flow models.

Rules of Thumb. Some alternative rules of thumb are shown in table 11.23. These include the gross income multiplier (GIM), the net income multiplier (NIM), equity dividend rate (EDR), after-tax rate (ATR), debt coverage ratio (DCR), and the operating expense ratio (OER). Each is calculated using the most likely, optimistic, and pessimistic assumptions.

How does the investor decide whether or not to invest, using these rules of thumb? Obviously, he needs a standard of comparison. To illustrate, suppose the investor decides that the purchase price should not exceed five times the estimated gross income in the first year. In this case, looking at column 1 of table 11.23, the investor sees that the asking price is 5.01 times the first year's effective gross income. Thus, if strictly applied he would conclude that it was a marginal investment decision.

The debt-coverage ratio (DCR) is widely used by mortgage lenders. It is the ratio of the NOI to the debt service. In this case, the DCR in the first year is 1.38 in the most likely outcome. This would fall in the acceptable range for most mortgage lenders.

The various other rules of thumb shown in the table are used in the same manner as the GIM or the DCR. The investor compares these to a standard and accepts or rejects the investment. Note that the rules of thumb do not always lead to the same accept/reject decision. An investment that may be acceptable using the GIM may be unacceptable using the EDR method. The investor should compute all the various rules of thumb and arrive at the investment decision after analyzing each one.

Discounted Cash Flow Models. The second major set of investment criteria are the discounted cash flow (DCF) models. As the name implies, the DCF models take the forecasted cash flows and discount them back to the present. Thus, the investor has the present worth of the expected cash flows.

The best DCF model is called the net present value (NPV) technique in which the investor calculates the total present value of the cash flows and compares this to the cost of investing. Under the NPV criterion, the investor invests if the NPV is positive. He does not invest if the NPV is negative. These decision rules make sense intuitively. They

Table 11.7 Reversion Decision Assumptions

1. Property values are expected to increase between 3 percent and 6 percent per year.
2. Selling expenses (brokerage fees, legal fees, etc.) are estimated to be 10 percent of the selling price.

Table 11.8 Tax Planning Assumptions

1. The investor is in a 28 percent marginal tax bracket that is not expected to change over time.
2. The building has a value of $400,000 (or 80 percent of the total cost). The depreciable amount is thus $400,000.
3. The useful life of the building for tax purposes is 27.5 years with a zero salvage value.
4. The investor will use the straight-line depreciation method.

Table 11.9 Depreciation Schedule

Total cost: $500,000
Depreciable amount: $400,000
Nondepreciable amount: $100,000
Useful life: 27.5 years
Straight-line percent: 3.63%

STRAIGHT-LINE METHOD

Year	Book Value	Amount	Cumulative
0	$400,000		
1	385,455	$14,545	$ 14,545
2	370,910	14,545	29,090
3	356,365	14,545	43,635
4	341,820	14,545	58,180
5	327,275	14,545	72,725
6	312,730	14,545	87,270
7	298,185	14,545	101,815

Table 11.10 Summary of Assumptions for Investment Inputs

Input		Assumptions
Purchase price		$500,000
Number of units		25
Rents	Optimistic	$375 per month expected to increase 7% per year
	Most likely	$350 per month expected to increase 5% per year
	Pessimistic	$300 per month expected to increase 3% per year
Vacancies	Optimistic	3% per year
	Most likely	5% per year
	Pessimistic	7% per year
Operating expenses	Optimistic	$49,106 in the first year, expected to increase 3% per year
	Most likely	$44,888 in the first year, expected to increase 5% per year
	Pessimistic	$37,665 in the first year, expected to increase 7% per year
Financing		70% of total value; 10.50% interest rate; monthly payments for 25 years; prepayment penalties of 5% of outstanding balance; 4% financing costs
Depreciation		Straight-line; useful life of 27.5 years; 80% of total cost is depreciable
Holding period		7 years
Reversion	Optimistic	Value is expected to be $725,000
	Most likely	Value is expected to be $700,000
	Pessimistic	Value is not expected to be $650,000
Selling expenses		10% of value
Tax rate		28% marginal tax rate; the minimum tax is not applicable
Equity		Total equity investment of $164,000; desired after-tax rate of return on equity is 15%

Table 11.11 Measurement of Expected Cash Flow from Operation: Most Likely Assumptions

		YEARS						
		1	2	3	4	5	6	7
	Potential gross income (PGI)	$ 105,000	110,250	115,763	121,551	127,628	134,010	140,710
Minus	Vacancy and bad debt allowance (VBD)	$ 5,250	5,513	5,788	6,078	6,381	6,700	7,036
Plus	Miscellaneous income (MI)	$ 0	0	0	0	0	0	0
Equals	Effective gross income (EGI)	$ 99,750	104,738	109,974	115,473	121,247	127,309	133,675
Minus	Operating expenses (OE)	$ 44,888	47,132	49,488	51,963	54,561	57,289	60,154
Equals	Net operating income (NOI)	$ 54,864	57,606	60,486	63,510	66,686	70,020	73,521
Minus	Debt service (DS)	$ 39,656	39,656	39,656	39,656	39,656	39,656	55,663[†]
Equals	Before-tax cash flow (BTCF)	$ 15,208	17,950	20,830	23,855	27,030	30,364	17,858
Minus	Taxes (savings) from operation (TO)*	$ 882	1,744	2,655	3,618	4,636	5,713	(453)
Equals	After-tax cash flow (ATCF)	$ 14,326	16,206	18,175	20,236	22,394	24,652	18,311

* See table 11.12.

[†] Includes prepayment penalty of $16,007.

Table 11.12 MEASUREMENT OF TAXABLE INCOME AND TAXES FROM OPERATION: MOST LIKELY ASSUMPTIONS

		YEARS						
		1	2	3	4	5	6	7
	Effective gross income (EGI)	$ 99,750	104,738	109,974	115,473	121,247	127,309	133,675
Minus	Operating expenses (OE)	$ 44,888	47,132	49,488	51,963	54,561	57,289	60,154
Equals	Net operating income (NOI)	$ 54,863	57,606	60,486	63,510	66,686	70,020	73,521
Minus	Interest on debt (I)	$ 36,606	36,270	35,897	35,483	35,023	34,512	49,953*
Minus	Depreciation deduction (D)	$ 14,545	14,545	14,545	14,545	14,545	14,545	14,545
Minus	Amortized financing costs (AFC)	$ 560	560	560	560	560	560	10,640
Plus	Replacement reserves (RR)	$ 0	0	0	0	0	0	0
Equals	Ordinary taxable income (OTI)	$ 3,151	6,230	9,484	12,922	16,558	20,402	(1,617)
Times	Investor's marginal tax rate (T)	0.28	0.28	0.28	0.28	0.28	0.28	0.28
Equals	Taxes (savings) from operation (TO)	$ 882	1,744	2,655	3,618	4,636	5,713	(453)

* Includes prepayment penalty of $16,007, deductible as interest for tax purposes.

199

Table 11.13 Measurement of Expected Cash Flow from Operation: Optimistic Assumptions

		YEARS						
		1	2	3	4	5	6	7
	Potential gross income (PGI)	$ 112,500	120,375	128,801	137,817	147,465	157,787	168,832
Minus	Vacancy and bad debt allowance (VBD)	$ 3,375	3,611	3,864	4,135	4,424	4,734	5,065
Plus	Miscellaneous income (MI)	$ 0	0	0	0	0	0	0
Equals	Effective gross income (EGI)	$ 109,125	116,764	124,937	133,683	143,041	153,053	163,767
Minus	Operating expenses (OE)	$ 49,106	50,579	52,097	53,660	55,270	56,928	58,635
Equals	Net operating income (NOI)	$ 60,019	66,184	72,840	80,023	87,771	96,126	105,132
Minus	Debt service (DS)	$ 39,656	39,656	39,656	39,656	39,656	39,656	55,663[†]
Equals	Before-tax cash flow (BTCF)	$ 20,363	26,529	33,185	40,367	48,115	56,470	49,469
Minus	Taxes (savings) from operation (TO)*	$ 2,326	4,147	6,115	8,242	10,540	13,022	8,398
Equals	After-tax cash flow (ATCF)	$ 18,037	22,382	27,070	32,126	37,575	43,448	41,071

* See table 11.14.

[†] Includes prepayment of $16,007.

Table 11.14 Measurement of Taxable Income and Taxes from Operation: Optimistic Assumptions

		YEARS						
		1	2	3	4	5	6	7
	Effective gross income (EGI)	$ 109,125	116,764	124,937	133,683	143,041	153,053	163,767
Minus	Operating expenses (OE)	$ 49,106	50,579	52,097	53,660	55,270	56,928	58,635
Equals	Net operating income (NOI)	$ 60,019	66,184	72,840	80,023	87,771	96,126	105,132
Minus	Interest on debt (I)	$ 36,606	36,270	35,897	35,483	35,023	34,512	49,953*
Minus	Depreciation deduction (D)	$ 14,545	14,545	14,545	14,545	14,545	14,545	14,545
Minus	Amortized financing costs (AFC)	$ 560	560	560	560	560	560	10,640
Plus	Replacement reserves (RR)	$ 0	0	0	0	0	0	0
Equals	Ordinary taxable income (OTI)	$ 8,307	14,809	21,838	29,435	37,643	46,508	29,994
Times	Investor's marginal tax rate (T)	0.28	0.28	0.28	0.28	0.28	0.28	0.28
Equals	Taxes (savings) from operation (TO)	$ 2,326	4,147	6,115	8,242	10,540	13,022	8,398

* Includes prepayment penalty of $16,007, deductible as interest for tax purposes.

201

Table 11.15 Measurement of Expected Cash Flow from Operation: Pessimistic Assumptions

		YEARS						
		1	**2**	**3**	**4**	**5**	**6**	**7**
	Potential gross income (PGI)	$ 90,000	92,700	95,481	98,345	101,296	104,335	107,465
Minus	Vacancy and bad debt allowance (VBD)	$ 6,300	6,489	6,684	6,884	7,091	7,303	7,523
Plus	Miscellaneous income (MI)	$ 0	0	0	0	0	0	0
Equals	Effective gross income (EGI)	$ 83,700	86,211	88,797	91,461	94,205	97,031	99,942
Minus	Operating expenses (OE)	$ 37,665	40,302	43,123	46,141	49,371	52,827	56,525
Equals	Net operating income (NOI)	$ 46,035	45,909	45,675	45,320	44,834	44,204	43,417
Minus	Debt service (DS)	$ 39,656	39,656	39,656	39,656	39,656	39,656	55,663†
Equals	Before-tax cash flow (BTCF)	$ 6,379	6,254	6,019	5,664	5,178	4,548	(12,246)
Minus	Taxes (savings) from operation (TO)*	$ (1,589)	(1,530)	(1,492)	(1,475)	(1,482)	(1,516)	(8,882)
Equals	After-tax cash flow (ATCF)	$ 7,969	7,784	7,511	7,139	6,661	6,064	(3,364)

* See table 11.16.

† Includes prepayment penalty of $16,007.

Table 11.16 Measurement of Taxable Income and Taxes from Operation: Pessimistic Assumptions

					YEARS			
		1	2	3	4	5	6	7
	Effective gross income (EGI)	$ 83,700	86,211	88,797	91,461	94,205	97,031	99,942
Minus	Operating expenses (OE)	$ 37,665	40,302	43,123	46,141	49,371	52,827	56,525
Equals	Net operating income (NOI)	$ 46,035	45,909	45,675	45,320	44,834	44,204	43,417
Minus	Interest on debt (I)	$ 36,606	36,270	35,897	35,483	35,023	34,512	49,953*
Minus	Depreciation deduction (D)	$ 14,545	14,545	14,545	14,545	14,545	14,545	14,545
Minus	Amortized financing costs (AFC)	$ 560	560	560	560	560	560	10,640
Plus	Replacement reserves (RR)	$ 0	0	0	0	0	0	0
Equals	Ordinary taxable income (OTI)	$ (5,676)	(5,466)	(5,328)	(5,268)	(5,294)	(5,413)	(31,721)
Times	Investor's marginal tax rate (T)	0.28	0.28	0.28	0.28	0.28	0.28	0.28
Equals	Taxes (savings) from operation (TO)	$ (1,589)	(1,530)	(1,492)	(1,475)	(1,482)	(1,516)	(8,882)

* Includes prepayment penalty of $16,007, deductible as interest for tax purposes.

203

Table 11.17 MEASUREMENT OF EXPECTED CASH FLOW
FROM THE SALE OF AN INVESTMENT: MOST LIKELY
ASSUMPTIONS

	Expected selling price (SP)	$ 700,000
Minus	Selling expenses (SE)	$ 70,000
Equals	Net sales proceeds (NSP)	$ 630,000
Minus	Unpaid mortgage balance (UM)	$ 320,146
Equals	Before-tax equity reversion (BTER)	$ 309,854
Minus	Taxes due on sale (TDS)*	$ 64,909
Equals	After-tax equity reversion (ATER)	$ 244,945

* See table 11.18 for calculation of taxes due on sale.

Table 11.18 MEASUREMENT OF TAXABLE INCOME
AND TAXES DUE ON SALE: MOST LIKELY ASSUMPTIONS

TAXABLE INCOME

	Expected selling price (SP)	$ 700,000
Minus	Selling expenses (SE)	$ 70,000
Equals	Amount realized (AR)	$ 630,000
Minus	Adjusted basis (AB)	$ 398,182
Equals	Capital gain on sale (CG)	$ 231,818

TAXES DUE ON SALE

	Capital gain on sale (CG)	$ 231,818
Times	Investor's marginal tax rate (T)	0.28
Equals	Taxes due on sale (TDS)	$ 64,909

Table 11.19 MEASUREMENT OF EXPECTED CASH FLOW
FROM THE SALE OF AN INVESTMENT: OPTIMISTIC
ASSUMPTIONS

	Expected selling price (SP)	$ 725,000
Minus	Selling expenses (SE)	$ 72,500
Equals	Net sales proceeds (NSP)	$ 652,500
Minus	Unpaid mortgage balance (UM)	$ 320,146
Equals	Before-tax equity reversion (BTER)	$ 332,354
Minus	Taxes due on sale (TDS)*	$ 71,209
Equals	After-tax equity reversion (ATER)	$ 261,145

* See table 11.20 for calculation of taxes due on sale.

Table 11.20 MEASUREMENT OF TAXABLE INCOME
AND TAXES DUE ON SALE: OPTIMISTIC ASSUMPTIONS

TAXABLE INCOME

	Expected selling price (SP)	$ 725,000
Minus	Selling expenses (SE)	$ 72,500
Equals	Amount realized (AR)	$ 652,500
Minus	Adjusted basis (AB)	$ 398,182
Equals	Capital gain on sale (CG)	$ 254,318

TAXES DUE ON SALE

	Capital gain on sale (CG)	$ 254,318
Times	Investor's marginal tax rate (T)	0.28
Equals	Taxes due on sale (TDS)	$ 71,209

Table 11.21 MEASUREMENT OF EXPECTED CASH FLOW
FROM THE SALE OF AN INVESTMENT: PESSIMISTIC
ASSUMPTIONS

	Expected selling price (SP)	$ 650,000
Minus	Selling expenses (SE)	$ 65,000
Equals	Net sales proceeds (NSP)	$ 585,000
Minus	Unpaid mortgage balance (UM)	$ 320,146
Equals	Before-tax equity reversion (BTER)	$ 264,854
Minus	Taxes due on sale (TDS)*	$ 52,309
Equals	After-tax equity reversion (ATER)	$ 212,545

* See table 11.22 for calculation of taxes due on sale.

Table 11.22 MEASUREMENT OF TAXABLE INCOME
AND TAXES DUE ON SALE: PESSIMISTIC ASSUMPTIONS

TAXABLE INCOME

	Expected selling price (SP)	$ 650,000
Minus	Selling expenses (SE)	$ 65,000
Equals	Amount realized (AR)	$ 585,000
Minus	Adjusted basis (AB)	$ 398,182
Equals	Capital gain on sale (CG)	$ 186,818

TAXES DUE ON SALE

	Capital gain on sale (CG)	$ 186,818
Times	Investor's marginal tax rate (T)	0.28
Equals	Taxes due on sale (TDS)	$ 52,309

Table 11.23 RULES OF THUMB USING FIRST-YEAR CASH FLOW
FROM OPERATIONS

	STATE OF THE WORLD		
Rule of Thumb	Most Likely	Optimistic	Pessimistic
1. GIM			
Gross income multiplier	5.01	4.58	5.97
2. NIM			
Net income multiplier	9.11	8.33	10.86
3. EDR			
Equity dividend rate (%)	9.27	12.42	3.89
4. ATR			
After-tax rate (%)	8.73	11.00	4.86
5. DCR			
Debt-coverage ratio	1.38	1.51	1.16
6. OER			
Operating expense ratio	.45	.45	.45

say compute the present worth of the expected cash flows at the desired rate of return; compare this present worth to how much it costs to invest; if the costs exceed the present worth of the cash flow, don't invest; if the present worth of the cash flows exceed the costs, do invest.

Tables 11.24, 11.25, and 11.26 give the net present value of the ATCF from operation and the ATER from the sale at the end of seven years. Recall that the equity invest-

ment was $164,000. These present values were calculated using a 15 percent rate of return. These cash flows are taken from the most likely, optimistic, and pessimistic outcomes. The after-tax cash flows represent the amount going to the equity position after all expenses, debt service, and taxes have been paid.

Column 5 of tables 11.24, 11.25, and 11.26 contains the present value factor at the desired 15 percent rate of return on equity.

Table 11.24 PRESENT VALUE OF AFTER-TAX FLOWS AT 15 PERCENT RATE:
MOST LIKELY ASSUMPTIONS

Year	Equity*	ATCF	ATER†	Present Value Factor at 15%	Present Value
0	$(164,000)			1.0	$(164,000)
1		14,325		.86957	12,457
2		16,206		.75614	12,254
3		18,175		.65752	11,950
4		20,236		.57177	11,570
5		22,394		.49718	11,134
6		24,652		.43233	10,658
7		18,311	244,945	.37594	98,968
				NPV = $	4,991

* This is the $150,000 plus the $14,000 financing costs.

† See table 11.17.

Table 11.25 PRESENT VALUE OF AFTER-TAX FLOWS AT 15 PERCENT RATE: OPTIMISTIC ASSUMPTIONS

Year	Equity*	ATCF	ATER†	Present Value Factor at 15%	Present Value
0	$(164,000)			1.0	$(164,000)
1		18,037		.86957	15,684
2		22,382		.75614	16,924
3		27,070		.65752	17,799
4		32,126		.57177	18,369
5		37,575		.49718	18,682
6		43,448		.43233	18,784
7		41,071	261,145	.37594	113,615
				NPV =	$ 55,857

* This is the $150,000 plus the $14,000 financing costs.

† See table 11.19.

Recall that the investor's major objective is to decide whether or not the investment would yield a 15 percent rate of return on the equity investment of $164,000. The present value factors were taken from the present value tables in appendix A. These factors, when multiplied by the expected cash flows in the respective years, give the present value of these cash flows as shown in column 6.

To interpret the present value numbers in column 6, look at table 11.24. This table gives the ATCF for the most likely assumptions. In year five, the investment is expected to generate $22,394 in ATCF. However, the present value of this $22,394 is $11,134. This means that at the desired rate of return of 15 percent, the investor is willing to pay $11,134 for the right to receive $22,394 five years later.

Table 11.26 PRESENT VALUE OF AFTER-TAX FLOWS AT 15 PERCENT RATE: PESSIMISTIC ASSUMPTIONS

Year	Equity*	ATCF	ATER†	Present Value Factor at 15%	Present Value
0	$(164,000)			1.0	$(164,000)
1		7,969		.86957	6,930
2		7,784		.75614	5,886
3		7,511		.65752	4,939
4		7,139		.57177	4,082
5		6,661		.49718	3,312
6		6,064		.43233	2,622
7		(3,364)	212,545	.37594	78,640
				NPV =	$ (57,589)

* This is the $150,000 plus the $14,000 financing costs.

† See table 11.21.

**Table 11.27 NET PRESENT VALUE OF CASH FLOWS
AT 15 PERCENT RATE OF RETURN**

	Most Likely Outcome	Optimistic Outcome	Pessimistic Outcome
Net present value of cash flows	$4,991	$55,857	$(57,589)

The net present value of the cash flow is found by adding the numbers in column 6. Notice that the net present value for the most likely assumption is $4,991. The net present value of the cash flows under the optimistic assumption is $55,857. Likewise, the net present value is − $57,589 for the pessimistic assumptions.

STEP 5: THE INVESTMENT DECISION

Now that the investor has established the objective, analyzed the investment environment, forecast the cash flows, and applied the investment criteria, should he pay $500,000 for the investment?

To make this decision, he examines the investment criteria, the best of which is the net present value (NPV) technique. The net present value of the expected after-tax cash flows under the three sets of assumptions is shown in table 11.27.

For the most likely outcome, the NPV of the investment is $4,991. Using the NPV decision rules, the investor should make the investment. Likewise, the investment would be made under the optimistic outcome. The investment should not be un-dertaken under the pessimistic assumption.

Suppose the investor assigned the probabilities in table 11.28 to the three possible "states of the world."

The investor believes that there is an 80 percent chance of the most likely assumption occurring. There is a 10 percent probability of the optimistic or pessimistic outcomes. Multiplying these probabilities times the net present value of each state, the resulting net present value is close to zero. Thus, it would appear that the project is one worth considering as an investment. The investor could obviously reassess the likelihood of the various states of the world and recalculate the expected NPV.

What should the investor do? Obviously, many assumptions have been made. This, however, is what investing is all about. Investment is giving up cash today (equity) in return for expected, but risky, cash inflow in the future. The investor must formulate the expectations explicitly. While no investor knows the actual outcome, this does not mean that he cannot form expectations about the future. The critical question is: How certain is he that his expectations are correct? Obviously, under some possible

Table 11.28 EXPECTED NET PRESENT VALUE

State of the World	Probability	Net Present Value	Expected NPV
Optimistic outcome	.10	$55,857	$5,586
Most likely outcome	.80	4,991	3,993
Pessimistic outcome	.10	(57,589)	(5,759)
		Expected NPV =	$3,820

outcomes the investor should invest, whereas under others, he should not. The important lesson for the investor is to examine each assumption and expectation carefully, thus reducing the risk as much as possible. The investment decision is only as good as the expectations on which it is based.

12

ALTERNATIVE FINANCING AND ACQUISITION METHODS

THIS chapter, like chapter 11, involves developing an investment strategy. This concept is explored by illustrating and explaining various financing techniques, types of real estate investments, and acquisition methods. The financing methods are different ways of funding and/or purchasing an investment and the acquisition methods are ways of possessing or owning an investment.

The various financing techniques explained are seller financing, first and second mortgages, installment sales, exchanges, leasebacks, buying second mortgages, and refinancing. The real estate types include vacant land, a triplex (residential) property, apartment building, office building, and a convenience store. The acquisition methods explained include an installment sale, sale and leaseback, refinancing, and an exchange. This chapter integrates the concepts from the previous chapters and presents them in consecutive subsections that include a brief introduction and background information, example data, and detailed calculations to show how to make the decision. Specifically, we examine decisions such as whether to refinance an investment, whether to sell or to continue to operate, whether to sell on an

installment basis, and others. We also examine how the tax-deferred exchange method works. The reader is encouraged to solve each problem and use the text solutions as a check.

VACANT LAND INVESTMENT WITH SELLER FINANCING

This section illustrates a common alternative financing strategy and acquisition method. Seller financing in this case refers to the owner in essence becoming a lender to the buyer. In this example, a purchase money mortgage will be extended to the buyer (borrower) from the seller (lender) for a percent of the total price of a parcel of vacant land. The concepts of property taxes, assessed value, and millage rates are also explained. The after-tax cash flows from operations, after-tax equity reversion, and net present values are calculated. Last, sensitivity analysis is conducted to determine the effect of changes in the expected property value rates of increase on the NPV and IRR calculations.

For instance, suppose an investor is considering the purchase of a parcel of vacant land. The asking price is $100,000 of which the seller will finance 80 percent with a purchase money mortgage (PMM). The PMM has an interest rate of 12 percent with interest-only payments (payable annually) for five years at which time the entire amount is due and payable. The property tax is based on an assessed value of 40 percent of the market value and a millage rate of 30. Property taxes (due to the investment being vacant land) are the only operating expenses expected by the investor. The investor expects property values to increase at a rate of 15 percent per year over the five-year holding period with selling expenses equating 10 percent of the selling price. We note that the investor is in a 28 percent marginal tax bracket. Should the investor buy the land if a 15 percent after-tax rate of return on equity is required?

AFTER-TAX CASH FLOWS FROM OPERATIONS (ATCF)

Tables 12.1 and 12.2 compute the ATCFs and the taxes for operations in years one through five. The standard format is used except for the fact that there is no effective gross income. The net operating income is −$1,200 and the debt service is interest only, amounting to $9,600 per year ($80,000 × .12). This results in a before-tax cash flow (BTCF) of −$10,800 per year. The after-tax cash flows are then derived by subtracting the taxes (from table 12.2) from the BTCF, which yields a −$7,776 per year in ATCFs. The tax computations from table 12.2 use the standard format, except that the effective gross income, depreciation, amortized financing costs, and replacement reserves are zero. Therefore, the taxable income is −$10,800, with taxes of −$3,024 each year.

AFTER-TAX CASH FLOWS FROM SALE (ATER)

Tables 12.3 and 12.4 compute the ATER and taxes due on sale of the investment in year five. The expected selling price is calculated using the 15 percent yearly expected growth in the market value as follows:

$$\text{Selling price} = \$100,000\,(1.15)^5$$
$$= \$201,136$$

Table 12.1 MEASUREMENT OF EXPECTED CASH FLOW FROM OPERATION: VACANT LAND EXAMPLE

				YEAR			
			1	2	3	4	5
	Potential gross income (PGI)	$	0	0	0	0	0
Minus	Vacancy and bad debt allowance (VBD)	$	0	0	0	0	0
Plus	Miscellaneous income (MI)	$	0	0	0	0	0
Equals	Effective gross income (EGI)	$	0	0	0	0	0
Minus	Operating expenses (OE)	$	1,200	1,200	1,200	1,200	1,200
Equals	Net operating income (NOI)	$	(1,200)	(1,200)	(1,200)	(1,200)	(1,200)
Minus	Debt service (DS)	$	9,600	9,600	9,600	9,600	9,600
Equals	Before-tax cash flow (BTCF)	$	(10,800)	(10,800)	(10,800)	(10,800)	(10,800)
Minus	Taxes (savings) from operation (TO)*	$	(3,024)	(3,024)	(3,024)	(3,024)	(3,024)
Equals	After-tax cash flow (ATCF)	$	(7,776)	(7,776)	(7,776)	(7,776)	(7,776)

* See table 12.2.

Table 12.2 Measurement of Taxable Income and Taxes from Operation: Vacant Land Example

			YEAR				
			1	2	3	4	5
	Effective gross income (EGI)	$	0	0	0	0	0
Minus	Operating expenses (OE)	$	1,200	1,200	1,200	1,200	1,200
Equals	Net operating income (NOI)	$	(1,200)	(1,200)	(1,200)	(1,200)	(1,200)
Minus	Interest on debt (I)	$	9,600	9,600	9,600	9,600	9,600
Minus	Depreciation deduction (D)	$	0	0	0	0	0
Minus	Amortized financing costs (AFC)	$	0	0	0	0	0
Plus	Replacement reserves (RR)	$	0	0	0	0	0
Equals	Ordinary taxable income (OTI)	$	(10,800)	(10,800)	(10,800)	(10,800)	(10,800)
Times	Investor's marginal tax rate (t)		0.28	0.28	0.28	0.28	0.28
Equals	Taxes (savings) from operation (TO)	$	(3,024)	(3,024)	(3,024)	(3,024)	(3,024)

Table 12.3 Measurement of Expected Cash Flow
from the Sale: Vacant Land Example

	Expected selling price (SP)	$	201,136*
Minus	Selling expenses (SE)	$	20,114
Equals	Net sales proceeds (NSP)	$	181,022
Minus	Unpaid mortgage balance (UM)	$	80,000
Equals	Before-tax equity reversion (BTER)	$	101,022
Minus	Taxes due on sale (TDS)†	$	22,686
Equals	After-tax equity reversion (ATER)	$	78,336

* At a 15% increase in property value.

† See table 12.4 for taxes due on sale computation.

Table 12.4 Measurement of Taxable Income
and Taxes Due on Sale: Vacant Land Example

	TAXABLE INCOME		
	Expected selling price (SP)	$	201,136
Minus	Selling expenses (SE)	$	20,114
Equals	Amount realized (AR)	$	181,022
Minus	Adjusted basis (AB)	$	100,000
Equals	Capital gain on sale (CG)	$	81,022

	TAXES DUE ON SALE		
	Capital gain on sale (CG)	$	81,022
Times	Investor's marginal tax rate (t)		0.28
Equals	Taxes due on sale (TDS)	$	22,686

Table 12.5 Net Present Value and Internal Rate of Return: Vacant Land Example

Year	Equity (E)	After-Tax Cash Flow (ATCF)*	After-Tax Equity Reversion (ATER)†	Present Value Factor at 15% (PVF)	Present Value
0	−$20,000			1.0	−$20,000
1		−$7,776		.86957	− 6,762
2		− 7,776		.75614	− 5,880
3		− 7,776		.65752	− 5,113
4		− 7,776		.57175	− 4,446
5		− 7,776	$84,818	.49718	35,081
			Net Present Value =		−$ 7,120
			IRR = 9.44%		

* See table 12.1.

† See table 12.3.

The standard ATER format is used in this case, but note the entire principal amount of the PMM is due on sale. The taxes due on sale are computed in the normal fashion (table 12.4) and the capital gain is $81,022, resulting in $22,686 taxes due on sale. Note also that the adjusted basis is simply the original cost of $100,000, since land is not a depreciable asset.

The net present value for the investment (table 12.5) is computed at a 15 percent required return on equity. The net present value is calculated as −$7,120, which signals to not invest or reject the project. With vacant land, the return on equity is solely in appreciation of the property value at the time of sale. The IRR is found to be 9.44 percent, which is less than the required rate

of 15 percent. If the NPV is less than zero and the IRR does not exceed the required rate of return, then the investor should reject the investment.

Table 12.6 contains the ATER at various property value growth rates. This analysis is performed to determine how sensitive the decision is with respect to the property value growth rate. Table 12.7 shows that, as the rate of growth in property value rises (from 5 percent to 25 percent), the net present value increases (from −$30,802 to $26,399) and the internal rate of return increases (from −22.25 percent to 30.28 percent). Note also that at a growth rate between 15 percent and 25 percent, the NPV equals zero and the IRR equals the 15 percent required rate of return.

Table 12.6 After-tax Equity Reversion at Various Rates of Increase in Property Value: Vacant Land Example

	RATE OF PROPERTY VALUE APPRECIATION					
	5%	10%	13%	14%	15%	25%
ATER	30,703	52,361	67,390	72,767	78,336	145,754

Table 12.7 SENSITIVITY ANALYSIS OF EFFECTS OF RATE
OF APPRECIATION ON NPV AND IRR: VACANT LAND EXAMPLE

Rate of Appreciation	Net Present Value	Internal Rate of Return
5%	− $30,802	− 22.25
10	− 20,034	− 3.90
13	− 12,562	4.46
14	− 9,889	7.00
15	− 7,120	9.44
25	26,399	30.28

TRIPLEX EXAMPLE WITH A FIRST AND SECOND MORTGAGE

In this section, the concepts and mechanics of an investment with a first and second mortgage are explained. Suppose an investor is considering the purchase of a triplex residential property with an asking price of $95,000. Each unit is expected to rent for $350 per month and increase by 5 percent per year. The vacancy and bad debt losses are estimated to be three months' rental for one unit per year. The operating expense ratio is estimated to be 30 percent of EGI in year one and the operating expenses should increase 7 percent per year. The straight-line method (with a useful life of 27.5 years) is used and 85 percent of the total cost is depreciable.

This project can be financed with a first mortgage of $70,000 at an interest rate of 12 percent for twenty years with monthly payments. Costs of placing the mortgage against the property (points, appraisal fees, etc.) are estimated at 4 percent of the amount borrowed. There are prepayment penalties of 6 percent of the amount outstanding if the loan is paid off within years one through eight of the mortgage loan. A second interest-only mortgage of $10,000 is available from the seller with interest payments of $1,500 per year with the entire balance payable at the end of three years. The investor is in the 28 percent marginal

income tax bracket and expects to sell the investment for $140,000 at the end of five years. The selling expenses at the time of sale (end of year five) will be 8 percent.

Given this data, should the investor buy the triplex if a 15 percent after-tax rate of return on equity is required? In order to make this decision, we must calculate the amortization schedules for the two loans, the depreciation schedules, the after-tax cash flow from operations and sale, and the present value of these flows at the appropriate rate of return.

AMORTIZATION SCHEDULES

In computing the schedule for the first mortgage (see table 12.8), we first determine debt service by multiplying the amount borrowed ($70,000) by the monthly mortgage constant (.01101). The debt service is $770.70 per month, or $9,249 per year. The interest payment can be found in several ways, but in this case the proportion outstanding (from table 3 of appendix A) was multiplied by the amount borrowed to yield the amount outstanding at the end of each year. The principal payment in year 1 ($897) is found by subtracting the amount outstanding from the amount borrowed ($70,000 − $69,103). The interest payment ($8,352) is the debt service minus the principal payment ($9,249 − $897).

Table 12.8 Mortgage Amortization Schedules: Triplex Example

Total cost:	$95,000
Loan-to-value ratio:	84.21%
Amount borrowed:	$70,000 on first mortgage
	$10,000 on second mortgage
Interest rate:	12% on first mortgage
	15% on second mortgage
Maturity term:	20 years on first mortgage
	3 years on second mortgage
Payments:	Monthly on first mortgage
	Yearly on second mortgage; interest only with
	balance due at end of three years
Annual mortgage constant:	.133879; for first mortgage
Debt service:	$9,249 yearly for first mortgage
	$1,500 yearly for second mortgage

AMORTIZATION SCHEDULE FOR FIRST MORTGAGE

Year	Proportion Outstanding	Amount Outstanding	Debt Service	Interest Payment	Principal Payment
0	1.0	$70,000			
1	.98718	69,103	$9,249	$8,352	$ 897
2	.97273	68,091	9,249	8,237	1,012
3	.95646	66,952	9,249	8,110	1,139
4	.93811	65,668	9,249	7,965	1,284
5	.91744	64,221	9,249	7,802	1,447

AMORTIZATION SCHEDULE FOR SECOND MORTGAGE

Year	Amount Outstanding	Debt Service	Interest Payment	Principal Payment
0	$10,000			
1	10,000	$1,500	$1,500	0
2	10,000	1,500	1,500	0
3	0	1,500	1,500	$10,000
	Debt service years 1 and 2 equals			$10,749
	Debt service in year 3 equals			$20,749
	Debt service after year 3 equals			$ 9,249

The schedule for the second mortgage (see table 12.8) is quite basic because the principal payments in years one and two are zero, and $10,000 in year three. The amount outstanding remains $10,000 until year 3. The total debt service is $10,749 in years one and two, $20,749 in year three, and $9,249 in year four. In year five, the debt service is $9,249, plus a prepayment penalty of $3,853.

Depreciation Schedules

In computing the depreciation deduction under the straight-line method (see table 12.9), the depreciable basis is divided by 27.5 years. In table 12.9, this is illustrated by multiplying the book value ($80,750) by the straight-line percentage (3.636 percent) to derive the straight-line deduction of $2,936.

Table 12.9 DEPRECIATION SCHEDULES: TRIPLEX EXAMPLE

Total cost	$95,000
Depreciable amount	80,750
Nondepreciable amount	14,250
Useful life	27.5 years

STRAIGHT-LINE METHOD

Year	Proportion	Book Value	Deduction
0		$80,750	$2,936
1	.03636	77,814	2,936
2	.03636	74,878	2,936
3	.03636	71,942	2,936
4	.03636	69,006	2,936
5	.03636	66,070	2,936

CASH FLOWS FROM OPERATIONS

Tables 12.10 and 12.11 illustrate the derivation of the ATCF and taxes for years one through five on this triplex investment. The potential gross income in each year (rent × number of units × 12) is growing at a 5 percent rate (e.g., $12,600 for year one to $13,230 for year two, and so forth).

The effective gross income is derived by subtracting the vacancy and bad debts from the potential gross income. The operating expenses ($3,465) in year one are found by multiplying the operating expenses ratio by the effective gross income. These expenses increase at a rate of 7 percent per year.

The net operating income is found by subtracting the operating expenses from the effective gross income. The debt service in years one and two is the sum of the debt service on the first mortgage ($9,249) and the interest on the second mortgage ($1,500). In year three, the debt service is the sum of the debt service on the first mortgage and the interest and principal repayment on the second mortgage. Debt service in year four is the debt service on the first mortgage. In year five, the debt service includes the prepayment penalty of $3,853 (.06 × $64,221).

The before-tax cash flow is the difference between the net operating income and the debt service. To compute the after-tax cash flow, we must use the taxes from table 12.11 and deduct them from the before-tax cash

Table 12.10 MEASUREMENT OF EXPECTED CASH FLOW FROM OPERATION: TRIPLEX EXAMPLE

		YEARS				
		1	2	3	4	5
	Potential gross income (PGI)	$ 12,600	13,230	13,892	14,586	15,315
Minus	Vacancy and bad debt allowance (VBD)	$ 1,050	1,103	1,158	1,216	1,276
Plus	Miscellaneous income (MI)	$ 0	0	0	0	0
Equals	Effective gross income (EGI)	$ 11,550	12,127	12,734	13,370	14,039
Minus	Operating expenses (OE)	$ 3,465	3,708	3,967	4,245	4,542
Equals	Net operating income (NOI)	$ 8,085	8,419	8,766	9,125	9,497
Minus	Debt service (DS)	$ 10,749	10,749	20,749	9,249	13,102[†]
Equals	Before-tax cash flow (BTCF)	$ (2,664)	(2,330)	(11,983)	(124)	(3,605)
Minus	Taxes (savings) from operation (TO)*	$ (1,356)	(1,231)	(1,097)	(537)	(2,054)
Equals	After-tax cash flow (ATCF)	$ (1,308)	(1,099)	(10,885)	413	(1,551)

* See table 12.11.

† This includes $3,853 in prepayment penalties.

Table 12.11 MEASUREMENT OF TAXABLE INCOME AND TAXES FROM OPERATION: TRIPLEX EXAMPLE

			YEARS			
		1	2	3	4	5
	Effective gross income (EGI)	$ 11,550	12,127	12,734	13,370	14,039
Minus	Operating expenses (OE)	$ 3,465	3,708	3,967	4,245	4,542
Equals	Net operating income (NOI)	$ 8,085	8,419	8,766	9,125	9,497
Minus	Interest on debt (I)	$ 9,852	9,738	9,610	7,965	11,656*
Minus	Depreciation deduction (D)	$ 2,936	2,936	2,936	2,936	2,936
Minus	Amortized financing costs (AFC)	$ 140	140	140	140	2,240
Plus	Replacement reserves (RR)	$ 0	0	0	0	0
Equals	Ordinary taxable income (OTI)	$ (4,843)	(4,395)	(3,920)	(1,916)	(7,334)
Times	Investor's marginal tax rate	0.28	0.28	0.28	0.28	0.28
Equals	Taxes (savings) from operations (TO)	$ (1,356)	(1,231)	(1,097)	(537)	(2,054)

* This figure includes $7,802 for interest deduction and $3,853 in prepayment penalties.

flow. This table computes the taxes by subtracting the operating expenses, depreciation deduction, interest, and amortized financing costs from effective gross income to derive the taxable income. This taxable income is then multiplied by the investor's tax rate to derive the taxes. Note that there were financing costs of $2,800 on the first mortgage. These are amortized for tax purposes at $\frac{1}{20}$ each year ($140). The remaining amount is deducted in year five.

CASH FLOW FROM SALE (ATER)

Tables 12.12 and 12.13 illustrate the derivation of the after-tax cash flow from sale (ATER) and taxes due on sale. Table 12.12 computes the ATER by subtracting the selling expenses, unpaid mortgage, and taxes due on sale from the expected selling price. The taxes due on sale are derived from table 12.13 by first computing the taxable income of $51,004. The taxes due on sale are com-

Table 12.12 MEASUREMENT OF EXPECTED CASH FLOW FROM THE SALE: TRIPLEX EXAMPLE

	Expected selling price (SP)	$ 140,000
Minus	Selling expenses (SE)	$ 11,200
Equals	Net sales proceeds (NSP)	$ 128,800
Minus	Unpaid mortgage balance (UM)	$ 64,221
Equals	Before-tax equity reversion (BTER)	$ 64,579
Minus	Taxes due on sale (TDS)*	$ 13,575
Equals	After-tax equity reversion (ATER)	$ 51,004

* See Table 12.13.

Table 12.13 MEASUREMENT OF TAXABLE INCOME
AND TAXES DUE ON SALE: TRIPLEX EXAMPLE

TAXABLE INCOME

	Expected selling price (SP)	$ 140,000
Minus	Selling expenses (SE)	$ 11,200
Equals	Amount realized (AR)	$ 128,800
Minus	Adjusted basis (AB)	$ 80,318
Equals	Capital gain on sale (CG)	$ 48,482

TAXES DUE ON SALE

	Capital gain on sale (CG)	$ 48,482
Times	Investor's marginal tax rate	0.28
Equals	Taxes due on sale (TDS)	$ 13,575

puted by multiplying the capital gain by the investor's marginal tax rate of 28 percent.

NET PRESENT VALUE AND IRR

Tables 12.14 and 12.15 compute the net present value at 15 percent and 11 percent required rates of return. At 11 percent, the net present value is a positive $1,791. (The investor would accept the investment at a required rate of 11 percent.) The internal rate of return is 12.73 percent.

SALE VERSUS CONTINUE TO OPERATE

Another decision facing the real estate investor is that of continuing to operate versus sale. In this section, we illustrate how to make this decision.

Consider a real estate investor (in a 40 percent tax bracket) who owns an apartment investment that was puchased five years ago for $500,000. The depreciable basis was $400,000. The investor has been using the straight-line depreciation method

Table 12.14 NET PRESENT VALUE AND INTERNAL RATE OF RETURN:
TRIPLEX EXAMPLE

Year	Equity (E)	After-Tax Cash Flow (ATCF)*	After-Tax Equity Reversion (ATER)†	Present Value Factor at 15% (PVF)	Present Value
0	− $17,800			1.0	− 17,800
1		− $1,308		.86956	− 1,137
2		− 1,099		.75614	− 831
3		− 10,885		.65752	− 7,157
4		413		.57175	236
5		− 1,551	$51,004	.49718	24,587
			Net present value =		− 2,102
			IRR = 12.73%		

* See table 12.10.

† See table 12.12.

Table 12.15 NET PRESENT VALUE AND INTERNAL RATE OF RETURN:
TRIPLEX EXAMPLE

Year	Equity (E)	After-Tax Cash Flow (ATCF)*	After-Tax Equity Reversion (ATER)†	Present Value Factor at 11% (PVF)	Present Value
0	− $17,800			1.0	− $17,800
1		− $1,308		.90090	− 1,178
2		− 1,099		.81162	− 892
3		− 10,885		.73119	− 7,959
4		413		.65873	272
5		− 1,551	$51,004	.59345	29,348
			Net present value =		− $ 1,791
			IRR = 12.73%		

* See table 12.10.

† See table 12.12.

with a 27.5-year life. The investment was financed with a $375,000 fixed-rate mortgage at an interest rate of 10 percent with monthly payments for 25 years. The investor estimates that the current selling price is $625,000. Selling expenses would be 7 percent of the selling price.

The investor is trying to decide whether to sell or continue to operate for five more years. The NOI next year is expected to be $68,750 and is expected to increase 2 percent per year. The value of the investment is expected to be $675,000 at the end of this additional five years with selling expenses of 7 percent.

Which option should the investor select (to sell or continue to operate) if the required after-tax rate of return is 12 percent?

ATER FROM SALE TODAY

In order to determine whether to sell or continue to operate, the investor must first compute the after-tax cash flow from sale *now* (or ATER). This is illustrated in table 12.16 by subtracting the selling expenses, unpaid mortgage (from table 12.18), and taxes (from table 12.17) from the selling price. Table 12.17 computes the taxes using the standard equations. Table 12.18 is an amortization

Table 12.16 MEASUREMENT OF EXPECTED CASH FLOW
FROM THE SALE OF AN INVESTMENT

	Expected selling price (SP)	$ 625,000
Minus	Selling expenses (SE)	$ 43,750
Equals	Net sales proceeds (NSP)	$ 581,250
Minus	Unpaid mortgage balance (UM)	$ 353,115
Equals	Before-tax equity reversion (BTER)	$ 228,135
Minus	Taxes due on sale (TDS)*	$ 43,114
Equals	After-tax equity reversion (ATER)	$ 185,021

* See table 12.17.

Table 12.17 Measurement of Taxable Income and Taxes Due on Sale

	TAXABLE INCOME	
	Expected selling price (SP)	$ 625,000
Minus	Selling expenses (SE)	$ 43,750
Equals	Amount realized (AR)	$ 581,250
Minus	Adjusted basis (AB)	$ 427,273
Equals	Capital gain on sale (CG)	$ 153,977

	TAXES DUE ON SALE	
	Capital gain on sale (CG)	$ 153,977
Times	Investor's marginal tax rate	0.28
Equals	Taxes due on sale (TDS)	$ 43,114

Table 12.18 Mortgage Amortization Schedule: $375,000 Loan at 10 Percent with Twenty-five-year Maturity, Monthly Payments

Year	Proportion Outstanding	Amount Outstanding	Debt Service	Interest	Principal
0	1.0	$375,000			
1	.99053	$371,449	$40,892	$37,341	$3,551
2	.98007	367,526	40,892	36,969	3,923
3	.96851	363,191	40,892	36,557	4,335
4	.95574	358,403	40,892	36,104	4,788
5	.94164	353,115	40,892	35,604	5,288
6	.92606	347,273	40,892	35,050	5,842
7	.90884	340,815	40,892	34,434	6,458
8	.88983	333,686	40,892	33,763	7,129
9	.86882	325,808	40,892	33,014	7,878
10	.84561	317,104	40,892	32,188	8,704

schedule for the loan that was originated *five years ago*. In other words, the amount outstanding today is the unpaid mortgage in year five of the loan ($353,115).

Cash Flows from Continuing to Operate

Tables 12.19 and 12.20 compute the after-tax cash flows and taxes from continuing to operate. Table 12.19 computes the after-tax flows (for years one to five) by subtracting debt service and taxes (table 12.20) from net operating income.

ATER from Continuing to Operate

Table 12.21 computes the after-tax cash flow (ATER) from sale five years from now. The ATER is equal to the selling price, minus the selling expenses, unpaid mortgage ($317,105), and taxes (from table 12.22).

Table 12.19 MEASUREMENT OF EXPECTED CASH FLOW FROM OPERATION

		YEARS				
		1	2	3	4	5
	Net operating income (NOI)	$ 68,750	70,125	71,528	72,958	74,417
Minus	Debt service (DS)	$ 40,892	40,892	40,892	40,892	40,892
Equals	Before-tax cash flow (BTCF)	$ 27,858	29,233	30,636	32,066	33,525
Minus	Taxes (savings) from operation (TO)*	$ 5,364	5,920	6,502	7,112	7,751
Equals	After-tax cash flow (ATCF)	$ 22,494	23,313	24,134	24,954	25,774

* See table 12.20.

Table 12.20 MEASUREMENT OF TAXABLE INCOME AND TAXES FROM OPERATION

		YEARS				
		1	2	3	4	5
Equals	Net operating income (NOI)	$ 68,750	70,125	71,528	72,958	74,417
Minus	Interest on debt (I)	$ 35,048	34,437	33,761	33,014	32,189
Minus	Depreciation deduction (D)	$ 14,545	14,545	14,545	14,545	14,545
Minus	Amortized financing costs (AFC)	$ 0	0	0	0	0
Plus	Replacement reserves (RR)	$ 0	0	0	0	0
Equals	Ordinary taxable income (OTI)	$ 19,157	21,143	23,221	25,399	27,683
Times	Investor's marginal tax rate (t)	0.28	0.28	0.28	0.28	0.28
Equals	Taxes (savings) from operation (TO)	$ 5,364	5,920	6,502	7,112	7,751

* See table 12.22.

Table 12.21 MEASUREMENT OF EXPECTED CASH FLOW FROM THE SALE

	Expected selling price (SP)	$ 675,000
Minus	Selling expenses (SE)	$ 47,250
Equals	Net sales proceeds (NSP)	$ 627,750
Minus	Unpaid mortgage balance (UM)	$ 317,105
Equals	Before-tax equity reversion (BTER)	$ 310,645
Minus	Taxes due on sale (TDS)*	$ 76,497
Equals	After-tax equity reversion (ATER)	$ 234,148

* See table 12.22.

Table 12.22 MEASUREMENT OF TAXABLE INCOME AND TAXES DUE ON SALE

	TAXABLE INCOME	
	Expected selling price (SP)	$ 675,000
Minus	Selling expenses (SE)	$ 47,250
Equals	Amount realized (AR)	$ 627,750
Minus	Adjusted basis (AB)	$ 354,545
Equals	Capital gain on sale (CG)	$ 273,205
	TAXES DUE ON SALE	
	Capital gain on sale (CG)	$ 273,205
Times	Investor's marginal tax rate	0.28
Equals	Taxes due on sale (TDS)	$ 76,497

DIFFERENTIAL CASH FLOWS

Table 12.23 illustrates the differential after-tax cash flows of continuing to operate versus selling. The cash flows from selling today are subtracted from the flows from continuing to operate to reach the differential flows. Notice the differential at time point zero is negative, which symbolizes the foregone flow from sale if the investor decides to continue to operate.

NPV AND IRR OF CONTINUING TO OPERATE

Table 12.24 illustrates the calculation of the NPV (at 15 percent) of continuing to op-

erate. This is done by multiplying the differential after-tax cash flows by present value factors. The NPV is found to be a positive $11,534, which indicates continued operation. The IRR is calculated to be 16.72 percent and, with this information, we can formulate the decision criteria:

1. If the opportunity rate is less than 16.72 percent, then continue to operate.
2. If the opportunity rate is greater than 16.72 percent, then sell (don't continue to operate).

Table 12.23 DIFFERENTIAL AFTER-TAX CASH FLOWS OF CONTINUING TO OPERATE VERSUS SALE

Year	ATCF from Continue to Operate	ATCF from Sale Today	Differential Cash Flows
0	$ 0	$185,021	−$185,021
1	22,495	0	22,495
2	23,314	0	23,314
3	24,134	0	24,134
4	24,955	0	24,955
5	259,923	0	259,923

Table 12.24 NET PRESENT VALUE AND IRR OF CONTINUING TO OPERATE

Year	Differential After-Tax Cash Flow	Present Value Factor at 15%	Present Value
0	−$185,021	1.0	−$185,021
1	22,495	.86957	19,561
2	23,314	.75614	17,629
3	24,134	.65752	15,869
4	24,955	.57175	14,268
5	259,923	.49718	129,228
		Net present value =	$ 11,534
		IRR =	16.72%

The opportunity rate referred to here is merely that rate of return an investor can receive on an alternative investment of equal risk. Since the NPV in this case is positive, the investor can conclude that continuing to operate is the best option, since the present value of the inflows from operating exceed the present value of the flow from selling.

INSTALLMENT SALE VERSUS OUTRIGHT SALE

An installment sale is the sale of property where the buyer agrees to pay the seller in a number of installments rather than a lump sum at the time of purchase. For a more detailed discussion of installment sales, review chapter 8.

To illustrate how an installment sale works, consider the following examples: A real estate investor (in the 28 percent marginal tax bracket) is considering the installment sale of a small apartment building. This complex was purchased eight years ago at a total price of $150,000. The investor's depreciable basis was 85 percent of total cost. The straight-line method of depreciation has been used with a recovery life of 27.5 years. The investment was financed with a 12 percent mortgage of $112,500 with monthly payments for 25 years.

The installment sale offer that the investor is considering is as follows: A sale price of $250,000 with the buyer assuming a balance of $102,924 of the existing mortgage, and the seller taking a purchase money mortgage for the remaining balance of $147,076 at 11 percent interest and annual payments over 5 years, with a balloon payment for the balance at the end of year 5. The annual payment will be $39,794. Table 12.25 gives the amortization schedule for

Table 12.25 MORTGAGE AMORTIZATION SCHEDULE: PURCHASE MONEY MORTGAGE*

Year	Amount Outstanding	Debt Service	Interest	Principal
0	$147,076			
1	123,460	$39,794	$16,178	$23,616
2	97,247	39,794	13,581	26,213
3	68,150	39,794	10,697	29,097
4	35,852	39,794	7,496	32,298
5	0	39,794	3,944	35,850

* Any differences due to rounding errors.

this purchase money mortgage. The selling expenses are $12,500 (or 5 percent of the selling price).

Alternatively, the investor could sell the investment outright for a price of $250,000 with selling expenses of 5 percent of the selling price. At a required rate of return of 12 percent, which is the better offer: installment or outright sale?

ATCF IN YEAR OF INSTALLMENT SALE

Table 12.26 shows the after-tax cash flow in the year of installment sale. This is computed by subtracting the selling expenses and the taxes (see table 12.27) from the amount of the down payment. Table 12.27 computes the taxes in the year of installment sale by deriving the taxable gain using the profit percentage (from table 12.28) and multiplying this gain by the investor's marginal tax rate.

Table 12.26 AFTER-TAX CASH FLOW IN YEAR OF INSTALLMENT SALE

	Down payment	$ 0
Minus	Selling expenses	− 12,500
Minus	Taxes*	− 11,281
Equals	ATCF	− 23,781

* See table 12.27.

Table 12.27 TAX IN YEAR OF INSTALLMENT SALE

	Excess of mortgage over adjusted basis and selling expenses	$21,664
Plus	Down payment	0
Equals	Payment received in year of sale	$21,664
Plus	Allocable installment indebtedness*	32,900
Equals	Taxable portion of gain from receipts	$54,564
Times	Profit percentage†	73.84%
Equals	Taxable income in year of sale	$40,290
Times	Marginal tax rate	.28
Equals	Tax in year of sale	$11,281

* See table 12.29.

† See table 12.28.

Table 12.28 PROFIT PERCENTAGE ON INSTALLMENT SALE

	TOTAL GAIN	
	Sale price	$250,000
Minus	Selling expense	− 12,500
Minus	Adjusted basis	−112,912
		$124,588

	CONTRACT PRICE	
	Sale price	$250,000
Plus	Excess mortgage over basis and selling expense	21,664
Minus	Morgage balance assured	−102,924
		$168,740

	PROFIT PERCENTAGE	
	Total gain	$124,588
Divided by	Contract price	$168,740
		73.84%

Table 12.28 computes the profit percentage by dividing the total gain (selling price minus selling expenses and the adjusted basis) by the contract price (sale price plus the excess mortgage over basis and selling expenses minus the assumed mortgage balance).

ATCF FROM INSTALLMENT RECEIPTS

Table 12.29 computes the investor's allocable installment indebtedness (AII). In the year of sale the investor has average quarterly indebtedness of $100,000 and an adjusted basis in his other assets of $300,000.

Table 12.29 ALLOCABLE INSTALLMENT INDEBTEDNESS

	Installments to be paid	$147,076
Divided by	Installments to be paid plus adjusted basis of assets	447,076
Equals	Installment percentage	32.90%
Times	Average quarterly indebtedness	$100,000
Equals	Allocable installment indebtedness	$32,900

Table 12.30 AFTER-TAX CASH FLOW FROM INSTALLMENT RECEIPTS

		YEARS				
		1	2	3	4	5
	BTCF (debt service)	$39,794	$39,794	$39,794	$39,794	$39,794
Minus	Taxes (.28)	(4,340)	(11,142)	(11,142)	(11,142)	(11,142)
Equals	ATCF	$35,454	$26,722	$26,722	$26,722	$26,722

By multiplying the installment percentage by the average quarterly indebtedness the seller must recognize a gain of $32,900 in the year of sale. When payments are received in preceding years, $24,293 will be shielded from tax to avoid double taxation; however, any amounts received over this will be taxed as ordinary income at the investor's marginal tax rate.

Table 12.30 computes the after-tax cash flow from the installment receipts for years one through five. This after-tax cash flow is simply the before-tax cash flow (or debt service) minus taxes determined by mul-

tiplying the BTCF times the seller's marginal tax rate. In year one, $24,293 (32,900 × 73.84 percent) is shielded from tax because it was previously taxed in the year of sale.

ATER FROM OUTRIGHT SALE

Tables 12.31 and 12.32 are needed to compare an outright sale to the installment sale. This is done by first computing the after-tax equity reversion from the outright sale (selling price $250,000). The after-tax equity reversion is selling price less selling

Table 12.31 EXPECTED CASH FLOW FROM SALE

	Expected selling price (SP)	$250,000
Minus	Selling expenses (SE)	− 12,500
Equals	Net sale proceeds (NSP)	237,500
Minus	Unpaid mortgage balance (UM)	− 102,924
Equals	Before-tax equity reversion (BTER)	134,576
Minus	Taxes due on sale (TDS)*	− 34,885
Equals	After-tax equity reversion (ATER)	$ 99,691

* See table 12.32.

Table 12.32 Expected Taxes Due on Sale

TAXABLE INCOME

	Expected selling price (SP)	$250,000
Minus	Selling expenses (SE)	−12,500
Equals	Amount realized (AR)	237,500
Minus	Adjusted basis (AB)	−112,912
Equals	Capital gain on sale (CG)	$124,588

TAXES DUE ON SALE

Equals	Capital gain on sale (CG)	$124,588
Times	Investor's marginal tax rate (t)	.28
Equals	Taxes due on sale (TDS)	$ 34,885

expenses, unpaid mortgage, and taxes due on sale (table 12.32).

DIFFERENTIAL CASH FLOWS

Table 12.33 computes the differential after-tax cash flows of installment sale versus outright sale. This differential is simply the installment sale cash flows minus the outright sale cash flows (for each year). Notice at time point zero, the differential is a negative because with the installment sale the investor loses the net of the outright sale proceeds and the installment sale proceeds.

Table 12.33 DIFFERENTIAL AFTER-TAX CASH FLOW OF INSTALLMENT SALE VERSUS OUTRIGHT SALE

Year	Installment Sale Cash Flow	Outright Sale Cash Flow	Differential
0	(24,987)	99,691	(124,678)
1	35,454	0	35,454
2	26,722	0	26,722
3	26,722	0	26,722
4	26,722	0	26,722
5	26,722	0	26,722

NPV AND IRR OF INSTALLMENT SALE

Table 12.34 calculates the NPV and IRR for the installment sale versus the outright sale. The NPV (−$20,411) is calculated by multiplying the differential flows (from table 12.33) by their respective present value factors at the 12 percent required rate of return. Thus, given the 12 percent required rate, since the NPV is negative, the investor should not pursue the installment sale, but instead sell outright. The IRR is computed to be 4.82 percent. From this we conclude:

1. If the required rate is less than 4.82 percent, then select the installment sale.
2. If the required rate is greater than 4.82 percent, then select outright sale.

REFINANCE VERSUS NOT REFINANCE

Another decision facing a real estate investor is whether or not to refinance an investment. To illustrate this decision-making process consider the following example.

A real estate investor owns an investment that was purchased five years ago for $500,000. The depreciable basis was $400,000. The investor has been using the straight-line depreciation method with a

Table 12.34 NET PRESENT VALUE AND IRR OF INSTALLMENT SALE VERSUS OUTRIGHT SALE

Year	Differential After-Tax Cash Flow	Present Value Factor at 12%	Present Value
0	−$124,678	.0	−$124,678
1	35,454	.892857	31,655
2	26,722	.7971194	21,301
3	26,722	.711780	19,020
4	26,722	.635518	16,982
5	26,722	.567427	− 15,163

Net present value = $− 20,557

IRR = 4.82%

27.5-year life. The investment was financed with a $375,000 fixed-rate mortgage at an interest rate of 10 percent with monthly payments for 25 years. The investor is in a 28 percent tax bracket. The estimated current selling price is $625,000. Selling expenses would be 7 percent of the selling price.

The investment is expected to generate $68,750 in net operating income next year. The NOI is expected to increase 2 percent per year. The investor expects to sell the investment for $675,000 five years from now, with selling expenses of 7 percent.

Now the investor is considering refinancing the investment. The new loan would be for $468,750 (75 percent of current value) with a 13 percent interest rate, twenty-five-year term, with monthly payments. Table 12.35 gives the mortgage amortization schedule for this new loan. There are origination fees of three points (3 percent of the loan amount) if the investor refinances. The proceeds could be reinvested at an opportunity rate of 15 percent. Should the investment be refinanced?

CASH FLOWS WITHOUT REFINANCING

Tables 12.19 and 12.20 calculate the ATCF without refinancing. See the explanation of these calculations in the "sale versus continue to operate" discussion.

Table 12.21 computes the ATER from future sale without refinancing, and table 12.22 calculates the taxes due on sale. A complete explanation of this procedure is also found in our discussion of sale versus continued operation.

CASH FLOWS WITH REFINANCING

Table 12.36 computes the ATCF from operations with refinancing by deducting the debt service and the taxes (from table 12.37) from the NOI. Table 12.37 computes the taxes from operations with refinancing by first deducting interest, depreciation, and amortized financing costs from NOI to derive the taxable income. The taxable income is multiplied by the marginal tax rate to compute the taxes (or savings). Table 12.38 computes the cash flow from sale in year five with refinancing. This is accomplished by deducting selling expenses, unpaid mortgage, and taxes due on sale (from table 12.27) from the selling price to arrive at the ATER. Notice that the taxes due on sale are the same under both options.

DIFFERENTIAL CASH FLOWS

Table 12.39 computes the net proceeds from refinancing by subtracting the origination fees and unpaid existing mortgage from the new loan amount. This difference equals the net proceeds from refinancing of $101,572.

Table 12.40 illustrates the differential

Table 12.35 MORTGAGE AMORTIZATION SCHEDULE: $468,750, 13 PERCENT, TWENTY-FIVE YEARS WITH MONTHLY PAYMENTS

Year	Proportion Outstanding	Amount Outstanding	Debt Service	Interest	Principal
0	1.0	$468,750			
1	.99433	466,092	$63,441	$60,783	$2,658
2	.98788	463,067	63,441	60,416	3,025
3	.98053	459,625	63,441	59,999	3,442
4	.97218	455,708	63,441	59,524	3,917
5	.96267	451,249	63,441	58,982	4,459

Table 12.36 MEASUREMENT OF EXPECTED CASH FLOW FROM OPERATION: WITH REFINANCING

			YEARS			
		1	2	3	4	5
	Net operating income (NOI)	$ 68,750	70,125	71,528	72,958	74,417
Minus	Debt service (DS)	$ 63,441	63,441	63,441	63,441	63,441
Equals	Before-tax cash flow (BTCF)	$ 5,309	6,684	8,087	9,517	10,976
Minus	Taxes (savings) from operation (TO)*	$ (3,018)	(2,530)	(2,020)	(1,487)	(4,077)
Equals	After-tax cash flow (ATCF)	$ 8,327	9,214	10,107	11,004	15,053

* See table 12.37.

Table 12.37 MEASUREMENT OF TAXABLE INCOME AND TAXES FROM OPERATION: WITH REFINANCING

			YEARS			
		1	2	3	4	5
	Net operating income (NOI)	$ 68,750	70,125	71,528	72,958	74,417
Minus	Interest on debt (I)	$ 60,783	60,416	59,999	59,524	58,982
Minus	Depreciation deduction (D)	$ 18,182	18,182	18,182	18,182	18,182
Minus	Amortized financing costs (AFC)	$ 563	563	563	563	11,813
Plus	Replacement reserves (RR)	$ 0	0	0	0	0
Equals	Ordinary taxable income (OTI)	$ (10,778)	(9,036)	(7,216)	(5,311)	(14,560)
Times	Investor's marginal tax rate (T)	0.28	0.28	0.28	0.28	0.28
Equals	Taxes (savings) from operation (TO)	$ (3,018)	(2,530)	(2,020)	(1,487)	(4,077)

Table 12.38 MEASUREMENT OF EXPECTED CASH FLOW FROM
THE SALE: IN YEAR FIVE WITH REFINANCING

	Expected selling price (SP)	$ 675,000
Minus	Selling expenses (SE)	$ 47,250
Equals	Net sales proceeds (NSP)	$ 627,750
Minus	Unpaid mortgage balance (UM)	$ 451,249
Equals	Before-tax equity reversion (BTER)	$ 176,501
Minus	Taxes due on sale (TDS)*	$ 76,497
Equals	After-tax equity reversion (ATER)	$ 100,004

* See table 12.22.

Table 12.39 CASH INFLOW FROM REFINANCING

	New loan amount	$ $468,750
Minus	Origination fees	$ − 14,063
Equals	Net new loan proceeds	$ 454,687
Minus	Unpaid existing mortgage	$ − 353,115
Equals	Net proceeds from refinancing	$ $101,572

Table 12.40 DIFFERENTIAL CASH FLOW OF REFINANCING VERSUS NOT REFINANCING

| Year | WITH REFINANCING | | WITHOUT REFINANCING | | Differential |
	ATCF	ATER	ATCF	ATER	
0	$101,572*		0		$101,572
1	8,327		$22,495		−14,168
2	9,214		23,314		−14,100
3	10,107		24,134		−14,027
4	11,004		24,955		−13,951
5	15,053	$100,004	25,775	$185,021	−95,739

* This is the net proceeds from refinancing in table 12.39.

cash flows of refinancing versus not refinancing. The ATCF and ATER from not refinancing is deducted from the ATCF and ATER from refinancing to reach the differential. The year 0 differential (from table 12.39) is the net proceeds from refinancing ($101,572). These differentials represent the net inflows from refinancing. In essence, the differential cash flow can be interpreted as follows: In year 0, the investor receives a net (after-tax) cash inflow of $101,572 from refinancing for which he must "pay" $14,168 in year one, $14,100 in year two, and so on.

NPV AND IRR FOR REFINANCING

Table 12.41 contains the computation of the NPV of refinancing at a 15 percent rate. The differential after-tax cash flows are multiplied by the appropriate present value factors to find the present value. The sum of these present values is the net present value (+$13,791 in this case). This positive net present value indicates that the decision to refinance should be accepted. The IRR is found to be 10.69 percent, which can be interpreted as follows:

1. If the opportunity rate is greater than 10.69 percent, then refinance.

2. If the opportunity rate is less than 10.69 percent, then don't refinance.

BUYING SECOND MORTGAGES

Many investors have become interested in buying mortgages. We will show how to determine the price (or value) an investor is willing to pay for a "second" mortgage. The risks should be considered when deciding whether to buy a mortgage. Obviously, the greater the risk, the greater the required rate of return on the investment. Data on the mortgage and the investor will be given and then we will show how to calculate the value of the mortgage, after-tax cash flows,

Table 12.41 NET PRESENT VALUE OF REFINANCING

	Differential After-Tax Cash Flow	Present Value Factor at 15%	Present Value
0	$101,572	1.0	$101,572
1	−14,168	.86957	−12,320
2	−14,100	.75614	−10,662
3	−14,027	.65752	−9,223
4	−13,951	.57175	−7,976
5	−95,739	.49718	−47,600
		NPV =	$13,791
		IRR =	10.69%

and NPV and IRR from buying a second mortgage.

SECOND MORTGAGE DATA

Assume a real estate investor in a 28 percent marginal tax bracket has decided to purchase a $20,000 second mortgage. The second mortgage has a 13 percent stated interest rate and the annual payments are based on a thirty-year amortization period with a balloon payment at the end of year five. The investor's required before-tax rate of return is 16 percent. How much should the investor pay for the mortgage to achieve the required rate of return?

BEFORE-TAX CASH FLOW AND VALUE

Table 12.42 shows the computation of the before-tax cash flow and total present value to the investor. The purchase price that will yield the required rate of return is the present value of all future mortgage payments (interest and principal payments) at the required rate of return. In table 12.42, the annual mortgage payment is $2,668 for five years with a balloon payment of $19,559 (in year five). The total present value of these flows is $18,048 at a 16 percent required

rate, or the value of the mortgage. The investor would be willing to pay $18,048 at the required rate of return of 16 percent. If the risks were higher, the investor would require a higher rate of return, and the present value (or amount he would have to pay) would be less.

TAX ASPECTS

The income the investor receives from the second mortgage is taxable. The stated interest payments on the mortgage are interest income and taxed as ordinary income. The collection of the discount (the difference between the face value of the note and the amount paid for the note) is also ordinary income. If the investor is a cash basis taxpayer, the stated interest income is reported when received. A portion of each principal payment is also reportable as ordinary taxable income which represents the discount.

AFTER-TAX CASH FLOW FROM SECOND MORTGAGE

Table 12.43 illustrates the derivation of the after-tax cash flows to the investor for years one through five. This table shows how to compute discounted income [principal

Table 12.42 How to Find the Value of a Mortgage

Year	Debt Service* Payment	Interest	Principal Reduction	Amount Outstanding	Balloon Payment	Present Value Factor at 16%	Present Value†
0				$20,000			
1	$2,668	$2,600	$ 68	19,932		.8621	$ 2,300
2	2,668	2,591	77	19,855		.7432	1,983
3	2,668	2,581	87	19,768		.6407	1,709
4	2,668	2,570	98	19,670		.5523	1,474
5	2,668	2,557	111	19,559	$19,559	.4761	10,582

Total present value = $18,048

* Amortization schedule based on a thirty-year payback at 13 percent annual.

† Equals debt service times present value factor in years one through four. In year five, it equals the balloon payment plus the debt service times the present value factors.

Table 12.43 After-tax Cash Flows: From Second Mortgage

Year	Principal[1] Payment	Discount[2] Proportion	Discount[3] Income	Interest[4] Income	Taxable[5] Income	Tax Rate	Tax[6]	After-Tax[7]
0								
1	$ 68	.0976	$ 7	$2,600	$2,607	.28	$ 730	$ 1,938
2	77	.0976	8	2,591	2,599	.28	728	1,940
3	87	.0976	9	2,581	2,590	.28	725	1,943
4	98	.0976	10	2,570	2,580	.28	722	1,946
5	19,670	.0976	1,920	2,557	4,477	.28	1,254	20,973

[1] From table 12.42.

[2] Face value − Amount paid = Discount
$20,000 − $18,048 = $1,952
Discount ÷ Face value = Discount proportion
$1,952 ÷ $20,000 = .0976

[3] Principal payment × .0976

[4] From table 12.42

[5] Discount income + Interest income

[6] Taxable income × .28

[7] Principal payment + Interest income − Tax

payment (table 12.42)] times the discount proportion [(face value − amount paid) ÷ face value] for each year. The tax is calculated by multiplying the tax rate by the sum of the discounted income and interest income. The after-tax cash flow is debt service minus the taxes.

NPV and IRR from Buying Second Mortgages

The required before-tax rate of return was 16 percent. The after-tax internal rate of return on the purchase of the mortgage is the discount rate that equates the present value of the after-tax cash inflows with the initial cost ($18,048 from table 12.42) of the mortgage. If the investor's after-tax required rate of return is greater than the after-tax IRR, the mortgage purchase should be rejected. If it is less, the purchase should be accepted.

Suppose the investor wants to earn a 9 percent after-tax rate of return. Should the mortgage be bought? Table 12.44 shows

NPV at 9 percent to be $1,872. Thus the investor would accept the investment.

Table 12.44 shows the necessary calculations for computing the after-tax rate of return. In determining the internal rate of return, we select a discount rate and calculate the present value of the future cash flows. If the present value of the future payments and the cash outflows are equal, the selected discount rate is the IRR. However, if the present value of the future payments is greater than the cash outflow, the internal rate of return is higher than the selected discount rate, and vice versa. This process is repeated until we find the IRR. In our example, the IRR is 11.62 percent, which is greater than the required 9 percent rate. Thus, the investment should be accepted.

Buy-and-Leaseback Decision

As a real estate developer in Anytown, U.S.A., you have just been approached by a representative of Dixieland Incorporated

Table 12.44 CALCULATION OF NPV AND **IRR**

Year	Cash Outflow	ATCF	Present Value Factor at 8%	Present Value at 8%	Present Value Factor at 9%	Present Value at 9%
0	−$18,048		1.0	−$18,048	1.0	−$18,048
1		$ 1,938	.9259	1,794	.9174	1,778
2		1,940	.8573	1,663	.8417	1,633
3		1,943	.7938	1,542	.7722	1,500
4		1,946	.7350	1,430	.7084	1,379
5		20,973	.6806	14,274	.6499	13,630

Net present value = $ 2,655

IRR = 11.62%

NPV = $ 1,872

(DI), a national convenience store chain, about constructing a Dixieland convenience store on Broad Street in Anytown. DI has purchased a site for $30,000, will construct the store at a cost of $60,000, and desires to sell the land and its improvements to you for $100,000. So, under the terms set forth in a fifteen-year lease, you will lease the property to DI for $17,000 per annum. DI will pay all costs related to maintaining the store, but you must pay the $2,000 per annum property taxes and you retain ownership of the land and building at the end of the fifteen years. At the end of year fifteen, you estimate the building and land will be worth $105,000. Selling expenses at that time will be $7,000. You have decided to use the straight-line depreciation method with a zero salvage value and the useful life is 31.5 years. The current

value (for depreciation purposes) of the building is $60,000. You tax rate is currently 28 percent and you plan to finance with your own equity (100 percent) and desire a 10 percent after-tax rate of return. Should you accept DI's offer?

ATCF FROM LEASE

The first step in solving this problem is to determine the annual cash flows to the lessor (buyer). These cash flows are computed in table 12.45 by subtracting the debt service (0) and operating expenses ($2,000) from the lease revenues ($17,000) to obtain the before-tax cash flows ($15,000). The after-tax cash flows ($11,334) are found by subtracting the taxes (table 12.45) from the before-tax cash flows. The taxes are computed by deducting depreciation expenses

Table 12.45 EXPECTED CASH FLOWS FROM OPERATION

	Effective gross income (EGI)	$17,000
Minus	Operating expenses (OE)	− 2,000
Equals	Net operating income (NOI)	15,000
Minus	Debt service (DS)	− 0
Equals	Before-tax cash flow (BTCF)	15,000
Minus	Taxes (savings) from operation (TO)*	− 3,666
Equals	After-tax cash flow (ATCF)	$11,334

* See table 12.46.

Table 12.46 MEASUREMENT OF TAXABLE INCOME AND TAXES FROM OPERATION

	Effective gross income (EGI)	$ 17,000
Minus	Operating expenses (OE)	$ 2,000
Equals	Net operating Income (NOI)	$ 15,000
Minus	Interest on debt (I)	$ 0
Minus	Depreciation deduction (D)	$ 1,905
Minus	Amortized financing costs (AFC)	$ 0
Plus	Replacement reserves (RR)	$ 0
Equals	Ordinary taxable income (OTI)	$ 13,095
Times	Investor's marginal tax rate	0.28
Equals	Taxes (savings) from operation (TO)	$ 3,666

Table 12.47 MEASUREMENT OF EXPECTED CASH FLOW FROM THE SALE OF INVESTMENT

	Expected selling price (SP)	$ 105,000
Minus	Selling expenses (SE)	$ 7,000
Equals	Net sales proceeds (NSP)	$ 98,000
Minus	Unpaid mortgage balance (UM)	$ 0
Equals	Before-tax equity reversion (BTER)	$ 98,000
Minus	Taxes due on sale (TDS)*	$ 7,441
Equals	After-tax equity reversion (ATER)	$ 90,559

* See table 12.48.

from the NOI and then multiplying this figure (taxable income of $13,095) by the investor's tax rate (28 percent). The annual cash flows are $11,334 for fifteen years.

ATER FROM SALE

The second step (table 12.47) is to compute the after-tax equity reversion from the sale in year fifteen. This figure is found to be $81,758, by deducting selling expenses, the unpaid mortgage, and taxes of $7,441 (from table 12.48) from the selling price of $105,000. Table 12.48 computes the taxes due on sale by deducting the selling expenses and adjusted basis from the selling price to calculate the capital gain. The cap-

ital gain ($26,575) is then taxed at the investor's marginal tax rate (28 percent) to yield the taxes ($7,441).

NPV AND IRR OF BUY AND LEASEBACK

In the third step (table 12.49), the net present value is computed by subtracting the present value of the investment from the sum of the present value of the cash flows and reversion. If this figure is negative, then a reject decision is made, and the reverse is true if it is positive. In this project, the NPV was positive, so the developer accepted the project. If the annual lease revenue was negotiated at a lower amount, one might have rejected the project (since this

Table 12.48 MEASUREMENT OF TAXABLE INCOME
AND TAXES DUE ON SALE

	TAXABLE INCOME		
	Expected selling price (SP)	$	105,000
Minus	Selling expenses (SE)	$	7,000
Equals	Amount realized (AR)	$	98,000
Minus	Adjusted basis (AB)	$	71,425
Equals	Capital gain on sale (CG)	$	26,575
	TAXES DUE ON SALE		
	Capital gain on sale (CG)	$	26,575
Times	Investor's marginal tax rate		0.28
Equals	Taxes due on sale (TDS)	$	7,441

may have made the NPV < 0. The IRR turned out to be 11.11 percent, which is greater than the required 10 percent, which further substantiates the decision not to buy and leaseback.

TAX-DEFERRED EXCHANGE

Sale of an investment is not the only means of disposing of property. Another method is the tax-deferred exchange. Of importance to this method is Section 1031 of the Internal Revenue Code which provides an exception to the requirement of recognition of gain or loss upon sale or exchange of property. According to this section, no gain or loss is recognized if the property held for productive use in a trade or business or for an investment is exchanged solely for property of a like kind to be held for productive use in a trade or business or for investment. The application of the section for deferring the taxes due on the disposition of a real estate investment is referred to as the deferred exchange. There are two basic motivations for exchanging real estate, rather than selling it and reinvesting the proceeds. The exchange is attractive as a method of marketing real estate when a sale does not appear possible. Another reason is the availability of income tax deferral.

In order to illustrate an exchange, the following steps are used (recall our discussion in chapter 8):

Step 1. Balance equity positions.
Step 2. Calculate the realized gain in an exchange.
Step 3. Calculate the recognized gain in an exchange.
Step 4. Identify the taxable gain.
Step 5. Calculate the ATCF and equity position after exchange.

To illustrate these concepts, assume a two-party exchange is being considered by Mr. Hewlett and Mr. Packard. Mr. Hewlett owns an apartment building with a market value of $660,000 and an outstanding mortgage of $240,000. The adjusted basis of the property is $300,000. Mr. Packard owns an office building with a market value of $750,000 and an outstanding mortgage debt of $450,000. The adjusted basis of the property is $525,000.

Mr. Hewlett and Mr. Packard have decided to exchange their investments. Mr.

Table 12.49 NPV AND IRR OF BUY AND LEASEBACK

Year	Equity (E)	After-Tax Cash Flow (ATCF)	After-Tax Equity Reversion (ATER)	Present Value Factor at 10% (PVF)	Present Value
0	– $100,000			1.0	– $100,000
1		$11,344		.90909	10,304
2		11,334		.82645	9,367
3		11,334		.75132	8,515
4		11,334		.68301	7,741
5		11,334		.62092	7,038
6		11,334		.56447	6,398
7		11,334		.51316	5,816
8		11,334		.46651	5,287
9		11,334		.42410	4,807
10		11,334		.38554	4,370
11		11,334		.35049	3,972
12		11,334		.31863	3,611
13		11,334		.28966	3,283
14		11,334		.26333	2,985
15		11,334	$90,559	.23939	24,392
		IRR = 11.11%	NPV =		$ 7,886

Hewlett's transaction costs are $49,500, while Mr. Packard's are $57,000. This includes brokerage fees, legal fees, appraisal fees, and other costs of the exchange. The differences in equities will be balanced by cash.

BALANCING EQUITY POSITIONS

Tables 12.50 and 12.51 explain the method of balancing the equities. The first table lists the pertinent data on each property. The second table computes the equity for both parties by deducting the mortgage debt from the market value. The net equity po-

Table 12.50 EXCHANGE PROPERTY DATA

Property 1:	Mr. Hewlett's Property
Market value	$660,000
Mortgage debt	240,000
Adjusted basis	300,000
Transaction costs	49,500

Property 2	Mr. Packard's Property
Market value	$750,000
Mortgage debt	450,000
Adjusted basis	525,000
Transaction costs	57,000

Table 12.51 BALANCE EQUITIES ON EXCHANGE

A. Mr. Hewlett's Equity:

Market value	$660,000
Mortgage debt	– 240,000
Equity	420,000

B. Mr. Packard's Equity:

Market value	$750,000
Mortgage debt	– 450,000
Equity	300,000

C. Net Equity Position:

Mr. Packard owes Mr. Hewlett the difference in equity of $120,000, to be paid in cash:

	Hewlett	Packard
Equity given	$420,000	300,000
Equity received	– 300,000	– 420,000
Net equity	120,000	– 120,000

sition is then computed for both parties by subtracting the equity received from the equity given. Notice that Mr. Packard owes Mr. Hewlett $120,000.

Table 12.52 REALIZED GAIN ON EXCHANGE

A. Mr. Hewlett's Realized Gain:

Market Value	$660,000
Adjusted Basis	− 300,000
Transaction Costs	− 49,500
Realized Gain	310,500

B. Mr. Packard's Realized Gain:

Market Value	$750,000
Adjusted Basis	− 525,000
Transaction Costs	− 57,000
Realized Gain	168,000

Table 12.53 RECOGNIZED GAIN ON EXCHANGE*

A. Mr. Hewlett's Recognized Gain:

Boot (or cash) Received	$120,000
Boot (or cash) Given	− 0
Net Loan Relief	+ 0
Transaction Costs	− 49,500
Recognized Gain	70,500

B. Mr. Packard's Recognized Gain:

Boot (or cash) Received	0
Boot (or cash) Given	− 120,000
Net Loan Relief	+ 210,000
Transaction Costs	− 57,000
Recognized Gain	33,000

* The recognized gain is the taxable gain because it is less than the realized gain.

CALCULATION OF REALIZED GAIN

Table 12.52 shows how to calculate the realized gain. The realized gain is the gain that the investor would have had if the property was sold rather than exchanged. The realized gain is the market value minus the adjusted basis and the transaction costs. The net realized gain is computed in table 12.52 for both parties.

CALCULATION OF RECOGNIZED GAIN

Steps 3 and 4 are calculated in table 12.53 by subtracting the boot (or cash) given and the transaction costs, and adding the net loan relief to (or from) the boot (or cash) received. The net mortgage relief is considered unlike property only to the extent that the difference between the two mortgage balances is positive. Thus, there is no negative net mortgage relief. The investor pays tax on the lower of the recognized gain or the realized gain.

ATCF AND EQUITY POSITION AFTER EXCHANGE

The ATCF is computed in table 12.54. Mr. Hewlett receives a positive cash flow of $50,760 while Mr. Packard pays out $186,240. Table 12.55 shows the amount of taxes both investors owe as a result of the exchange.

Table 12.54 CASH FLOW FROM EXCHANGE

		Hewlett	Packard
	Cash outflow	0	− $120,000
Minus	Transaction costs	− $ 49,500	− 57,000
Plus	Cash inflows	+ 120,000	+ 0
Minus	Tax on gain* (28% bracket)	− 19,740	− 9,240
	Net cash flow	$ 50,760	− $186,240

* See table 12.55.

Table 12.55 TAXES DUE ON EXCHANGE

		Hewlett	Packard
	Taxable gain	$70,500	$33,000
Times	Marginal income tax rate	.28	.28
Equals	Tax on gain	$19,740	$ 9,240

Table 12.56 EQUITY POSITION AFTER EXCHANGE

		Hewlett	Packard
	Market value of property given	$660,000	$750,000
Minus	Mortgage debt	− 240,000	− 450,000
	Original equity	420,000	300,000
Minus	Transactions cost	− 49,500	− 57,000
Minus	Taxes on recognized gain	− 19,740	− 9,240
Plus	Cash given	0	+ 120,000
	New equity position	$350,760	$353,760

The equity positions after the exchange are shown in table 12.56. Mr. Hewlett received an office building with a market value of $750,000, with equity of $300,000, and an after-tax cash inflow from the exchange of $50,760. Thus, his new equity position is $350,760 after the exchange. Mr. Hewlett has deferred taxes on the unrecognized gain (the realized gain minus the rec-ognized gain). Had the investment been sold outright, Mr. Hewlett would have had to pay tax on the total realized gain of $310,500.

This chapter has illustrated investment strategies for various types of investments. We illustrated and discussed various financing techniques, types of investments, and acquisition methods.

APPENDIX A ——————————————

REAL ESTATE INVESTMENT TABLES

THE tables presented in this appendix are used in making real estate investment decisions. There are three sets of tables:

Table 1 Present Value of $1 (Annual Compounding)

Table 2 Mortgage Constant (Monthly Compounding)

Table 3 Proportion Outstanding on Mortgages

Table 1 provides the factors for finding the present value of a payment to be made in the future at various rates of discount. Table 2 provides the mortgage constant factors for monthly payments. The mortgage constant, when multiplied by the amount borrowed, tells the investor the payment necessary to fully amortize the loan. Table 3 contains the proportion outstanding on mortgages at various interest rates, mortgage maturities, and holding periods.

Table 1 PRESENT VALUE OF $1 (ANNUAL COMPOUNDING)

YEAR	6.00	INTEREST RATE (%) 6.25	6.50	6.75
1	0.94339623	0.94117647	0.93896714	0.93676815
2	0.88999644	0.88581315	0.88165928	0.87753457
3	0.83961928	0.83370649	0.82784909	0.82204643
4	0.79209366	0.78466493	0.77732309	0.77006692
5	0.74725817	0.73850817	0.72988084	0.72137416
6	0.70496054	0.69506652	0.68533412	0.67576034
7	0.66505711	0.65418025	0.64350621	0.63303076
8	0.62741237	0.61569906	0.60423119	0.59300305
9	0.59189846	0.57948147	0.56735323	0.55550637
10	0.55839478	0.54539432	0.53272604	0.52038068
11	0.52678753	0.51331230	0.50021224	0.48747605
12	0.49696936	0.48311746	0.46968285	0.45665203
13	0.46883902	0.45469879	0.44101676	0.42777708
14	0.44230096	0.42795180	0.41410025	0.40072794
15	0.41726506	0.40277817	0.38882652	0.37538917
16	0.39364628	0.37908533	0.36509533	0.35165262
17	0.37136442	0.35678619	0.34281251	0.32941698
18	0.35034379	0.33579877	0.32188969	0.30858733
19	0.33051301	0.31604590	0.30224384	0.28907478
20	0.31180473	0.29745497	0.28379703	0.27079605
21	0.29415540	0.27995762	0.26647608	0.25367312
22	0.27750510	0.26348952	0.25021228	0.23763289
23	0.26179726	0.24799014	0.23494111	0.22260693
24	0.24697855	0.23340248	0.22060198	0.20853108
25	0.23299863	0.21967292	0.20713801	0.19534527
26	0.21981003	0.20675099	0.19449579	0.18299323
27	0.20736795	0.19458917	0.18262515	0.17142223
28	0.19563014	0.18314274	0.17147902	0.16058289
29	0.18455674	0.17236964	0.16101316	0.15042893
30	0.17411013	0.16223025	0.15118607	0.14091703
31	0.16425484	0.15268729	0.14195875	0.13200659
32	0.15495740	0.14370569	0.13329460	0.12365957
33	0.14618622	0.13525241	0.12515925	0.11584034
34	0.13791153	0.12729639	0.11752042	0.10851554
35	0.13010522	0.11980837	0.11034781	0.10165391
36	0.12274077	0.11276081	0.10361297	0.09522614
37	0.11579318	0.10612783	0.09728917	0.08920482
38	0.10923885	0.09988501	0.09135134	0.08356423
39	0.10305552	0.09400942	0.08577590	0.07828031
40	0.09722219	0.08847946	0.08054075	0.07333050
41	0.09171905	0.08327478	0.07562512	0.06869368
42	0.08652740	0.07837627	0.07100950	0.06435005
43	0.08162962	0.07376590	0.06667559	0.06028108
44	0.07700908	0.06942673	0.06260619	0.05646939
45	0.07265007	0.06534280	0.05878515	0.05289873
46	0.06853781	0.06149911	0.05519733	0.04955384
47	0.06465831	0.05788151	0.05182848	0.04642046
48	0.06099840	0.05447672	0.04866524	0.04348521
49	0.05754566	0.05127221	0.04569506	0.04073556
50	0.05428836	0.04825619	0.04290616	0.03815978

Table 1 (cont.)

YEAR	INTEREST RATE (%)			
	7.00	7.25	7.50	7.75
1	0.93457944	0.93240093	0.93023256	0.92807425
2	0.87343873	0.86937150	0.86533261	0.86132181
3	0.81629788	0.81060280	0.80496057	0.79937059
4	0.76289521	0.75580680	0.74880053	0.74187525
5	0.71298618	0.70471497	0.69655863	0.68851532
6	0.66634222	0.65707689	0.64796152	0.63899333
7	0.62274974	0.61265911	0.60275490	0.59303326
8	0.58200910	0.57124392	0.56070223	0.55037889
9	0.54393374	0.53262837	0.52158347	0.51079247
10	0.50834929	0.49662319	0.48519393	0.47405334
11	0.47509280	0.46305192	0.45134319	0.43995670
12	0.44401196	0.43175004	0.41985413	0.40831248
13	0.41496445	0.40256414	0.39056198	0.37894430
14	0.38781724	0.37535118	0.36331347	0.35168844
15	0.36244602	0.34997779	0.33796602	0.32639299
16	0.33873460	0.32631962	0.31438699	0.30291692
17	0.31657439	0.30426072	0.29245302	0.28112940
18	0.29586392	0.28369298	0.27204932	0.26090895
19	0.27650833	0.26451560	0.25306913	0.24214288
20	0.25841900	0.24663459	0.23541315	0.22472657
21	0.24151309	0.22996232	0.21898897	0.20856294
22	0.22571317	0.21441708	0.20371067	0.19356190
23	0.21094688	0.19992269	0.18949830	0.17963981
24	0.19714662	0.18640810	0.17627749	0.16671908
25	0.18424918	0.17380709	0.16397906	0.15472769
26	0.17219549	0.16205789	0.15253866	0.14359878
27	0.16093037	0.15110293	0.14189643	0.13327033
28	0.15040221	0.14088851	0.13199668	0.12368476
29	0.14056282	0.13136458	0.12278761	0.11478864
30	0.13136712	0.12248446	0.11422103	0.10653238
31	0.12277301	0.11420462	0.10625212	0.09886996
32	0.11474113	0.10648449	0.09883918	0.09175866
33	0.10723470	0.09928624	0.09194343	0.08515885
34	0.10021934	0.09257458	0.08552877	0.07903374
35	0.09366294	0.08631663	0.07956164	0.07334918
36	0.08753546	0.08048171	0.07401083	0.06807348
37	0.08180884	0.07504122	0.06884729	0.06317724
38	0.07645686	0.06996850	0.06404399	0.05863317
39	0.07145501	0.06523870	0.05957580	0.05441594
40	0.06678038	0.06082862	0.05541935	0.05050203
41	0.06241157	0.05671666	0.05155288	0.04686963
42	0.05832857	0.05288267	0.04795617	0.04349850
43	0.05451268	0.04930785	0.04461039	0.04036984
44	0.05094643	0.04597468	0.04149804	0.03746621
45	0.04761349	0.04286684	0.03860283	0.03477142
46	0.04449859	0.03996908	0.03590961	0.03227046
47	0.04158747	0.03726721	0.03340428	0.02994938
48	0.03886679	0.03474798	0.03107375	0.02779525
49	0.03632410	0.03239905	0.02890582	0.02579606
50	0.03394776	0.03020890	0.02688913	0.02394066

Table 1 (cont.)

		INTEREST RATE (%)		
YEAR	8.00	8.25	8.50	8.75
1	0.92592593	0.92378753	0.92165899	0.91954023
2	0.85733882	0.85338340	0.84945529	0.84555423
3	0.79383224	0.78834494	0.78290810	0.77752114
4	0.73502985	0.72826322	0.72157428	0.71496196
5	0.68058320	0.67276048	0.66504542	0.65743629
6	0.63016963	0.62148775	0.61294509	0.60453912
7	0.58349040	0.57412263	0.56492635	0.55589804
8	0.54026888	0.53036732	0.52066945	0.51117061
9	0.50024897	0.48994672	0.47987968	0.47004194
10	0.46319349	0.45260667	0.44228542	0.43222247
11	0.42888286	0.41811240	0.40763633	0.39744595
12	0.39711376	0.38624702	0.37570168	0.36546754
13	0.36769792	0.35681018	0.34626883	0.33606211
14	0.34046104	0.32961679	0.31914178	0.30902263
15	0.31524170	0.30449588	0.29413989	0.28415874
16	0.29189047	0.28128950	0.27109667	0.26129539
17	0.27026895	0.25985173	0.24985869	0.24027162
18	0.25024903	0.24004779	0.23028450	0.22093942
19	0.23171206	0.22175315	0.21224378	0.20316269
20	0.21454821	0.20485280	0.19561639	0.18681627
21	0.19865575	0.18924046	0.18029160	0.17178507
22	0.18394051	0.17481798	0.16616738	0.15796328
23	0.17031528	0.16149467	0.15314965	0.14525360
24	0.15769934	0.14918676	0.14115176	0.13356652
25	0.14601790	0.13781687	0.13009378	0.12281979
26	0.13520176	0.12731350	0.11990210	0.11293774
27	0.12518682	0.11761063	0.11050885	0.10385080
28	0.11591372	0.10864723	0.10185148	0.09549498
29	0.10732752	0.10036696	0.09387233	0.08781148
30	0.09937733	0.09271774	0.08651828	0.08074619
31	0.09201605	0.08565149	0.07974035	0.07424937
32	0.08520005	0.07912378	0.07349341	0.06827528
33	0.07888893	0.07309356	0.06773586	0.06278187
34	0.07304531	0.06752292	0.06242936	0.05773045
35	0.06763454	0.06237683	0.05753858	0.05308547
36	0.06262458	0.05762294	0.05303095	0.04881423
37	0.05798572	0.05323135	0.04887645	0.04488665
38	0.05369048	0.04917446	0.04504742	0.04127508
39	0.04971341	0.04542675	0.04151836	0.03795410
40	0.04603093	0.04196467	0.03826577	0.03490032
41	0.04262123	0.03876644	0.03526799	0.03209225
42	0.03946411	0.03581195	0.03250506	0.02951011
43	0.03654084	0.03308263	0.02995858	0.02713573
44	0.03383411	0.03056132	0.02761160	0.02495240
45	0.03132788	0.02823217	0.02544848	0.02294474
46	0.02900730	0.02608053	0.02345482	0.02109861
47	0.02685861	0.02409287	0.02161734	0.01940102
48	0.02486908	0.02225669	0.01992382	0.01784002
49	0.02302693	0.02056045	0.01836297	0.01640461
50	0.02132123	0.01899349	0.01692439	0.01508470

Table 1 (cont.)

YEAR	INTEREST RATE (%)			
	9.00	9.25	9.50	9.75
1	0.91743119	0.91533181	0.91324201	0.91116173
2	0.84167999	0.83783232	0.83401097	0.83021570
3	0.77218348	0.76689457	0.76165385	0.75646077
4	0.70842521	0.70196299	0.69557429	0.68925811
5	0.64993139	0.64252906	0.63522767	0.62802561
6	0.59626733	0.58812728	0.58011659	0.57223290
7	0.54703424	0.53833161	0.52978684	0.52139672
8	0.50186628	0.49275204	0.48382360	0.47507674
9	0.46042778	0.45103162	0.44184803	0.43287175
10	0.42241081	0.41284359	0.40351419	0.39441617
11	0.38753285	0.37788887	0.36850611	0.35937692
12	0.35553473	0.34589370	0.33653526	0.32745050
13	0.32617865	0.31660751	0.30733813	0.29836036
14	0.29924647	0.28980092	0.28067410	0.27185454
15	0.27453804	0.26526400	0.25632337	0.24770346
16	0.25186976	0.24280458	0.23408527	0.22569791
17	0.23107318	0.22224675	0.21377651	0.20564730
18	0.21199374	0.20342952	0.19522969	0.18737795
19	0.19448967	0.18620551	0.17829195	0.17073162
20	0.17843089	0.17043983	0.16282370	0.15556411
21	0.16369806	0.15600900	0.14869744	0.14174407
22	0.15018171	0.14280000	0.13579675	0.12915177
23	0.13778139	0.13070938	0.12401530	0.11767815
24	0.12640494	0.11964245	0.11325598	0.10722383
25	0.11596784	0.10951254	0.10343012	0.09769825
26	0.10639251	0.10024031	0.09445673	0.08901891
27	0.09760781	0.09175315	0.08626185	0.08111062
28	0.08954845	0.08398457	0.07877795	0.07390489
29	0.08215454	0.07687375	0.07194333	0.06733931
30	0.07537114	0.07036499	0.06570167	0.06135700
31	0.06914783	0.06440731	0.06000153	0.05590615
32	0.06343838	0.05895406	0.05479592	0.05093955
33	0.05820035	0.05396253	0.05004193	0.04641417
34	0.05339481	0.04939362	0.04570039	0.04229081
35	0.04898607	0.04521155	0.04173552	0.03853377
36	0.04494135	0.04138357	0.03811463	0.03511050
37	0.04123059	0.03787970	0.03480788	0.03199134
38	0.03782623	0.03467249	0.03178802	0.02914928
39	0.03470296	0.03173684	0.02903015	0.02655971
40	0.03183758	0.02904973	0.02651156	0.02420019
41	0.02920879	0.02659015	0.02421147	0.02205029
42	0.02679706	0.02433881	0.02211093	0.02009138
43	0.02458446	0.02227808	0.02019263	0.01830650
44	0.02255455	0.02039184	0.01844076	0.01668018
45	0.02069224	0.01866530	0.01684087	0.01519834
46	0.01898371	0.01708494	0.01537979	0.01384815
47	0.01741625	0.01563839	0.01404547	0.01261790
48	0.01597821	0.01431432	0.01282692	0.01149695
49	0.01465891	0.01310235	0.01171408	0.01047558
50	0.01344854	0.01199300	0.01069779	0.00954495

Table 1 (cont.)

YEAR	INTEREST RATE (%)			
	10.00	10.25	10.50	10.75
1	0.90909091	0.90702948	0.90497738	0.90293454
2	0.82644628	0.82270247	0.81898405	0.81529078
3	0.75131480	0.74621540	0.74116204	0.73615420
4	0.68301346	0.67683936	0.67073487	0.66469905
5	0.62092132	0.61391325	0.60699989	0.60017973
6	0.56447393	0.55683742	0.54932116	0.54192301
7	0.51315812	0.50506795	0.49712323	0.48932100
8	0.46650738	0.45811152	0.44988527	0.44182483
9	0.42409762	0.41552065	0.40713599	0.39893890
10	0.38554329	0.37688948	0.36844886	0.36021571
11	0.35049390	0.34184987	0.33343788	0.32525121
12	0.31863082	0.31006791	0.30175374	0.29368055
13	0.28966438	0.28124073	0.27308031	0.26517431
14	0.26333125	0.25509364	0.24713150	0.23943504
15	0.23939205	0.23137745	0.22364842	0.21619417
16	0.21762914	0.20986617	0.20239676	0.19520918
17	0.19784467	0.19035480	0.18316449	0.17626111
18	0.17985879	0.17265741	0.16575972	0.15915225
19	0.16350799	0.15660536	0.15000879	0.14370406
20	0.14864363	0.14204568	0.13575456	0.12975536
21	0.13513057	0.12883962	0.12285481	0.11716059
22	0.12284597	0.11686133	0.11118082	0.10578835
23	0.11167816	0.10599668	0.10061613	0.09551995
24	0.10152560	0.09614211	0.09105532	0.08624826
25	0.09229600	0.08720373	0.08240301	0.07787654
26	0.08390545	0.07909635	0.07457286	0.07031741
27	0.07627768	0.07174272	0.06748675	0.06349202
28	0.06934335	0.06507276	0.06107398	0.05732914
29	0.06303941	0.05902291	0.05527057	0.05176446
30	0.05730855	0.05353552	0.05001861	0.04673992
31	0.05209868	0.04855830	0.04526571	0.04220309
32	0.04736244	0.04404381	0.04096445	0.03810662
33	0.04305676	0.03994903	0.03707190	0.03440779
34	0.03914251	0.03623495	0.03354923	0.03106798
35	0.03558410	0.03286617	0.03036129	0.02805235
36	0.03234918	0.02981058	0.02747628	0.02532944
37	0.02940835	0.02703908	0.02486542	0.02287082
38	0.02673486	0.02452524	0.02250264	0.02065086
39	0.02430442	0.02224512	0.02036438	0.01864637
40	0.02209493	0.02017698	0.01842930	0.01683645
41	0.02008630	0.01830111	0.01667810	0.01520221
42	0.01826027	0.01659965	0.01509330	0.01372660
43	0.01660025	0.01505637	0.01365910	0.01239423
44	0.01509113	0.01365657	0.01236118	0.01119117
45	0.01371921	0.01238691	0.01118658	0.01010490
46	0.01247201	0.01123530	0.01012361	0.00912406
47	0.01133819	0.01019074	0.00916163	0.00823843
48	0.01030745	0.00924331	0.00829107	0.00743876
49	0.00937041	0.00838395	0.00750323	0.00671672
50	0.00851855	0.00760449	0.00679026	0.00606475

Table 1 (cont.)

| YEAR | INTEREST RATE (%) | | | |
	11.00	11.25	11.50	11.75
1	0.90090090	0.89887640	0.89686099	0.89485459
2	0.81162243	0.80797879	0.80435963	0.80076473
3	0.73119138	0.72627307	0.72139877	0.71656799
4	0.65873097	0.65282973	0.64699441	0.64122415
5	0.59345133	0.58681324	0.58026405	0.57380237
6	0.53464084	0.52747257	0.52041619	0.51346969
7	0.48165841	0.47413265	0.46674097	0.45948070
8	0.43392650	0.42618665	0.41860177	0.41116841
9	0.39092477	0.38308912	0.37542760	0.36793594
10	0.35218448	0.34434977	0.33670636	0.32924916
11	0.31728331	0.30952789	0.30197880	0.29463013
12	0.28584082	0.27822731	0.27083301	0.26365112
13	0.25751426	0.25009197	0.24289956	0.23592941
14	0.23199482	0.22480177	0.21784714	0.21112252
15	0.20900435	0.20206901	0.19537860	0.18892395
16	0.18829220	0.18163506	0.17522744	0.16905947
17	0.16963262	0.16326747	0.15715466	0.15128364
18	0.15282218	0.14675728	0.14094588	0.13537686
19	0.13767764	0.13191665	0.12640886	0.12114260
20	0.12403391	0.11857677	0.11337118	0.10840501
21	0.11174226	0.10658586	0.10167818	0.09700672
22	0.10066870	0.09580751	0.09119120	0.08680691
23	0.09069252	0.08611911	0.08178583	0.07767956
24	0.08170498	0.07741044	0.07335052	0.06951191
25	0.07360809	0.06958242	0.06578522	0.06220305
26	0.06631359	0.06254599	0.05900020	0.05566269
27	0.05974197	0.05622112	0.05291497	0.04981001
28	0.05382160	0.05053584	0.04745738	0.04457272
29	0.04848793	0.04542547	0.04256267	0.03988610
30	0.04368282	0.04083188	0.03817280	0.03569226
31	0.03935389	0.03670282	0.03423569	0.03193938
32	0.03545395	0.03299130	0.03070466	0.02858110
33	0.03194050	0.02965510	0.02753781	0.02557593
34	0.02877522	0.02665627	0.02469759	0.02288674
35	0.02592363	0.02396069	0.02215030	0.02048030
36	0.02335462	0.02153770	0.01986574	0.01832689
37	0.02104020	0.01935973	0.01781681	0.01639990
38	0.01895513	0.01740200	0.01597920	0.01467553
39	0.01707670	0.01564225	0.01433112	0.01313247
40	0.01538441	0.01406045	0.01285302	0.01175165
41	0.01385983	0.01263861	0.01152738	0.01051601
42	0.01248633	0.01136055	0.01033845	0.00941030
43	0.01124895	0.01021173	0.00927216	0.00842085
44	0.01013419	0.00917908	0.00831583	0.00753544
45	0.00912990	0.00825086	0.00745815	0.00674312
46	0.00822513	0.00741650	0.00668892	0.00603411
47	0.00741003	0.00666652	0.00599903	0.00539965
48	0.00667570	0.00599238	0.00538030	0.00483191
49	0.00601415	0.00538641	0.00482538	0.00432385
50	0.00541815	0.00484171	0.00432769	0.00386922

Table 1 (cont.)

YEAR	12.00	12.25	12.50	12.75
		INTEREST RATE (%)		
1	0.89285714	0.89086860	0.88888889	0.88691796
2	0.79719388	0.79364686	0.79012346	0.78662347
3	0.71178025	0.70703506	0.70233196	0.69767048
4	0.63551808	0.62987533	0.62429508	0.61877648
5	0.56742686	0.56113615	0.55492896	0.54880397
6	0.50663112	0.49989858	0.49327018	0.48674410
7	0.45234922	0.44534395	0.43846239	0.43170208
8	0.40388323	0.39674294	0.38974434	0.38288433
9	0.36061002	0.35344582	0.34643942	0.33958699
10	0.32197324	0.31487378	0.30794615	0.30118580
11	0.28747610	0.28051117	0.27372991	0.26712710
12	0.25667509	0.24989859	0.24331547	0.23691982
13	0.22917419	0.22262681	0.21628042	0.21012844
14	0.20461981	0.19833123	0.19224926	0.18636669
15	0.18269626	0.17668706	0.17088823	0.16529196
16	0.16312166	0.15740496	0.15190065	0.14660041
17	0.14564434	0.14022713	0.13502280	0.13002254
18	0.13003959	0.12492395	0.12002027	0.11531932
19	0.11610678	0.11129082	0.10668468	0.10227878
20	0.10366677	0.09914550	0.09483083	0.09071289
21	0.09255961	0.08832561	0.08429407	0.08045489
22	0.08264251	0.07868651	0.07492806	0.07135689
23	0.07378796	0.07009934	0.06660272	0.06328770
24	0.06588210	0.06244930	0.05920242	0.05613100
25	0.05882331	0.05563412	0.05262437	0.04978359
26	0.05252081	0.04956269	0.04677722	0.04415396
27	0.04689358	0.04415385	0.04157975	0.03916094
28	0.04186927	0.03933528	0.03695978	0.03473254
29	0.03738327	0.03504256	0.03285314	0.03080492
30	0.03337792	0.03121832	0.02920279	0.02732143
31	0.02980172	0.02781142	0.02595803	0.02423187
32	0.02660868	0.02477632	0.02307381	0.02149168
33	0.02375775	0.02207245	0.02051005	0.01906136
34	0.02121227	0.01966365	0.01823116	0.01690586
35	0.01893953	0.01751773	0.01620547	0.01499411
36	0.01691029	0.01560599	0.01440486	0.01329855
37	0.01509848	0.01390289	0.01280432	0.01179472
38	0.01348078	0.01238565	0.01138162	0.01046095
39	0.01203641	0.01103398	0.01011700	0.00927800
40	0.01074680	0.00982983	0.00899289	0.00822883
41	0.00959536	0.00875709	0.00799368	0.00729830
42	0.00856728	0.00780141	0.00710549	0.00647299
43	0.00764936	0.00695003	0.00631599	0.00574101
44	0.00682978	0.00619157	0.00561421	0.00509181
45	0.00609802	0.00551587	0.00499041	0.00451601
46	0.00544466	0.00491392	0.00443592	0.00400533
47	0.00486131	0.00437766	0.00394304	0.00355240
48	0.00434045	0.00389992	0.00350493	0.00315069
49	0.00387540	0.00347431	0.00311549	0.00279440
50	0.00346018	0.00309516	0.00276932	0.00247841

Table 1 (cont.)

YEAR	13.00	13.25	13.50	13.75
		INTEREST RATE (%)		
1	0.88495575	0.88300221	0.88105727	0.87912088
2	0.78314668	0.77969290	0.77626191	0.77285352
3	0.69305016	0.68847055	0.68393120	0.67943167
4	0.61331873	0.60792102	0.60258255	0.59730256
5	0.54275994	0.53679560	0.53090974	0.52510115
6	0.48031853	0.47399170	0.46776188	0.46162739
7	0.42506064	0.41853572	0.41212501	0.40582628
8	0.37615986	0.36956796	0.36310573	0.35677035
9	0.33288483	0.32632933	0.31991695	0.31364427
10	0.29458835	0.28814952	0.28186515	0.27573122
11	0.26069765	0.25443666	0.24833934	0.24240107
12	0.23070589	0.22466813	0.21880118	0.21309985
13	0.20416450	0.19838246	0.19277637	0.18734052
14	0.18067655	0.17517215	0.16984702	0.16469497
15	0.15989075	0.15467739	0.14964495	0.14478678
16	0.14149624	0.13658048	0.13184577	0.12728508
17	0.12521791	0.12060086	0.11616368	0.11189898
18	0.11081231	0.10649083	0.10234685	0.09837273
19	0.09806399	0.09403164	0.09017344	0.08648152
20	0.08678229	0.08303014	0.07944796	0.07602771
21	0.07679849	0.07331580	0.06999821	0.06683754
22	0.06796327	0.06473801	0.06167243	0.05875828
23	0.06014448	0.05716381	0.05433694	0.05165563
24	0.05322521	0.05047577	0.04787396	0.04541154
25	0.04710195	0.04457022	0.04217970	0.03992224
26	0.04168314	0.03935560	0.03716273	0.03509647
27	0.03688774	0.03475108	0.03274249	0.03085404
28	0.03264402	0.03068528	0.02884801	0.02712443
29	0.02888851	0.02709517	0.02541675	0.02384565
30	0.02556505	0.02392510	0.02239361	0.02096321
31	0.02262394	0.02112591	0.01973005	0.01842920
32	0.02002119	0.01865423	0.01738331	0.01620149
33	0.01771786	0.01647172	0.01531569	0.01424307
34	0.01567953	0.01454457	0.01349400	0.01252138
35	0.01387569	0.01284289	0.01188899	0.01100781
36	0.01227937	0.01134030	0.01047488	0.00967719
37	0.01086670	0.01001351	0.00922897	0.00850742
38	0.00961655	0.00884195	0.00813125	0.00747905
39	0.00851022	0.00780746	0.00716410	0.00657499
40	0.00753117	0.00689400	0.00631198	0.00578021
41	0.00666475	0.00608742	0.00556121	0.00508151
42	0.00589801	0.00537521	0.00489975	0.00446726
43	0.00521948	0.00474632	0.00431696	0.00392726
44	0.00461901	0.00419101	0.00380349	0.00345254
45	0.00408762	0.00370067	0.00335109	0.00303520
46	0.00361736	0.00326770	0.00295250	0.00266830
47	0.00320120	0.00288539	0.00260132	0.00234576
48	0.00283292	0.00254780	0.00229192	0.00206221
49	0.00250701	0.00224972	0.00201931	0.00181293
50	0.00221859	0.00198650	0.00177913	0.00159378

Table 1 (cont.)

YEAR	INTEREST RATE (%) 14.00	14.25	14.50	14.75
1	0.87719298	0.87527352	0.87336245	0.87145969
2	0.76946753	0.76610374	0.76276196	0.75944200
3	0.67497152	0.67055032	0.66616765	0.66182309
4	0.59208028	0.58691494	0.58180581	0.57675215
5	0.51936866	0.51371111	0.50812734	0.50261625
6	0.45558655	0.44963773	0.44377934	0.43800981
7	0.39963732	0.39355600	0.38758021	0.38170789
8	0.35055905	0.34446915	0.33849800	0.33264304
9	0.30750794	0.30150472	0.29563144	0.28988501
10	0.26974381	0.26389910	0.25819340	0.25262310
11	0.23661738	0.23098390	0.22549642	0.22015085
12	0.20755910	0.20217409	0.19694010	0.19185259
13	0.18206939	0.17695763	0.17200009	0.16719180
14	0.15970999	0.15488633	0.15021842	0.14570092
15	0.14009648	0.13556790	0.13119513	0.12697248
16	0.12289165	0.11865899	0.11458090	0.11065139
17	0.10779969	0.10385908	0.10007065	0.09642823
18	0.09456113	0.09090510	0.08739795	0.08403332
19	0.08294836	0.07956683	0.07633009	0.07323165
20	0.07276172	0.06964274	0.06666383	0.06381843
21	0.06382607	0.06095644	0.05822169	0.05561519
22	0.05598778	0.05335356	0.05084863	0.04846640
23	0.04911209	0.04669896	0.04440929	0.04223651
24	0.04308078	0.04087436	0.03878540	0.03680742
25	0.03779016	0.03577625	0.03387372	0.03207618
26	0.03314926	0.03131400	0.02958403	0.02795310
27	0.02907830	0.02740832	0.02583758	0.02436000
28	0.02550728	0.02398977	0.02256557	0.02122876
29	0.02237481	0.02099761	0.01970792	0.01850001
30	0.01962702	0.01837866	0.01721216	0.01612201
31	0.01721669	0.01608635	0.01503246	0.01404968
32	0.01510236	0.01407996	0.01312878	0.01224373
33	0.01324768	0.01232381	0.01146618	0.01066992
34	0.01162077	0.01078671	0.01001414	0.00929840
35	0.01019366	0.00944132	0.00874597	0.00810318
36	0.00894181	0.00826374	0.00763840	0.00706160
37	0.00784369	0.00723303	0.00667109	0.00615390
38	0.00688043	0.00633088	0.00582628	0.00536287
39	0.00603547	0.00554125	0.00508846	0.00467353
40	0.00529427	0.00485011	0.00444407	0.00407279
41	0.00464410	0.00424517	0.00388128	0.00354927
42	0.00407377	0.00371569	0.00338976	0.00309305
43	0.00357348	0.00325224	0.00296049	0.00269547
44	0.00313463	0.00284660	0.00258558	0.00234899
45	0.00274968	0.00249156	0.00225815	0.00204705
46	0.00241200	0.00218079	0.00197218	0.00178392
47	0.00211579	0.00190879	0.00172243	0.00155462
48	0.00185595	0.00167071	0.00150431	0.00135479
49	0.00162803	0.00146233	0.00131381	0.00118064
50	0.00142810	0.00127994	0.00114743	0.00102888

Table 1 (*cont.*)

YEAR	INTEREST RATE (%)			
	15.00	15.25	15.50	15.75
1	0.86956522	0.86767896	0.86580087	0.86393089
2	0.75614367	0.75286678	0.74961114	0.74637657
3	0.65751623	0.65324666	0.64901397	0.64481778
4	0.57175325	0.56680838	0.56191686	0.55707799
5	0.49717674	0.49180771	0.48650810	0.48127688
6	0.43232760	0.42673120	0.42121914	0.41578996
7	0.37593704	0.37026568	0.36469189	0.35921379
8	0.32690177	0.32127174	0.31575056	0.31033589
9	0.28426241	0.27876073	0.27337711	0.26810876
10	0.24718471	0.24187482	0.23669014	0.23162744
11	0.21494322	0.20986969	0.20492652	0.20011010
12	0.18690715	0.18209952	0.17742556	0.17288129
13	0.16252796	0.15800392	0.15361521	0.14935749
14	0.14132866	0.13709668	0.13300018	0.12903455
15	0.12289449	0.11895590	0.11515167	0.11147693
16	0.10686477	0.10321553	0.09969841	0.09630836
17	0.09292589	0.08955795	0.08631897	0.08320377
18	0.08080512	0.07770754	0.07473504	0.07188231
19	0.07026532	0.06742520	0.06470566	0.06210134
20	0.06110028	0.05850343	0.05602222	0.05365127
21	0.05313068	0.05076219	0.04850409	0.04635099
22	0.04620059	0.04404529	0.04199488	0.04004405
23	0.04017443	0.03821717	0.03635920	0.03459529
24	0.03493428	0.03316023	0.03147983	0.02988794
25	0.03037764	0.02877244	0.02725526	0.02582112
26	0.02641534	0.02496524	0.02359763	0.02230766
27	0.02296986	0.02166181	0.02043085	0.01927228
28	0.01997379	0.01879550	0.01768905	0.01664991
29	0.01736851	0.01630846	0.01531519	0.01438438
30	0.01510305	0.01415051	0.01325991	0.01242711
31	0.01313309	0.01227810	0.01148044	0.01073616
32	0.01142008	0.01065345	0.00993977	0.00927530
33	0.00993050	0.00924377	0.00860586	0.00801322
34	0.00863522	0.00802063	0.00745097	0.00692287
35	0.00750889	0.00695933	0.00645105	0.00598088
36	0.00652947	0.00603846	0.00558533	0.00516707
37	0.00567780	0.00523945	0.00483578	0.00446399
38	0.00493722	0.00454616	0.00418682	0.00385658
39	0.00429323	0.00394461	0.00362495	0.00333182
40	0.00373324	0.00342265	0.00313849	0.00287846
41	0.00324630	0.00296976	0.00271731	0.00248679
42	0.00282287	0.00257680	0.00235265	0.00214841
43	0.00245467	0.00223584	0.00203692	0.00185608
44	0.00213449	0.00193999	0.00176357	0.00160353
45	0.00185608	0.00168329	0.00152690	0.00138534
46	0.00161398	0.00146055	0.00132199	0.00119683
47	0.00140346	0.00126729	0.00114458	0.00103398
48	0.00122040	0.00109960	0.00099098	0.00089329
49	0.00106122	0.00095410	0.00085799	0.00077174
50	0.00092280	0.00082785	0.00074285	0.00066673

Table 1 (cont.)

YEAR	16.00	16.25	16.50	16.75
		INTEREST RATE (%)		
1	0.86206897	0.86021505	0.85836910	0.85653105
2	0.74316290	0.73996994	0.73679751	0.73364544
3	0.64065767	0.63653328	0.63244421	0.62839010
4	0.55229110	0.54755551	0.54287057	0.53823563
5	0.47611302	0.47101549	0.46598332	0.46101553
6	0.41044225	0.40517462	0.39998568	0.39487411
7	0.35382953	0.34853731	0.34333535	0.33822194
8	0.30502546	0.29981704	0.29470846	0.28969759
9	0.26295298	0.25790713	0.25296863	0.24813498
10	0.22668360	0.22185559	0.21714046	0.21253532
11	0.19541690	0.19084352	0.18638666	0.18204310
12	0.16846284	0.16416647	0.15998855	0.15592557
13	0.14522659	0.14121847	0.13732923	0.13355509
14	0.12519534	0.12147825	0.11787916	0.11439408
15	0.10792701	0.10449742	0.10118383	0.09798208
16	0.09304053	0.08989026	0.08685307	0.08392470
17	0.08020735	0.07732495	0.07455199	0.07188411
18	0.06914427	0.06651609	0.06399313	0.06157097
19	0.05960713	0.05721814	0.05492972	0.05273745
20	0.05138546	0.04921990	0.04714998	0.04517126
21	0.04429781	0.04233970	0.04047208	0.03869059
22	0.03818776	0.03642125	0.03473999	0.03313969
23	0.03292049	0.03133011	0.02981973	0.02838517
24	0.02837973	0.02695063	0.02559634	0.02431278
25	0.02446528	0.02318334	0.02197110	0.02082465
26	0.02109076	0.01994266	0.01885932	0.01783696
27	0.01818169	0.01715497	0.01618825	0.01527791
28	0.01567387	0.01475697	0.01389550	0.01308601
29	0.01351196	0.01269416	0.01192747	0.01120857
30	0.01164824	0.01091971	0.01023817	0.00960049
31	0.01004159	0.00939330	0.00878813	0.00822312
32	0.00865654	0.00808026	0.00754346	0.00704335
33	0.00746253	0.00695076	0.00647507	0.00603285
34	0.00643322	0.00597915	0.00555800	0.00516732
35	0.00554588	0.00514335	0.00477082	0.00442597
36	0.00478093	0.00442439	0.00409512	0.00379098
37	0.00412149	0.00380593	0.00351512	0.00324710
38	0.00355301	0.00327392	0.00301727	0.00278124
39	0.00306294	0.00281627	0.00258994	0.00238222
40	0.00264047	0.00242260	0.00222312	0.00204044
41	0.00227626	0.00208396	0.00190826	0.00174770
42	0.00196230	0.00179265	0.00163799	0.00149696
43	0.00169163	0.00154206	0.00140600	0.00128219
44	0.00145831	0.00132651	0.00120687	0.00109824
45	0.00125716	0.00114108	0.00103594	0.00094068
46	0.00108376	0.00098158	0.00088922	0.00080572
47	0.00093427	0.00084437	0.00076328	0.00069012
48	0.00080541	0.00072634	0.00065517	0.00059111
49	0.00069432	0.00062481	0.00056238	0.00050631
50	0.00059855	0.00053747	0.00048273	0.00043367

Table 1 (*cont.*)

YEAR	INTEREST RATE (%) 17.00	17.25	17.50	17.75
1	0.85470085	0.85287846	0.85106383	0.84925690
2	0.73051355	0.72740168	0.72430964	0.72123728
3	0.62437056	0.62038522	0.61643374	0.61251574
4	0.53365005	0.52911320	0.52462446	0.52018322
5	0.45611115	0.45126925	0.44648890	0.44176919
6	0.38983859	0.38487783	0.37999055	0.37517553
7	0.33319538	0.32825401	0.32339622	0.31862041
8	0.28478237	0.27996078	0.27523082	0.27059058
9	0.24340374	0.23877252	0.23423900	0.22980092
10	0.20803738	0.20364394	0.19935234	0.19516001
11	0.17780973	0.17368353	0.16966156	0.16574099
12	0.15197413	0.14813094	0.14439282	0.14075668
13	0.12989242	0.12633769	0.12288751	0.11953858
14	0.11101916	0.10775070	0.10458511	0.10151896
15	0.09488817	0.09189825	0.08900861	0.08621568
16	0.08110100	0.07837804	0.07575201	0.07321926
17	0.06931709	0.06684694	0.06446979	0.06218196
18	0.05924538	0.05701231	0.05486791	0.05280846
19	0.05063708	0.04862458	0.04669609	0.04484795
20	0.04327955	0.04147085	0.03974135	0.03808743
21	0.03699107	0.03536960	0.03382243	0.03234601
22	0.03161630	0.03016597	0.02878505	0.02747008
23	0.02702248	0.02572790	0.02449791	0.02332915
24	0.02309614	0.02194278	0.02084929	0.01981244
25	0.01974029	0.01871452	0.01774407	0.01682585
26	0.01687204	0.01596121	0.01510134	0.01428947
27	0.01442055	0.01361297	0.01285220	0.01213543
28	0.01232525	0.01161021	0.01093805	0.01030610
29	0.01053440	0.00990210	0.00930898	0.00875253
30	0.00900376	0.00844529	0.00792253	0.00743314
31	0.00769553	0.00720280	0.00674258	0.00631265
32	0.00657737	0.00614312	0.00573837	0.00536106
33	0.00562169	0.00523933	0.00488372	0.00455292
34	0.00480486	0.00446851	0.00415635	0.00386660
35	0.00410672	0.00381110	0.00353732	0.00328373
36	0.00351002	0.00325040	0.00301049	0.00278873
37	0.00300001	0.00277220	0.00256212	0.00236835
38	0.00256411	0.00236435	0.00218052	0.00201134
39	0.00219155	0.00201650	0.00185577	0.00170814
40	0.00187312	0.00171983	0.00157938	0.00145065
41	0.00160096	0.00146681	0.00134415	0.00123198
42	0.00136834	0.00125101	0.00114396	0.00104626
43	0.00116952	0.00106696	0.00097358	0.00088855
44	0.00099959	0.00090999	0.00082858	0.00075461
45	0.00085435	0.00077611	0.00070517	0.00064085
46	0.00073021	0.00066193	0.00060015	0.00054425
47	0.00062411	0.00056454	0.00051076	0.00046221
48	0.00053343	0.00048149	0.00043469	0.00039253
49	0.00045592	0.00041065	0.00036995	0.00033336
50	0.00038968	0.00035023	0.00031485	0.00028311

Table 1 (cont.)

YEAR	18.00	INTEREST RATE (%) 18.25	18.50	18.75
1	0.84745763	0.84566596	0.84388186	0.84210526
2	0.71818443	0.71515092	0.71213659	0.70914127
3	0.60863087	0.60477879	0.60095915	0.59717160
4	0.51578888	0.51144084	0.50713852	0.50288135
5	0.43710922	0.43250811	0.42796500	0.42347903
6	0.37043154	0.36575738	0.36115189	0.35661392
7	0.31392503	0.30930857	0.30476953	0.30030646
8	0.26603816	0.26157173	0.25718948	0.25288965
9	0.22545607	0.22120231	0.21703753	0.21295970
10	0.19106447	0.18706326	0.18315404	0.17933449
11	0.16191904	0.15819303	0.15456037	0.15101852
12	0.13721953	0.13377846	0.13043069	0.12717349
13	0.11628773	0.11313189	0.11006809	0.10709346
14	0.09854893	0.09567179	0.09288447	0.09018397
15	0.08351604	0.08090638	0.07838352	0.07594439
16	0.07077630	0.06841977	0.06614643	0.06395317
17	0.05997992	0.05786027	0.05581977	0.05385530
18	0.05083044	0.04893046	0.04710529	0.04535184
19	0.04307664	0.04137883	0.03975130	0.03819102
20	0.03650563	0.03499266	0.03354540	0.03216086
21	0.03093698	0.02959211	0.02830836	0.02708283
22	0.02621778	0.02502504	0.02388891	0.02280659
23	0.02221845	0.02116282	0.02015942	0.01920555
24	0.01882920	0.01789668	0.01701217	0.01617310
25	0.01595695	0.01513461	0.01435626	0.01361945
26	0.01352284	0.01279883	0.01211499	0.01146901
27	0.01146003	0.01082353	0.01022362	0.00965811
28	0.00971189	0.00915309	0.00862752	0.00813315
29	0.00823042	0.00774046	0.00728061	0.00684897
30	0.00697493	0.00654584	0.00614398	0.00576755
31	0.00591096	0.00553560	0.00518479	0.00485689
32	0.00500929	0.00468126	0.00437535	0.00409001
33	0.00424516	0.00395879	0.00369228	0.00344422
34	0.00359759	0.00334781	0.00311585	0.00290039
35	0.00304881	0.00283113	0.00262941	0.00244244
36	0.00258373	0.00239419	0.00221891	0.00205679
37	0.00218960	0.00202469	0.00187250	0.00173203
38	0.00185560	0.00171221	0.00158017	0.00145855
39	0.00157254	0.00144796	0.00133347	0.00122826
40	0.00133266	0.00122449	0.00112529	0.00103432
41	0.00112937	0.00103551	0.00094962	0.00087101
42	0.00095710	0.00087569	0.00080136	0.00073348
43	0.00081110	0.00074054	0.00067626	0.00061767
44	0.00068737	0.00062625	0.00057068	0.00052014
45	0.00058252	0.00052960	0.00048159	0.00043801
46	0.00049366	0.00044787	0.00040640	0.00036885
47	0.00041836	0.00037874	0.00034296	0.00031061
48	0.00035454	0.00032029	0.00028941	0.00026157
49	0.00030046	0.00027086	0.00024423	0.00022027
50	0.00025462	0.00022906	0.00020610	0.00018549

Table 1 (cont.)

	INTEREST RATE (%)			
YEAR	19.00	19.25	19.50	19.75
1	0.84033613	0.83857442	0.83682008	0.83507307
2	0.70616482	0.70320706	0.70026785	0.69734703
3	0.59341581	0.58969146	0.58599820	0.58233572
4	0.49866875	0.49450017	0.49037507	0.48629288
5	0.41904937	0.41467520	0.41035570	0.40609009
6	0.35214233	0.34773602	0.34339389	0.33911490
7	0.29591792	0.29160253	0.28735891	0.28318572
8	0.24867052	0.24453042	0.24046770	0.23648077
9	0.20896683	0.20505696	0.20122820	0.19747872
10	0.17560238	0.17195552	0.16839180	0.16490916
11	0.14756502	0.14419750	0.14091364	0.13771120
12	0.12400422	0.12092034	0.11791937	0.11499891
13	0.10420523	0.10140070	0.09867729	0.09603250
14	0.08756742	0.08503203	0.08257514	0.08019415
15	0.07358606	0.07130569	0.06910054	0.06696798
16	0.06183703	0.05979513	0.05782472	0.05592315
17	0.05196389	0.05014266	0.04838888	0.04669992
18	0.04366713	0.04204836	0.04049279	0.03899784
19	0.03669507	0.03526068	0.03388518	0.03256605
20	0.03083619	0.02956870	0.02835580	0.02719503
21	0.02591277	0.02479556	0.02372870	0.02270984
22	0.02177544	0.02079292	0.01985665	0.01896437
23	0.01829869	0.01743641	0.01661645	0.01583664
24	0.01537705	0.01462173	0.01390498	0.01322475
25	0.01292189	0.01226141	0.01163596	0.01104363
26	0.01085873	0.01028210	0.00973721	0.00922224
27	0.00912498	0.00862231	0.00814829	0.00770124
28	0.00766805	0.00723045	0.00681865	0.00643110
29	0.00644374	0.00606327	0.00570599	0.00537044
30	0.00541491	0.00508450	0.00477488	0.00448471
31	0.00455034	0.00426373	0.00399572	0.00374506
32	0.00382382	0.00357546	0.00334370	0.00312740
33	0.00321329	0.00299829	0.00279807	0.00261161
34	0.00270025	0.00251429	0.00234148	0.00218088
35	0.00226911	0.00210842	0.00195940	0.00182120
36	0.00190682	0.00176806	0.00163967	0.00152083
37	0.00160237	0.00148265	0.00137211	0.00127001
38	0.00134653	0.00124332	0.00114821	0.00106055
39	0.00113154	0.00104261	0.00096084	0.00088563
40	0.00095087	0.00087431	0.00080405	0.00073957
41	0.00079905	0.00073317	0.00067285	0.00061759
42	0.00067147	0.00061482	0.00056305	0.00051574
43	0.00056426	0.00051557	0.00047117	0.00043068
44	0.00047417	0.00043235	0.00039429	0.00035965
45	0.00039846	0.00036255	0.00032995	0.00030033
46	0.00033484	0.00030403	0.00027611	0.00025080
47	0.00028138	0.00025495	0.00023105	0.00020944
48	0.00023645	0.00021379	0.00019335	0.00017489
49	0.00019870	0.00017928	0.00016180	0.00014605
50	0.00016698	0.00015034	0.00013540	0.00012196

Table 1 (*cont.*)

YEAR	20.00	20.25	20.50	20.75
		INTEREST RATE (%)		
1	0.83333333	0.83160083	0.82987552	0.82815735
2	0.69444444	0.69155994	0.68869338	0.68584460
3	0.57870370	0.57510182	0.57152977	0.56798724
4	0.48225309	0.47825515	0.47429857	0.47038281
5	0.40187757	0.39771738	0.39360877	0.38955098
6	0.33489798	0.33074211	0.32664628	0.32260951
7	0.27908165	0.27504541	0.27107575	0.26717144
8	0.23256804	0.22872799	0.22495913	0.22125999
9	0.19380670	0.19021039	0.18668808	0.18323809
10	0.16150558	0.15817912	0.15492786	0.15174997
11	0.13458799	0.13154189	0.12857084	0.12567285
12	0.11215665	0.10939034	0.10669779	0.10407689
13	0.09346388	0.09096910	0.08854589	0.08619205
14	0.07788657	0.07564998	0.07348206	0.07138058
15	0.06490547	0.06291059	0.06098097	0.05911435
16	0.05408789	0.05231649	0.05060661	0.04895598
17	0.04507324	0.04350644	0.04199719	0.04054326
18	0.03756104	0.03617999	0.03485244	0.03357620
19	0.03130086	0.03008731	0.02892318	0.02780637
20	0.02608405	0.02502063	0.02400264	0.02302805
21	0.02173671	0.02080718	0.01991921	0.01907085
22	0.01811393	0.01730327	0.01653046	0.01579367
23	0.01509494	0.01438941	0.01371822	0.01307964
24	0.01257912	0.01196625	0.01138442	0.01083200
25	0.01048260	0.00995114	0.00944765	0.00897060
26	0.00873550	0.00827538	0.00784037	0.00742907
27	0.00727958	0.00688181	0.00650653	0.00615244
28	0.00606632	0.00572292	0.00539961	0.00509519
29	0.00505526	0.00475918	0.00448101	0.00421962
30	0.00421272	0.00395774	0.00371868	0.00349451
31	0.00351060	0.00329126	0.00308604	0.00289400
32	0.00292550	0.00273702	0.00256103	0.00239669
33	0.00243792	0.00227610	0.00212534	0.00198483
34	0.00203160	0.00189281	0.00176376	0.00164376
35	0.00169300	0.00157406	0.00146370	0.00136129
36	0.00141083	0.00130899	0.00121469	0.00112736
37	0.00117569	0.00108856	0.00100804	0.00093363
38	0.00097974	0.00090525	0.00083655	0.00077319
39	0.00081645	0.00075280	0.00069423	0.00064033
40	0.00068038	0.00062603	0.00057613	0.00053029
41	0.00056698	0.00052061	0.00047811	0.00043916
42	0.00047248	0.00043294	0.00039677	0.00036370
43	0.00039374	0.00036003	0.00032927	0.00030120
44	0.00032811	0.00029940	0.00027326	0.00024944
45	0.00027343	0.00024898	0.00022677	0.00020658
46	0.00022786	0.00020706	0.00018819	0.00017108
47	0.00018988	0.00017219	0.00015617	0.00014168
48	0.00015823	0.00014319	0.00012960	0.00011733
49	0.00013186	0.00011908	0.00010756	0.00009717
50	0.00010988	0.00009903	0.00008926	0.00008047

Table 1 *(cont.)*

YEAR	INTEREST RATE (%) 21.00	21.25	21.50	21.75
1	0.82644628	0.82474227	0.82304527	0.82135524
2	0.68301346	0.68019981	0.67740351	0.67462442
3	0.56447393	0.56098953	0.55753376	0.55410630
4	0.46650738	0.46267178	0.45887552	0.45511811
5	0.38554329	0.38158497	0.37767532	0.37381365
6	0.31863082	0.31470926	0.31084389	0.30703380
7	0.26333125	0.25955403	0.25583859	0.25218382
8	0.21762914	0.21406518	0.21056674	0.20713250
9	0.17985879	0.17654860	0.17330596	0.17012936
10	0.14864363	0.14560709	0.14263865	0.13973664
11	0.12284597	0.12008832	0.11739807	0.11477342
12	0.10152560	0.09904192	0.09662392	0.09426975
13	0.08390545	0.08168405	0.07952586	0.07742895
14	0.06934335	0.06736829	0.06545338	0.06359668
15	0.05730855	0.05556148	0.05387110	0.05223546
16	0.04736244	0.04582390	0.04433835	0.04290387
17	0.03914251	0.03779291	0.03649247	0.03523932
18	0.03234918	0.03116941	0.03003496	0.02894400
19	0.02673486	0.02570673	0.02472013	0.02377331
20	0.02209493	0.02120143	0.02034578	0.01952633
21	0.01826027	0.01748571	0.01674550	0.01603805
22	0.01509113	0.01442121	0.01378231	0.01317294
23	0.01247201	0.01189378	0.01134346	0.01081966
24	0.01030745	0.00980930	0.00933618	0.00888679
25	0.00851855	0.00809015	0.00768410	0.00729921
26	0.00704013	0.00667228	0.00632436	0.00599524
27	0.00581829	0.00550292	0.00520524	0.00492422
28	0.00480850	0.00453849	0.00428415	0.00404454
29	0.00397397	0.00374308	0.00352605	0.00332200
30	0.00328427	0.00308708	0.00290210	0.00272854
31	0.00271427	0.00254604	0.00238856	0.00224110
32	0.00224320	0.00209983	0.00196589	0.00184074
33	0.00185388	0.00173182	0.00161802	0.00151190
34	0.00153214	0.00142830	0.00133170	0.00124181
35	0.00126623	0.00117798	0.00109605	0.00101997
36	0.00104647	0.00097153	0.00090210	0.00083776
37	0.00086485	0.00080126	0.00074247	0.00068809
38	0.00071475	0.00066084	0.00061108	0.00056517
39	0.00059070	0.00054502	0.00050295	0.00046421
40	0.00048819	0.00044950	0.00041395	0.00038128
41	0.00040346	0.00037072	0.00034070	0.00031316
42	0.00033344	0.00030575	0.00028041	0.00025722
43	0.00027557	0.00025217	0.00023079	0.00021127
44	0.00022774	0.00020797	0.00018995	0.00017353
45	0.00018822	0.00017152	0.00015634	0.00014253
46	0.00015555	0.00014146	0.00012867	0.00011707
47	0.00012855	0.00011667	0.00010590	0.00009615
48	0.00010624	0.00009622	0.00008716	0.00007897
49	0.00008780	0.00007936	0.00007174	0.00006487
50	0.00007257	0.00006545	0.00005905	0.00005328

Table 1 (cont.)

| | INTEREST RATE (%) | | | |
YEAR	22.00	22.25	22.50	22.75
1	0.81967213	0.81799591	0.81632653	0.81466395
2	0.67186240	0.66911731	0.66638900	0.66367735
3	0.55070689	0.54733522	0.54399102	0.54067401
4	0.45139909	0.44771797	0.44407431	0.44046763
5	0.36999925	0.36623147	0.36250964	0.35883310
6	0.30327808	0.29957585	0.29592623	0.29232839
7	0.24858859	0.24505182	0.24157244	0.23814940
8	0.20376114	0.20045138	0.19720199	0.19401173
9	0.16701733	0.16396841	0.16098122	0.15805436
10	0.13689945	0.13412549	0.13141324	0.12876119
11	0.11221266	0.10971410	0.10727611	0.10489710
12	0.09197759	0.08974569	0.08757234	0.08545589
13	0.07539147	0.07341160	0.07148762	0.06961783
14	0.06179629	0.06005039	0.05835724	0.05671514
15	0.05065269	0.04912098	0.04763856	0.04620378
16	0.04151860	0.04018076	0.03888862	0.03764055
17	0.03403164	0.03286769	0.03174582	0.03066440
18	0.02789479	0.02688564	0.02591495	0.02498118
19	0.02286458	0.02199234	0.02115506	0.02035127
20	0.01874146	0.01798965	0.01726944	0.01657944
21	0.01536185	0.01471546	0.01409750	0.01350668
22	0.01259168	0.01203718	0.01150816	0.01100340
23	0.01032105	0.00984637	0.00939442	0.00896408
24	0.00845988	0.00805429	0.00766891	0.00730271
25	0.00693433	0.00658837	0.00626034	0.00594925
26	0.00568387	0.00538926	0.00511048	0.00484664
27	0.00465891	0.00440840	0.00417182	0.00394838
28	0.00381878	0.00360605	0.00340557	0.00321661
29	0.00313015	0.00294973	0.00278006	0.00262045
30	0.00256570	0.00241287	0.00226943	0.00213479
31	0.00210303	0.00197372	0.00185260	0.00173914
32	0.00172379	0.00161449	0.00151233	0.00141681
33	0.00141295	0.00132065	0.00123455	0.00115422
34	0.00115815	0.00108029	0.00100780	0.00094031
35	0.00094931	0.00088367	0.00082269	0.00076603
36	0.00077812	0.00072284	0.00067158	0.00062406
37	0.00063780	0.00059128	0.00054823	0.00050840
38	0.00052279	0.00048366	0.00044754	0.00041417
39	0.00042852	0.00039563	0.00036534	0.00033741
40	0.00035124	0.00032363	0.00029823	0.00027488
41	0.00028790	0.00026473	0.00024346	0.00022393
42	0.00023599	0.00021654	0.00019874	0.00018243
43	0.00019343	0.00017713	0.00016224	0.00014862
44	0.00015855	0.00014489	0.00013244	0.00012107
45	0.00012996	0.00011852	0.00010811	0.00009864
46	0.00010652	0.00009695	0.00008826	0.00008035
47	0.00008731	0.00007931	0.00007204	0.00006546
48	0.00007157	0.00006487	0.00005881	0.00005333
49	0.00005866	0.00005306	0.00004801	0.00004345
50	0.00004808	0.00004341	0.00003919	0.00003539

Table 1 (cont.)

	INTEREST RATE (%)			
YEAR	23.00	23.25	23.50	23.75
1	0.81300813	0.81135903	0.80971660	0.80808081
2	0.66098222	0.65830347	0.65564097	0.65299459
3	0.53738392	0.53412046	0.53088338	0.52767240
4	0.43689749	0.43336346	0.42986508	0.42640194
5	0.35520122	0.35161335	0.34806889	0.34456722
6	0.28878148	0.28528467	0.28183716	0.27843816
7	0.23478169	0.23146829	0.22820823	0.22500053
8	0.19087942	0.18780389	0.18478399	0.18181861
9	0.15518652	0.15237638	0.14962266	0.14692413
10	0.12616790	0.12363195	0.12115195	0.11872657
11	0.10257553	0.10030990	0.09809875	0.09594066
12	0.08339474	0.08138734	0.07943218	0.07752781
13	0.06780060	0.06603435	0.06431756	0.06264873
14	0.05512244	0.05357757	0.05207899	0.05062524
15	0.04481499	0.04347064	0.04216923	0.04090928
16	0.03643495	0.03527030	0.03414512	0.03305801
17	0.02962191	0.02861688	0.02764787	0.02671354
18	0.02408286	0.02321856	0.02238694	0.02158670
19	0.01957956	0.01883859	0.01812708	0.01744380
20	0.01591834	0.01528486	0.01467780	0.01409600
21	0.01294174	0.01240151	0.01188486	0.01139071
22	0.01052174	0.01006208	0.00962336	0.00920461
23	0.00855426	0.00816396	0.00779220	0.00743807
24	0.00695468	0.00662390	0.00630947	0.00601056
25	0.00565421	0.00537436	0.00510888	0.00485702
26	0.00459692	0.00436054	0.00413675	0.00392486
27	0.00373733	0.00353796	0.00334959	0.00317161
28	0.00303848	0.00287056	0.00271222	0.00256291
29	0.00247031	0.00232905	0.00219613	0.00207104
30	0.00200838	0.00188970	0.00177824	0.00167357
31	0.00163283	0.00153322	0.00143987	0.00135238
32	0.00132751	0.00124399	0.00116589	0.00109283
33	0.00107927	0.00100933	0.00094404	0.00088310
34	0.00087746	0.00081893	0.00076440	0.00071361
35	0.00071338	0.00066444	0.00061895	0.00057666
36	0.00057998	0.00053910	0.00050118	0.00046599
37	0.00047153	0.00043740	0.00040581	0.00037655
38	0.00038336	0.00035489	0.00032859	0.00030429
39	0.00031167	0.00028795	0.00026607	0.00024589
40	0.00025339	0.00023363	0.00021544	0.00019870
41	0.00020601	0.00018956	0.00017444	0.00016056
42	0.00016749	0.00015380	0.00014125	0.00012975
43	0.00013617	0.00012478	0.00011437	0.00010485
44	0.00011071	0.00010125	0.00009261	0.00008472
45	0.00009001	0.00008215	0.00007499	0.00006846
46	0.00007318	0.00006665	0.00006072	0.00005532
47	0.00005949	0.00005408	0.00004916	0.00004471
48	0.00004837	0.00004388	0.00003981	0.00003613
49	0.00003932	0.00003560	0.00003223	0.00002919
50	0.00003197	0.00002888	0.00002610	0.00002359

Table 1 (cont.)

YEAR	24.00	24.25	24.50	24.75
		INTEREST RATE (%)		
1	0.80645161	0.80482897	0.80321285	0.80160321
2	0.65036420	0.64774968	0.64515088	0.64256770
3	0.52448726	0.52132771	0.51819348	0.51508433
4	0.42297360	0.41957964	0.41621966	0.41289325
5	0.34110774	0.33768985	0.33431298	0.33097655
6	0.27508689	0.27178258	0.26852448	0.26531187
7	0.22184426	0.21873849	0.21568232	0.21267484
8	0.17890666	0.17604708	0.17323881	0.17048084
9	0.14427957	0.14168779	0.13914764	0.13665798
10	0.11635449	0.11403444	0.11176517	0.10954548
11	0.09383427	0.09177822	0.08977122	0.08781201
12	0.07567280	0.07386577	0.07210540	0.07039039
13	0.06102645	0.05944931	0.05791598	0.05642516
14	0.04921488	0.04784653	0.04651886	0.04523059
15	0.03968942	0.03850827	0.03736455	0.03625698
16	0.03200759	0.03099257	0.03001168	0.02906372
17	0.02581258	0.02494372	0.02410577	0.02329757
18	0.02081659	0.02007543	0.01936207	0.01867540
19	0.01678758	0.01615729	0.01555186	0.01497026
20	0.01353837	0.01300385	0.01249145	0.01200021
21	0.01091804	0.01046588	0.01003330	0.00961941
22	0.00880487	0.00842324	0.00805887	0.00771095
23	0.00710070	0.00677927	0.00647299	0.00618112
24	0.00572637	0.00545615	0.00519919	0.00495481
25	0.00461804	0.00439127	0.00417606	0.00397179
26	0.00372423	0.00353422	0.00335426	0.00318380
27	0.00300341	0.00284444	0.00269419	0.00255214
28	0.00242210	0.00228929	0.00216400	0.00204581
29	0.00195331	0.00184249	0.00173816	0.00163992
30	0.00157525	0.00148289	0.00139611	0.00131457
31	0.00127036	0.00119347	0.00112137	0.00105376
32	0.00102449	0.00096054	0.00090070	0.00084470
33	0.00082620	0.00077307	0.00072345	0.00067711
34	0.00066629	0.00062219	0.00058109	0.00054278
35	0.00053733	0.00050076	0.00046674	0.00043509
36	0.00043333	0.00040302	0.00037489	0.00034877
37	0.00034946	0.00032436	0.00030112	0.00027958
38	0.00028182	0.00026106	0.00024186	0.00022411
39	0.00022728	0.00021011	0.00019427	0.00017965
40	0.00018329	0.00016910	0.00015604	0.00014401
41	0.00014781	0.00013610	0.00012533	0.00011543
42	0.00011920	0.00010953	0.00010067	0.00009253
43	0.00009613	0.00008816	0.00008086	0.00007417
44	0.00007753	0.00007095	0.00006495	0.00005946
45	0.00006252	0.00005710	0.00005216	0.00004766
46	0.00005042	0.00004596	0.00004190	0.00003821
47	0.00004066	0.00003699	0.00003365	0.00003063
48	0.00003279	0.00002977	0.00002703	0.00002455
49	0.00002644	0.00002396	0.00002171	0.00001968
50	0.00002133	0.00001928	0.00001744	0.00001578

Table 1 (*cont.*)

YEAR	INTEREST RATE (%) 25.00	25.25	25.50	25.75
1	0.80000000	0.79840319	0.79681275	0.79522863
2	0.64000000	0.63744766	0.63491056	0.63238857
3	0.51200000	0.50894025	0.50590483	0.50289350
4	0.40960000	0.40633952	0.40311142	0.39991530
5	0.32768000	0.32442277	0.32120432	0.31802410
6	0.26214400	0.25902018	0.25593969	0.25290187
7	0.20971520	0.20680254	0.20393601	0.20111481
8	0.16777216	0.16511180	0.16249881	0.15993225
9	0.13421773	0.13182579	0.12948113	0.12718270
10	0.10737418	0.10525013	0.10317221	0.10113933
11	0.08589935	0.08403204	0.08220893	0.08042889
12	0.06871948	0.06709145	0.06550513	0.06395935
13	0.05497558	0.05356603	0.05219532	0.05086231
14	0.04398047	0.04276729	0.04158990	0.04044717
15	0.03518437	0.03414554	0.03313936	0.03216474
16	0.02814750	0.02726191	0.02640586	0.02557832
17	0.02251800	0.02176599	0.02104053	0.02034062
18	0.01801440	0.01737804	0.01676536	0.01617544
19	0.01441152	0.01387468	0.01335885	0.01286317
20	0.01152922	0.01107759	0.01064451	0.01022916
21	0.00922337	0.00884438	0.00848168	0.00813452
22	0.00737870	0.00706138	0.00675831	0.00646881
23	0.00590296	0.00563783	0.00538511	0.00514418
24	0.00472237	0.00450126	0.00429092	0.00409080
25	0.00377789	0.00359382	0.00341906	0.00325312
26	0.00302231	0.00286932	0.00272435	0.00258697
27	0.00241785	0.00229087	0.00217080	0.00205724
28	0.00193428	0.00182904	0.00172972	0.00163597
29	0.00154743	0.00146031	0.00137826	0.00130097
30	0.00123794	0.00116592	0.00109822	0.00103457
31	0.00099035	0.00093087	0.00087507	0.00082272
32	0.00079228	0.00074321	0.00069727	0.00065425
33	0.00063383	0.00059338	0.00055559	0.00052028
34	0.00050706	0.00047376	0.00044270	0.00041374
35	0.00040565	0.00037825	0.00035275	0.00032902
36	0.00032452	0.00030200	0.00028108	0.00026164
37	0.00025961	0.00024111	0.00022397	0.00020807
38	0.00020769	0.00019251	0.00017846	0.00016546
39	0.00016615	0.00015370	0.00014220	0.00013158
40	0.00013292	0.00012271	0.00011331	0.00010464
41	0.00010634	0.00009797	0.00009028	0.00008321
42	0.00008507	0.00007822	0.00007194	0.00006617
43	0.00006806	0.00006245	0.00005732	0.00005262
44	0.00005445	0.00004986	0.00004567	0.00004185
45	0.00004356	0.00003981	0.00003639	0.00003328
46	0.00003484	0.00003179	0.00002900	0.00002646
47	0.00002788	0.00002538	0.00002311	0.00002104
48	0.00002230	0.00002026	0.00001841	0.00001673
49	0.00001784	0.00001618	0.00001467	0.00001331
50	0.00001427	0.00001292	0.00001169	0.00001058

Table 2 MORTGAGE CONSTANT (MONTHLY COMPOUNDING)

YEAR	INTEREST RATE 6.00	6.25	6.50	6.75
1	0.08606643	0.08618138	0.08629642	0.08641154
2	0.04432061	0.04443334	0.04454625	0.04465933
3	0.03042194	0.03053534	0.03064900	0.03076292
4	0.02348503	0.02359982	0.02371495	0.02383043
5	0.01933280	0.01944926	0.01956615	0.01968346
6	0.01657289	0.01669115	0.01680993	0.01692921
7	0.01460855	0.01472870	0.01484944	0.01497076
8	0.01314143	0.01326350	0.01338623	0.01350964
9	0.01200575	0.01212976	0.01225452	0.01238002
10	0.01110205	0.01122801	0.01135480	0.01148241
11	0.01036703	0.01049495	0.01062377	0.01075349
12	0.00975850	0.00988837	0.01001921	0.01015103
13	0.00924723	0.00937904	0.00951190	0.00964580
14	0.00881236	0.00894610	0.00908096	0.00921693
15	0.00843857	0.00857423	0.00871107	0.00884909
16	0.00811438	0.00825194	0.00839075	0.00853080
17	0.00783101	0.00797045	0.00811121	0.00825327
18	0.00758162	0.00772293	0.00786561	0.00800965
19	0.00736083	0.00750398	0.00764856	0.00779455
20	0.00716431	0.00730928	0.00745573	0.00760364
21	0.00698857	0.00713534	0.00728363	0.00743343
22	0.00683074	0.00697928	0.00712939	0.00728105
23	0.00668847	0.00683875	0.00699065	0.00714414
24	0.00655978	0.00671177	0.00686543	0.00702071
25	0.00644301	0.00659669	0.00675207	0.00690912
26	0.00633677	0.00649211	0.00664918	0.00680795
27	0.00623985	0.00639682	0.00655555	0.00671601
28	0.00615124	0.00630980	0.00647016	0.00663227
29	0.00607005	0.00623018	0.00639213	0.00655585
30	0.00599551	0.00615717	0.00632068	0.00648598
31	0.00592695	0.00609012	0.00625515	0.00642199
32	0.00586380	0.00602844	0.00619496	0.00636330
33	0.00580553	0.00597161	0.00613959	0.00630940
34	0.00575170	0.00591919	0.00608858	0.00625982
35	0.00570190	0.00587076	0.00604154	0.00621417
36	0.00565577	0.00582598	0.00599811	0.00617208
37	0.00561300	0.00578453	0.00595797	0.00613325
38	0.00557331	0.00574611	0.00592083	0.00609739
39	0.00553643	0.00571048	0.00588644	0.00606424
40	0.00550214	0.00567740	0.00585457	0.00603357

Table 2 (cont.)

YEAR	7.00	7.25	7.50	7.75
		INTEREST RATE		
1	0.08652675	0.08664204	0.08675742	0.08687288
2	0.04477258	0.04488600	0.04499959	0.04511336
3	0.03087710	0.03099153	0.03110622	0.03122116
4	0.02394624	0.02406240	0.02417890	0.02429574
5	0.01980120	0.01991936	0.02003795	0.02015696
6	0.01704901	0.01716931	0.01729011	0.01741142
7	0.01509268	0.01521518	0.01533828	0.01546195
8	0.01363372	0.01375846	0.01388387	0.01400994
9	0.01250628	0.01263328	0.01276102	0.01288950
10	0.01161085	0.01174010	0.01187018	0.01200106
11	0.01088410	0.01101561	0.01114801	0.01128129
12	0.01028381	0.01041756	0.01055226	0.01068792
13	0.00978074	0.00991671	0.01005370	0.01019172
14	0.00935401	0.00949218	0.00963143	0.00977177
15	0.00898828	0.00912863	0.00927012	0.00941276
16	0.00867208	0.00881458	0.00895828	0.00910317
17	0.00839661	0.00854122	0.00868709	0.00883421
18	0.00815502	0.00830172	0.00844973	0.00859904
19	0.00794192	0.00809068	0.00824079	0.00839224
20	0.00775299	0.00790376	0.00805593	0.00820949
21	0.00758472	0.00773747	0.00789166	0.00804727
22	0.00743424	0.00758893	0.00774510	0.00790273
23	0.00729919	0.00745579	0.00761389	0.00777348
24	0.00717760	0.00733605	0.00749605	0.00765756
25	0.00706779	0.00722807	0.00738991	0.00755329
26	0.00696838	0.00713043	0.00729407	0.00745927
27	0.00687815	0.00704194	0.00720734	0.00737430
28	0.00679609	0.00696157	0.00712868	0.00729736
29	0.00672130	0.00688843	0.00705720	0.00722756
30	0.00665302	0.00682176	0.00699215	0.00716412
31	0.00659059	0.00676089	0.00693284	0.00710639
32	0.00653341	0.00670523	0.00687870	0.00705377
33	0.00648098	0.00665427	0.00682921	0.00700575
34	0.00643283	0.00660755	0.00678392	0.00696188
35	0.00638856	0.00656467	0.00674243	0.00692176
36	0.00634783	0.00652528	0.00670437	0.00688503
37	0.00631031	0.00648906	0.00666944	0.00685138
38	0.00627571	0.00645573	0.00663735	0.00682052
39	0.00624379	0.00642502	0.00660785	0.00679220
40	0.00621431	0.00639672	0.00658071	0.00676620

Table 2 *(cont.)*

| YEAR | INTEREST RATE | | | |
	8.00	8.25	8.50	8.75
1	0.08698843	0.08710406	0.08721978	0.08733559
2	0.04522729	0.04534140	0.04545567	0.04557012
3	0.03133637	0.03145182	0.03156754	0.03168351
4	0.02441292	0.02453044	0.02464830	0.02476650
5	0.02027639	0.02039625	0.02051653	0.02063723
6	0.01753324	0.01765556	0.01777838	0.01790171
7	0.01558621	0.01571106	0.01583649	0.01596249
8	0.01413668	0.01426407	0.01439213	0.01452084
9	0.01301871	0.01314867	0.01327935	0.01341077
10	0.01213276	0.01226526	0.01239857	0.01253268
11	0.01141545	0.01155048	0.01168639	0.01182317
12	0.01082453	0.01096207	0.01110056	0.01123997
13	0.01033074	0.01047077	0.01061179	0.01075381
14	0.00991318	0.01005566	0.01019919	0.01034376
15	0.00955652	0.00970140	0.00984740	0.00999449
16	0.00924925	0.00939650	0.00954491	0.00969447
17	0.00898257	0.00913214	0.00928292	0.00943489
18	0.00874963	0.00890148	0.00905457	0.00920890
19	0.00854501	0.00869909	0.00885446	0.00901109
20	0.00836440	0.00852066	0.00867823	0.00883711
21	0.00820428	0.00836266	0.00852239	0.00868345
22	0.00806178	0.00822223	0.00838406	0.00854724
23	0.00793453	0.00809700	0.00826087	0.00842610
24	0.00782054	0.00798497	0.00815082	0.00831806
25	0.00771816	0.00788450	0.00805227	0.00822144
26	0.00762598	0.00779417	0.00796380	0.00813483
27	0.00754280	0.00771278	0.00788421	0.00805705
28	0.00746759	0.00763930	0.00781247	0.00798705
29	0.00739946	0.00757286	0.00774770	0.00792396
30	0.00733765	0.00751267	0.00768913	0.00786700
31	0.00728148	0.00745807	0.00763610	0.00781552
32	0.00723038	0.00740848	0.00758801	0.00776892
33	0.00718382	0.00736338	0.00754435	0.00772670
34	0.00714137	0.00732232	0.00750469	0.00768840
35	0.00710261	0.00728491	0.00746861	0.00765363
36	0.00706719	0.00725079	0.00743576	0.00762204
37	0.00703480	0.00721964	0.00740584	0.00759332
38	0.00700516	0.00719119	0.00737855	0.00756718
39	0.00697800	0.00716518	0.00735366	0.00754338
40	0.00695312	0.00714139	0.00733094	0.00752171

Table 2 (cont.)

YEAR	INTEREST RATE 9.00	9.25	9.50	9.75
1	0.08745148	0.08756745	0.08768351	0.08779966
2	0.04568474	0.04579953	0.04591449	0.04602962
3	0.03179973	0.03191621	0.03203295	0.03214994
4	0.02488504	0.02500392	0.02512314	0.02524269
5	0.02075836	0.02087990	0.02100186	0.02112424
6	0.01802554	0.01814986	0.01827469	0.01840002
7	0.01608908	0.01621624	0.01634398	0.01647230
8	0.01465020	0.01478022	0.01491089	0.01504220
9	0.01354291	0.01367577	0.01380936	0.01394367
10	0.01266758	0.01280327	0.01293976	0.01307702
11	0.01196080	0.01209930	0.01223865	0.01237884
12	0.01138031	0.01152156	0.01166373	0.01180681
13	0.01089681	0.01104078	0.01118572	0.01133163
14	0.01048938	0.01063602	0.01078368	0.01093235
15	0.01014267	0.01029192	0.01044225	0.01059363
16	0.00984516	0.00999697	0.01014990	0.01030392
17	0.00958804	0.00974235	0.00989781	0.01005440
18	0.00936445	0.00952119	0.00967911	0.00983820
19	0.00916897	0.00932808	0.00948840	0.00964991
20	0.00899726	0.00915867	0.00932131	0.00948517
21	0.00884581	0.00900945	0.00917434	0.00934047
22	0.00871174	0.00887754	0.00904461	0.00921293
23	0.00859268	0.00876057	0.00892974	0.00910017
24	0.00848664	0.00865655	0.00882775	0.00900020
25	0.00839196	0.00856382	0.00873697	0.00891137
26	0.00830723	0.00848096	0.00865599	0.00883227
27	0.00823125	0.00840679	0.00858361	0.00876169
28	0.00816300	0.00834027	0.00851882	0.00869861
29	0.00810158	0.00828051	0.00846071	0.00864215
30	0.00804623	0.00822675	0.00840854	0.00859154
31	0.00799628	0.00817834	0.00836164	0.00854613
32	0.00795116	0.00813468	0.00831942	0.00850534
33	0.00791035	0.00809526	0.00828138	0.00846865
34	0.00787341	0.00805965	0.00824708	0.00843563
35	0.00783993	0.00802744	0.00821612	0.00840589
36	0.00780957	0.00799830	0.00818815	0.00837909
37	0.00778203	0.00797190	0.00816288	0.00835491
38	0.00775701	0.00794798	0.00814002	0.00833309
39	0.00773428	0.00792628	0.00811934	0.00831338
40	0.00771361	0.00790661	0.00810062	0.00829559

Table 2 (cont.)

	INTEREST	RATE	
YEAR	10.00	10.25	10.50	10.75
1	0.08791589	0.08803220	0.08814860	0.08826509
2	0.04614493	0.04626040	0.04637604	0.04649185
3	0.03226719	0.03238469	0.03250244	0.03262045
4	0.02536258	0.02548281	0.02560338	0.02572428
5	0.02124704	0.02137026	0.02149390	0.02161795
6	0.01852584	0.01865216	0.01877897	0.01890628
7	0.01660118	0.01673064	0.01686067	0.01699127
8	0.01517416	0.01530677	0.01544002	0.01557390
9	0.01407869	0.01421442	0.01435086	0.01448801
10	0.01321507	0.01335390	0.01349350	0.01363387
11	0.01251988	0.01266175	0.01280446	0.01294799
12	0.01195078	0.01209565	0.01224141	0.01238804
13	0.01147848	0.01162628	0.01177502	0.01192469
14	0.01108203	0.01123269	0.01138434	0.01153696
15	0.01074605	0.01089951	0.01105399	0.01120948
16	0.01045902	0.01061519	0.01077242	0.01093070
17	0.01021210	0.01037091	0.01053081	0.01069178
18	0.00999844	0.01015980	0.01032228	0.01048585
19	0.00981259	0.00997642	0.01014139	0.01030747
20	0.00965022	0.00981643	0.00998380	0.01015229
21	0.00950780	0.00967631	0.00984599	0.01001679
22	0.00938246	0.00955318	0.00972507	0.00989810
23	0.00927182	0.00944466	0.00961867	0.00979382
24	0.00917389	0.00934877	0.00952481	0.00970199
25	0.00908701	0.00926383	0.00944182	0.00962093
26	0.00900977	0.00918846	0.00936829	0.00954924
27	0.00894098	0.00912144	0.00930304	0.00948574
28	0.00887960	0.00906176	0.00924504	0.00942940
29	0.00882477	0.00900854	0.00919341	0.00937934
30	0.00877572	0.00896101	0.00914739	0.00933481
31	0.00873178	0.00891853	0.00910634	0.00929517
32	0.00869238	0.00888051	0.00906968	0.00925983
33	0.00865703	0.00884646	0.00903690	0.00922831
34	0.00862527	0.00881594	0.00900759	0.00920017
35	0.00859672	0.00878856	0.00898134	0.00917503
36	0.00857105	0.00876398	0.00895783	0.00915256
37	0.00854793	0.00874190	0.00893676	0.00913246
38	0.00852712	0.00872206	0.00891787	0.00911448
39	0.00850836	0.00870423	0.00890092	0.00909839
40	0.00849146	0.00868818	0.00888570	0.00908397

Table 2 (*cont.*)

		INTEREST RATE		
YEAR	11.00	11.25	11.50	11.75
1	0.08838166	0.08849831	0.08861505	0.08873188
2	0.04660784	0.04672399	0.04684032	0.04695681
3	0.03273872	0.03285723	0.03297601	0.03309503
4	0.02584552	0.02596710	0.02608901	0.02621125
5	0.02174242	0.02186731	0.02199261	0.02211832
6	0.01903408	0.01916237	0.01929116	0.01942043
7	0.01712244	0.01725417	0.01738646	0.01751932
8	0.01570843	0.01584358	0.01597937	0.01611579
9	0.01462586	0.01476441	0.01490366	0.01504360
10	0.01377500	0.01391689	0.01405954	0.01420295
11	0.01309235	0.01323752	0.01338350	0.01353029
12	0.01253555	0.01268393	0.01283317	0.01298326
13	0.01207527	0.01222677	0.01237918	0.01253248
14	0.01169054	0.01184508	0.01200055	0.01215696
15	0.01136597	0.01152345	0.01168190	0.01184131
16	0.01109000	0.01125033	0.01141165	0.01157396
17	0.01085381	0.01101687	0.01118096	0.01134606
18	0.01065050	0.01081620	0.01098295	0.01115073
19	0.01047464	0.01064288	0.01081218	0.01098251
20	0.01032188	0.01049256	0.01066430	0.01083707
21	0.01018871	0.01036171	0.01053578	0.01071088
22	0.01007223	0.01024746	0.01042374	0.01060106
23	0.00997008	0.01014742	0.01032581	0.01050523
24	0.00988027	0.01005962	0.01024002	0.01042142
25	0.00980113	0.00998240	0.01016469	0.01034798
26	0.00973127	0.00991435	0.01009844	0.01028351
27	0.00966950	0.00985429	0.01004008	0.01022682
28	0.00961480	0.00980121	0.00998859	0.01017691
29	0.00956629	0.00975423	0.00994312	0.01013292
30	0.00952323	0.00971261	0.00990291	0.01009410
31	0.00948497	0.00967570	0.00986733	0.01005981
32	0.00945093	0.00964294	0.00983581	0.01002950
33	0.00942063	0.00961383	0.00980786	0.01000269
34	0.00939364	0.00958796	0.00978308	0.00997896
35	0.00936958	0.00956494	0.00976107	0.00995794
36	0.00934811	0.00954445	0.00974153	0.00993931
37	0.00932896	0.00952621	0.00972417	0.00992280
38	0.00931186	0.00950996	0.00970874	0.00990816
39	0.00929659	0.00949548	0.00969502	0.00989517
40	0.00928294	0.00948257	0.00968282	0.00988364

Table 2 (cont.)

YEAR	INTEREST RATE 12.00	12.25	12.50	12.75
1	0.08884879	0.08896578	0.08908286	0.08920003
2	0.04707347	0.04719031	0.04730731	0.04742448
3	0.03321431	0.03333384	0.03345363	0.03357366
4	0.02633384	0.02645675	0.02658000	0.02670358
5	0.02224445	0.02237099	0.02249794	0.02262530
6	0.01955019	0.01968044	0.01981118	0.01994240
7	0.01765273	0.01778671	0.01792124	0.01805632
8	0.01625284	0.01639051	0.01652881	0.01666772
9	0.01518423	0.01532555	0.01546755	0.01561023
10	0.01434709	0.01449199	0.01463762	0.01478398
11	0.01367788	0.01382626	0.01397543	0.01412538
12	0.01313419	0.01328597	0.01343857	0.01359200
13	0.01268666	0.01284173	0.01299766	0.01315446
14	0.01231430	0.01247254	0.01263168	0.01279172
15	0.01200168	0.01216299	0.01232522	0.01248837
16	0.01173725	0.01190150	0.01206670	0.01223283
17	0.01151216	0.01167923	0.01184726	0.01201624
18	0.01131950	0.01148927	0.01166001	0.01183170
19	0.01115386	0.01132620	0.01149951	0.01167378
20	0.01101086	0.01118565	0.01136141	0.01153812
21	0.01088700	0.01106410	0.01124218	0.01142120
22	0.01077938	0.01095869	0.01113896	0.01132016
23	0.01068565	0.01086704	0.01104937	0.01123262
24	0.01060382	0.01078717	0.01097144	0.01115662
25	0.01053224	0.01071744	0.01090354	0.01109052
26	0.01046952	0.01065646	0.01084427	0.01103294
27	0.01041449	0.01060305	0.01079247	0.01098272
28	0.01036613	0.01055621	0.01074713	0.01093885
29	0.01032359	0.01051510	0.01070741	0.01090049
30	0.01028613	0.01047896	0.01067258	0.01086693
31	0.01025311	0.01044718	0.01064201	0.01083754
32	0.01022398	0.01041921	0.01061515	0.01081178
33	0.01019827	0.01039457	0.01059156	0.01078919
34	0.01017557	0.01037286	0.01057080	0.01076936
35	0.01015550	0.01035371	0.01055254	0.01075196
36	0.01013776	0.01033682	0.01053647	0.01073668
37	0.01012206	0.01032191	0.01052232	0.01072325
38	0.01010817	0.01030875	0.01050986	0.01071146
39	0.01009588	0.01029713	0.01049887	0.01070108
40	0.01008500	0.01028686	0.01048919	0.01069196

Table 2   (cont.)

YEAR	INTEREST RATE 13.00	13.25	13.50	13.75
1	0.08931728	0.08943461	0.08955203	0.08966953
2	0.04754182	0.04765933	0.04777701	0.04789486
3	0.03369395	0.03381449	0.03393529	0.03405633
4	0.02682750	0.02695174	0.02707632	0.02720123
5	0.02275307	0.02288126	0.02300985	0.02313884
6	0.02007411	0.02020629	0.02033896	0.02047211
7	0.01819196	0.01832815	0.01846489	0.01860218
8	0.01680726	0.01694740	0.01708816	0.01722953
9	0.01575359	0.01589762	0.01604231	0.01618768
10	0.01493107	0.01507889	0.01522743	0.01537668
11	0.01427611	0.01442761	0.01457987	0.01473289
12	0.01374625	0.01390131	0.01405717	0.01421383
13	0.01331210	0.01347059	0.01362992	0.01379007
14	0.01295264	0.01311442	0.01327707	0.01344056
15	0.01265242	0.01281736	0.01298319	0.01314987
16	0.01239988	0.01256783	0.01273668	0.01290640
17	0.01218614	0.01235697	0.01252869	0.01270129
18	0.01200433	0.01217787	0.01235231	0.01252764
19	0.01184898	0.01202510	0.01220211	0.01238001
20	0.01171576	0.01189431	0.01207375	0.01225405
21	0.01160114	0.01178198	0.01196370	0.01214627
22	0.01150226	0.01168525	0.01186911	0.01205379
23	0.01141676	0.01160177	0.01178761	0.01197428
24	0.01134267	0.01152956	0.01171727	0.01190577
25	0.01127835	0.01146700	0.01165645	0.01184666
26	0.01122244	0.01141273	0.01160378	0.01179558
27	0.01117376	0.01136557	0.01155812	0.01175138
28	0.01113133	0.01132456	0.01151849	0.01171310
29	0.01109432	0.01128885	0.01148406	0.01167992
30	0.01106200	0.01125774	0.01145412	0.01165113
31	0.01103375	0.01123060	0.01142807	0.01162613
32	0.01100904	0.01120693	0.01140539	0.01160441
33	0.01098743	0.01118626	0.01138564	0.01158554
34	0.01096851	0.01116820	0.01136842	0.01156913
35	0.01095193	0.01115242	0.01135341	0.01155485
36	0.01093741	0.01113863	0.01134031	0.01154243
37	0.01092468	0.01112657	0.01132889	0.01153161
38	0.01091352	0.01111601	0.01131891	0.01152220
39	0.01090373	0.01110678	0.01131021	0.01151400
40	0.01089514	0.01109870	0.01130261	0.01150685

Table 2   (cont.)

YEAR	14.00	INTEREST RATE 14.25	14.50	14.75
1	0.08978712	0.08990479	0.09002255	0.09014039
2	0.04801288	0.04813107	0.04824943	0.04836795
3	0.03417763	0.03429918	0.03442098	0.03454303
4	0.02732648	0.02745205	0.02757795	0.02770419
5	0.02326825	0.02339806	0.02352828	0.02365890
6	0.02060574	0.02073985	0.02087443	0.02100948
7	0.01874001	0.01887839	0.01901730	0.01915676
8	0.01737150	0.01751408	0.01765726	0.01780103
9	0.01633370	0.01648038	0.01662772	0.01677571
10	0.01552664	0.01567731	0.01582868	0.01598074
11	0.01488666	0.01504118	0.01519644	0.01535243
12	0.01437127	0.01452949	0.01468849	0.01484825
13	0.01395103	0.01411280	0.01427538	0.01443874
14	0.01360490	0.01377006	0.01393603	0.01410282
15	0.01331741	0.01348580	0.01365501	0.01382504
16	0.01307699	0.01324843	0.01342070	0.01359379
17	0.01287476	0.01304908	0.01322424	0.01340022
18	0.01270383	0.01288087	0.01305874	0.01323743
19	0.01255876	0.01273835	0.01291876	0.01309998
20	0.01243521	0.01261719	0.01279998	0.01298355
21	0.01232967	0.01251388	0.01269889	0.01288465
22	0.01223929	0.01242558	0.01261264	0.01280045
23	0.01216173	0.01234995	0.01253892	0.01272860
24	0.01209504	0.01228505	0.01247578	0.01266720
25	0.01203761	0.01222928	0.01242163	0.01261465
26	0.01198808	0.01218127	0.01237512	0.01256961
27	0.01194532	0.01213992	0.01233514	0.01253097
28	0.01190836	0.01210425	0.01230074	0.01249779
29	0.01187639	0.01207346	0.01227110	0.01246928
30	0.01184872	0.01204687	0.01224556	0.01244476
31	0.01182474	0.01202388	0.01222353	0.01242366
32	0.01180396	0.01200401	0.01220452	0.01240549
33	0.01178594	0.01198681	0.01218812	0.01238985
34	0.01177030	0.01197192	0.01217395	0.01237637
35	0.01175673	0.01195903	0.01216171	0.01236475
36	0.01174495	0.01194786	0.01215113	0.01235473
37	0.01173472	0.01193818	0.01214198	0.01234609
38	0.01172583	0.01192980	0.01213408	0.01233864
39	0.01171811	0.01192253	0.01212724	0.01233222
40	0.01171140	0.01191623	0.01212133	0.01232667

Table 2 (*cont.*)

YEAR	15.00	15.25	15.50	15.75
1	0.09025831	0.09037632	0.09049442	0.09061259
2	0.04848665	0.04860551	0.04872454	0.04884374
3	0.03466533	0.03478788	0.03491068	0.03503373
4	0.02783075	0.02795764	0.02808486	0.02821241
5	0.02378993	0.02392136	0.02405319	0.02418542
6	0.02114501	0.02128102	0.02141749	0.02155443
7	0.01929675	0.01943728	0.01957835	0.01971994
8	0.01794541	0.01809037	0.01823592	0.01838206
9	0.01692434	0.01707361	0.01722353	0.01737407
10	0.01613350	0.01628693	0.01644105	0.01659585
11	0.01550915	0.01566659	0.01582474	0.01598361
12	0.01500877	0.01517003	0.01533204	0.01549478
13	0.01460287	0.01476778	0.01493346	0.01509988
14	0.01427040	0.01443876	0.01460790	0.01477780
15	0.01399587	0.01416750	0.01433990	0.01451308
16	0.01376770	0.01394239	0.01411787	0.01429411
17	0.01357700	0.01375458	0.01393292	0.01411203
18	0.01341691	0.01359717	0.01377819	0.01395997
19	0.01328198	0.01346475	0.01364826	0.01383250
20	0.01316790	0.01335299	0.01353881	0.01372534
21	0.01307117	0.01325841	0.01344636	0.01363500
22	0.01298897	0.01317820	0.01336812	0.01355869
23	0.01291899	0.01311004	0.01330176	0.01349410
24	0.01285929	0.01305203	0.01324539	0.01343936
25	0.01280831	0.01300258	0.01319745	0.01339290
26	0.01276470	0.01296039	0.01315663	0.01335342
27	0.01272738	0.01292434	0.01312183	0.01331984
28	0.01269540	0.01289352	0.01309215	0.01329126
29	0.01266797	0.01286716	0.01306681	0.01326692
30	0.01264444	0.01284459	0.01304517	0.01324617
31	0.01262424	0.01282525	0.01302667	0.01322848
32	0.01260688	0.01280868	0.01301086	0.01321339
33	0.01259197	0.01279447	0.01299733	0.01320051
34	0.01257916	0.01278229	0.01298575	0.01318952
35	0.01256813	0.01277184	0.01297585	0.01318014
36	0.01255865	0.01276287	0.01296737	0.01317212
37	0.01255050	0.01275517	0.01296011	0.01316528
38	0.01254348	0.01274857	0.01295389	0.01315943
39	0.01253744	0.01274289	0.01294856	0.01315443
40	0.01253224	0.01273802	0.01294400	0.01315016

Table 2 (cont.)

YEAR	INTEREST RATE			
	16.00	16.25	16.50	16.75
1	0.09073086	0.09084921	0.09096764	0.09108615
2	0.04896311	0.04908265	0.04920235	0.04932222
3	0.03515703	0.03528058	0.03540438	0.03552843
4	0.02834028	0.02846848	0.02859701	0.02872586
5	0.02431806	0.02445109	0.02458452	0.02471835
6	0.02169184	0.02182972	0.02196806	0.02210686
7	0.01986206	0.02000471	0.02014789	0.02029159
8	0.01852879	0.01867609	0.01882397	0.01897243
9	0.01752525	0.01767706	0.01782948	0.01798253
10	0.01675131	0.01690744	0.01706423	0.01722167
11	0.01614317	0.01630343	0.01646438	0.01662601
12	0.01565825	0.01582244	0.01598734	0.01615294
13	0.01526704	0.01543494	0.01560357	0.01577291
14	0.01494845	0.01511985	0.01529198	0.01546482
15	0.01468701	0.01486168	0.01503709	0.01521321
16	0.01447110	0.01464884	0.01482730	0.01500647
17	0.01429188	0.01447246	0.01465376	0.01483575
18	0.01414247	0.01432569	0.01450961	0.01469421
19	0.01401746	0.01420312	0.01438945	0.01457644
20	0.01391256	0.01410046	0.01428901	0.01447820
21	0.01382430	0.01401426	0.01420484	0.01439603
22	0.01374990	0.01394173	0.01413417	0.01432719
23	0.01368706	0.01388061	0.01407473	0.01426940
24	0.01363391	0.01382901	0.01402466	0.01422084
25	0.01358889	0.01378541	0.01398245	0.01417997
26	0.01355072	0.01374853	0.01394681	0.01414555
27	0.01351833	0.01371729	0.01391670	0.01411654
28	0.01349082	0.01369083	0.01389124	0.01409206
29	0.01346745	0.01366838	0.01386971	0.01407140
30	0.01344757	0.01364935	0.01385148	0.01405396
31	0.01343066	0.01363319	0.01383605	0.01403922
32	0.01341627	0.01361947	0.01382297	0.01402676
33	0.01340402	0.01360781	0.01381189	0.01401623
34	0.01339358	0.01359791	0.01380250	0.01400733
35	0.01338469	0.01358950	0.01379454	0.01399980
36	0.01337712	0.01358235	0.01378779	0.01399343
37	0.01337067	0.01357627	0.01378206	0.01398804
38	0.01336517	0.01357110	0.01377721	0.01398348
39	0.01336048	0.01356670	0.01377309	0.01397962
40	0.01335648	0.01356297	0.01376959	0.01397635

Table 2   (cont.)

YEAR	INTEREST RATE 17.00	17.25	17.50	17.75
1	0.09120475	0.09132344	0.09144220	0.09156106
2	0.04944226	0.04956247	0.04968285	0.04980339
3	0.03565273	0.03577727	0.03590207	0.03602711
4	0.02885504	0.02898455	0.02911437	0.02924453
5	0.02485258	0.02498720	0.02512221	0.02525762
6	0.02224613	0.02238586	0.02252605	0.02266669
7	0.02043580	0.02058054	0.02072579	0.02087156
8	0.01912145	0.01927105	0.01942121	0.01957193
9	0.01813619	0.01829046	0.01844533	0.01860081
10	0.01737977	0.01753850	0.01769788	0.01785788
11	0.01678832	0.01695130	0.01711494	0.01727923
12	0.01631923	0.01648621	0.01665387	0.01682220
13	0.01594295	0.01611369	0.01628512	0.01645723
14	0.01563838	0.01581264	0.01598759	0.01616321
15	0.01539004	0.01556757	0.01574578	0.01592467
16	0.01518634	0.01536690	0.01554813	0.01573002
17	0.01501843	0.01520179	0.01538579	0.01557045
18	0.01487947	0.01506539	0.01525195	0.01543913
19	0.01476409	0.01495236	0.01514124	0.01533072
20	0.01466801	0.01485842	0.01504942	0.01524099
21	0.01458782	0.01478018	0.01497310	0.01516656
22	0.01452077	0.01471489	0.01490955	0.01510472
23	0.01446461	0.01466033	0.01485655	0.01505325
24	0.01441751	0.01461467	0.01481229	0.01501037
25	0.01437797	0.01457641	0.01477530	0.01497460
26	0.01434473	0.01454434	0.01474434	0.01494474
27	0.01431678	0.01451742	0.01471843	0.01491980
28	0.01429326	0.01449481	0.01469672	0.01489895
29	0.01427344	0.01447582	0.01467852	0.01488151
30	0.01425675	0.01445986	0.01466325	0.01486692
31	0.01424269	0.01444643	0.01465045	0.01485471
32	0.01423082	0.01443514	0.01463970	0.01484449
33	0.01422082	0.01442564	0.01463068	0.01483593
34	0.01421238	0.01441765	0.01462311	0.01482876
35	0.01420526	0.01441092	0.01461675	0.01482276
36	0.01419925	0.01440525	0.01461141	0.01481773
37	0.01419418	0.01440048	0.01460693	0.01481351
38	0.01418990	0.01439646	0.01460316	0.01480998
39	0.01418629	0.01439308	0.01459999	0.01480702
40	0.01418324	0.01439023	0.01459733	0.01480453

Table 2   (cont.)

YEAR	INTEREST RATE 18.00	18.25	18.50	18.75
1	0.09167999	0.09179901	0.09191812	0.09203731
2	0.04992410	0.05004498	0.05016603	0.05028724
3	0.03615240	0.03627793	0.03640371	0.03652974
4	0.02937500	0.02950580	0.02963692	0.02976836
5	0.02539343	0.02552962	0.02566621	0.02580319
6	0.02280779	0.02294935	0.02309135	0.02323381
7	0.02101784	0.02116463	0.02131192	0.02145972
8	0.01972321	0.01987505	0.02002744	0.02018038
9	0.01875689	0.01891356	0.01907082	0.01922866
10	0.01801852	0.01817978	0.01834165	0.01850414
11	0.01744418	0.01760977	0.01777599	0.01794285
12	0.01699120	0.01716084	0.01733114	0.01750208
13	0.01663001	0.01680345	0.01697753	0.01715226
14	0.01633950	0.01651645	0.01669405	0.01687228
15	0.01610421	0.01628440	0.01646523	0.01664669
16	0.01591256	0.01609573	0.01627952	0.01646393
17	0.01575573	0.01594163	0.01612812	0.01631521
18	0.01562691	0.01581529	0.01600425	0.01619377
19	0.01552078	0.01571141	0.01590259	0.01609431
20	0.01543312	0.01562578	0.01581897	0.01601266
21	0.01536055	0.01555504	0.01575003	0.01594550
22	0.01530038	0.01549652	0.01569312	0.01589016
23	0.01525041	0.01544802	0.01564606	0.01584452
24	0.01520887	0.01540779	0.01560711	0.01580682
25	0.01517430	0.01537439	0.01557484	0.01577565
26	0.01514551	0.01534663	0.01554809	0.01574987
27	0.01512151	0.01532354	0.01552589	0.01572853
28	0.01510149	0.01530433	0.01550746	0.01571086
29	0.01508479	0.01528835	0.01549216	0.01569622
30	0.01507085	0.01527503	0.01547945	0.01568408
31	0.01505922	0.01526394	0.01546888	0.01567402
32	0.01504950	0.01525470	0.01546010	0.01566568
33	0.01504137	0.01524700	0.01545280	0.01565875
34	0.01503459	0.01524058	0.01544673	0.01565301
35	0.01502892	0.01523523	0.01544168	0.01564825
36	0.01502418	0.01523077	0.01543748	0.01564430
37	0.01502022	0.01522705	0.01543398	0.01564102
38	0.01501691	0.01522394	0.01543107	0.01563830
39	0.01501414	0.01522135	0.01542866	0.01563604
40	0.01501182	0.01521920	0.01542664	0.01563416

Table 2 (*cont.*)

YEAR	INTEREST RATE			
	19.00	19.25	19.50	19.75
1	0.09215658	0.09227593	0.09239537	0.09251490
2	0.05040862	0.05053016	0.05065188	0.05077376
3	0.03665602	0.03678254	0.03690931	0.03703632
4	0.02990012	0.03003220	0.03016460	0.03029732
5	0.02594055	0.02607830	0.02621645	0.02635497
6	0.02337672	0.02352008	0.02366388	0.02380813
7	0.02160802	0.02175682	0.02190612	0.02205591
8	0.02033386	0.02048789	0.02064246	0.02079756
9	0.01938708	0.01954608	0.01970566	0.01986580
10	0.01866724	0.01883093	0.01899522	0.01916010
11	0.01811033	0.01827842	0.01844713	0.01861643
12	0.01767365	0.01784584	0.01801865	0.01819207
13	0.01732762	0.01750361	0.01768021	0.01785742
14	0.01705115	0.01723062	0.01741071	0.01759139
15	0.01682876	0.01701143	0.01719470	0.01737855
16	0.01664893	0.01683451	0.01702067	0.01720739
17	0.01650288	0.01669110	0.01687988	0.01706919
18	0.01638384	0.01657445	0.01676558	0.01695722
19	0.01628655	0.01647930	0.01667255	0.01686627
20	0.01620685	0.01640152	0.01659665	0.01679223
21	0.01614143	0.01633780	0.01653461	0.01673184
22	0.01608764	0.01628554	0.01648384	0.01668252
23	0.01604337	0.01624261	0.01644222	0.01664219
24	0.01600689	0.01620732	0.01640809	0.01660918
25	0.01597680	0.01617827	0.01638006	0.01658215
26	0.01595197	0.01615436	0.01635704	0.01655998
27	0.01593146	0.01613465	0.01633811	0.01654181
28	0.01591451	0.01611841	0.01632254	0.01652690
29	0.01590051	0.01610502	0.01630974	0.01651466
30	0.01588892	0.01609397	0.01629920	0.01650461
31	0.01587935	0.01608485	0.01629053	0.01649636
32	0.01587142	0.01607733	0.01628338	0.01648958
33	0.01586486	0.01607112	0.01627750	0.01648401
34	0.01585944	0.01606599	0.01627266	0.01647944
35	0.01585495	0.01606176	0.01626867	0.01647568
36	0.01585123	0.01605826	0.01626538	0.01647259
37	0.01584815	0.01605537	0.01626267	0.01647005
38	0.01584560	0.01605299	0.01626044	0.01646797
39	0.01584349	0.01605102	0.01625861	0.01646625
40	0.01584175	0.01604939	0.01625709	0.01646484

Table 3   PROPORTION OUTSTANDING ON MORTGAGES

```
PROPORTION OUTSTANDING OF $1 (MONTHLY COMPOUNDING, TERM =15 YEARS)
```

YEAR	6.00	6.25	6.50	6.75
1	0.95758333	0.95843190	0.95926784	0.96009119
2	0.91255049	0.91419007	0.91580777	0.91740361
3	0.86474012	0.86710253	0.86943710	0.87174379
4	0.81398091	0.81698623	0.81996090	0.82290476
5	0.76009099	0.76364635	0.76717119	0.77066517
6	0.70287725	0.70687556	0.71084605	0.71478825
7	0.64213470	0.64645317	0.65074871	0.65502074
8	0.57764567	0.58214430	0.58662655	0.59109173
9	0.50917911	0.51369897	0.51821000	0.52271149
10	0.43648968	0.44085111	0.44521147	0.44957006
11	0.35931692	0.36331755	0.36732410	0.37133595
12	0.27738431	0.28079688	0.28422046	0.28765456
13	0.19039829	0.19296834	0.19555122	0.19814661
14	0.09804715	0.09949050	0.10094363	0.10240640
15	0.00000000	0.00000000	0.00000000	0.00000000

YEAR	7.00	7.25	7.50	7.75
1	0.96090202	0.96170040	0.96248639	0.96326008
2	0.91897765	0.92052992	0.92206051	0.92356946
3	0.87402255	0.87627338	0.87849625	0.88069117
4	0.82581765	0.82869944	0.83155000	0.83436920
5	0.77412802	0.77755944	0.78095918	0.78432698
6	0.71870174	0.72258608	0.72644086	0.73026571
7	0.65926868	0.66349200	0.66769015	0.67186261
8	0.59553921	0.59996833	0.60437846	0.60876899
9	0.52720273	0.53168304	0.53615173	0.54060814
10	0.45392619	0.45827919	0.46262838	0.46697308
11	0.37535250	0.37937312	0.38339721	0.38742417
12	0.29109870	0.29455238	0.29801513	0.30148644
13	0.20075419	0.20337363	0.20600461	0.20864680
14	0.10387866	0.10536027	0.10685108	0.10835093
15	0.00000000	0.00000000	0.00000000	0.00000000

YEAR	8.00	8.25	8.50	8.75
1	0.96402153	0.96477083	0.96550805	0.96623329
2	0.92505686	0.92652279	0.92796733	0.92939057
3	0.88285815	0.88499720	0.88710835	0.88919164
4	0.83715696	0.83991319	0.84263780	0.84533075
5	0.78766260	0.79096583	0.79423647	0.79747432
6	0.73406023	0.73782407	0.74155690	0.74525837
7	0.67600889	0.68012849	0.68422093	0.68828576
8	0.61313932	0.61748884	0.62181698	0.62612318
9	0.54505160	0.54948147	0.55389709	0.55829786
10	0.47131264	0.47564640	0.47997371	0.48429393
11	0.39145337	0.39548424	0.39951616	0.40354855
12	0.30496583	0.30845282	0.31194690	0.31544761
13	0.21129987	0.21396349	0.21663732	0.21932103
14	0.10985968	0.11137716	0.11290323	0.11443773
15	0.00000000	0.00000000	0.00000000	0.00000000

Table 3   (cont.)

PROPORTION OUTSTANDING OF $1 (MONTHLY COMPOUNDING, TERM =15 YEARS)

YEAR	9.00	9.25	9.50	9.75
1	0.96694663	0.96764816	0.96833797	0.96901616
2	0.93079262	0.93217358	0.93353356	0.93487268
3	0.89124712	0.89327485	0.89527490	0.89724734
4	0.84799198	0.85062146	0.85321916	0.85578507
5	0.80067921	0.80385098	0.80698948	0.81009459
6	0.74892817	0.75256602	0.75617163	0.75974473
7	0.69232253	0.69633082	0.70031022	0.70426033
8	0.63040689	0.63466757	0.63890471	0.64311778
9	0.56268314	0.56705233	0.57140484	0.57574009
10	0.48860643	0.49291059	0.49720578	0.50149141
11	0.40758081	0.41161237	0.41564264	0.41967105
12	0.31895444	0.32246691	0.32598455	0.32950688
13	0.22201429	0.22471677	0.22742812	0.23014801
14	0.11598050	0.11753137	0.11909020	0.12065681
15	0.00000000	0.00000000	0.00000000	0.00000000

YEAR	10.00	10.25	10.50	10.75
1	0.96968283	0.97033807	0.97098199	0.97161469
2	0.93619106	0.93748882	0.93876610	0.94002304
3	0.89919225	0.90110974	0.90299991	0.90486286
4	0.85831920	0.86082155	0.86329215	0.86573105
5	0.81316619	0.81620418	0.81920847	0.82217899
6	0.76328508	0.76679245	0.77026661	0.77370737
7	0.70818077	0.71207117	0.71593119	0.71976050
8	0.64730631	0.65146981	0.65560782	0.65971990
9	0.58005750	0.58435652	0.58863661	0.59289723
10	0.50576686	0.51003157	0.51428494	0.51852641
11	0.42369703	0.42772001	0.43173946	0.43575480
12	0.33303340	0.33656366	0.34009718	0.34363348
13	0.23287612	0.23561209	0.23835560	0.24110632
14	0.12223105	0.12381275	0.12540175	0.12699789
15	0.00000000	0.00000000	0.00000000	0.00000000

YEAR	11.00	11.25	11.50	11.75
1	0.97223628	0.97284686	0.97344655	0.97403545
2	0.94125978	0.94247646	0.94367325	0.94485029
3	0.90669871	0.90850760	0.91028966	0.91204502
4	0.86813828	0.87051390	0.87285799	0.87517062
5	0.82511567	0.82801848	0.83088739	0.83372236
6	0.77711455	0.78048796	0.78382746	0.78713290
7	0.72355878	0.72732573	0.73106107	0.73476452
8	0.66380561	0.66786453	0.67189627	0.67590043
9	0.59713787	0.60135801	0.60555718	0.60973488
10	0.52275541	0.52697141	0.53117386	0.53536223
11	0.43976551	0.44377104	0.44777087	0.45176447
12	0.34717211	0.35071259	0.35425448	0.35779732
13	0.24386390	0.24662803	0.24939837	0.25217458
14	0.12860100	0.13021091	0.13182747	0.13345050
15	0.00000000	0.00000000	0.00000000	0.00000000

Table 3   (cont.)

PROPORTION OUTSTANDING OF $1 (MONTHLY COMPOUNDING, TERM =15 YEARS)

YEAR	12.00	12.25	12.50	12.75
1	0.97461368	0.97518135	0.97573857	0.97628547
2	0.94600774	0.94714577	0.94826454	0.94936424
3	0.91377385	0.91547629	0.91715251	0.91880269
4	0.87745189	0.87970190	0.88192075	0.88410857
5	0.83652340	0.83929052	0.84202373	0.84472307
6	0.79040416	0.79364113	0.79684372	0.80001183
7	0.73843584	0.74207479	0.74568114	0.74925469
8	0.67987664	0.68382455	0.68774381	0.69163411
9	0.61389066	0.61802407	0.62213465	0.62622201
10	0.53953601	0.54369470	0.54783779	0.55196481
11	0.45575133	0.45973095	0.46370283	0.46766648
12	0.36134066	0.36488405	0.36842706	0.37196924
13	0.25495635	0.25774334	0.26053524	0.26333171
14	0.13507985	0.13671534	0.13835681	0.14000410
15	0.00000000	0.00000000	0.00000000	0.00000000

YEAR	13.00	13.25	13.50	13.75
1	0.97682216	0.97734876	0.97786538	0.97837216
2	0.95044502	0.95150708	0.95255059	0.95357573
3	0.92042699	0.92202559	0.92359870	0.92514650
4	0.88626548	0.88839164	0.89048717	0.89255224
5	0.84738859	0.85002032	0.85261836	0.85518277
6	0.80314541	0.80624440	0.80930876	0.81233847
7	0.75279524	0.75630263	0.75977669	0.76321727
8	0.69549512	0.69932655	0.70312812	0.70689957
9	0.63028571	0.63432537	0.63834061	0.64233104
10	0.55607529	0.56016876	0.56424478	0.56830290
11	0.47162142	0.47556717	0.47950327	0.48342927
12	0.37551017	0.37904942	0.38258658	0.38612122
13	0.26613245	0.26893713	0.27174543	0.27455705
14	0.14165705	0.14331548	0.14497925	0.14664817
15	0.00000000	0.00000000	0.00000000	0.00000000

YEAR	14.00	14.25	14.50	14.75
1	0.97886921	0.97935665	0.97983460	0.98030320
2	0.95458269	0.95557167	0.95654285	0.95749643
3	0.92666919	0.92816697	0.92964006	0.93108867
4	0.89458702	0.89659167	0.89856638	0.90051134
5	0.85771364	0.86021108	0.86267519	0.86510610
6	0.81533351	0.81829388	0.82121959	0.82411067
7	0.76662425	0.76999749	0.77333691	0.77664241
8	0.71064064	0.71435110	0.71803072	0.72167929
9	0.64629633	0.65023613	0.65415011	0.65803796
10	0.57234272	0.57636380	0.58036575	0.58434819
11	0.48734471	0.49124917	0.49514221	0.49902342
12	0.38965294	0.39318133	0.39670601	0.40022657
13	0.27737168	0.28018900	0.28300871	0.28583052
14	0.14832210	0.15000087	0.15168432	0.15337229
15	0.00000000	0.00000000	0.00000000	0.00000000

Table 3 (*cont.*)

PROPORTION OUTSTANDING OF $1 (MONTHLY COMPOUNDING, TERM =15 YEARS)

YEAR	15.00	15.25	15.50	15.75
1	0.98076256	0.98121280	0.98165406	0.98208646
2	0.95843261	0.95935157	0.96025353	0.96113868
3	0.93251302	0.93391332	0.93528982	0.93664273
4	0.90242673	0.90431277	0.90616965	0.90799760
5	0.86750395	0.86986886	0.87220100	0.87450051
6	0.82696716	0.82978911	0.83257657	0.83532962
7	0.77991391	0.78315135	0.78635469	0.78952389
8	0.72529663	0.72888255	0.73243689	0.73595949
9	0.66189938	0.66573408	0.66954179	0.67332224
10	0.58831073	0.59225301	0.59617468	0.60007538
11	0.50289238	0.50674869	0.51059197	0.51442183
12	0.40374264	0.40725383	0.41075977	0.41426010
13	0.28865413	0.29147924	0.29430555	0.29713279
14	0.15506462	0.15676116	0.15846175	0.16016623
15	0.00000000	0.00000000	0.00000000	0.00000000

YEAR	16.00	16.25	16.50	16.75
1	0.98251011	0.98292515	0.98333171	0.98372990
2	0.96200723	0.96285937	0.96369533	0.96451529
3	0.93797229	0.93927875	0.94056233	0.94182329
4	0.90979684	0.91156759	0.91331008	0.91502456
5	0.87676758	0.87900238	0.88120508	0.88337589
6	0.83804835	0.84073284	0.84338320	0.84599955
7	0.79265892	0.79575977	0.79882645	0.80185897
8	0.73945021	0.74290894	0.74633556	0.74972997
9	0.67707520	0.68080044	0.68449772	0.68816684
10	0.60395480	0.60781262	0.61164852	0.61546222
11	0.51823789	0.52203981	0.52582721	0.52959977
12	0.41775446	0.42124250	0.42472386	0.42819822
13	0.29996067	0.30278891	0.30561722	0.30844535
14	0.16187445	0.16358625	0.16530149	0.16702002
15	0.00000000	0.00000000	0.00000000	0.00000000

YEAR	17.00	17.25	17.50	17.75
1	0.98411985	0.98450169	0.98487554	0.98524152
2	0.96531948	0.96610809	0.96688133	0.96763942
3	0.94306187	0.94427831	0.94547288	0.94664582
4	0.91671126	0.91837044	0.92000235	0.92160723
5	0.88551501	0.88762264	0.88969899	0.89174430
6	0.84858202	0.85113073	0.85364583	0.85612747
7	0.80485735	0.80782164	0.81075188	0.81364812
8	0.75309208	0.75642183	0.75971915	0.76298399
9	0.69180761	0.69541985	0.69900339	0.70255807
10	0.61925343	0.62302188	0.62676732	0.63048948
11	0.53335714	0.53709901	0.54082505	0.54453496
12	0.43166523	0.43512458	0.43857594	0.44201901
13	0.31127302	0.31409996	0.31692592	0.31975064
14	0.16874168	0.17046633	0.17219382	0.17392401
15	0.00000000	0.00000000	0.00000000	0.00000000

Table 3 (cont.)

PROPORTION OUTSTANDING OF $1 (MONTHLY COMPOUNDING, TERM =20 YEARS)

YEAR	6.00	6.25	6.50	6.75
1	0.97330201	0.97405373	0.97478893	0.97550780
2	0.94495735	0.94643855	0.94788944	0.94931026
3	0.91486445	0.91704710	0.91918843	0.92128864
4	0.88291549	0.88576515	0.88856526	0.89131592
5	0.84899598	0.85247109	0.85589121	0.85925628
6	0.81298440	0.81703549	0.82102891	0.82496438
7	0.77475170	0.77932061	0.78383182	0.78828481
8	0.73416089	0.73917983	0.74414357	0.74905132
9	0.69106652	0.69645714	0.70179733	0.70708608
10	0.64531420	0.65098644	0.65661507	0.66219889
11	0.59673996	0.60259098	0.60840688	0.61418629
12	0.54516978	0.55108264	0.55697010	0.56283068
13	0.49041886	0.49626119	0.50208850	0.50789928
14	0.43229102	0.43791352	0.44353138	0.44914313
15	0.37057798	0.37581283	0.38105258	0.38629590

YEAR	7.00	7.25	7.50	7.75
1	0.97621050	0.97689721	0.97756813	0.97822344
2	0.95070125	0.95206268	0.95339481	0.95469794
3	0.92334794	0.92536660	0.92734486	0.92928303
4	0.89401726	0.89666942	0.89927259	0.90182698
5	0.86256626	0.86582115	0.86902098	0.87216585
6	0.82884166	0.83266054	0.83642087	0.84012254
7	0.79267911	0.79701427	0.80128993	0.80550574
8	0.75390236	0.75869602	0.76343168	0.76810876
9	0.71232244	0.71750550	0.72263440	0.72770832
10	0.66773671	0.67322741	0.67866991	0.68406320
11	0.61992787	0.62563030	0.63129235	0.63691281
12	0.56866292	0.57446540	0.58023675	0.58597563
13	0.51369203	0.51946527	0.52521757	0.53094753
14	0.45474728	0.46034241	0.46592710	0.47149995
15	0.39154142	0.39678781	0.40203377	0.40727797

YEAR	8.00	8.25	8.50	8.75
1	0.97886334	0.97948803	0.98009771	0.98069259
2	0.95597234	0.95721834	0.95843623	0.95962637
3	0.93118140	0.93304031	0.93486008	0.93664109
4	0.90433283	0.90679041	0.90920002	0.91156195
5	0.87525584	0.87829111	0.88127183	0.88419821
6	0.84376547	0.84734964	0.85087505	0.85434175
7	0.80966142	0.81375673	0.81779147	0.82176548
8	0.77272675	0.77728517	0.78178360	0.78622166
9	0.73272652	0.73768829	0.74259296	0.74743994
10	0.68940629	0.69469826	0.69993823	0.70512537
11	0.64249050	0.64802433	0.65351320	0.65895611
12	0.59168073	0.59735080	0.60298463	0.60858104
13	0.53665377	0.54233496	0.54798979	0.55361700
14	0.47705960	0.48260469	0.48813391	0.49364597
15	0.41251914	0.41775600	0.42298731	0.42821183

Table 3 (cont.)

PROPORTION OUTSTANDING OF $1 (MONTHLY COMPOUNDING, TERM =20 YEARS)

YEAR	9.00	9.25	9.50	9.75
1	0.98127290	0.98183883	0.98239061	0.98292847
2	0.96078906	0.96192467	0.96303354	0.96411603
3	0.93838370	0.94008831	0.94175532	0.94338515
4	0.91387657	0.91614422	0.91836529	0.92054019
5	0.88707049	0.88988894	0.89265385	0.89536557
6	0.85774982	0.86109939	0.86439062	0.86762370
7	0.82567867	0.82953096	0.83332233	0.83705281
8	0.79059902	0.79491541	0.79917059	0.80336437
9	0.75222866	0.75695863	0.76162937	0.76624048
10	0.71025890	0.71533809	0.72036227	0.72533081
11	0.66435208	0.66970018	0.67499952	0.68024927
12	0.61413889	0.61965710	0.62513462	0.63057045
13	0.55921535	0.56478365	0.57032075	0.57582552
14	0.49913961	0.50461360	0.51006674	0.51549785
15	0.43342835	0.43863568	0.44383266	0.44901814

YEAR	10.00	10.25	10.50	10.75
1	0.98345262	0.98396328	0.98446070	0.98494509
2	0.96517250	0.96620334	0.96720891	0.96818960
3	0.94497823	0.94653500	0.94805592	0.94954145
4	0.92266934	0.92475319	0.92679220	0.92878684
5	0.89802443	0.90063082	0.90318514	0.90568784
6	0.87079887	0.87391637	0.87697651	0.87997961
7	0.84072244	0.84433132	0.84787960	0.85136743
8	0.80749661	0.81156721	0.81557610	0.81952328
9	0.77079160	0.77528242	0.77971265	0.78408208
10	0.73024311	0.73509864	0.73989692	0.74463751
11	0.68544865	0.69059691	0.69569336	0.70073736
12	0.63596363	0.64131324	0.64661842	0.65187833
13	0.58129688	0.58673379	0.59213525	0.59750029
14	0.52090581	0.52628949	0.53164784	0.53697981
15	0.45419100	0.45935015	0.46449452	0.46962306

YEAR	11.00	11.25	11.50	11.75
1	0.98541668	0.98587572	0.98632242	0.98675702
2	0.96914580	0.97007790	0.97098630	0.97187139
3	0.95099208	0.95240827	0.95379053	0.95513936
4	0.93073762	0.93264504	0.93450962	0.93633190
5	0.90813934	0.91054014	0.91289072	0.91519159
6	0.88292602	0.88581612	0.88865032	0.89142905
7	0.85479504	0.85816265	0.86147055	0.86471903
8	0.82340877	0.82723263	0.83099497	0.83469593
9	0.78839052	0.79263785	0.79682396	0.80094879
10	0.74932001	0.75394406	0.75850938	0.76301569
11	0.70572829	0.71066561	0.71554881	0.72037741
12	0.65709220	0.66225927	0.66737886	0.67245031
13	0.60282799	0.60811746	0.61336786	0.61857838
14	0.54228439	0.54756061	0.55280753	0.55802424
15	0.47473476	0.47982862	0.48490368	0.48995901

279

Table 3 (cont.)

PROPORTION OUTSTANDING OF $1 (MONTHLY COMPOUNDING, TERM =20 YEARS)

YEAR	12.00	12.25	12.50	12.75
1	0.98717975	0.98759084	0.98799054	0.98837906
2	0.97273357	0.97357325	0.97439083	0.97518671
3	0.95645525	0.95773872	0.95899030	0.96021049
4	0.93811243	0.93985177	0.94155049	0.94320917
5	0.91744329	0.91964636	0.92180137	0.92390890
6	0.89415278	0.89682198	0.89943716	0.90199884
7	0.86790845	0.87103916	0.87411156	0.87712607
8	0.83833568	0.84191444	0.84543245	0.84888998
9	0.80501235	0.80901465	0.81295576	0.81683578
10	0.76746278	0.77185048	0.77617864	0.78044717
11	0.72515099	0.72986918	0.73453163	0.73913805
12	0.67747301	0.68244638	0.68736990	0.69224308
13	0.62374826	0.62887676	0.63396319	0.63900691
14	0.56320987	0.56836358	0.57348458	0.57857209
15	0.49499369	0.50000685	0.50499763	0.50996521

YEAR	13.00	13.25	13.50	13.75
1	0.98875663	0.98912350	0.98947988	0.98982600
2	0.97596132	0.97671504	0.97744828	0.97816146
3	0.96139983	0.96255884	0.96368806	0.96478801
4	0.94482838	0.94640874	0.94795084	0.94945528
5	0.92596954	0.92798390	0.92995258	0.93187623
6	0.90450757	0.90696391	0.90936844	0.91172176
7	0.88008314	0.88298325	0.88582688	0.88861456
8	0.85228736	0.85562490	0.85890300	0.86212203
9	0.82065484	0.82441313	0.82811084	0.83174822
10	0.78465602	0.78880517	0.79289464	0.79692449
11	0.74368819	0.74818182	0.75261878	0.75699891
12	0.69706547	0.70183666	0.70655630	0.71122403
13	0.64400730	0.64896378	0.65387582	0.65874291
14	0.58362537	0.58864373	0.59362650	0.59857303
15	0.51490878	0.51982759	0.52472089	0.52958797

YEAR	14.00	14.25	14.50	14.75
1	0.99016210	0.99048838	0.99080509	0.99111243
2	0.97885498	0.97952924	0.98018464	0.98082158
3	0.96585924	0.96690227	0.96791764	0.96890589
4	0.95092268	0.95235366	0.95374883	0.95510881
5	0.93375547	0.93559096	0.93738335	0.93913329
6	0.91402448	0.91627723	0.91848064	0.92063537
7	0.89134682	0.89402422	0.89664734	0.89921677
8	0.86528243	0.86838463	0.87142911	0.87441636
9	0.83532553	0.83884307	0.84230116	0.84570018
10	0.80089480	0.80480571	0.80865736	0.81244994
11	0.76132213	0.76558836	0.76979757	0.77394977
12	0.71583959	0.72040269	0.72491314	0.72937074
13	0.66356459	0.66834043	0.67307004	0.67775305
14	0.60348274	0.60835505	0.61318942	0.61798535
15	0.53442814	0.53924076	0.54402519	0.54878084

Table 3 (cont.)

PROPORTION OUTSTANDING OF $1 (MONTHLY COMPOUNDING, TERM =20 YEARS)

YEAR	15.00	15.25	15.50	15.75
1	0.99141062	0.99169988	0.99198043	0.99225247
2	0.98144045	0.98204167	0.98262560	0.98319265
3	0.96986754	0.97080314	0.97171320	0.97259827
4	0.95643423	0.95772572	0.95898389	0.96020938
5	0.94084146	0.94250852	0.94413515	0.94572204
6	0.92274207	0.92480142	0.92681411	0.92878080
7	0.90173313	0.90419703	0.90660911	0.90897003
8	0.87734690	0.88022126	0.88303999	0.88580367
9	0.84904048	0.85232249	0.85554663	0.85871335
10	0.81618368	0.81985881	0.82347562	0.82703441
11	0.77804499	0.78208330	0.78606481	0.78998963
12	0.73377534	0.73812682	0.74242511	0.74667014
13	0.68238914	0.68697801	0.69151941	0.69601311
14	0.62274238	0.62746004	0.63213794	0.63677569
15	0.55350713	0.55820351	0.56286947	0.56750451

YEAR	16.00	16.25	16.50	16.75
1	0.99251622	0.99277188	0.99301965	0.99325973
2	0.98374320	0.98427763	0.98479632	0.98529963
3	0.97345885	0.97429548	0.97510867	0.97589894
4	0.96140281	0.96256479	0.96369597	0.96479694
5	0.94726986	0.94877929	0.95025102	0.95168574
6	0.93070221	0.93257903	0.93441196	0.93620171
7	0.91128045	0.91354103	0.91575247	0.91791544
8	0.88851288	0.89116822	0.89377031	0.89631979
9	0.86182312	0.86487645	0.86787384	0.87081582
10	0.83053550	0.83397925	0.83736603	0.84069624
11	0.79385794	0.79766990	0.80142575	0.80512571
12	0.75086190	0.75500039	0.75908565	0.76311774
13	0.70045890	0.70485662	0.70920613	0.71350732
14	0.64137293	0.64592935	0.65044465	0.65491857
15	0.57210818	0.57668002	0.58121963	0.58572662

YEAR	17.00	17.25	17.50	17.75
1	0.99349232	0.99371762	0.99393582	0.99414710
2	0.98578794	0.98626162	0.98672101	0.98716649
3	0.97666679	0.97741273	0.97813726	0.97884087
4	0.96586833	0.96691075	0.96792480	0.96891110
5	0.95308412	0.95444686	0.95577462	0.95706810
6	0.93794900	0.93965454	0.94131905	0.94294323
7	0.92003066	0.92209883	0.92412064	0.92609683
8	0.89881729	0.90126347	0.90365898	0.90600452
9	0.87370295	0.87653578	0.87931490	0.88204088
10	0.84397029	0.84718863	0.85035172	0.85346002
11	0.80877004	0.81235904	0.81589302	0.81937230
12	0.76709676	0.77102282	0.77489607	0.77871666
13	0.71776011	0.72196444	0.72612028	0.73022764
14	0.65935085	0.66374129	0.66808970	0.67239591
15	0.59020061	0.59464128	0.59904829	0.60342137

Table 3 (*cont.*)

PROPORTION OUTSTANDING OF $1 (MONTHLY COMPOUNDING, TERM =25 YEARS)

YEAR	6.00	6.25	6.50	6.75
1	0.98219961	0.98285404	0.98348901	0.98410484
2	0.96330133	0.96460523	0.96587224	0.96710293
3	0.94323745	0.94518261	0.94707565	0.94891721
4	0.92193607	0.92451070	0.92702022	0.92946525
5	0.89932087	0.90250913	0.90562163	0.90865890
6	0.87531081	0.87909239	0.88278995	0.88640384
7	0.84981986	0.85416943	0.85842918	0.86259922
8	0.82275669	0.82764339	0.83243693	0.83713712
9	0.79402432	0.79941114	0.80470393	0.80990215
10	0.76351981	0.76936294	0.77511359	0.78077086
11	0.73113384	0.73738199	0.74354154	0.74961123
12	0.69675037	0.70334396	0.70985505	0.71628201
13	0.66024621	0.66711655	0.67391252	0.68063215
14	0.62149055	0.62855893	0.63556284	0.64250006
15	0.58034452	0.58752121	0.59464482	0.60171291

YEAR	7.00	7.25	7.50	7.75
1	0.98470187	0.98528044	0.98584091	0.98638363
2	0.96829783	0.96945753	0.97058261	0.97167369
3	0.95070794	0.95244856	0.95413977	0.95578234
4	0.93184648	0.93416462	0.93642044	0.93861472
5	0.91162152	0.91451015	0.91732550	0.92006832
6	0.88993450	0.89338242	0.89674817	0.90003239
7	0.86667973	0.87067099	0.87457337	0.87838732
8	0.84174386	0.84625715	0.85067709	0.85500387
9	0.81500537	0.82001329	0.82492567	0.82974243
10	0.78633396	0.79180223	0.79717511	0.80245216
11	0.75558990	0.76147652	0.76727019	0.77297013
12	0.72262333	0.72887765	0.73504368	0.74112031
13	0.68727362	0.69383522	0.70031535	0.70671254
14	0.64936847	0.65616607	0.66289096	0.66954137
15	0.60872315	0.61567330	0.62256122	0.62938488

YEAR	8.00	8.25	8.50	8.75
1	0.98690896	0.98741726	0.98790890	0.98838426
2	0.97273137	0.97375628	0.97474907	0.97571037
3	0.95737704	0.95892466	0.96042602	0.96188194
4	0.94074832	0.94282209	0.94483694	0.94679380
5	0.92273941	0.92533965	0.92786993	0.93033119
6	0.90323578	0.90635911	0.90940319	0.91236891
7	0.88211336	0.88575208	0.88930416	0.89277034
8	0.85923778	0.86337919	0.86742856	0.87138642
9	0.83446355	0.83908913	0.84361936	0.84805452
10	0.80763306	0.81271759	0.81770563	0.82259717
11	0.77857566	0.78408622	0.78950137	0.79482077
12	0.74710651	0.75300137	0.75880411	0.76451406
13	0.71302543	0.71925279	0.72539349	0.73144653
14	0.67611564	0.68261222	0.68902968	0.69536669
15	0.63614236	0.64283185	0.64945163	0.65600012

Table 3 (cont.)

PROPORTION OUTSTANDING OF $1 (MONTHLY COMPOUNDING, TERM =25 YEARS)

YEAR	9.00	9.25	9.50	9.75
1	0.98884369	0.98928757	0.98971628	0.99013018
2	0.97664084	0.97754114	0.97841192	0.97925387
3	0.96329327	0.96466088	0.96598564	0.96726842
4	0.94869362	0.95053738	0.95232608	0.95406073
5	0.93272441	0.93505061	0.93731083	0.93950616
6	0.91525719	0.91806900	0.92080536	0.92346735
7	0.89615141	0.89944825	0.90266177	0.90579294
8	0.87525339	0.87903015	0.88271746	0.88631615
9	0.85239498	0.85664121	0.86079373	0.86485318
10	0.82739230	0.83209120	0.83669413	0.84120146
11	0.80004420	0.80517151	0.81020269	0.81513781
12	0.77013065	0.77565343	0.78108205	0.78641626
13	0.73741101	0.74328614	0.74907125	0.75476577
14	0.70162204	0.70779463	0.71388346	0.71988765
15	0.66247581	0.66887732	0.67520336	0.68145276

YEAR	10.00	10.25	10.50	10.75
1	0.99052966	0.99091507	0.99128679	0.99164518
2	0.98006764	0.98085391	0.98161334	0.98234661
3	0.96851012	0.96971163	0.97087386	0.97199770
4	0.95574238	0.95737206	0.95895084	0.96047979
5	0.94163768	0.94370654	0.94571387	0.94766084
6	0.92605604	0.92857258	0.93101814	0.93339389
7	0.90884280	0.91181241	0.91470288	0.91751537
8	0.88982711	0.89325127	0.89658963	0.89984325
9	0.86882022	0.87269563	0.87648024	0.88017492
10	0.84561364	0.84993119	0.85415472	0.85828490
11	0.81997703	0.82472059	0.82936885	0.83392222
12	0.79165593	0.79680099	0.80185149	0.80680758
13	0.76036924	0.76588128	0.77130163	0.77663012
14	0.72580642	0.73163908	0.73738507	0.74304388
15	0.68762443	0.69371739	0.69973078	0.70566381

YEAR	11.00	11.25	11.50	11.75
1	0.99199061	0.99232343	0.99264401	0.99295270
2	0.98305437	0.98373730	0.98439604	0.98503126
3	0.97308405	0.97413383	0.97514793	0.97612726
4	0.96195997	0.96339248	0.96477840	0.96611881
5	0.94954863	0.95137844	0.95315146	0.95486892
6	0.93570107	0.93794090	0.94011466	0.94222360
7	0.92025107	0.92291120	0.92549701	0.92800978
8	0.90301323	0.90610070	0.90910684	0.91203288
9	0.88378063	0.88729838	0.89072921	0.89407423
10	0.86232247	0.86626826	0.87012312	0.87388800
11	0.83838119	0.84274636	0.84701835	0.85119790
12	0.81166946	0.81643744	0.82111191	0.82569333
13	0.78186667	0.78701129	0.79206408	0.79702520
14	0.74861514	0.75409856	0.75949392	0.76480111
15	0.71151579	0.71728613	0.72297433	0.72857997

Table 3 (*cont.*)

PROPORTION OUTSTANDING OF $1 (MONTHLY COMPOUNDING, TERM =25 YEARS)

YEAR	12.00	12.25	12.50	12.75
1	0.99324985	0.99353579	0.99381088	0.99407544
2	0.98564360	0.98623371	0.98680222	0.98734975
3	0.97707270	0.97798515	0.97886550	0.97971461
4	0.96741479	0.96866744	0.96987783	0.97104703
5	0.95653202	0.95814199	0.95970004	0.96120742
6	0.94426904	0.94625225	0.94817456	0.95003728
7	0.93045080	0.93282140	0.93512292	0.93735670
8	0.91488007	0.91764968	0.92034303	0.92296144
9	0.89733458	0.90051145	0.90360605	0.90661964
10	0.87756388	0.88115179	0.88465282	0.88806809
11	0.85528576	0.85928279	0.86318988	0.86700797
12	0.83018222	0.83457919	0.83888490	0.84310008
13	0.80189492	0.80667357	0.81136156	0.81595935
14	0.77002009	0.77515090	0.78019368	0.78514861
15	0.73410273	0.73954235	0.74489867	0.75017161

YEAR	13.00	13.25	13.50	13.75
1	0.99432980	0.99457429	0.99480922	0.99503490
2	0.98787693	0.98838436	0.98887265	0.98934239
3	0.98053335	0.98132258	0.98208315	0.98281590
4	0.97217612	0.97326615	0.97431818	0.97533324
5	0.96266532	0.96407497	0.96543757	0.96675434
6	0.95184172	0.95358920	0.95528105	0.95691858
7	0.93952411	0.94162652	0.94366530	0.94564184
8	0.92550627	0.92797888	0.93038066	0.93271300
9	0.90955352	0.91240898	0.91518736	0.91789001
10	0.89139876	0.89464604	0.89781116	0.90089539
11	0.87073806	0.87438120	0.87793846	0.88141096
12	0.84722552	0.85126204	0.85521055	0.85907198
13	0.82046748	0.82488655	0.82921723	0.83346021
14	0.79001596	0.79479606	0.79948932	0.80409620
15	0.75536114	0.76046732	0.76549028	0.77043021

YEAR	14.00	14.25	14.50	14.75
1	0.99525164	0.99545974	0.99565949	0.99585117
2	0.98979416	0.99022852	0.99064605	0.99104728
3	0.98352164	0.98420119	0.98485535	0.98548490
4	0.97631237	0.97725658	0.97816688	0.97904426
5	0.96802646	0.96925511	0.97044147	0.97158670
6	0.95850310	0.96003593	0.96151835	0.96295165
7	0.94755752	0.94941372	0.95121182	0.95295320
8	0.93497729	0.93717496	0.93930742	0.94137607
9	0.92051831	0.92307365	0.92555741	0.92797102
10	0.90390000	0.90682632	0.90967567	0.91244941
11	0.88479988	0.88810638	0.89133170	0.89447708
12	0.86284730	0.86653754	0.87014376	0.87366706
13	0.83761628	0.84168624	0.84567095	0.84957131
14	0.80861721	0.81305293	0.81740398	0.82167104
15	0.77528736	0.78006204	0.78475463	0.78936555

Table 3 (*cont.*)

PROPORTION OUTSTANDING OF $1 (MONTHLY COMPOUNDING, TERM =25 YEARS)

YEAR	15.00	15.25	15.50	15.75
1	0.99603507	0.99621146	0.99638059	0.99654274
2	0.99143276	0.99180301	0.99215855	0.99249987
3	0.98609061	0.98667325	0.98723354	0.98777222
4	0.97988969	0.98070413	0.98148852	0.98224379
5	0.97269194	0.97375832	0.97478696	0.97577895
6	0.96433712	0.96567601	0.96696958	0.96821907
7	0.95463922	0.95627124	0.95785062	0.95937869
8	0.94338234	0.94532763	0.94721335	0.94904091
9	0.93031587	0.93259338	0.93480499	0.93695210
10	0.91514890	0.91777551	0.92033063	0.92281565
11	0.89754377	0.90053308	0.90344630	0.90628475
12	0.87710854	0.88046938	0.88375074	0.88695382
13	0.85338826	0.85712278	0.86077587	0.86434857
14	0.82585483	0.82995611	0.83397569	0.83791440
15	0.79389528	0.79834434	0.80271329	0.80700276

YEAR	16.00	16.25	16.50	16.75
1	0.99669814	0.99684706	0.99698972	0.99712636
2	0.99282747	0.99314183	0.99344341	0.99373267
3	0.98829000	0.98878757	0.98926561	0.98972479
4	0.98297085	0.98367059	0.98434389	0.98499159
5	0.97673537	0.97765729	0.97854575	0.97940178
6	0.96942570	0.97059066	0.97171516	0.97280035
7	0.96085678	0.96228620	0.96366825	0.96500421
8	0.95081169	0.95252708	0.95418845	0.95579715
9	0.93903613	0.94105849	0.94302059	0.94492384
10	0.92523197	0.92758099	0.92986410	0.93208270
11	0.90904977	0.91174269	0.91436485	0.91691762
12	0.89007984	0.89313005	0.89610569	0.89900802
13	0.86784195	0.87125711	0.87459514	0.87785720
14	0.84177313	0.84555277	0.84925426	0.85287857
15	0.81121340	0.81534589	0.81940097	0.82337939

YEAR	17.00	17.25	17.50	17.75
1	0.99725721	0.99738248	0.99750239	0.99761714
2	0.99401005	0.99427598	0.99453087	0.99477515
3	0.99016576	0.99058913	0.99099554	0.99138558
4	0.98561453	0.98621354	0.98678941	0.98734291
5	0.98022637	0.98102052	0.98178519	0.98252132
6	0.97384738	0.97485738	0.97583147	0.97677073
7	0.96629534	0.96754289	0.96874808	0.96991212
8	0.95735454	0.95886195	0.96032068	0.96173203
9	0.94676961	0.94855929	0.95029424	0.95197582
10	0.93423819	0.93633195	0.93836537	0.94033982
11	0.91940235	0.92182039	0.92417310	0.92646183
12	0.90183832	0.90459787	0.90728796	0.90990988
13	0.88104441	0.88415796	0.88719901	0.89016876
14	0.85642667	0.85989959	0.86329834	0.86662398
15	0.82728194	0.83110944	0.83486273	0.83854267

Table 3 (cont.)

PROPORTION OUTSTANDING OF $1 (MONTHLY COMPOUNDING, TERM =30 YEARS)

YEAR	6.00	6.25	6.50	6.75
1	0.98771988	0.98828204	0.98882275	0.98934252
2	0.97468236	0.97581037	0.97689693	0.97794298
3	0.96084070	0.96253649	0.96417242	0.96574972
4	0.94614532	0.94840881	0.95059572	0.95270746
5	0.93054357	0.93337241	0.93610977	0.93875710
6	0.91397953	0.91736885	0.92065367	0.92383540
7	0.89639386	0.90033591	0.90416245	0.90787473
8	0.87772354	0.88220738	0.88656677	0.89080276
9	0.85790168	0.86291278	0.86779269	0.87254210
10	0.83685725	0.84237713	0.84776126	0.85300999
11	0.81451484	0.82052058	0.82638830	0.83211790
12	0.79079441	0.79725818	0.80358395	0.80977113
13	0.76561095	0.77249951	0.77925235	0.78586841
14	0.73887423	0.74614830	0.75329121	0.76030139
15	0.71048844	0.71810215	0.72559141	0.73295419

YEAR	7.00	7.25	7.50	7.75
1	0.98984190	0.99032143	0.99078166	0.99122312
2	0.97894947	0.97991738	0.98084767	0.98174133
3	0.96726963	0.96873345	0.97014248	0.97149804
4	0.95474545	0.95671119	0.95860622	0.96043208
5	0.94131590	0.94378777	0.94617437	0.94847738
6	0.92691552	0.92989563	0.93277740	0.93556256
7	0.91147414	0.91496216	0.91834039	0.92161051
8	0.89491650	0.89890930	0.90278260	0.90653793
9	0.87716191	0.88165315	0.88601701	0.89025483
10	0.85812383	0.86310350	0.86794987	0.87266399
11	0.83770950	0.84316341	0.84848013	0.85366036
12	0.81581940	0.82172863	0.82749891	0.83313051
13	0.79234688	0.79868715	0.80488885	0.81095183
14	0.76717752	0.77391851	0.78052352	0.78699192
15	0.74018866	0.74729326	0.75426665	0.76110772

YEAR	8.00	8.25	8.50	8.75
1	0.99164636	0.99205193	0.99244038	0.99281223
2	0.98259937	0.98342278	0.98421255	0.98496968
3	0.97280149	0.97405417	0.97525746	0.97641271
4	0.96219039	0.96388275	0.96551081	0.96707624
5	0.95069857	0.95283972	0.95490266	0.95688925
6	0.93825293	0.94085038	0.94335684	0.94577427
7	0.92477432	0.92783366	0.93079047	0.93364676
8	0.91017698	0.91370150	0.91711336	0.92041448
9	0.89436808	0.89835833	0.90222731	0.90597680
10	0.87724704	0.88170037	0.88602546	0.89022391
11	0.85870496	0.86361496	0.86839153	0.87303600
12	0.83862391	0.84397976	0.84919891	0.85428234
13	0.81687613	0.82266199	0.82830984	0.83382030
14	0.79332330	0.79951745	0.80557437	0.81149425
15	0.76781560	0.77438960	0.78082928	0.78713439

Table 3 (cont.)

PROPORTION OUTSTANDING OF $1 (MONTHLY COMPOUNDING, TERM =30 YEARS)

YEAR	9.00	9.25	9.50	9.75
1	0.99316803	0.99350831	0.99383359	0.99414438
2	0.98569517	0.98639001	0.98705517	0.98769163
3	0.97752131	0.97858462	0.97960401	0.98058084
4	0.96858068	0.97002583	0.97141335	0.97274492
5	0.95880136	0.96064090	0.96240978	0.96410990
6	0.94810468	0.95035010	0.95251262	0.95459432
7	0.93640456	0.93906600	0.94163320	0.94410835
8	0.92360690	0.92669270	0.92967402	0.93255307
9	0.90960873	0.91312508	0.91652793	0.91981940
10	0.89429744	0.89824786	0.90207711	0.90578719
11	0.87754984	0.88193463	0.88619208	0.89032401
12	0.85923120	0.86404678	0.86873051	0.87328395
13	0.83919414	0.84443232	0.84953592	0.85450618
14	0.81727747	0.82292458	0.82843630	0.83381351
15	0.79330487	0.79934084	0.80524261	0.81101066

YEAR	10.00	10.25	10.50	10.75
1	0.99444121	0.99472458	0.99499496	0.99525286
2	0.98830035	0.98888228	0.98943835	0.98996949
3	0.98151646	0.98241220	0.98326939	0.98408933
4	0.97402221	0.97524688	0.97642058	0.97754495
5	0.96574320	0.96731160	0.96881701	0.97026133
6	0.95659728	0.95852364	0.96037550	0.96215497
7	0.94649367	0.94879137	0.95100370	0.95313293
8	0.93533207	0.93801331	0.94059911	0.94309177
9	0.92300171	0.92607710	0.92904789	0.93191639
10	0.90938019	0.91285828	0.91622368	0.91947867
11	0.89433233	0.89821903	0.90198620	0.90563600
12	0.87770876	0.88200672	0.88617971	0.89022968
13	0.85934448	0.86405231	0.86863128	0.87308311
14	0.83905722	0.84416861	0.84914896	0.85399969
15	0.81664563	0.82214830	0.82751962	0.83276064

YEAR	11.00	11.25	11.50	11.75
1	0.99549874	0.99573307	0.99595629	0.99616886
2	0.99047660	0.99096056	0.99142225	0.99186252
3	0.98487330	0.98562258	0.98633841	0.98702202
4	0.97862160	0.97965213	0.98063811	0.98158110
5	0.97164645	0.97297426	0.97424660	0.97546531
6	0.96386415	0.96550516	0.96708005	0.96859091
7	0.95518130	0.95715107	0.95904450	0.96086382
8	0.94549367	0.94780714	0.95003456	0.95217827
9	0.93468500	0.93735609	0.93993208	0.94241538
10	0.92262556	0.92566673	0.92860457	0.93144150
11	0.90917062	0.91259235	0.91590351	0.91910644
12	0.89415869	0.89796884	0.90166232	0.90524134
13	0.87740960	0.88161265	0.88569425	0.88965644
14	0.85872232	0.86331848	0.86778991	0.87213839
15	0.83787257	0.84285671	0.84771449	0.85244743

Table 3 (cont.)

PROPORTION OUTSTANDING OF $1 (MONTHLY COMPOUNDING, TERM =30 YEARS)

YEAR	12.00	12.25	12.50	12.75
1	0.99637121	0.99656374	0.99674688	0.99692100
2	0.99228219	0.99268208	0.99306298	0.99342566
3	0.98767459	0.98829730	0.98889129	0.98945768
4	0.98248262	0.98334416	0.98416719	0.98495314
5	0.97663219	0.97774902	0.97881755	0.97983949
6	0.97003977	0.97142864	0.97275953	0.97403437
7	0.96261127	0.96428904	0.96589933	0.96744428
8	0.95424065	0.95622402	0.95813072	0.95996306
9	0.94480842	0.94711364	0.94933344	0.95147023
10	0.93417996	0.93682239	0.93937124	0.94182899
11	0.92220353	0.92519721	0.92808990	0.93088405
12	0.90870820	0.91206521	0.91531472	0.91845912
13	0.89350132	0.89723108	0.90084791	0.90435407
14	0.87636583	0.88047418	0.88446546	0.88834173
15	0.85705713	0.86154530	0.86591370	0.87016419

YEAR	13.00	13.25	13.50	13.75
1	0.99708651	0.99724378	0.99739315	0.99753498
2	0.99377087	0.99409934	0.99441176	0.99470883
3	0.98999756	0.99051200	0.99100202	0.99146863
4	0.98570342	0.98641939	0.98710239	0.98775372
5	0.98081654	0.98175033	0.98264248	0.98349456
6	0.97525511	0.97642363	0.97754180	0.97861141
7	0.96892603	0.97034667	0.97170827	0.97301286
8	0.96172333	0.96341377	0.96503662	0.96659409
9	0.95352641	0.95550436	0.95740643	0.95923494
10	0.94419806	0.94648092	0.94867997	0.95079763
11	0.93358210	0.93618651	0.93869974	0.94112422
12	0.92150079	0.92444214	0.92728561	0.93003360
13	0.90775186	0.91104357	0.91423156	0.91731816
14	0.89210513	0.89575781	0.89930197	0.90273983
15	0.87429865	0.87831905	0.88222739	0.88602571

YEAR	14.00	14.25	14.50	14.75
1	0.99766961	0.99779737	0.99791856	0.99803349
2	0.99499120	0.99525953	0.99551442	0.99575648
3	0.99191279	0.99233546	0.99273755	0.99311995
4	0.98837465	0.98896640	0.98953018	0.99006713
5	0.98430810	0.98508461	0.98582554	0.98653230
6	0.97963426	0.98061208	0.98154656	0.98243935
7	0.97426241	0.97545888	0.97660418	0.97770016
8	0.96808832	0.96952145	0.97089556	0.97221269
9	0.96099218	0.96268042	0.96430190	0.96585879
10	0.95283629	0.95479829	0.95668599	0.95850166
11	0.94346237	0.94571662	0.94788934	0.94998291
12	0.93268854	0.93525285	0.93772891	0.94011911
13	0.92030573	0.92319664	0.92599324	0.92869791
14	0.90607364	0.90930565	0.91243814	0.91547338
15	0.88971610	0.89330065	0.89678151	0.90016082

Table 3 (*cont.*)

PROPORTION OUTSTANDING OF $1 (MONTHLY COMPOUNDING, TERM =30 YEARS)

YEAR	15.00	15.25	15.50	15.75
1	0.99814245	0.99824572	0.99834357	0.99843625
2	0.99598628	0.99620439	0.99641133	0.99660763
3	0.99348351	0.99382905	0.99415739	0.99446928
4	0.99057840	0.99106506	0.99152816	0.99196873
5	0.98720628	0.98784880	0.98846117	0.98904463
6	0.98329208	0.98410629	0.98488352	0.98562524
7	0.97874865	0.97975142	0.98071020	0.98162667
8	0.97347485	0.97468398	0.97584202	0.97695081
9	0.96735325	0.96878740	0.97016329	0.97148295
10	0.96024759	0.96192599	0.96353905	0.96508893
11	0.95199966	0.95394189	0.95581188	0.95761188
12	0.94242583	0.94465140	0.94679814	0.94886834
13	0.93131297	0.93384077	0.93628362	0.93864382
14	0.91841366	0.92126126	0.92401843	0.92668744
15	0.90344074	0.90662344	0.90971109	0.91270587

YEAR	16.00	16.25	16.50	16.75
1	0.99852403	0.99860713	0.99868578	0.99876021
2	0.99679379	0.99697027	0.99713754	0.99729605
3	0.99476548	0.99504669	0.99531361	0.99556690
4	0.99238775	0.99278617	0.99316490	0.99352482
5	0.98960041	0.99012967	0.99063357	0.99111318
6	0.98633289	0.98700785	0.98765148	0.98826508
7	0.98250247	0.98333920	0.98413839	0.98490154
8	0.97801219	0.97902792	0.97999972	0.98092929
9	0.97274836	0.97396144	0.97512409	0.97623814
10	0.96657772	0.96800750	0.96938027	0.97069801
11	0.95934407	0.96101062	0.96261365	0.96415524
12	0.95086426	0.95278812	0.95464212	0.95642839
13	0.94092364	0.94312533	0.94525110	0.94730316
14	0.92927053	0.93176994	0.93418785	0.93652647
15	0.91560994	0.91842546	0.92115459	0.92379945

YEAR	17.00	17.25	17.50	17.75
1	0.99883062	0.99889722	0.99896019	0.99901972
2	0.99744620	0.99758842	0.99772308	0.99785055
3	0.99580720	0.99603511	0.99625123	0.99645612
4	0.99386680	0.99419163	0.99450012	0.99479302
5	0.99156957	0.99200377	0.99241675	0.99280947
6	0.98884991	0.98940718	0.98993808	0.99044374
7	0.98563012	0.98632552	0.98698910	0.98762219
8	0.98181824	0.98266815	0.98348057	0.98425699
9	0.97730538	0.97832755	0.97930634	0.98024339
10	0.97196265	0.97317606	0.97434007	0.97545647
11	0.96563743	0.96706220	0.96843150	0.96974723
12	0.95814906	0.95980619	0.96140182	0.96293794
13	0.94928364	0.95119466	0.95303833	0.95481666
14	0.93878794	0.94097439	0.94308792	0.94513061
15	0.92636216	0.92884483	0.93124951	0.93357828

APPENDIX B

USING SPREADSHEETS FOR REAL ESTATE INVESTMENT ANALYSIS

INTRODUCTION

Real estate investment analysis has enjoyed a long history of computerized financial analysis. As early as 1974, Dasso noted that there were at least 112 articles written about computerized real estate analysis in actual practice using mainframes and canned software.* Now, with the development of microcomputers, a new generation of real estate computer users has arrived. In particular, it was the development of the computerized spreadsheet in the late 1970s that has had a major impact on real estate investment analysis.

There are several advantages of spreadsheets over hand-calculated analyses for real estate investors. These include the ability to perform long sets of mathematical calculations, the rapid speed of computers, accuracy and reliability, extensive storage capabilities, and the very inexpensive cost

of processing.† Also, spreadsheets are considerably easier to learn and use than other computer software that preceeded them. In effect, once an investor understands the benefits and power of spreadsheets, it is unlikely that the investor will revert to hand calculations again.

This real estate investment book contains numerous calculations. A set of templates have been developed that can be used with Lotus 1-2-3, the best-selling and most widely used spreadsheet program. With the use of this specially prepared diskette and Lotus 1-2-3, the reader of this book can calculate all of the important analyses found in the book. In fact, use of the diskette may simplify some of the concepts taught in the book and the investor may be able to concentrate on the investment choices rather than on performing the calculations. If so, this is the real value of computerized real estate investment analysis!

---

* See Jerome Dasso, "Computer Applications in Real Estate," *CREUES Real Estate Report 13* (Storrs, CT: Center for Real Estate and Urban Economic Studies, June 1974).

† For more discussion, see Austin J. Jaffe, "Computer Technology and Real Estate Education: Some Observation," *Proceedings of the Real Estate Educators Association Annual Conference* (August 1985, 15–31).

Description of Computer Software

The real estate software that accompanies this book consists of a single diskette. This IBM or 100 percent compatible diskette contains a special file that automatically welcomes you when initially called by Lotus 1-2-3. The introductory file provides an overview of all of the computerized applications and provides instructions for access and usage. (Written instructions are also provided with the diskette.)

Each application has its own menu so that use, even for computer novices, is quite easy. It is also easy to print or graph your results if you have the proper hardware.

There are five applications included in the software. Each is briefly described below.

1. *Present Value* (pv.wk1). This template calculates a detailed table of present value factors for up to several discount rates and for scores of years. The template is automated to provide as large a table as the user indicates based on only a few required inputs.

2. *Effective Cost of Borrowing* (effcost.-wk1). The effective cost of borrowing is calculated for any loan from the borrower's point of view. This template evaluates the impact of several types of mortgage or other loan provisions on the borrower's cost of borrowing including closing costs, early repayment with and without penalties, prepaid interest, discount points, and mortgage insurance.

3. *After-tax Financial Analysis* (cashflow.wk1). A complete discounted cash flow analysis is provided for either simple or complex real estate investments. The user can input up to five rental types, three mortgages with prepayment penalties and amortized financing costs, various growth rates, and depreciation and capital gains tax treatment for holding periods of up to ten years. This template uses the current tax law following the Tax Reform Act of 1986. Various criteria are also reported including financial ratios, net present value, and the internal rate of return.

4. *Risk Analysis* (risk.wk1). This template calculates the expected rate of return, the variance, and the standard deviation of return for up to ten investments. The user is permitted to compare both the expected return for any investment with the expected level of risk. Both risk and return are merged into an analysis that in most cases can evaluate which investment is preferred for the wealth-maximizing investor.

5. *Comparable Sales Analysis* (comp.-wk1). This template calculates several units of comparison for up to 20 market comparables. This template also provides several rules of thumb and uses regression analysis to provide an indicated value for the subject property.

Instructions for Obtaining Diskette

The diskette containing the real estate templates is available for $29.95 plus $2 shipping from JS & Associates, Calder Square, P.O. Box 10096, State College, PA 16805. Pennsylvania residents please add 6 percent sales tax. You will need an IBM or 100 percent compatible computer and Lotus 1-2-3, release 2.0 or later. Please allow 3 to 4 weeks for delivery.

GLOSSARY

Accounting rate of return. *See* Average rate of return method.

Adjusted average rate of return method. A modified rule of thumb that results in using an average income or cash flow figure taking into account the expected selling price or equity reversion.

Adjusted basis. A tax term that is equal to the original basis (typically cost) plus any capital improvements less the total accumulated depreciation deductions.

Adjusted internal rate of return. A financial criterion that modifies the internal rate of return method to account for the reinvestment assumption.

Ad valorem. Literally, "according to value." This phrase is often used in describing the property tax base.

After-tax cash flow (ATCF). A measure of income from operations, a major source of value to the equity investor. Specifically, it is defined as net operating income less debt service less income taxes for any year of operation.

After-tax cash flow multiplier. A payback method equal to equity divided by after-tax cash flow. It is also equal to the reciprocal of the after-tax rate of return.

After-tax equity reversion (ATER). The second measure of income from operations. (*See* After-tax cash flow.) Specifically, it is defined as expected net selling price less unpaid outstanding mortgage less taxes due on sale.

After-tax rate (ATR). A rate of return measure equal to after-tax cash flow divided by equity. It is also the reciprocal to the after-tax cash flow multiplier.

Air rights. The property rights associated with the use, control, and regulation of air space over a parcel of real estate.

Alternative minimum tax (AMT). A tax that ensures both individuals and corporations pay at least some tax according to the minimum tax schedule.

Amortization. The process by which the debt is reduced by a series of regular periodic payments.

Amortized financing costs. The allowance for tax purposes for the financing costs of an investment.

Assessed value. The value placed on property by the government for purposes of levying property taxes.

At-risk amount. The amount an investor is personally liable for (cash and certain nonrecourse loans) from a real estate investment. This limits the amount of real estate losses a taxpayer can deduct in any taxable year.

Average rate of return method. Rules of thumb that result in average income or cash flow figures as percentages of total or equity cost.

Average rate on after-tax cash flow. An average rate of return measure that equals average after-tax cash flow divided by equity costs.

Average rate on before-tax cash flow. An average rate of return measure that equals average before-tax cash flow divided by equity costs.

Average rate on net operating income. An average rate of return measure that equals average net operating income divided by total investment costs.

Bad debt allowance. The amount that reduces potential gross income based on the probability that some of the rental income is uncollectable.

Balloon mortgage. A financing arrangement

specifying that the mortgagor may make payments at a level that would amortize the loan over a long period. However, in this method, repayment takes place at an agreed upon early date. Hence, the level-payments are smaller than they ordinarily would have been to amortize the loan.

Basic ownership rights. The general and private property rights associated with ownership of real and personal property: possession, control, enjoyment, and disposition.

Before-tax cash flow. A measure of annual income from operation equal to net operating income less debt service.

Before-tax cash flow multiplier. A payback method equal to equity divided by before-tax cash flow. It is also the reciprocal of the equity dividend rate.

Before-tax equity reversion (BTER). The remaining value of the expected selling price less selling expenses less the unpaid mortgage principal at the time of sale.

Benefit/cost ratio. An alternative financial technique that measures the ratio of benefits per dollar of costs typically on a discounted cash-flow basis. Also known as *profitability index*.

Book value. The value of an asset less the accumulated depreciation taken by the investor.

Break-even analysis. A financial technique that indicates how many units or how much revenue is needed to meet all expenses.

Break-even cash flow ratio. The percentage of total operating expenses and debt service to effective gross income. If this ratio is 1.00, before-tax cash flow is zero.

Break-even point (BEP). The number of units, BEP(Q), or amount of revenue, BEP($) or BEP($ per unit), necesssary for gross income to equal total costs.

Bundle of rights theory. A doctrine that views interests in real property as a collection of property rights.

Business risk. The likelihood of downward changes in demand or supply that will result in declining net income from an investment.

Capital gain. The accounting measure of the difference between amount realized and the adjusted basis.

Capital improvements. Expenditures made by the investor, often upon recommendation of the property manager, that result in permanent improvements or rehabilitation of the existing property.

Capitalization. The process of converting an expected income stream into a present value sum.

Capitalization rate. *See* Overall capitalization rate.

Cash-on-cash return. Another name for the equity dividend rate.

Certainty-equivalent approach. A valuation technique that seeks to account for risk by adjusting the size of the benefit by the amount of uncertainty and risk in the estimate.

Closing costs. Charges assessed to the buyer when making a real estate purchase.

Concurrent estates. Estates in land with more than one owner.

Conservatism. A method of adjusting for risk by understanding inflows and overestimating costs to provide acceptable projects with a margin of safety.

Contingent estates. Future interests that become possessory estates dependent on the occurrence of a specific event.

Conventional life estate. A type of life estate consisting of ordinary life estates and *pur autre vie* estates. *See* Life estate.

Corporate income tax rates. The federal tax rates that are applied to corporations to measure tax liability on corporate income.

Correlation. A statistical measure that shows relationships between two variables.

Cost approach. One of the three approaches traditionally used in estimating value. It seeks to value property according to the equivalent reproduction cost less loss in value of the improvements plus the estimated value of the land.

Covariance. A statistical measure of the relationship of the variability of one variable with another.

Covenant. A promise to do or not to do a specific thing.

Curtesy rights. A legal life estate of the husband's interest in his wife's property.

Debt coverage ratio. The ratio of net operating income to debt service. Traditionally, typical values of well-run investments vary between 1.2 and 1.5. It is used as a measurement of financial risk by lenders.

Debt service. The required periodic payment of interest only (in "interest-only" loans) or interest and principal reduction (in level-payment amortization loans). This is also referred to as the *mortgage payment*.

Decision tree. A quantitative tool used to assist in the assessment of risk and uncertainty.

Declining-balance depreciation method. An accelerated depreciation technique that enables investors to take more depreciation in the early years of the life of the asset.

Deed of trust. A device used in some states instead of the mortgage document in pledging real estate as security for a debt.

Defeasance clause. The clause, which originated in feudal times, that permitted the mortgagor to extinguish the mortgage.

Defeasible fees. Fee estates that are subject to revocation depending on the occurrence of some event.

Degree of operating leverage (DOL). A measure that, at any occupancy level, is the percentage change in net operating income from a change in occupancy level. It can be used to demonstrate percentage increases in net operating income resulting from increases in occupancy.

Depreciation allowance. An accounting concept that permits the reduction of taxable income in determining tax liability. Since it is not a cash expense and since the actual depreciation (loss in value) of the property bears no relationship to the depreciation allowance for tax purposes, this amount forms the basis of tax shelter for real estate.

Direct sales comparison approach. One of the three approaches traditionally used in estimating value. It seeks to value property according to what buyers are willing to pay for similar property after any necessary adjustments.

Discounted cash flow techniques. Investment criteria that evaluate alternative cash flows and adjust the value of the cash flows according to timing as well as magnitude, based on the mechanics of the time value of money.

Discount points. Charges to raise the return to the mortgagee. Typically one point equals one percent of the amount of the loan.

Discount rate. The rate used in financial calculations to calculate present (and future) values. This rate may be equivalent to the overall capitalization rate or the weighted average cost of capital depending on the assumptions and market conditions. It typically includes adjustment for risk and a risk-free component.

Diversification. The reduction of risk through acquisition of different types of investment or, in the case of the real estate, through investments in different geographical areas, whose expected returns tend to be inversely related to one another. A common measure of the relationship of the returns on diversified investments is called the *correlation* between the investments.

Dower rights. A legal life estate of a wife's interest in her husband's property.

Early repayment. The making of additional loan payments prior to the required time, or in greater amounts than the agreed promissory note. Also called *prepayment*.

Easement. An interest in someone else's land.

Effective cost of borrowing. The true cost of the borrower of making and holding the loan.

Effective gross income. The amount of income available to pay expenses after bad debts and vacancy losses have been deducted.

Eminent domain. A governmental power that permits taking for public purpose with compensation.

Equitable right of redemption. The doctrine that enables mortgagors who had previously defaulted to regain their interests in the property within a specified period of time.

Equity buildup. The amount of net worth that results from paying off the mortgage debt.

Typically, when using a level-payment amortized loan, the equity buildup grows at a very slow pace, due to the necessity of satisfying the interest.

Equity dividend rate. A simple rate of return measure equal to before-tax cash flow dividend by equity. It is also the reciprocal to the before-tax cash flow multiplier.

Equity investor. The owner who maintains an interest in the net worth of the investment. The equity investor concentrates his or her decision-making effort on the portion of the investment representing the difference between the total investment in land and improvements and the mortgage indebtedness.

Equity participation. A financing technique where the institutional lender acquires an equity interest in the property.

Estates. Property interests that are alienable. Also called *estates in land*.

Estimated selling price. The price that is expected at the end of the holding period based on expected growth rates in real property.

Executory interests. Future interests created by will or deed that permit a transfer of property after the death of the grantor.

Expected cash flow. The most likely cash flow under all possible states of the world.

Feasibility. In reference to real estate investments, the analysis of the profitability and investment potential of one or more investment projects.

Fee simple. *See* Fee simple absolute.

Fee simple absolute. The most complete estate in land available. Also called *fee* or *fee simple*.

Fee simple determinable. A defeasible fee estate, the duration of which is determined by the occurrence or nonoccurrence of an event. Also called *qualified fee*.

Fee simple subject to condition subsequent. A defeasible fee that terminates if a stated condition occurs.

Fee simple subject to executory devise. A defeasible fee that shifts or changes property rights by will at some time in the future.

Fee simple subject to executory limitation. A defeasible fee that shifts or changes property rights by deed at some time in the future.

Fee tail. An estate of inheritance limited to some particular class of heirs of the person to whom it is granted.

Financial leverage. The increase in the rate of return to the equity investor due to borrowing funds. *Favorable financial leverage* exists when the rate of return on the investment is greater than the cost of borrowing. *Unfavorable financial leverage* exists when the cost of borrowing is greater than the rate of return on the investment.

Financial management rate of return (FMRR). A complex and specialized investment criterion developed to serve as an alternative to the internal rate of return.

Financial risk. The risk associated with financial leverage.

Fixed expenses. Operating expenses paid by the investor that tend to be fixed in amount each income period. In addition, fixed expenses tend not to vary with occupancy in the short run. Examples include property taxes and property insurance premiums.

Fixture. An asset, which formerly was movable (personalty), that has become permanently attached and part of the improvements (realty).

Foreclosure. The process by which the mortgage lender takes a property as a result of default by the borrower. *See* Strict foreclosure; Statutory foreclosure.

Free and clear rate of return. Another name for overall capitalization rate.

Freehold estates. Estates in fee or life estates.

Future interests. Estates that may become possessory at a future date.

Future value. The estimated worth of an asset at some future period.

General partnership. A joint ownership form characterized by personal income tax rates and unlimited liability.

Gross income multiplier (GIM). The ratio of selling price (or market value) to effective gross income.

Holding period. The amount of time (generally years) during which the investor anticipates maintaining equity interest in an investment.

Income approach. One of the three approaches traditionally used in estimating market value. The value of the property based on a capitalized income concept.

Inflation. Increases in all prices at the same rate of change. *See* Relative price change.

Inflation hedge. An investment strategy that seeks to offset any decreases in value due to declining values of money's buying power.

Inflation risk. The likelihood of losses in real estate due to changes in nominal prices. Also called *purchasing power risk*.

Installment land sales contract. A financing arrangement where the buyer agrees to purchase the property as per the terms of a contract.

Installment sale. A method of deferring taxes that enables the seller to spread the gain from the sale of property over a period of time rather than take the gain in only one year.

Interest expenses. Payments made for use of borrowed capital. These expenses are tax deductible.

Interest rate. The cost of borrowing.

Internal rate of return (IRR). A financial criterion where a rate is calculated such that present value of inflows equals the present value of outflows. If the IRR is greater than the required rate of return, the investor would be willing to accept the investment.

Internal rate of return on equity. A discounted cash flow technique that finds the rate to equate the present value of each after-tax cash flow plus the after-tax equity reversion with the cost of equity.

Internal rate of return on total investment. A discounted cash flow technique that finds the rate to equate the present value of the net operating income plus expected net selling price with the total cost of an investment.

Investment. The sacrifice of certain outflows in return for expected but uncertain inflows. An investment is also defined as the choice among marked alternatives made by the financial decision maker in order to achieve some financial objective or goal.

Investment value of equity (E). A discounted cash flow technique that values after-tax cash flow and after-tax equity reversion.

Investor. An economic entity who foregoes current consumption and wealth in the expectation of future benefits and increases in net worth.

Joint tenancy. A concurrent estate with right of survivorship.

Joint venture. A special ownership arrangement created for large projects; it has a limited duration.

Junior lien. A secondary claim by creditors against the asset(s) pledged as security for which there exists a senior lien.

Just compensation. The required payment in eminent domain cases.

Land trust. An ownership form that permits limited liability, ordinary tax treatment, and private ownership of real property.

Lateral support. The property right that entitles the owner of property to receive support from adjoining land.

Lease. The document that links the landlord/lessor/equity investor to the tenant/lessee/user of real estate.

Leasehold estate. The rights created between landlord and tenant during the term of the lease; nonfreehold estates.

Legal environment. The climate with respect to federal, state, and local authority for purposes of many real estate decisions.

Legal life estate. A form of life estate other than the conventional life estates. Common ones are dower, curtesy, and homestead interests. *See* Life estate.

Leverage. *See* Financial leverage; Operating leverage.

Leverage gains. The increases in the value of the investment or in its rate of return due to the use of leverage.

License. A privilege to go onto another's land.

Lien theory. A theory of mortgages that views the existence of a mortgage as a lien on the property by the mortgagee.

Life estate. An estate that is extinguished at the death of the life tenant in a conventional life estate or at the death of the person designated in *pur autre vie*.

Limited partnership. A special partnership arrangement for passive investors that permits limited liability and personal tax treatment.

Listing agreement. A document signed between the equity investor wishing to sell and the brokerage agent.

Loan-to-value ratio. The ratio of the amount borrowed to the total value of the real estate.

Management agreement. A contract between the equity investor and a property manager.

Management expenses. The fees, charges, or foregone rental income paid to property management for managerial services rendered to the investor.

Marginal tax rate. The income tax rate charged on the last dollar of income. It is the relevant tax rate of making investment decisions.

Market analysis. The study of the economic forces of supply and demand and their impact on real estate returns, risk, and values.

Market risk. The likelihood of failing to meet expectations in net income due to changes in economic conditions in the market.

Market value. The price, typically expressed in terms of money, that an informed buyer is willing and able to pay and an informed seller is willing and able to accept, each acting in their own best interests and neither under any duress.

Mortgage. A conveyance of real property used as security until the completion of payment of a debt.

Mortgage constant. The ratio of debt service to initial loan value. Also equal to the reciprocal of the present value factor of an annuity.

Mortgagee. The entity to whom property is mortgaged. Typically, this is the lender (financial institution).

Mortgage insurance. Insurance paid by the mortgagor that insures the holder of the mortgage against a mortgagor default.

Mortgage lender. Typically a financial institution or other intermediary who lends money to the equity investor and retains a lien against the real estate as collateral.

Morgage note. The specified amount of the loan for which the property is held as security.

Mortgagor. The entity who mortgages the prop-

erty. Typically this is the borrower (owner-investor).

Net income before interest and taxes. An accounting measure equivalent to net operating income plus the reserve for replacement allowance.

Net income multiplier (NIM). The ratio of selling price (or market value) to net operating income. The reciprocal is the overall capitalization rate used in traditional investment analysis and market valuation.

Net operating income (NOI). The amount of income left over after total operating expenses have been paid out of effective gross income.

Net present value (NPV). A financial decision criterion where the present value of the benefits, typically cash flows, are compared to the outflow, typically the initial investment. If the present value of the benefits is greater than the present value of the costs, the net present value is positive and the investor would be willing to accept this project.

Nonresidential property. In terms of IRS classifications, any income-producing real estate where more than 20 percent of its income is derived from the rental of nonresidential units.

Nuisance. The legal theory that deals with interference by neighboring users.

Objective probability distributions. The range of outcomes of a statistical event for which data exists to objectively measure the distribution.

Occupancy rate. The percentage of rental units occupied by tenants paying rent.

Operating expense analysis. The area of real estate investment analysis concerned with changes in income, occupancy, and expenses and their impact on net operating income. Techniques available for the analysis include income multipliers, break-even analysis, and operating leverage.

Operating expenses. The regular required outlays associated with the ownership of income-producing real estate. Traditionally, operating expenses have been divided into fixed expenses, variable expenses, and a reserve for replacement.

Operating expense ratio (OER). The ratio of total operating expenses to effective gross income.

Operating leverage. A financial technique where a small increase in gross income results in a large increase in net operating income.

Overall capitalization rate. A widely used investment and market value rule of thumb equal to net operating income divided by total costs. It is also the reciprocal of the net income multiplier.

Passive activity. a trade or business activity in which the taxpayer does not materially participate, or any rental activity.

Payback methods. Rules of thumb that result in multipliers (or, as reciprocals, rates of return) for real estate investment criteria.

Payback period. The amount of time, usually in years, for the benefits of an investment, usually income or cash flow, to repay the total cost or equity cost of investment.

Percentage leases. Leasing arrangements that allow for a varying rent schedule according to volume of sales or income.

Personal income tax rates. The federal tax rates that are applied to personal income to measure tax liability.

Personal property. The legal rights associated with personalty.

Personalty. All assets that are not permanently attached to the land.

Portfolio analysis. A type of investment analysis, originally introduced for common stock securities, where combinations of different investments are included to reduce the overall risk by diversification.

Possibility of a reverter. Future interest that may become a possessory interest if the determinable fee is extinguished.

Potential gross income. The amount of rental income that would result from 100 percent occupancy.

Preference taxes. *See* Tax preference items.

Prepaid interest. Interest charges that are assessed at the time of the origination of a loan.

Prepayment. *See* Early repayment.

Prepayment penalties. Clauses in some mortgages that assess the mortgagor a charge in the event that he or she wishes to prepay the mortgage note before maturity.

Present value. The current worth of an asset.

Present value of future selling price. The amount of the expected future selling price times the present value of $1.00 factor.

Present value of $1.00. A valuation factor that enables the investor to convert an expected future amount into a percent amount. It is equivalent to the reciprocal of the compound (or future) value of $1.00. Mathematically, it is represented by the term $1/(1 + k)^n$ where k is the discount rate and n is the period of the expected future amount.

Present value of $1.00 per period. A valuation factor, sometimes called an *annuity*, that enables the analyst to convert a series of expected equal periodic payments into an amount today. It is closely related to the present value of $1.00 factor and assists in calculating present values. Mathematically, it is represented by the term $[1 - (1 + k)^{-n}]/k$ where k is the discount rate and n is the number of expected periodic payments.

Prior appropriation doctrine. The legal theory of water rights that maintains the first to use the water has the best claim to the water.

Probabilistic modeling. A method of financial decision making involving random elements incorporated into parameter estimates. Also called simulation or Monte Carlo methods.

Profitability index. *See* Benefit/cost ratio.

Promissory note. A written promise of one person to repay an amount of money to another.

Property management. The activity of renting, maintaining, managing, and budgeting real estate operations for others.

Property rights. The legal rights and responsibilities associated with ownership of real estate, typically viewed as a "bundle of rights."

Pur autre vie. A conventional life estate meaning "for another's life." *See* Life estate.

Purchase-money mortgage. A financing technique where the seller of the property takes back a note from the buyer.

Purchase option. A contingent security that

gives the holder of the option the right to purchase property at a fixed, determined price within a specified period of time.

Qualified fee. *See* Fee simple determinable.

Real estate. The physical land and improvements, the field of study, or one profession dealing with land and its improvements.

Real estate investment process. The general framework by which the equity investor identifies objectives, analyzes the investment climate, forecasts cash flows, compares the costs and benefits of the investment, and accepts or rejects an investment opportunity.

Real estate investment strategy. An overall investment plan in which the real estate investor makes a set of decisions that helps to achieve his or her goals. The real estate investment process forms the basis for a general real estate investment strategy.

Real estate investment trust (REIT). A special ownership form that requires 100 shareholders and "pass through" tax treatment.

Real estate participants. The major actors involved in a real estate investment. Specifically, the equity investor, the tenant, the mortgage lender, and the government.

Real property. The legal rights associated with real estate.

Realty. The physical land and improvements. Also called real estate.

Rehabilitation tax credit. A tax credit for expenditures to rehabilitate nonresidential buildings placed in service before 1936. The rehabilitated property must be depreciated using the straight-line method in order to qualify for this credit.

Relative price change. An increase or decrease in the price of a good (or investment) due to changes in market conditions relative to the price of other goods (or investments).

Remainders. Future estates that are the grant of revisionary interacts.

Reserve for replacement. An allowance that takes into account the wearing out of furniture, appliances, and other assets with short lives. It reduces the expected net operating income but not taxable income. Failure to deduct a reserve when these expenditures are expected result in overvaluing the property.

Residential property. In terms of IRS classifications, any income-producing real estate where no more than 20 percent of its income is derived from nonresidential components.

Reversion. The legal interest in real property at a specified future period, typically in real estate investment analysis at the end of one holding period; the disposition of a real estate investment.

Right of reentry. Future interest that may result in a possessory interest if a condition subsequent occurs.

Riparian rights theory. A legal theory of water rights. It maintains that the use of water belongs to natural users, especially those adjacent to it.

Risk. The probability or likelihood of not achieving an expected rate of return or of not achieving an expected increase in the value of the real estate.

Risk-adjusted discount rates. A well-known technique for accounting for risk in discounted cash flow models. Under this method the required rate of return is the sum of an allowance for the time value of money and an allowance for the expected types of risk of the investment: market, financial, and inflation.

Risk-return tradeoff. A market relationship that results from investors valuing investment assets according to the expected risks and returns.

Rules of thumb. Shorthand and easy-to-calculate methods of techniques for making investment decisions. Common examples in real estate investment include gross income multiplier and overall capitalization method.

Sale-leaseback. A commercial financing arrangement where the owner of the property sells to a buyer (investor) who then leases the property back to the original owner.

Second mortgage. *See* Junior lien.

Selling expenses. The transaction costs associated with the conveyance of interests in real property.

Sensitivity analysis. An operations research

method that analyzes the effects on outputs due to a change in inputs.

Simulation. *See* Probabilistic modeling.

Sociopolitical analysis. The study of behavioral and political factors for purposes of making real estate decisions.

Speculation. Formerly thought to be risky and unsecured gambles by opportunistic individuals. Modern thinking tends to regard speculation and investment as very similar or even identical.

Standard deviation. The square root of the variance.

Statutory foreclosure. A well-represented doctrine whereby the mortgagee is limited to recover only the amount of the mortgage after a default.

Straight-line depreciation method. An accounting method for depreciation that allows for equal amounts of depreciation each year over the entire expected useful life of the depreciable assets.

Strict foreclosure. A minority-held doctrine whereby most of the rights rest with the mortgagee after a default has occurred.

Subchapter S corporation. A form of business entity that attempts to avoid double taxation of corporations but retain other corporate characteristics.

Subjective probability distributions. The range of outcomes of a statistical event that is estimated based on personal judgment and beliefs.

Syndication. A mechanism for raising capital in larger projects, typically in the form of a partnership.

Taxable income. An accounting measure that is multiplied by the taxpayer's income tax rate to determine tax liability.

Tax capitalization theory. The principle that values reflect expected tax burdens and thus the taxes are accounted for in the value of the property.

Tax-deferred exchange. A method of tax planning that enables the investor to defer the recognition of the gain or loss by exchanging one investment for another of like kind.

Tax planning. The strategy, methods, and techniques of achieving financial objectives under the constraint of federal, state, and local taxation authority.

Tenancy at sufferance. The legal term for holdover tenants.

Tenancy at will. A leasehold estate that exists for as long as both parties desire.

Tenancy by the entirety. A concurrent estate similar to joint tenancy for husbands and wives.

Tenancy for years. A leasehold estate in which the beginning and ending dates are clearly specified.

Tenancy from period to period. A leasehold estate characterized by an implication of renewal and continual use.

Tenancy in common. A concurrent estate where each tenant owns an undivided portion of the property.

Tenancy in coparcenary. An extinct concurrent estate where property was left to more than one nonmale heir.

Term of mortgage. The amount of time over which the borrower is expected to repay the mortgage. Also known as the *mortgage maturity*.

Terminal value. The economic worth of an investment at the time of sale. Also called *expected selling price*.

"Three approaches to value." Cost, comparison, and income—the traditional framework developed in the 1930s for estimating the market value of real property.

Time value of money. The concept that the value of money is related to when the money is received. In other words, a payment due in the future is worth less today than the face amount to be paid in the future.

Title theory. A theory of mortgage law that views the existence of a mortgage as a conveyance to title from the borrower to the lender.

Trust deed. *See* Deed of trust.

Uncertainty factors. Unknown, unexpected, and immeasurable conditions.

Unpaid mortgage principal. The outstanding balance of a loan. It becomes especially important at the time of sale when the unpaid balance usually becomes due.

Useful life. The number of years that a depreciable asset is expected to be useful in the taxpayer's trade or business.

User of real estate. In the identification of real estate participants, the tenant who leases the property.

Vacancy allowance. The account that reduces potential gross income based on the probability of the occurrence of vacancies.

Variable expenses. Operating expenses, paid by the investor, that tend to vary with the occupancy of the real estate. Examples are utilities, maintenance, administration, payroll, and management fees.

Variance. A statistical measure of dispersion around the mean value.

Vested estates. Future interests that definitely become possessory estates at a specific time.

Water rights. The property rights associated with the use, control, and regulation of water.

Wraparound mortgage. A financing arrangement whereby the financing gains of the original loan are captured by the investor by maintaining the older loan and supplementing that loan with a new loan that "wraps around" the original loan.

Zoning. Land-use controls regarding the location of types of property.

BIBLIOGRAPHY _____

CHAPTER 1

Case, Fred. "Comparative Real Estate Investment Experience." *The Appraisal Journal* 28 (July 1960), 337–44.

Kau, James B., and Sirmans, C. F. *Real Estate.* New York: McGraw-Hill Book Company, 1985.

Landauer, James D. "Real Estate as an Investment." *The Appraisal Journal* 28 (October 1960), 426–34.

McMahon, John. *Property Development—Effective Decision Making in Uncertain Times.* New York: McGraw-Hill Book Company, 1976.

Maisel, Sherman J., and Roulac, Stephen E. *Real Estate Investment and Finance.* New York: McGraw-Hill Book Company, 1976.

Messner, Stephen D., Schreiber, Irving, Lyon, Victor L., and Ward, Robert L. *Marketing Investment Real Estate.* 2nd ed. Chicago: Realtors National Marketing Institute of the National Association of Realtors, 1982.

Seldin, Maury, and Swesnik, Richard H. *Real Estate Investment Strategy.* 2nd ed. New York: John Wiley & Sons, Inc., 1979.

Smith, Halbert C., Tschappat, Carl J., and Racster, Ronald L. *Real Estate and Urban Development.* rev. ed. Homewood, Ill.: Richard D. Irwin, Inc., 1977.

Wendt, Paul F., and Cerf, Alan R. *Real Estate Investment Analysis and Taxation.* 2nd ed. New York: McGraw-Hill Book Company, 1979.

Weston, J. Fred, and Brigham, Eugene F. *Essentials of Managerial Finance.* 5th ed. Hinsdale, Ill.: The Dryden Press, 1979.

CHAPTER 2

Bedford, E. W. "Why Buy Real Estate?" *The Appraisal Journal* 13 (April 1945), 135–37.

Roulac, Stephen E. "Can Real Estate Returns Outperform Common Stocks?" *Journal of Portfolio Management* 2 (Winter 1976), 26–43.

CHAPTER 4

Bowes, W. A. "What Is Market Analysis?" *The Real Estate Appraiser,* 34 (July–August 1968), 11–14.

Donato, Frank R. "Feasibility Study: Predicting Success." *Real Estate Today* 7 (September 1974), 18–21.

Eldred, Gary W., and Zerbst, Robert H. "A Critique of Real Estate Market and Investment Analysis." *The Appraisal Journal* 46 (July 1978), 443–52.

Gibbons, James E. "Apartment Feasibility Studies." *The Appraisal Journal* 36 (July 1968), 325–32.

Graaskamp, James A. *A Guide to Feasibility Analysis.* Chicago: Society of Real Estate Appraisers, 1970.

Hanford, Lloyd D. *Feasibility Study Guidelines.* Chicago: Institute of Real Estate Management, 1972.

Jaffe, Austin J., and Bussa, Robert G. "Using a Simple Model to Estimate Market Rents: A Case Study." *The Appraisal Journal* 45 (January 1977), 7–13.

Messner, Stephen C., Boyce, Byrl N., Trimble, Harold G., and Ward, Robert L. *Analyzing Real Estate Opportunities—Market and*

Feasibility Studies. Chicago: Realtors National Marketing Institute of the National Association of Realtors, 1982.

Redman, Arnold L., and Sirmans, C. F. "Regional/Local Economic Analysis: A Discussion of Data Sources." The Appraisal Journal 45 (April 1977), 261–72.

Sumichrast, Michael, and Seldin, Maury. Housing Markets: The Complete Guide to Analysis and Strategy for Home Builders, Lenders, and Other Investors. Homewood, Ill.: Dow-Jones-Irwin, 1977.

Chapter 5

Atteberry, William, Pearson, Karl, and Litka, Michael. Real Estate Law. Columbus, Ohio: Grid, Inc., 1974.

Bergfield, Philip B. Principles of Real Estate Law. New York: McGraw-Hill Book Company, 1979.

Cribbet, John E. Principles of the Law of Property. 2nd ed. Mineola, N.Y.: The Foundation Press, Inc., 1975.

Kratovil, Robert, and Werner, Raymond J. Real Estate Law. 8th ed. Englewood Cliffs, N.J.: Prentice-Hall, Inc., 1983.

Chapter 6

Buildings Owners and Managers Association. Office Building Income and Expense Analysis. Washington: Buildings Owners and Managers Association, annual.

Downs, James C., Jr. Principles of Real Estate Management. 11th ed. Chicago: Institute of Real Estate Management, 1975.

Hanford, Lloyd D., Jr. "Expense Ratios and Their Use." The Appraisal Journal 41 (January 1973), 100–103.

Institute of Real Estate Management. Income/Expense Analysis for Apartments, Condominiums and Cooperatives. Chicago: Institute of Real Estate Management, annual.

Jaffe, Austin J. Property Management in Real Estate Investment Decision-Making. Lexington, Mass.: D. C. Heath & Co., 1979.

Jaffe, Austin J. "A Reexamination of Management Fee Assessment." Journal of Property Management 44 (January/February 1979), 39–47.

Jaffe, Austin J., and Sirmans, C. F. "The Relationship Between Growth Factors, Operating Expense Ratio, and Valuation." The Real Estate Appraiser 44 (July–August 1978), 30–34.

Ratcliff, Richard U. "Don't Underrate the Gross Income Multiplier." The Appraisal Journal 39 (April 1971), 264–71.

Urban Land Institute. Dollars and Cents of Shopping Centers. Washington: Urban Land Institute, annual.

Walters, David W. "Just How Important is Property Management?" Journal of Property Management 38 (July/August 1973), 164–68.

Chapter 7

Atteberry, William. Modern Real Estate Finance. 2nd ed. Columbus, Ohio: Grid, Inc., 1976.

Ellwood, L. W. Ellwood Tables for Real Estate Appraising and Financing. Chicago: American Institute of Real Estate Appraisers, 1967.

Bruggeman, William B., and Stone, Leo D. Real Estate Finance. 7th ed. Homewood, Ill.: Richard D. Irwin, Inc., 1981.

Messner, Stephen D., and Boyce, Byrl N. "Calculation of Amortization Schedule and Mortgage Balances." The Appraisal Journal 40 (January 1972), 76–82.

Montgomery, J. Thomas. "Leverage." The Appraisal Journal 45 (October 1977), 589–600.

Nelson, Roland D., and Pollakowski, Arthur J. "The Effect of Financing on Value." The Appraisal Journal 40 (April 1972), 279–85.

Pyle, Jack L. "The Effects of Leverage." Real Estate Today 6 (April 1973), 32–38.

Sirmans, C. F. Real Estate Finance. New York: McGraw-Hill Book Co., 1985.

Sirota, David. Essentials of Real Estate Finance. Chicago: Real Estate Education Company, 1977.

Chapter 8

Anderson, Paul Edwards. Tax Factors in Real Estate Operations. 5th ed. Englewood Cliffs, N.J.: Prentice-Hall, Inc., 1978.

Greer, Gaylon E. *The Real Estate Investor and the Federal Income Tax.* New York: John Wiley & Sons, Inc., 1978.

Kau, James B., and Sirmans, C. F. *Tax Planning for Real Estate Investors.* 2nd ed. Englewood Cliffs, N.J.: Prentice-Hall, Inc., 1982.

CHAPTER 9

Davis, Irving F. *A Study of Real Estate Investment Returns to Capital and Management.* Fresno, Calif.: California State University, Bureau of Business Research and Service, Study no. 14, July 1973.

Gettel, Ronald E. *Real Estate Guidelines and Rules of Thumb.* New York: McGraw-Hill Book Co., 1976.

Jaffe, Austin J. "Evaluating Rules of Thumb." *Real Estate Today* 11 (October 1978), 22–25.

Jaffe, Austin J., and Sirmans, C. F. "Some Myths About Real Estate." *Real Estate Review* 8 (Spring 1978), 39–42.

Shenkel, William M. *Modern Real Estate Appraisal.* New York: McGraw-Hill Book Company, 1978.

Sirmans, C. F., and Webb, James R. "Mortgage Equity Analysis, Again?!" *The Appraisal Journal* 47 (January 1979), 44–52.

Wendt, Paul F. *Real Estate Appraisal—Review and Outlook.* Athens, Ga.: University of Georgia Press, 1974.

Wiley, Robert J. "Real Estate Investment Analysis: An Empirical Study." *The Appraisal Journal* 44 (October 1976), 586–92.

CHAPTER 10

Clettenberg, Karel J., and Kroncke, Charles O. "How To Calculate Real Estate Return on Investment." *Real Estate Review* 2 (Winter 1973), 105–109.

Cooper, James R., and Morrison, Cathy A. "Using Computer Simulation to Minimize Risk in Urban Housing Development." *The Real Estate Appraiser* 39 (March–April 1973), 15–26.

Cooper, James R., and Pyhrr, Stephen A. "Forecasting the Rates of Return on an Apartment Investment: A Case Study." *The Appraisal Journal* 41 (July 1973), 312–37.

Diamond, Arnold H. "Motivations of Investors in Multifamily Housing." *The Real Estate Appraiser* 38 (May–June 1972), 17–24.

Hanford, Lloyd D., Jr. "The Use of Discount Cash Flow Analysis." *The Real Estate Appraiser* 39 (November–December 1973), 31–34.

Hemmer, Edgar H. "How a Computer 'Thinks' About Real Estate." *Real Estate Review* 4 (Winter 1975), 113–23.

Jaffe, Austin J. "Is There a 'New' Internal Rate of Return Literature?" *American Real Estate and Urban Economics Journal* 5 (Winter 1977), 482–502.

Jaffe, Austin J., and Sirmans, C. F. *Real Estate Investment Decision Making.* Englewood Cliffs, N.J.: Prentice-Hall, Inc., 1982.

Montgomery, J. Thomas. "Real Estate Investment Risk—Basic Concepts." *The Appraisal Journal* 44 (January 1976), 9–22.

Pyhrr, Stephen A. "A Computer Simulation Model to Measure the Risk in Real Estate Investment." *American Real Estate and Urban Economics Association Journal* 1 (June 1973), 48–78; also in *The Real Estate Appraiser* 39 (May–June 1973), 13–31.

Van Horne, James C. *Financial Management and Policy.* 5th ed. Englewood Cliffs, N.J.: Prentice-Hall, Inc., 1982.

INDEX_____

definition of, 129–30
determining, 130–32
Direct sales comparison approach, 15
Discounted cash flow (DCF) models, 15–16
   advantages of, 165–66
   basic, 166–67
   comparison of NPV and IRR, 182–84
   forecasting future cash flows, 169–70
   importance of, 167–69
   internal rate of return of equity, 180–82
   investment value of equity, 174–78
   net present value of equity, 178–80
   real estate investment tables and, 172–74
   risk and, 170–72
Diversification, 22, 189–90

E

Easements, 72
Economic trends, market analysis and, 48
Effective gross income (EGI), 9, 10
Eminent domain, 8, 77
Environment for investment, analyzing, 7–8
Equitable mortgage, 73
Equitable right of redemption, 105
Equity
   buildup, 21
   dividend rate (EDR), 150
   internal rate of return on, 180–82
   investment value of, 174–78
   net present value of, 178–80
Equity investor
   government and the, 80
   legal environment/risk and the, 60–63
   mortgage lender and the, 78
   objectives of the, 5, 39–40
   property rights and the, 69–73
   tenant and the, 78, 80
Escheat, 8, 68
Estates in land, 59
Executory interests, 72
Expected rate of return, 19

F

Federal credit agencies, 65
Fee simple estate, 69
Fee tail estate, 70
Financial leverage, 21, 109–14
   definition of, 109
   impact of, 109–12
   increase of wealth and, 112–13

operating leverage and, 113–14
Financial management rate of return (FMRR),
   184–85
Financial risk, 7, 19
Financing
   comparing types of, 104–5
   creative, 114–19
   financial leverage, 21, 109–14
   reasons for, 103–5
   refinancing, 226–29
   seller, 210–13
   See also Mortgage
Fixed expenses, 88, 91
Fixture, definition of, 59
Foreclosure, 105
Freehold estates, 69–70
Future interests estates, 71–72

G

General partnerships, 61
Government
   equity investor and the, 80
   legal environment/risk and the, 67–68
   mortgage lender and the, 81
   objectives of the, 7
   property rights and the, 76–78
   tenants and the, 81–82
Gross income multiplier (GIM), 38, 95, 149

H

Holding period, 11
Hypothesis testing, 171

I

Income
   approach to valuation, 15, 162–63
   demand and market analysis and, 48
   equity participations and, 116–17
   taxation, 7
Individual/proprietorship ownership, 61
Inflation
   hedge, 21–22
   market analysis and, 42–43
   risk, 7, 19, 40
Installment land sales contract, 115
Installment sale, 137–39
   versus outright sale of real estate, 223–26
Institute of Real Estate Management (IREM), 89

Reserve for replacement expenses, 88, 89
Reversions, 71–72, 134, 152, 154
Reversion values, 17
Right of reentry, 72
Rights, ownership, 59
Riparian rights theory, 76
Risk
    adjusted discount rates, 170
    definition of, 43
    discounted cash flow models and, 15–16
    financial leverage and, 111–12
    over time, 41
    versus uncertainty, 40–41
Risk and return
    analyzing, 3, 5
    categories of, 7, 19
    measuring, 43–46
    rate of return and, 19–20, 22–23
    trade-off, 18–19
    See also under type of return
Rules-of-thumb investment criteria, 15
    average rate of return methods, 151–52, 154
    characteristics of, 147–58
    how to use, 154–55
    limitations of, 155–56
    payback period methods, 149–50

S

Sale-leaseback, 115–16
Sales contract, 82
Savings and loan associations, 63
Security, investment, 20
Selling versus operation of real estate,
    218–23
Sensitivity analysis, risk and, 171
Services, as expenses, 90
Simulation, risk and, 172
Sociopolitical environment, 8, 53
    importance of, 56
    rental and vacancy forecasts and, 56
Standard deviation, 44, 45, 171
Statutory foreclosure, 105
Strict foreclosure, 105
Subchapter S corporation, 61–62
Subjective probability distributions, 41
Supplies, as expenses, 91
Supply and demand analysis, 39–40
    market analysis and, 48
Syndication, 62–63

T

Tax(es)

alternative minimum, 132–34
analyzing the impact of, 122–23
capitalization theory, 80
classifying real estate for, 123, 125–26
deferred exchange, 139–42, 234–37
deferring, 137–42
mortgage financing and, 127–29
on sale of an investment, 134–37
operating expenses and, 126–27
real estate, 91
shelter benefits, 21, 120–22
Taxable income, cash flow versus, 120–22
Tax Reform Act (TRA) of 1986, 122–23, 129,
    131, 135, 137, 138, 143
Tenancy, types of, 71, 74
Tenants
    commercial, 66–67
    equity investors and, 78, 80
    government and, 81–82
    industrial, 67
    legal environment/risk and, 66–67
    mortgage lender and, 81
    objectives of, 7, 39
    property rights of, 74–76
    residential, 66
    special-purpose, 67
Title theory, 73
Traditional valuation models, 15
Triplex residential property, investing in, 214–18
Trust deed, 73

U

Uncertainty, risk versus, 40–41
Utility expenses, 90

V

Vacancies, 9, 56
Vacant land investment, 210–13
Value, operating expenses and, 92–97
Variable expenses, 88, 90–91
Variance, 44–45, 171
    mean, 46
Vested estates, 71

W

Water rights, 76
Wraparound mortgage, 117–18